AF729412

Classroom Companion: Business

The Classroom Companion series in Business features foundational and introductory books aimed at students to learn the core concepts, fundamental methods, theories and tools of the subject. The books offer a firm foundation for students preparing to move towards advanced learning. Each book follows a clear didactic structure and presents easy adoption opportunities for lecturers.

More information about this series at https://link.springer.com/bookseries/16374

Susan E. Reid • Charles B. Crawford

Entrepreneurial Vision

A Guide for Charting and Implementing the Visioning Process

Springer

Susan E. Reid
Williams School of Business
Bishop's University
Sherbrooke, QC, Canada

Charles B. Crawford
Université de Sherbrooke
Sherbrooke, QC, Canada

ISSN 2662-2866 ISSN 2662-2874 (electronic)
Classroom Companion: Business
ISBN 978-3-030-77802-6 ISBN 978-3-030-77803-3 (eBook)
https://doi.org/10.1007/978-3-030-77803-3

© The Editor(s) (if applicable) and The Author(s), under exclusive license to Springer Nature Switzerland AG 2022
This work is subject to copyright. All rights are solely and exclusively licensed by the Publisher, whether the whole or part of the material is concerned, specifically the rights of translation, reprinting, reuse of illustrations, recitation, broadcasting, reproduction on microfilms or in any other physical way, and transmission or information storage and retrieval, electronic adaptation, computer software, or by similar or dissimilar methodology now known or hereafter developed.
The use of general descriptive names, registered names, trademarks, service marks, etc. in this publication does not imply, even in the absence of a specific statement, that such names are exempt from the relevant protective laws and regulations and therefore free for general use.
The publisher, the authors and the editors are safe to assume that the advice and information in this book are believed to be true and accurate at the date of publication. Neither the publisher nor the authors or the editors give a warranty, expressed or implied, with respect to the material contained herein or for any errors or omissions that may have been made. The publisher remains neutral with regard to jurisdictional claims in published maps and institutional affiliations.

This Springer imprint is published by the registered company Springer Nature Switzerland AG
The registered company address is: Gewerbestrasse 11, 6330 Cham, Switzerland

This book is dedicated to all of the hardworking and visionary entrepreneurs who dare to dream and follow their North Star. We hope that our audience gets as much out of reading about entrepreneurial vision as we have during our own journey and the journeys of those brave souls who inspired us to explore, research, and write about it.

Preface

» He that rules by mind is like the North Star, steady in his seat, whilst the stars all bend to him. –Confucius

Night Sky with North Star. (Source: Image licensed and downloaded from Adobe Stock, May 28, 2020. Credit: by romvo/stock.adobe.com)

The North Star, fixed in the northern sky, has guided explorers for centuries. Perfectly aligned with the Earth's rotational axis, the North Star, also known as Polaris, sits virtually motionless above the North Pole, while all other stars rotate around it. The North Star provides a clear direction for navigation and lights the way forward.

Vision is the North Star of all businesses, setting the direction and guiding key decisions, priorities, and allocation of resources. The most successful entrepreneurs and business leaders are also great visionaries—they view the future of their business with insight and clarity that illuminates the way forward for virtually every step. A clear, compelling, and well-conceived vision that is expertly communicated to employees and stakeholders is fixed like the North Star and sets the organization off unambiguously down the right path.

The reality, however, is that far too many start-ups lack clear vision or have poorly conceived or communicated vision that inevitably sets the organization off in the wrong direction or, worse, in multiple directions at the same time. Without a clear, magnetic, and refined vision, employees become discouraged and even doubtful of their leaders, and often work in opposing directions to one another. The result is that the majority of new businesses fail, while many larger, established companies simply stagnate.

Research has consistently confirmed that vision is among the most important leadership traits in all organizational spheres, but most importantly for entrepreneurs who build businesses based on their view of the future. But what is this "vision" concept that is so often spoken about in elusive or magical terms? Is vision something you are born with or can it be taught? Do great visions appear like a flash or in a dream or are they built slowly over time? How do you know if the vision is a good one or a poor one? How does vision tie into strategy, finance, and execution? How should leaders go about communicating their vision to employees and stakeholders?

While many texts on entrepreneurship and biographies of great entrepreneurs and leaders talk about vision and its importance, few delve into what vision really is, how it comes to be, and how it can and should be developed. This book, based on evidence-based research, delves into the entire *visioning process*. Starting with understanding the elements which differentiate strong and sustainable vision from weak and poorly conceived vision, we take you through steps focusing on how successful entrepreneurs build and implement their vision and, in turn, build great businesses.

While Entrepreneurial Vision and the process suggested to achieve it are based on research, the authors and publisher of this textbook do not provide any guarantees of success or performance levels based on the use of the text or its worksheets. This is due to the numerous factors such as, but not limited to, environmental changes and competition, which can obviously have an impact on success and performance levels.

In this textbook, wherever needed and where it makes sense to do so, the masculine gender may be interpreted for the feminine or other gender, and the singular for the plural, indifferently.

Susan E. Reid
Sherbrooke, QC, Canada

Charles B. Crawford
Sherbrooke, QC, Canada

Acknowledgments

This textbook owes much to the efforts and support of many important people.

Our research efforts over the years have involved many individuals including our dissertation supervisors (Dr. Ulrike de Brentani and Dr. Jacques Baronet), our many colleagues, and research assistants. We would like to thank them all for their assistance, advice, and inspiration over the years. Our work has been all the better with their involvement. In completing this book, we are particularly indebted to the hard work of Haley Crawford and Gillian Regnier, for their invaluable assistance in editing and research. And to all our friends and colleagues, your good humor, advice, and friendship have been a "True North" guiding us during this process.

Our families including our parents, Mary Jean and Clyde Reid and Denise and Walter Crawford, have always encouraged us and have been a source of strength. They instilled in us the importance of knowledge and a strong work ethic. Our children, Haley and Scott, have, through most of their lives, been our test subjects growing up in a live case of family entrepreneurship. Through all its ups and downs, thank you for living the dream with us!

We also want to express our sincere gratitude to the numerous research organizations, professional societies, publishers, institutions, companies, and universities that have provided invaluable support during our various research efforts over our 20+ years in academia. These include the Canadian Foundation for Innovation (CFI), the Social Sciences and Humanities Research Council of Canada (SSHRC), the National Science and Research Council (NSERC), Fonds de recherche – Nature et technologies (FRQNT), Fonds de recherche – Société et culture (FQRSC), the Kauffman Foundation, the Canada Research Chair on the Management of Technology, MELS, TechnoCap, MANCEF, Canadian Microelectronics Corporation (CMC), and the Product Development and Management Association (PDMA). Importantly, the formation and support of our research would not have been possible without the strong support from several universities including: Athabasca, Bishop's, Concordia, McGill, Nottingham, Sherbrooke, and Western (Ivey).

Finally, thanks to Springer Nature, our publisher, and the team there who have helped to bring this work to life, particularly our editor, Nitza Jones-Sepulveda. Thank you for believing in us and carefully guiding us through the publication process.

Contents

About the Authors

Susan E. Reid
is a retired Professor of Marketing and Entrepreneurship at the Williams School of Business, Bishop's University. Her teaching and research interests lie at the intersection of marketing, innovation, and entrepreneurship, with an in-depth focus on the topic of vision. Susan has published in refereed journals including: *Journal of Product Innovation Management, Industrial Marketing Management, Technological Forecasting and Social Change, R&D Management, Journal of Consumer Marketing, World Development, Business History,* and *International Journal of Technology Marketing*. She has been associated to the Canada Research Chair on the Management of Technology; held grants through the Canadian Foundation for Innovation, SSHRC, FQRSC, FQRNT, and MELS; and has more than 25 years of experience working and consulting for the biopharma, nanotech, and aviation sectors. She has been a keynote speaker locally and internationally, including on the topic of the Power of Entrepreneurial Vision, and was a contributor to Forbes.com. In 2019, she won the Business Division Teaching Award at Bishop's University and the 2019 Dean's Award for Distinguished Contributions to Scholarly Activity and Research. She, along with her husband and co-author Charles, is the co-founder of Domaine Pinnacle, a pioneering Canadian producer of craft ciders and spirits.

Susan holds a Bachelor of Science degree from Queen's University, an MBA from McGill University, and a PhD from Concordia University's John Molson School of Business.

Charles B. Crawford
is an experienced entrepreneur who has spearheaded the start-up, launch, and development of several high-growth companies. He, along with his wife and co-author Susan, is a co-founder of Domaine Pinnacle, a family-owned apple farm that they built into an award-winning producer of ice cider and craft spirits, sold in over 60 countries worldwide. Prior to co-founding Domaine Pinnacle, he worked for several multi-national companies and was a consultant and entrepreneur with experience in the technology, communications, airline, pharmaceutical, and consumer products industries. He is currently an associate professor at the Université de Sherbrooke, where he teaches entrepreneurship. He is actively involved in several non-profit organizations providing mentoring and incubation services to

aspiring young entrepreneurs. His research focuses on entrepreneurial teams, ecosystems, and strategic alliances.

Charles holds a Bachelor of Science degree from Concordia University, an MBA from The Ivey School of Business (Western), and a Doctorate in Business Administration from Athabasca University.

The Entrepreneurial Vision Imperative

Contents

© The Author(s), under exclusive license to Springer Nature Switzerland AG 2022
S. E. Reid, C. B. Crawford, *Entrepreneurial Vision*, Classroom Companion: Business,
https://doi.org/10.1007/978-3-030-77803-3_1

1.1 Why Entrepreneurs and Their Visions Are Important

There is a rapidly growing interest in understanding how entrepreneurs envision future products and markets and how they transform their vision into reality (◘ Fig. 1.1). Without a doubt, entrepreneurs capable of bringing well-developed visions to life provide one of the most important sets of activities in our economy.

The entrepreneur's unique skill is the ability to utilize their vision to combine existing skills, ideas, and resources in a new way, and it is this skill which is of importance to the economy. Indeed, the French roots of the word "entrepreneur" (Etymonline, 2020, online) mean "undertaker" or more loosely applied, "between parts." The latter idea demonstrates the notion that the entrepreneur is an individual who brings together or combines skills, ideas, and resources in a new way that is capable of bringing new value-added combinations together, much as a general contractor coordinates the work of engineers, plumbers, and so on in the building industry.

According to Navale (2013, p. 1), "The term (entrepreneur) first appeared in the French Dictionary *Dictionnaire Universel de Commerce* of Jacques des Bruslons published in 1723," and the concept was further developed through "the work of Richard Cantillon in his *Essai sur la Nature du Commerce en Général* (1755) and Jean-Baptiste Say in his *Treatise on Political Economy*." The first edition of Say's work was published in 1803.

◘ **Fig. 1.1** Conceptual image to portray "vision." (Source: Image licensed and downloaded from Adobe Stock on July 28, 2020. Credit: by grufnar/7 stock.adobe.com. License Link: ▸ https://stock.adobe.com/ca/images/hands-creating-a-square-turning-a-drawing-of-a-clean-landscape-into-reality/140404199?prev_url=detail)

Joseph Schumpeter (1911/1934) was one of the first economists to study entrepreneurs, venture capital, and innovation and to show their impacts on the economy. Nathan Rosenberg (1982, p. 106) described Schumpeter's contributions eloquently when he compared the study of innovation to "a series of footnotes upon Schumpeter." Scherer (1999, p. 27) provides an excellent overview of Schumpeter's main contributions:

> "The heir to Marx's view of capitalist dynamics was Joseph A. Schumpeter, an Austrian economist who spent the last eighteen years of his professional life (between 1932 and 1950) as a distinguished member of the Harvard economics faculty. As a twenty-eight-year-old, Schumpeter completed an influential book, *The Theory of Economic Development*, published at first in German (1911) and later in English (1934) and Japanese (1937), among other languages. The book advanced two main themes. First, innovation – including the introduction of new products and production methods, the opening of new markets, the development of new supply sources, and the creation of new industrial organization forms – lay at the heart of economic development, facilitating the growth of material prosperity. Second, innovations did not just happen, but required acts of entrepreneurship – heroic efforts to break out of static economic routines. … Successful innovations displaced inferior technologies (a process Schumpeter later called "the process of creative destruction") and through imitation and diffusion spread throughout the economic system[1]."

Schumpeter (1911/1934) began writing *The Theory of Economic Development* to investigate what he believed to be the strongly related issues of entrepreneurial profits, money, interest, and credit. As a result, he came to the conclusion that these phenomena were components of a distinct "equilibrium process" where money was the means through which the various elements of economic development were related. Issues of financing existed for entrepreneurs in that they would need venture capital or other forms of investment to fuel their initial actions. Once entrepreneurial firms grew to a certain size, they would require scaling up, which usually meant further financing (i.e., through equity or debt on which interest would be paid or credit given) to achieve the scale required to further encourage their actions.

Building on this work, another theme advanced by the work of Schumpeter (1911/1934) proposed that market changes come from producers and that consumers would be educated by the producers if necessary. In an ever-increasing world of "open innovation" (Chesbrough, 2006), however, where the lines between producers and consumers are becoming increasingly blurred, this manufacturer-led paradigm necessitates some re-thinking and balance with a more co-evolutionary approach to understanding the origins of disequilibrium, as will be explored in this book.

A key takeaway from Schumpeter's work (1911/1934, p. 74) is that entrepreneurs and capitalists are both required for the development of "new combina-

---

1 Used with permission of Brookings Institution Press from (New perspectives on growth and technological innovation, F.M. Scherer, 1999); permission conveyed through Copyright Clearance Center, Inc.

tions," whereby the attributes from old products and technologies are reconfigured in a novel way. As such, the entrepreneur's function is to provide a new combination of existing productive factors, while the capitalist is responsible for the financing of this effort through credit or lending. The entrepreneur facilitates this process of combinatorial action by exercising control over productive assets and resources. These actions are the mainstay on which the global economy is dependent for continued growth.

A key question, therefore, is related to why and how entrepreneurs are inspired to "start" to bring about new combinations from productive factors in the first place. Another related question is whether entrepreneurial inspiration is linked to the entrepreneurial processes they follow and therefore the subsequent levels of value-add they bring to the making of such new combinations.

1.2 A Process Approach to Studying Entrepreneurial Vision

There has been an abundance of research on why entrepreneurship is necessary, the nature of various entrepreneurial activities, and what makes entrepreneurs tick. These ideas have also been illustrated through excellent entrepreneurial biographies, including some recent works on Steve Jobs of Apple (*Steve Jobs*, Isaacson, 2011), Phil Knight of Nike (*Shoe Dog*, Knight, 2016), and Jeff Bezos of Amazon (*The Everything Store*, Stone, 2013). Such works have laid the foundation for understanding entrepreneurship and, to a certain extent, the types of actions which may lead to success in given environments.

There has been remarkably little research, however, about the entrepreneurial visioning process from a "how-to" perspective. Indeed, it seems that most how-to-style advice still attempts to focus on specific aspects of business planning, often treated in silos, rather than on the overarching imperative of how to develop a vision by building a visioning competence through to refinement and implementation in a logical, fun, and straightforward way.

This book, based on the latest research on the topic of vision, is a response to what we saw as an unmet need in the marketplace. We hope it will be helpful for you to not only understand the stage you are at in your journey but, also, for you to be able to take advantage of some proven tools, moving forward, to help you better understand the authors' suggested process and thereby hopefully improve your chances for success.

1.3 The Need for Teaching a Process Approach

Never have there been so many life coaches, wellness practices, and entrepreneurship schools and incubators dedicated to helping the individual seek out their life's purpose and passion and trying to assist aspiring entrepreneurs in bringing their ideas to success in the marketplace. While some of these approaches may be successful in helping to shape the piece of the puzzle they aim at serving, there is very little cohesion in terms of stringing together the pieces of the jigsaw during the various need and interest stages of entrepreneurs. Life coaches tend to focus on people once they have become dissatisfied with their current activity train and are looking to refocus their aptitudes and skills. Most young people we work with do not necessarily know what a life coach is, never mind having had access to one. Entrepreneurship school programs at the undergraduate level and even some at pre-university levels do focus on younger audiences; however, these are groups which often do not really know yet what they want to do. For example, our undergrad marketing and entrepreneurship students often ask what they should focus on bringing to market. In other words, "I know I'm a marketing student, but the marketing of what?" Graduate students are often focused mainly on researching why entrepreneurs do what they do, rather than doing it themselves. In the case of executive education and incubators, such programs tend to be involved with people who may already have an extant idea or business, are on a particular trajectory, and are looking for support in their journey. As a result, very few institutions or consultants are genuinely able to focus on a holistic view of the entire potential journey. The reality is that individuals view entrepreneurship from various perspectives—either in terms of age, experience, interest, opportunity, or necessity. Their entry points differ, so it is vital to meet them on the path where they are to help focus or refocus their visioning competence and vision accordingly. Additionally, and importantly, there are far more people—including students—who would like to start the entrepreneurial journey from the very beginning, and this, therefore, involves learning about and moving through an entrepreneurial visioning process from A to Z.

1.4 Statistics That Support the Need for a Better Approach

Research from the Organisation for Economic Co-operation and Development (OECD, 2015) shows that **while only 4% of the population are currently self-identified entrepreneurs with paid personnel, over 50% of individuals surveyed internationally state that they want to be their own boss** (from a survey of over 2000 individuals across more than 40 OECD countries). Let's drill down a little into the nature of this huge gap.

Compared to the 4% of "self-identified entrepreneurs" globally, the number of individuals who consider themselves to be "self-employed" in the workforce is much higher. "Self-employed" is defined by the OECD (2001, online) as "persons who are the sole owners, or joint owners, of the unincorporated enterprises in which they work, excluding those unincorporated enterprises that are classified as quasi-corporations." In Canada, for 2018, the numbers sat at approximately 2.9 million of 19.3 million laborers in the Canadian population or approximately 15% (Statistics Canada, 2019). Based on the OECD definition, the "self-employed" category incorporates the self-identified entrepreneurs with paid personnel. As a result, there is a fundamental difference as to how people think about themselves in terms of such a classification—i.e., am I an entrepreneur or am I self-employed? Some of these declarations may be related to the solo acts who work part-time or make little money through their self-employment activities.

What about the "intrapreneurs" out there—a type of entrepreneur, but one who work for others as a choice? What about those business owners, who have inherited, bought, or franchised their businesses? Do they consider themselves to be entrepreneurs? These are essential questions because according to the OECD (2018), 70–95% of all enterprises are micro-businesses (i.e., less than ten employees). In Canada (Statistics Canada, 2014), the number of small businesses in 2014 was estimated to be 97.1% taking into account firms with 1–49 employees (compared to 2.5% for medium-sized with 50–249 employees and 0.4% for large businesses with 250+ employees). As noted in GEM's annual survey (Bosma et al., 2019/2020, Figure 1.2, p. 26), "Total Early-Stage Entrepreneurial Activity (TEA)" includes potential or would-be entrepreneurship, nascent (setting up) entrepreneurial activity, and owner-managers of a new business up to 3.5 years. As such, of the large number of micro-businesses employing up to ten people, only a portion would be considered "TEA," as many micro-businesses have existed more than 3.5 years.

So, for our purposes, we know that there are at least 50% would-be entrepreneurs and 4% self-identified entrepreneurs and that "the rest" category of entrepreneurship potential includes some self-employed as well as franchisors, other new business owners, and intrapreneurs (◘ Fig. 1.2). This data highlights a critical gap in our understanding, not only for statistics agencies but in terms of framing one's own experience and seeking the appropriate support—because each one of these types of activities is, in its own way, a form of entrepreneurship.

In sum, there is a vast difference in percentage terms between the number of self-identified entrepreneurs/self-employed/business owners and those who are potential or "would-be" entrepreneurs. The OECD (2015) asked their participants whether "I would rather take a risk and build my own business than work for someone else." This question was used to determine "preference for risk." The number of participants, 18 to 64 years old, who stated that they agreed with this statement was remarkably high globally. In the USA, 69% of men and 58% of women agreed with

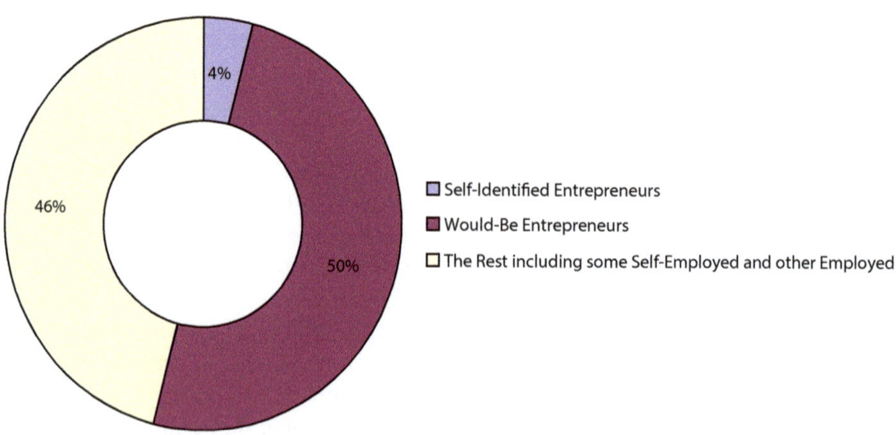

◘ **Fig. 1.2** Global entrepreneurship potential. (Figure by the authors)

this statement. These numbers are remarkable, particularly when compared to the 4% of the population who are self-identified entrepreneurs with paid personnel and up to approximately 11% more (Canadian data) who are self-employed. We have started to see growing evidence of this trend very clearly with our own students. In one class, recently, we asked the students how many might be interested in eventually running their own business and almost every hand in the class went up. The problem is, however, that most aspiring entrepreneurs don't know where to start, and so in most cases, based on the data, they don't.

1.5 Our Objectives

Clearly, the chasm between would-be entrepreneurs and reality is immense. Therefore, we felt it was important to find ways to help reduce this gap. In this book, we share our combined insights on how to tackle this opportunity from over 50+ combined years of academic teaching, research, writing, consulting, and personal entrepreneurial startup experience.

Many people question whether there is such a thing as an entrepreneurial process. Our research suggests that there is a process, and there are some fundamentals including vision as a key starting point which, if put in place, can help to guide entrepreneurial activity in a way that is more likely to achieve a higher degree of success than if no process including visioning is actively utilized.

The objectives of this book are *(1) to distinctly convey what the entrepreneurial visioning process looks like, (2) to give examples to illustrate this process,* and *(3) to provide worksheets aimed at helping would-be and early-stage entrepreneurs move through this process successfully.*

To achieve these objectives, ► Chap. 2 of this book begins by developing an understanding of how vision and the visioning process work, including the key building blocks. ► Chapters 3 and 4 aim at helping both would-be entrepreneurs and students to gain a better sense of their underlying motivations and how these can potentially impact the visioning process. ► Chapter 5 provides a how-to guide to getting started with framing a vision depending on primary motivations. ► Chapters 6 and 7 aim at gaining a better understanding of how to set a strong early context for your future entrepreneurial activities through effective networking and entrepreneurial team development. ► Chapters 8, 9, 10, 11, and 12 focus on building industry and market context through opportunity analysis, market learning, and early vision construction. ► Chapters 13, 14, 15, 16, 17, 18, 19, and 20 show a path for moving the vision through concept testing with specific market niche refinement and building the value proposition to be communicated to your market. In sum, our aim with this book is to help you develop a vision capable of powering you through the entrepreneurial process from getting started through to successful launch and beyond.

1

Chapter Review Questions

1. Define the term "new combinations" and explain why it is important for entrepreneurs. Provide one or two examples to illustrate this concept.
2. Why do you think an entrepreneur can be compared to a general contractor?
3. Who was Joseph Schumpeter, and why was he such an influential figure in the study of entrepreneurship?
4. Why do you think there is such an expansive gap between self-identified entrepreneurs and would-be entrepreneurs?
5. Why do you think that the "visioning process" should be the first step in the entrepreneurial journey?

References

Bosma, N., Hill, S., Ionescu-Somers, A., Kelley, D., Levie, J., & Tamawa, A. (2020). *Global entrepreneurship monitor (GEM) 2019/2020 global report*. Global Entrepreneurship Research Association: London Business School.

Cantillon, R. (1755). *Essai sur la nature du commerce en général*. Macmillan.

Chesbrough, H. (2006). *Open innovation: The new imperative for creating and profiting from technology*. Harvard University Press.

Etymonline. (2020, online). https://www.etymonline.com/word/entrepreneur. Etymology of the word "entrepreneur". Accessed on 25 Aug 2020.

Isaacson, W. (2011). *Steve Jobs*. Simon & Schuster Paperbacks.

Knight, P. (2016). *Shoe dog: A memoir by the creator of Nike*. Scribner.

Navale, A. B. (2013). Developing entrepreneur skills for corporate work. *Research Directions, 1*(4), 1–3.

OECD. (2001, online). *OECD Glossary of statistical terms.* Source Publication: https://stats.oecd.org/glossary/detail.asp?ID=2424#:~:text=French%20Equivalent%3A%20Travailleurs%20ind%C3%A9pendants%20%E2%80%93%20SCN.%20Definition%3A%20Self-employed,enterprises%20that%20are%20classified%20as%20quasi-corporations.%20Source%20Publication%3A. SNA 7.24, created September 24, 2001; updated November 22, 2001. Accessed on 25 Aug 2020.

OECD. (2015). *Entrepreneurship at a glance, 2015*. OECD Publishing. https://doi.org/10.1787/entrepreneur_aag-2015-en

OECD. (2018). *Entrepreneurship at a glance, 2018*. OECD Publishing.

Rosenberg, N. (1982). *Inside the black box: Technology and economics*. Cambridge University Press.

Scherer, F. M. (1999). *New perspectives on economic growth and technological innovation*. British-North American Committee Brookings Institution Press.

Schumpeter, J. A. (1934). *The theory of economic development*. (translated from the German 1911 version), Cambridge, MA: Harvard University Press.

Statistics Canada. (2014). *Entrepreneurship indicator database*. Center for Special Business Projects.

Statistics Canada. (2019). *Labour statistics at a glance: Self-employed Canadians: Who and why?* by L. Yssaad and V. Ferrao, Released May 28, 2019.

Stone, B. (2013). *The everything store: Jeff Bezos and the age of Amazon*. Little, Brown and Company, Hachette Book Group, Inc.

Understanding Entrepreneurial Vision

Contents

© The Author(s), under exclusive license to Springer Nature Switzerland AG 2022
S. E. Reid, C. B. Crawford, *Entrepreneurial Vision*, Classroom Companion: Business,
https://doi.org/10.1007/978-3-030-77803-3_2

Learning Objectives

In the pursuit of all things in life, having a clear, tangible, and magnetic long-term future goal in front of you—i.e., a vision—helps to power you more successfully along the path to that goal. The academic research we have performed, in addition to our 50+ years of combined entrepreneurial experience, indicates that, when bringing new innovations and ideas to market, there are significant competencies that are critical to focus on building as early on in the process as possible. For entrepreneurs, developing a strong vision starts with building a visioning competence and supporting processes and resources. These resources, in turn, are significantly linked to early success with lead customers, access to capital, and competitive advantage. For the startup entrepreneur, vision is key!

In this chapter, we focus on building an understanding of:

1. What vision is
2. The components of vision
3. Types of vision
4. How vision is created and evolves over the long term
5. Why vision is important

2.1 Vision: A Definition

At its core, vision is a clear mental image of the future that one person or a group of people have that they are passionate about (Reid, 2005). In other words, as noted in Reid and Roberts (2011), vision blends insight, foresight, and passion together to foster a desirable image of the future. Entrepreneurship offers us the opportunity to pursue both our shorter- and longer-term goals—i.e., visions—those which we are passionate about and which may look out over a very long time horizon (◘ Fig. 2.1).

2.2 Vision: The Main Components

Vision is comprised of three underlying components (◘ Fig. 2.2): (► Sect. 2.2.1) a potential future goal, (► Sect. 2.2.2) passion, and (► Sect. 2.2.3) clarity/specificity.

2.2.1 A Potential Future Goal

The mental image of how we see ourselves or something of interest to us in a future state acts as a North Star in guiding our visioning journey. In other words, a potential future goal, while not yet enacted, allows the visioning individual to form an idea which both excites them to action and provides a focus for the future. As a result, such focused foresight may lead a visionary to think about how, potentially, to manifest such an imagining in the future. Collins and Porras (1991) note that

■ **Fig. 2.1** Conceptual image to portray "long-term time horizon." (Source: Image licensed and downloaded from Adobe Stock on July 28, 2020. Credit: by AR Pictures/► stock.adobe.com. License Link: ► https://stock.adobe.com/ca/images/old-wooden-breakwater-at-the-beach-in-the-evening-long-time-exposure-german-baltic-sea-coast-europe/103133558?prev_url=detail)

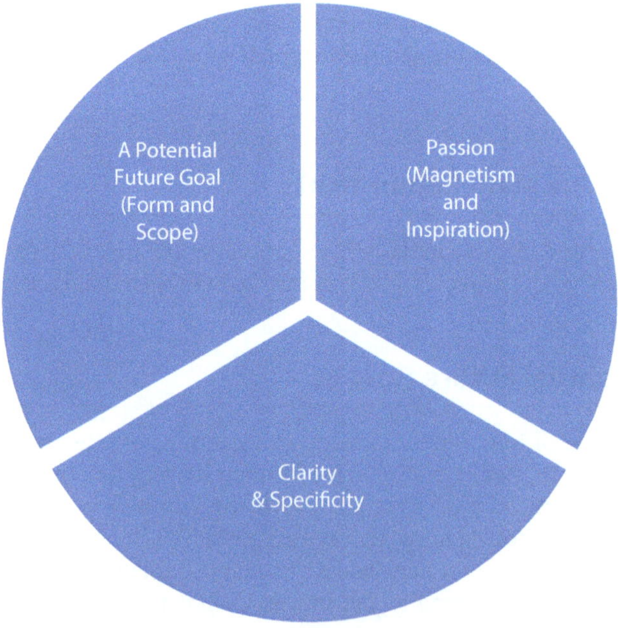

■ **Fig. 2.2** The basic building blocks of vision. (Figure by the authors)

goals should be driven by a guiding philosophy comprised of core beliefs, values, and purpose, and they describe the type of goal that should be part of a vision as a "big, hairy, audacious goal" (Collins & Porras, 1991; p. 42). To demonstrate how purpose ties in notably with vision, they quote Merck's "1989 Statement of Corporate Purpose" (Collins & Porras, 1991, p. 38): "We are in the business of preserving and improving human life. All of our actions must be measured by our success in achieving this." Breaking this down further, as shown in empirical research (Reid, 2005; Reid & de Brentani, 2010), a potential future goal is comprised of two core dimensions: "vision form" (based on the work of Collins & Porras, 1991, 1995) and "vision scope" (based on the work of Cooper, 1985).

2.2.1.1 Vision Form

Vision form is what the mental image of the goal looks like to the visionary (Collins & Porras, 1995). Individuals create representations in their minds, or mental models, structure them into patterns that they store in their memory, and later retrieve them to process new data encountered in the environment (McCulloch & Pitts, 1943; Gardner, 1985). In other words, the vision's form is made up of the characteristics or attributes comprising the mental model representation, and these may get more detailed over time with the addition of new information. Characteristics of vision form may include how a product might be produced or used, how it plans to replace an old technology, or who the potential customer might be (Reid, 2005). Many other characteristics might be included in such imagery, and these are described in more detail in later chapters. For an example of a visionary using vision form to convey a mental model, at a presentation at South by Southwest (SXSW) in 2018, Elon Musk conveyed his overall vision form for the future using high-touch (i.e., very tangible and, therefore, easy to understand) imagery. He described the future as a time when "anyone can move to Mars and gas cars will be like steam engines" (Clifford, 2018).

2.2.1.2 Vision Scope

Vision scope relates more specifically to the size or grandiosity of the goal. Scope is a vital goal component (Cooper, 1985), because as noted in Reid and de Brentani (2010, p. 505), "markets that have good potential size typically offer better performance outcomes." It may also have to do with the potential for the goal to impact others or society. Such impact is often a key aspect of the vision statements of not-for-profits and charitable organizations. For example, Habitat for Humanity aims to create "a world where everyone has a decent place to live" (Habitat for Humanity website, 2020).

2.2.2 Passion (Magnetism and Inspiration)

Research on vision demonstrates that "passion" is a crucial aspect of both having and realizing a vision (e.g., Collins & Porras, 1991, 1995; Breugst et al., 2012). This is particularly important for entrepreneurs as a vision with magnetic quality helps to infuse tangibility of value (Selznick, 1957) in the absence of other organizational cues of value for startups. The goals of any vision will involve the hopes and dreams of the visionary projected into the future. It is important, however, to consider that it is the level of passion that an individual or group has for the vision that can elevate it from being an unrealized hope or dream. Vision passion is key to the realization of a vision in three ways. First, it helps visionaries overcome the natural state of inertia that exists in moving toward new goals, particularly those which have a large scope. Second, it helps the visionary speed up the process to realize the vision. Third, passion may help attract others to share in and help realize the vision. Walt Disney, for example, knew how to motivate himself and others with possibly one of the most attractive visions ever created—and all in four words—"To make people happy" (Rasmus, 2012, online). Passion acts as an incentive: the more passionate someone is about their vision, the more they will be inspired to make it happen.

In the case where an entrepreneur creates a new vision with new imagery that is different and distinctive from other visions and products in a similar market space, we speak about the passion of the vision in terms of its ability to inspire others through the promise of the new vision. During the early days of vision creation for entrepreneurial teams, the ability to inspire, even through the early versions of the vision, is critical. When visions already exist, we speak about whether such extant visions are magnetic to others. The distinction is subtle, but we believe it is beneficial to distinguish between visions in creation and visions in play.

2.2.3 Vision Clarity and Vision Specificity

All visions inherently have a certain level of clarity, and often, as an entrepreneur moves along their journey, their vision will either become more precise and more focused or change and adapt to their desires or external conditions. Clarity is required to help zoom in on the desired mental map of the vision and enables providing direction to others (Giordan, 1995; Hamel & Prahalad, 1994; Lynn & Akgün, 2001; Neimes, 1996; Rice et al., 1998; Vaughan, 1997). It does this by providing specificity through a high level of tangibility by using the kinds of vivid description that will resonate with the senses (Collins & Porras, 1991). An effective vision is characterized by clear imagery that enables a comprehensive understanding of its specific building blocks. In sum, a clear vision details the "who," "when," and "what" involved in bringing it to life (but not the "how," which comes later with the action plan) (Lynn & Akgün, 2001).

An example of vision clarity, based on a service focus, is showcased by FedEx's vision (◘ Fig. 2.3). Pioneer Frederick W. Smith in the 1970s had a clear vision to facilitate package and mail delivery for (1) businesses—the who, (2) overnight—the when, and (3) using a "Super Hub," the what: the first of which was centrally located in the USA in Memphis, Tennessee. His initial expectation for success was based on two underlying assumptions according to Nayak and Ketteringham (1986): first, he believed that with the exponential increase of businesses using electronic machines in the 1970s, there would be a related breakdown of parts and

Fig. 2.3 FedEx jet takeoff. (Source: ▶ https://commons.wikimedia.org/wiki/File:FedEx_767.jpg. Credit: Scott Kerhaert/CC BY-SA (▶ https://creativecommons.org/licenses/by-sa/4.0), August 1, 2016. Downloaded via Wikimedia Commons on June 13, 2020)

entire machines; second, he believed that these breakdowns would necessitate faster delivery for replacements. Up until that time, the business delivery model had been very laissez-faire, but his vision was to overhaul the delivery time model.

Clarity of vision, in many ways, works in the same way that vision magnetism does: the clearer the vision, the higher the likelihood of achieving it. As noted by Gerber (2001, Forward XV), "the simple truth about the greatest business people I have known is that they have a genuine fascination for the truly astonishing impact little things done exactly right can have on the world." Additionally, clarity allows the ideas underlying a vision to be more easily shared and understood because it imbues meaning for people and reduces their variance in understanding. Without a consistent understanding of the vision, as noted in Reid (2015, p. 138), "not only is it difficult for the individual to pursue the goal, but it also becomes more difficult to share and build further meaning with others." As a result, just as with magnetism, clarity helps to overcome inertia in building toward new goals, speeds up the process, and helps to move forward with others in realizing the vision.

These three main components of vision—goal, passion, and clarity—are present regardless of whether a vision pertains to the business world (e.g., Michael Dell's vision of customizable home computers) or some other non-business-related future objective (e.g., a utopian vision of world peace).

2.3 Types of Vision

2

Vision has been discussed as an important component of strategic management paradigms by many distinguished researchers (e.g., Christensen, 1997; Collins & Porras, 1991, 1995; Cummings & Davies, 1994; Day & Schoemaker, 2005; Hamel & Prahalad, 1994; Jolly, 1997; Moenart et al., 2009; Rice et al., 1998; Sturken et al., 2004; Tellis & Golder, 2002), and it has been primarily examined from the perspectives of Organizational Vision, Market Vision, Project Vision, and Technology Vision.

2.3.1 Organizational Vision

"Organizational Vision" consists of a "guiding philosophy" and a "tangible image" (Collins & Porras, 1991, p. 33). In other words, Organizational Vision involves an understanding from an organization's perspective of where we are now (mission statement) in comparison to where we should/would want to go (vision statement). To elucidate this distinction, MASKargo Logistics, a Malaysian cargo airline, is a useful example. Their mission is to "deliver the right products and services meeting customers' satisfaction," while their vision is to be one of "the most viable total logistics providers" (MASKargo Logistics website, 2020). In other words, this vision is focused on offering a greater scope of service provision in the future, while the mission is about what they provide to customers today.

2.3.2 Market Vision

"Market Vision," on the other hand, is "a clear and specific mental model or image" of what a specific product or service/market interface looks like (Reid, 2005, p. 1). As noted in Reid (2005, p. 1), "This image includes potential users, a potential product concept and the potential interaction of user and product in the use environment and the marketplace." Market Vision doesn't include the action steps to achieve the vision; this comes later with the Project Vision (Lynn & Akgün, 2001). It is the Market Vision, however, which sets the trajectory for all future-related Project Visions. For entrepreneurs, Market Vision—sometimes accompanied by vision for a specific technology (i.e., Technology Vision, Reid & Roberts, 2011; Reid et al., 2015)—occurs first and therefore importantly sets the course for future potential Organizational Vision, as per ◘ Fig. 2.4.

2.3.3 Project Vision

"Project Vision" (Lynn & Akgün, 2001) facilitates the bridging between Organizational Vision, Market Vision, and project strategy's action-oriented focus.

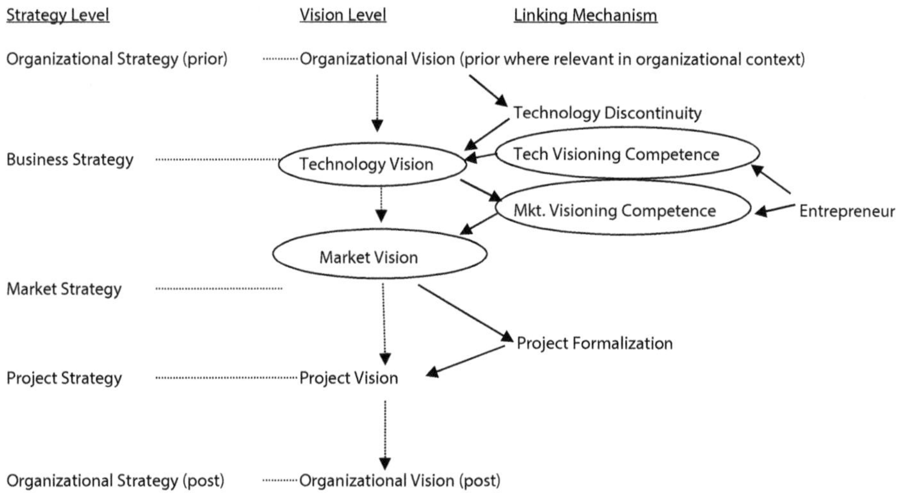

Fig. 2.4 Sequence of emergent strategies, visions, and linking mechanisms with the entrepreneur. (Source: Adapted from Reid (2005) PhD Thesis, "Market Vision for radically-new, high-tech products")

Brown and Eisenhardt (1995, p. 370) describe "vision" from the perspective of new product teams and define it as

> "The cognitive ability to mesh a variety of factors together to create an effective, holistic view and to communicate it to others. Specifically, in the case of product development, this means meshing together firm competencies (e.g., particular technical, marketing, or other skills) and strategies with the needs of the market (e.g., consumer preferences for style and cost) to create an effective product concept."

In other words, once the product concept has become clear enough, mainly through the market visioning process, briefly described later in this chapter, it will include more detailed aspects of project strategy, including action-oriented details. For example, in discussing the "Project Vision" for the IBM PC, Lynn and Akgün (2001, pp. 376–377) note that "the (project) vision, or blueprint, was a plan of when the PC should be launched, what features and benefits it should provide, who the target market would be, and where it would be sold."

In summary, as noted in Reid (2005) and Reid and Roberts (2011, p. 428), "just as there are corporate strategies, project strategies, market strategies, and so on," there are also visions at each level, "which embody the long-range goal component for each particular strategic level." For entrepreneurs, to achieve the higher-level organizational strategies and goals, the elements of product/market vision (and possibly technology vision, if relevant), and Project Vision must first be achieved and then incorporated into a broader Organizational Vision.

Since vision should come before strategy, it is useful to conceive of the different potential ways in which visions may be "born" or created.

2.4 How Visions Are Created: A Long-Term View

We suggest thinking of the vision creation process as being a function of two main factors. The first relates to "who" is initiating the vision (i.e., the "initiation point"): either an individual entrepreneur working largely on their own or an individual from within an organizational context. The second relates to "where" or how far away from development the eventual target market is (i.e., the "exploitation point"). In other words, as questioned in Reid (2015), is there a "low-market context" or a "high-market context" for the innovation? If there is not much known about the potential markets and their needs, then there will likely be a low level of understanding about or context for the market that needs to be developed. Building understanding usually takes quite some time in the "low-market context" case. At the other end of the spectrum, in a "high-market context" case, customer needs are usually better understood. The "high-market context" would indicate that potential routes of distribution may already be developed and, therefore, the "work" involved with getting to market is likely a lot less extensive than it might be in the "low-market context" case.

Based on the above concepts, we utilize a 2 × 2 matrix showing four potential "birth routes," as were represented by archetypes of vision creation in Reid (2015): value-driven vision (high individual focus/low-market context), technology-enabled vision (high organizational focus/low-market context), bottom-up market vision (high individual focus/high-market context), and top-down market vision (high organizational focus/high-market context). The matrix shows "initiation points" (individual or organizational) and "exploitation points" (low- to high-market context) which help us understand the typical sources of vision and the market situation in which the visioning process unfolds. As such, we can think of the location as a starting point for a given innovation or idea which becomes "a vector which will have a directionality and speed behind it" (Reid, 2015, p. 141), as represented in ◘ Fig. 2.5.

Quadrant 1 (Q1) is the realm of the *artist*, inspired or intuitive thinker, and/or pattern recognizer. It is the domain of the radical visionary who works with a *value-driven vision*. This is the quadrant from which all other quadrants and visions originally stem. Typically, the value-driven vision is the fuel for many other ancillary visions, possibly hundreds or thousands. For example, the research comprising the key scientific discoveries related to recombinant DNA ("rDNA") (e.g., Herbert Boyer or Watson and Crick) laid the foundation for many applications of this generic technology. We can think of others from a variety of disciplines who fall in this category from Leonardo da Vinci to Elon Musk.

In *Quadrant 2 (Q2)*, the archetype is the *bench-level scientist*. This individual sometimes works solo, but more often works within some form of institutional context, such as at a research center, corporation, or university, and usually has resources provided by their organization to move forward with their vision. Most scientific exploits contribute incrementally to the forward march of science, usually

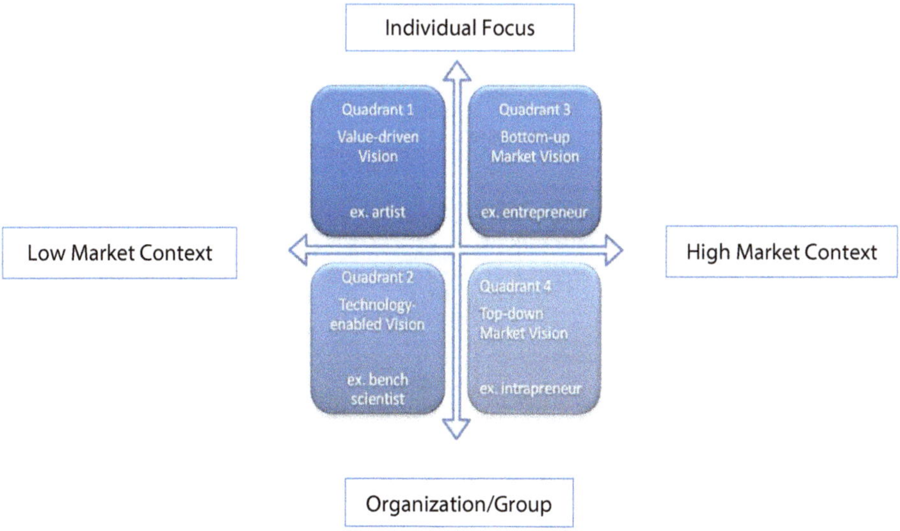

Fig. 2.5 Vision typology. (Source: Reid, 2015. Permission granted on December 3, 2020, by Springer Nature for reprint)

begun by a vision from Quadrant 1. Each scientist or firm, however, would have their own *technology-enabled vision* they are trying to enact and possibly relate to a potential market. The collective sum of these efforts in joining technology vision to markets is part of what drives the continued rise to market growth in a given field. The original visions underlying the numerous innovations for blades and razors made by Gillette, including the Trac IIR (the first twin-blade shaving system) to the Atra (the pivoting head) to the Mach 3R (three-blade technology) to the Fusion ProShield™ (provides lubrication before and after the blades), just to name a few, provide a great example of technology-enabled vision (Q2). The base vision for the detachable razor with disposable blades, however, was of the more radical type affiliated with Quadrant 1 and was patented by King C. Gillette in 1904 (Fig. 2.6).

In *Quadrant 3 (Q3)*, the archetype is the *entrepreneur*. This type of vision is known as "bottom-up vision" because the individual, often working on their own or perhaps with a small team, usually starts with some knowledge of the market if they are at the stage where they are trying to make a go of a certain product/market opportunity. The vision is considered *bottom-up market vision* because the entrepreneur is not being directed through any organizational context. While they may have formed a team, the visioning exercise has usually been performed by one individual and then is shared with others (Reid & de Brentani, 2004).

In *Quadrant 4 (Q4)*, *top-down market vision* initiatives usually are driven by CEOs, Directors of Marketing, or other group-level initiatives whereby the market (or potential market awareness developed through market research) is established. In this case, the firm may simply be going through a re-positioning exercise, or it may also be involved with innovation, driven by the efforts of an *intrapreneur* (Pinchot & Pinchot, 1978).

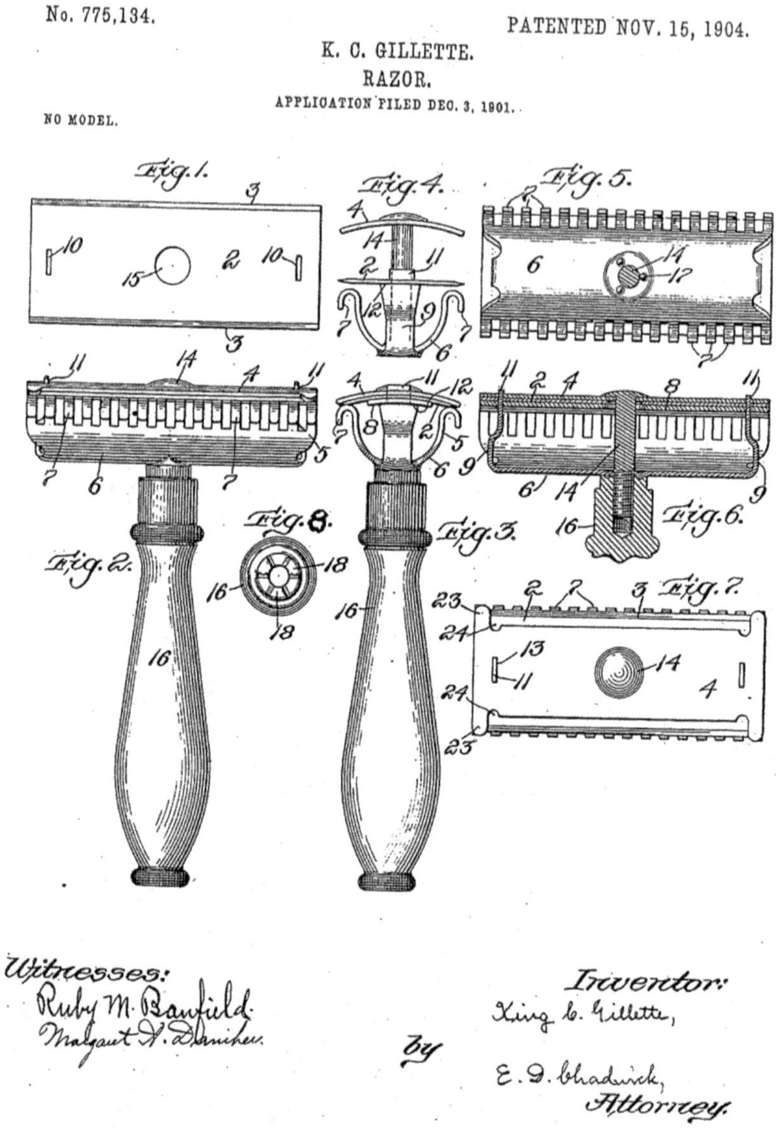

■ **Fig. 2.6** The original Gillette razor patent, Inventor K.C. Gillette, November 15, 1904. (Source: The United States Patent and Trademark Office (USPTO). Website: ► https://pdfpiw.uspto.gov/.piw?Docid=775134&idkey=NONE&homeurl=http%3A%252F%252Fpatft.uspto.gov%252Fnetahtml%252FPTO%252Fpatimg.htm, accessed August 28, 2020. Public Domain)

The likelihood of radical innovation projects decreases as vision moves through the Quadrants 1 to 4. Additionally, as noted in Reid (2015, p. 144), "Some ideas and information may begin in Quadrant 1, but not travel much further through the exploitation processes offered in Quadrants 2 through 4, and therefore, not result in new products in the market. An example of this would be an artist who has painted a large canvas and keeps it hanging in their own living room with no intention to sell it. In other words, no attempts are made by some individuals from Quadrant 1 to commercialize their efforts."

An interesting point to note: it is possible to arrive at the entrepreneurial path from any other quadrant. For example, one potential path may be that an individual has a radical idea, develops it, and then brings it to market on their own and starts a firm. This route is much like the Gillette example provided above where the individual moves from Q1 to Q3.

Another potential path would be that an individual "intrapreneur" working within a company may begin to work on a market-driven product idea while employed for a company, but then decide to pursue it on their own, particularly if the idea does not receive support internally; this would be an example of movement from Q4 to Q3. In the case where this would stem from a technology-related vision, the movement would be from Q2 to Q3. For example, Steve Wozniak presented one of his early-stage computers to his then-employer HP, which famously turned down the option to be further involved (Livingston, 2007). As a result, Steve Wozniak and Steve Jobs were free to pursue the development of the home computer on their own and started one of the largest ever consumer goods companies to date on the planet, Apple Computer.

The intrapreneur who would prefer to start their idea within the extant firm for which they already work, or bring it to another firm, would likely remain in Q4. Related to this, in the case where the original vision was technology-enabled, the movement would be from Q2 to Q4. In other words, situations involving highly complex technologies or possibly a lack of marketing skills by the intrapreneur would most likely invoke the intrapreneurial route.

Another potential pathway might involve movement from Quadrant 1 to 2 to 3. As described by Reid (2015, p. 145), "An example of this is provided by the story of the first elevator. While several underlying technologies and firms contributed to the technological developments required for vertical transportation of this nature (Q2), it was the Otis Elevator corporation (Q3) through the entrepreneurial efforts of Elisha G. Otis (Q1), which built the first passenger lift for an urban structure in New York's Haughwout Department Store on Broadway in 1857 (Hitchcock, 1968)."

2.5 The Visioning Skills Required to Develop a Strong Entrepreneurial Vision

The next logical question, then, is: how to go about developing a successful vision in the first place? For our purposes, we start by looking at how to develop Market Vision, as this is the type of vision which all entrepreneurs need to focus on.

The various exploratory learning processes, involving a set of capabilities to enable the linking of product ideas to new markets, is known as "Market Visioning Competence" (MVC). "Market Visioning Competence" was originally defined as "a set of organizational capabilities that enable the linking of advanced technologies to a given market opportunity of the future" (Colarelli O'Connor & Veryzer, 2001, p. 231). Schilling further elaborates this definition (Schilling, 2013), stating that MVC is "a harmonized combination of multiple resources and skills that distinguish a firm in the marketplace" (Schilling, 2013, p. 117) and therefore offer a foundation for a company's competitiveness. Individual entrepreneurs and their teams also need to work on developing the capabilities underlying MVC (◘ Fig. 2.7) as such skills and resources have been shown to significantly impact the potential for success of both small (startup) and large firms in the marketplace (Reid & de Brentani, 2012). These capabilities include *networking*, *idea driving*, *proactive market orientation*, and *market learning tools* (Reid, 2005) (the foci of Chapters 6–10 of this text book).

Effective visioning, in essence, begins by putting certain building blocks in place so that when shifts or discontinuities occur in the environment (whether they stem from changes in technology, demographics, or social changes), the entrepreneur is already well set up to respond to and/or influence these changes. Further, according to Reid (2015, p. 135), visioning "enables risk reduction to entrepreneurs by offering different points of convergence around technology development goals and specific market goals." "Market Visioning Competence requires a subtle balance

◘ **Fig. 2.7** Conceptual image to portray "team harmony." (Source: Image licensed and downloaded from Shutterstock on September 24, 2018. Credit: by Rawpixel/Shutterstock.com. Signed model release on file with Shutterstock, Inc. License Link: ▸ https://www.shutterstock.com/image-photo/team-teamwork-togetherness-collaboration-concept-343048862)

between the dynamic learning capabilities of individuals (e.g., networking, idea driving) and of the organizations in which they participate (e.g., proactive market orientation, market learning tools)" (Reid & de Brentani, 2012, p. 501). Each of these components underlying Market Visioning Competence has been shown to have a statistically significant impact on the formation of Market Vision (Reid, 2005; Reid & de Brentani, 2010). These findings have been consistent across dissertation research (Reid, 2005) in subsequent related research (Reid & de Brentani, 2010) and with other data samples (Reid et al., 2015).

2.6 Why Is Vision Important?

In this chapter, we have begun to build an understanding of why vision plays a vital role in ensuring success with innovation (Reid & de Brentani, 2010; Reid & Roberts, 2011; Reid et al., 2015). Understanding vision's importance is specifically critical for new ventures and entrepreneurial firms, as research (Baron & Hannan, 2002; Bird, 1992; Breugst et al., 2012; Filion, 1991; Kirkpatrick & Locke, 1996; Reid & de Brentani, 2010, 2012) has specifically shown that the vision itself and the passion behind it exert a significant influence on gaining support from potential partners very early in the entrepreneurial process and that this is a critical success factor for entrepreneurial firms. Any skills, capabilities, processes, or resources that entrepreneurs can arm themselves with to help develop these abilities to create a strong vision are clearly desirable to enable more likelihood of success.

The question is: how do we measure success in the very early stages of entrepreneurship with idea and vision development?

Entrepreneurs need to try to get a handle on their early performance on some level, even though doing so requires looking at different factors from those which existing companies might typically use to assess their performance. Indeed, several studies on best practices of firms (Cooper & Kleinschmidt, 1995; Griffin, 1997) show that "measuring performance" is one of the discriminating factors for firms benchmarked as "best" performers. As one might imagine, performance is typically accounted for in extant companies using measures such as market share, profitability, return on investment, and speed to market, to name a few (Griffin & Page, 1996; Hultink & Robben, 1995). None of these performance measurements would be useful for an early-stage entrepreneur, however, who doesn't have products in the pipeline yet or may not even have capital secured. The early stages of entrepreneurial involvement deal primarily with the pre-project and pre-market stages of innovation, and as such, the use of standard performance tools is not relevant in the very early stages of the entrepreneurial process when vision formation is nascent.

Nevertheless, it is important that prospective investors, customers, and partners can discern those startups with great potential at an early stage. It is the ability of entrepreneurs to communicate and champion their product/market vision which can help develop some of these early relationships. Moreover, having some level of early performance information can help gain further commitment from additional potential early investors and/or distributors and the interest of early customers and, also, help to secure key advisory or team members in the early going stages.

2

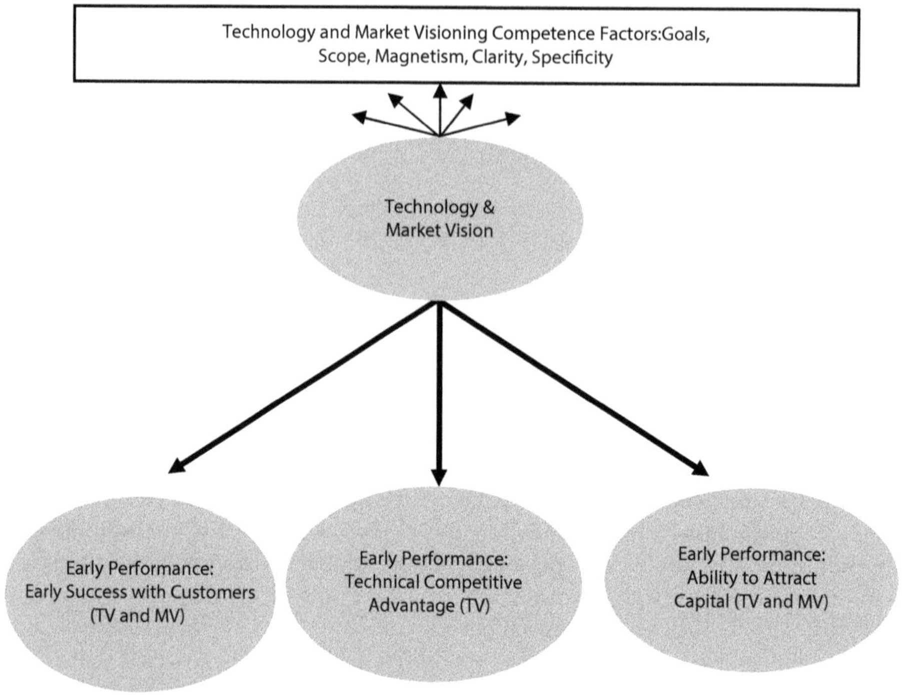

Fig. 2.8 Technology Vision and Market Vision impacts on three early performance factors. (Source: Adapted from Reid (2005) PhD thesis)

So, what types of significant advantage are specifically achieved by crafting a solid vision?

Based on empirical research, three types of competitive advantage have been found as specific outcomes of having developed a solid Technology Vision and/or Market Vision (Reid, 2005; Reid & de Brentani, 2010; Reid & Roberts, 2011; Reid et al., 2015) (Fig. 2.8), particularly in the early days of an innovative product initiation before launch: *early success with customers, ability to attract capital and technical competitive advantage*.

2.6.1 Early Success with Customers

Both "customer acceptance" and "customer satisfaction" are useful metrics for rating performance with "new-to-the-world products" (Griffin & Page, 1996). Taken together, "early success with customers" ("ESC") (Reid, 2005; Reid & de Brentani, 2010) is a first early success metric for innovation. Additionally, this metric is related to the "lead user" concept (von Hippel, 1986). "Lead users" are positioned to obtain outsized gains from their involvement in finding solutions to their needs (von Hippel, 2005), and as such, are more likely to be involved in creating or co-creating promising ideas for successful product delivery in the future. Therefore, early success with customers, such as lead users, provides a useful early metric for understanding the future promise of a given vision.

2.6.2 Ability to Attract Capital

Secondly, an entrepreneur's "ability to attract capital" ("AAC") (Reid, 2005; Reid & de Brentani, 2010) provides another critical measure of early vision performance. New ventures, such as those housed in entrepreneurial startups, in addition to downstream marketing efforts to early customers, need to market their ideas upstream to potential investors (Timmons & Spinelli, 2004), such as venture capitalists (Hellmann & Puri, 2000; Kaplan & Strömberg, 2004; Zider, 1998), incubators, corporate partners, and institutional investors (Song & di Benedetto, 2008). As such, the ability to attract capital provides an important early proxy indicator of the value of the vision.

2.6.3 Technical Competitive Advantage

Lastly, an important measure that can be applied in the case of new entrepreneurial initiatives, particularly those involving a vision for the technical side of a product, is "technical competitive advantage" ("TCA") (Griffin & Page, 1996; Reid, 2005; Reid & de Brentani, 2010). Effectively, TCA accounts for a product's quality, performance, and innovativeness. In entrepreneurial new product development scenarios involving high levels of technical uncertainty, the ability to create robust Technology Vision as well as a strong Market Vision, helps to achieve a significant competitive advantage with customers, employees, financiers, and the competition. This, in turn, can ultimately lead to superior financial results.

In sum, our suggested entrepreneurial process takes the ideas underlying how to build a successful Market Vision (and, where relevant, Technology Vision) through creating a Visioning Competence, as a basis for building a more refined understanding of what the beginning of a successful entrepreneurial process might look like. In later chapters, we provide worksheets aimed at understanding how to build better networking and championing skills. Additionally, we demonstrate how to develop market learning tools and, also, how to use your own proactive inspiration to move you actively toward new markets, and perhaps even those that you will play a large role in building.

Chapter Review Questions

1. What are the three essential building blocks of vision and why do you think it is important that they all be present?
2. What are the main differences between low-market context and high-market context types of vision? Please provide two examples of each to illustrate the differences.
3. What do you understand by the term Market Visioning Competence? Do you think this is a skill that can be taught? Why or why not?
4. A strong market vision has been shown to create competitive advantage in several different ways. Please provide an example of an entrepreneur who has a compelling vision and how this has worked in their favor.

References

2

Baron, J. N., & Hannan, M. T. (2002). The economic sociology of organizational entrepreneurship: Lessons from the Stanford project on emerging companies. In V. Nee & R. Swedberg (Eds.), *The economic sociology of capitalism* (pp. 168–203). Princeton University Press.

Bird, B. (1992). The emergence of the new venture. *Entrepreneurship Theory and Practice, 17*(1), 11–20.

Breugst, N., Domurath, A., Patzelt, H., & Klaukien, A. (2012). Perceptions of entrepreneurial passion and employees' commitment to entrepreneurial ventures. *Entrepreneurship Theory and Practice, 36*(1), 171–192.

Brown, S. L., & Eisenhardt, K. M. (1995). Product development: Past research, present findings and future directions. *Academy of Management Review, 20*(4), 343–378.

Christensen, C. M. (1997). *The innovator's dilemma*. Harvard Business School Press.

Clifford, C. C. (2018). Anyone can move to mars and gas cars will be like steam engines. Entrepreneurs section, *CNBC.com*. https://www.cnbc.com/2018/05/15/what-elon-musk-thinks-the-future-of-cars-and-mars-will-be.html. Uploaded May 15, 2018. Accessed on August 29, 2020.

Colarelli O'Connor, G., & Veryzer, R. (2001). The nature of market visioning for technology-based radical innovation. *The Journal of Product Innovation Management, 18*(4), 231–246.

Collins, J. C., & Porras, J. I. (1991). Organizational vision and visionary organizations. *California Management Review*, 34(1), 30–52.

Collins, J. C., & Porras, J. I. (1995). Building a visionary company. *California Management Review, 37*(2), 80–100.

Cooper, R. G. (1985). Selecting winning new product projects: Using the NewProd system. *The Journal of Product Innovation Management*, 2(1), 34–44.

Cooper, R. G., & Kleinschmidt, E. J. (1995). Benchmarking the firm's critical success factors in new product development. *The Journal of Product Innovation Management, 12*(5), 374–391.

Cummings, S., & Davies, J. (1994). Mission, vision, fusion. *Long Range Planning, 27*(6), 147–150.

Day, G., & Schoemaker, P. J. H. (2005). Scanning the periphery. *Harvard Business Review*, 83(11), 135-140.

Filion, L. J. (1991). Visions and relations: Elements for an entrepreneurial metamodel. International Small Business Journal, 9(2), 112–131.

Gardner, H. (1985). *The mind's new science: A history of the cognitive revolution*. Basic Books.

Gerber, M. E. (2001). *The E-Myth revisited*. Harper Business, a division of Harper Collins Publishers.

Giordan, J. C. (1995). That vision thing. *Research-Technology Management, 38*(5), 8–9.

Griffin, A. (1997). PDMA research on new product development practices: Updating trends and benchmarking best practices. *The Journal of Product Innovation Management, 14*(6), 429–458.

Griffin, A., & Page, A. L. (1996). PDMA success measurement project: Recommended measures for product development success and failure. *The Journal of Product Innovation Management, 13*(6), 478–496.

Hamel, G., & Prahalad, C. K. (1994). *Competing for the future*. Harvard Business School Press.

Hellmann, T., & Puri, M. (2000). The interaction between product market and financing strategy: The role of venture capital. *Review of Financial Studies, 13*(4), 959–984.

Hitchcock, H. R. (1968). *Architecture: Nineteenth and twentieth centuries* (3rd ed.). Penguin.

Hultink, E.-J., & Robben, H. S. J. (1995). Measuring new product success: The difference that time perspective makes. *The Journal of Product Innovation Management, 12*(5), 392–405.

Jolly, V. K. (1997). *Commercializing new technologies*. Harvard Business School Press.

Kaplan, S. N., & Strömberg, P. (2004). Characteristics, contracts, and actions: Evidence from venture capitalist analyses. *The Journal of Finance, 59*(5), 2177–2210.

Kirkpatrick, S. A., & Locke, E. A. (1996). Direct and indirect effects of three core charismatic leadership components on performance and attitudes. *Journal of Applied Psychology, 81(1)*, 36–51.

Livingston, J. (2007). *Founders at work: Stories of startups' early days*. Springer-Verlag.

Lynn, G., & Akgün, A. E. (2001). Project visioning: Its components and impact on new product success. *The Journal of Product Innovation Management, 18*(6), 374–387.

MasKargo Logistics website. (2020, online). *MasKargo vision statement*, www.maskargologistics.com. Accessed on August 25, 2020.

McCulloch, W. S., & Pitts, W. (1943). A logical calculus of ideas imminent in nervous activity. *Bulletin of Mathematical Biophysics, 5*.

Moenart, R. K., Robben, H., & Gouw, P. (2009). *Visionary Marketing: Building sustainable business*. Editions Lannoo sa.

Nayak, P. R., & Ketteringham, J. M. (1986). *Breakthroughs! How the vision and drive of innovators in sixteen companies created commercial breakthroughs that swept the world*. Arthur D. Little and Rawson Associates.

Neimes, J. (1996). Team members must have vision, trust, confidence. *Orlando Business Journal, 12*(42), 15.

Pinchot, G., & Pinchot, E. (1978). *Intra-corporate entrepreneurship*. The School for Entrepreneurs.

Rasmus, D. W. (2012). *Defining your company's vision*. www.FastCompany.com/1821021. Uploaded February 28, 2012. Accessed on 20 July 2020.

Reid, S. E. (2005). *Market Vision for radically-new, high-tech products*. Ph.D. Thesis, John Molson School of Business, Concordia University.

Reid, S. E. (2015). Vision and radical innovation: A typology. In A. Brem & E. Viardot (Eds.), *Adoption of innovation: Balancing internal and external stakeholders in the marketing of innovation* (pp. 133–154). Springer International Publications.

Reid, S. E., & de Brentani, U. (2004). The fuzzy front-end of new product development for discontinuous innovation: A theoretical model. *The Journal of Product Innovation Management, 21*(3), 170–184.

Reid, S. E., & de Brentani, U. (2010). Market Vision and Market Visioning Competence: Impact on early performance for radically-new, high-tech products. *The Journal of Product Innovation Management, 27*(4), 500–518.

Reid, S. E., & de Brentani, U. (2012). Market Vision and the front end of NPD for radical innovation: The impact of moderating effects. *The Journal of Product Innovation Management, 29*(S1, Dec), 124–139.

Reid, S. E., & Roberts, D. L. (2011). Technology Vision: A scale development. *R&D Management, 41*(5), 427–442.

Reid, S. E., Roberts, D. L., & Moore, K. (2015). Vision for technology-enabled radical innovation and its impact on early success. *The Journal Product Innovation Management, 32*(4), 593–609.

Rice, M. P., O'Connor, G. C., Peters, L. S., & Morone, J. G. (1998). Managing discontinuous innovation. *Research-Technology Management, 41*, 52–58.

Schilling, M. A. (2013). *Strategic management of technological innovation*. McGraw Hill.

Selznick, P. (1957). *Leadership in administration: A sociological interpretation*. Row, Peterson & Company.

Song, M., & di Benedetto, A. (2008). Supplier's involvement and success of radical new product development in new ventures. *Journal of Operations Management, 26*(1), 1–22.

Sturken, M., Thomas, D., & Ball-Rokeach, S. J. (Eds.). (2004). *Technological Visions: The hopes and fears that shape new technologies*. Temple University Press.

Tellis, G. J., & Golder, P. N. (2002). *Will and Vision: How latecomers grow to dominate markets*. McGraw-Hill.

Timmons, J. A., & Spinelli, S. (2004). *New venture creation: Entrepreneurship for the 21st century*. McGraw-Hill Irwin.

Vaughan, J. A. (1997). Vision and meaning. *Executive Excellence, 14*(3), 11–12.

Von Hippel, E. (1986). Lead users: A source of novel product concepts. *Management Science, 32*(7), 791–805.

Von Hippel, E. (2005). *Democratizing innovation*. MIT Press.

Zider, B. (1998). How venture capital works. *Harvard Business Review*, 76(6), 131–139.

The Motivational Roots of Entrepreneurial Vision

Contents

© The Author(s), under exclusive license to Springer Nature Switzerland AG 2022
S. E. Reid, C. B. Crawford, *Entrepreneurial Vision*, Classroom Companion: Business, https://doi.org/10.1007/978-3-030-77803-3_3

Learning Objectives

There is a growing interest in and focus on understanding what underlies the initial decision of any given individual to undertake a business initiative. Specifically, there is an increasing degree of importance being accorded to understanding the triggers which motivate any given individual to become an entrepreneur. Motivation types and levels are key indicators of the likelihood of a given individual's active participation in processes involved with entrepreneurship (Shane et al., 2003). As such, entrepreneurial motivation serves as a good basis for understanding why and how entrepreneurs get started on a given entrepreneurial path.

In order to better understand "why" entrepreneurs get started on a given path, in this chapter, we provide a general framework of entrepreneurial motivation by breaking it down into intrinsic, extrinsic, and hybrid types of motivational triggers. We also offer an overview of the "what," related to the "why," otherwise known as the interests, values, and personal missions that underlie an entrepreneur's desire to create something new, and how this is influenced by cultural context. Finally, we discuss "how" entrepreneurs experience and follow through with these motivational triggers based on cognitive style, mindset, and the creation of an actionable vision.

3.1 An Entrepreneurial Motivation Framework

The entrepreneurial motivation framework and associated literature review we use for understanding entrepreneurial motivational triggers and their outcomes (◘ Fig. 3.1) were developed by Lalonde and Reid (2019/2020).

In general, entrepreneurial drive has been primarily classified by researchers into two broad types of motivations: intrinsic and extrinsic (Carsrud & Brännback, 2009, 2011). Intrinsic motivations are triggered through latent, or underdeveloped, personality traits, while extrinsic motivations stem from an interaction between the individual and social and informational cues from the environment.

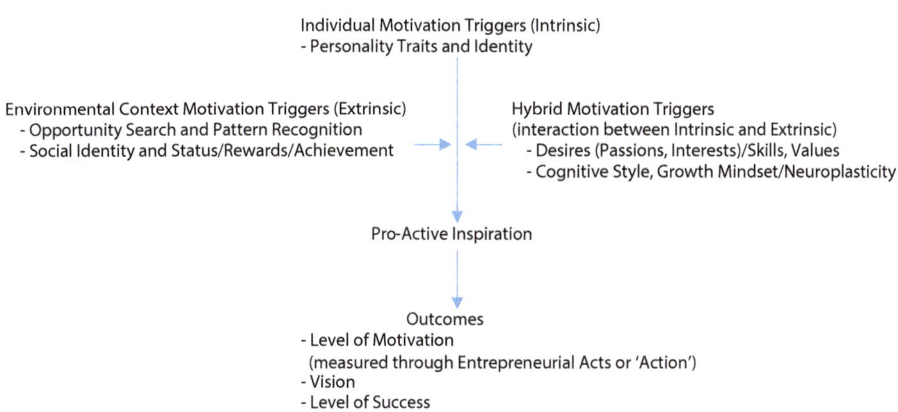

◘ **Fig. 3.1** An entrepreneurial motivation framework. (Source: Lalonde and Reid (2019/2020))

Rather than solely focusing on either intrinsic or extrinsic perspectives, we suggest considering a hybrid approach, as first put forward by Gibb and Ritchie (1982). Using such a dynamic approach accounts for both internal psychosocial "entrepreneurial potential" along with external social and environmental triggers, and how they evolve together through various focusing and filtering mechanisms such as values, cognitive style, skills, and desires. The overall outcome of these interactions

results in certain levels of entrepreneurial activity, entrepreneurial vision, and success. In effect, "entrepreneurial potential," captured by measuring psychosocial traits when blended with environmental triggers, provides a foundation for understanding how to start building a successful vision tailored to your motivations.

To build a better basis for understanding, each of these three perspectives on motivation—intrinsic, extrinsic, and hybrid—is briefly described.

3.2 Intrinsic Motivations

According to the intrinsic motivational perspective, individuals engage in entrepreneurial activities primarily because they are drawn to them (Eccles & Wigfield, 2002). This key argument in the entrepreneurship literature is mostly psychological in nature and springs from research such as that from McClelland (1961) and Brockhaus (1982) who launched "the psychological traits school." Certain personality traits have been associated with higher levels of entrepreneurship including adventuring, creativity, flexibility, imagination, innovation, initiative, pioneering, proactivity, and risk taking (Cromie, 2000; Chell et al., 1991; Dandridge & Ford, 1987; Gibb & Ritchie, 1982; Hornaday, 1982) (■ Fig. 3.2). This research on entrepreneurial traits has not shown consensus across authors, however.

Research based on demographic indicators has been spotty historically but more recently finds that the impact from factors such as age, gender, and education varies depending on location. One recent study (Crawford, 2018 based on 2004 to 2011 data from the National Opinion Research Center ("NORC data enclave")/Kauffman Foundation's survey of American entrepreneurs, which started in 1996) found that for American entrepreneurs there was no impact related to age, gender, or education. Recent research from the Global Report of the GEM group (Bosma et al., 2019/2020), an important source for data on entrepreneurship in 50 economies with surveys from more than 150,000 adults, shows some interesting recent trends from a global perspective. As relates to age, Bosma et al. (2019/2020, p. 19) found for 38/50 of the countries studied that "levels of early-stage entrepreneurship generally increase with age and then decline." As relates to gender, they found (2019/2020, p. 19) that "women are taking a stronger and more robust role in some economies, though they still lag significantly behind men in others."

As such, based on the direction provided by these researchers, we suggest considering a fuller framework of entrepreneurial experience over time, one which includes values, cognitive style, skills, desires, mindsets, and other external motivational triggers such as specific opportunities, expertise, advisors, and networks—including family, friends, and alliances. For example, Crawford (2018) specifically found that founders' first alliances and partners, as well as their networks, were key

Fig. 3.2 Conceptual image to portray the question "Personality traits of entrepreneurs?" (Source: Image licensed and downloaded from Shutterstock on May 28, 2020. Credit: by canadastock/▶ Shutterstock.com. License Link: ▶ https://www.shutterstock.com/image-photo/fearless-hiker-standing-on-overhanging-rock-1181662462)

determinants in entrepreneurial success (Crawford, 2018). These findings align with the research reported by the GEM group (Bosma et al., 2019/2020).

3.3 Extrinsic Motivations

According to the extrinsic motivational perspective, a person's desire to seek what they consider to be a higher and/or new social identity is a major determining factor impacting entrepreneurial motivation (Mahto & McDowell, 2018). We refer to this as the "I'll show them" approach. According to this perspective, extrinsic motivation is mostly related to external triggering mechanisms, i.e., social and informational cues from the environment. For example, individuals may be motivated to engage in entrepreneurial activities for rewards, the desire to change circumstances, the need for recognition from others, or due to the identification of alluring commercial opportunities (Hamdi-Kidar & Vellera, 2012), familial obligations, or sometimes out of necessity. As an illustration, in the Global Report of the GEM group (Bosma et al., 2019/2020, p. 18): "in 35 of the 50 economies (surveyed), over half of adults starting a new business agree with the motive 'to earn a living because jobs are scarce.'" As such, we can see that this perspective suggests that many individuals are primarily motivated through external pressures from the environment to bring about change.

There are many examples of very successful entrepreneurs whereby at least part of their motivation may have come about in such a way. J.K. Rowling, now one of the world's foremost authors, was struggling financially (▶ https://www.biography.

com/news/jk-rowling-harry-potter-author-rags-to-riches-billionaire, Tim Ott, February 25, 2020) when she wrote the first of the Harry Potter series. Clearly, such motivations can have powerful outcomes when coupled with passion, skill, and perseverance.

3.4 Hybrid Approaches to Understanding Motivation

A dynamic hybrid approach (Lalonde & Reid, 2019/2020) suggests that identity and desire for upward mobility and/or basic psychosocial traits are not sufficient for understanding entrepreneurial motivation. A full framework should be inclusive of "values," defined by Usunier and Valette-Florence (2007, p. 353) as "inferred constructs held collectively by societies and individually by persons." Such a values-inclusive framework includes a more elaborate consideration of culture, spirituality, and concern for the environment and for others, the latter of which has led to a great deal of interest in "social entrepreneurship."

Additionally, while there has been some recognition of the importance of cognitive style, there has been little research on their relationship specific to entrepreneurship beyond the basic innovative traits perspective already described. For example, there has been some interest in the relationship between entrepreneurial orientation ("EO") and emotional intelligence ("EQ") with some data pointing to a significant positive relationship between the two (e.g., Pradhan & Nath, 2012). Further, in order to provide a broader level of understanding, we suggest that a focus on "cognitive style" and how different cognitive styles come into play in the overall visioning and entrepreneurial process may be a useful perspective to examine. A particularly important facet of this level of understanding is that many of these skills can be learned or balanced out through the creation of strong entrepreneurial team structures. These approaches may be useful in aiding the creation of better cross-functional entrepreneurial teams in the first place and understanding when to emphasize which skills over the journey of building a business.

Last, we feel strongly that a framework of motivation, particularly one aimed at getting to the heart of how to build a strong and compelling vision, must begin and end with what we refer to as proactive inspiration and related passions, interests, skills, and mindsets.

These last hybrid perspectives of motivation offer new avenues for research and support for practice in the field.

3.5 Passion, Skills, Proactive Inspiration, and Their Relationships to Motivation

In general, the field of positive psychology underscores the motivational aspect of passion. Vallerand and Verner-Filion (2013, p. 35) state that "Passion is defined as a strong inclination toward a self-defining activity that people like (or love), find important, and in which they invest time and energy." In other words, there is a "natural" aspect to passion—similar in a way to pre-existing psychosocial traits, where individuals hold certain activities near and dear (◘ Fig. 3.3).

According to Vallerand and Verner-Filion (2013, p. 36), "Descartes (1596–1650) defined passions as strong emotions with inherent behavioral tendencies… Rousseau (1712–1778)…further suggesting that passion could lead to knowledge and truth…Hegel (1770–1831) passions are highly energetic and necessary to reach the highest levels of achievement."

◘ **Fig. 3.3** Lewis Carroll's "Alice's Adventures in Wonderland": "But what am I to do?" said Alice. "Anything you like," said the Footman and began whistling. (Image illustrated by A.E. Jackson, New York: Henry Frowde, 1914. Source: Downloaded from the collection of Dave Neal who has posted some images from his collection for public use at ► http://www.exit109.com/~dnn/alice/jackson/jack6.jpg. Public Domain)

While, for some, the pursuit of passion may seem self-serving or even narcissistic, research finds many positive outcomes related to the importance of understanding and pursuing one's passion. The research of Vallerand et al. (2003) found relationships between passion and psychological/physical health, relationships, and performance.

3

Additionally, Chen et al. (2009) found a strong correlation between entrepreneurial passion and its impact on the ability to secure entrepreneurial financing. Further, Baum and Locke (2004) demonstrated a relationship between passion and company performance; so, passion plays an essential role in extant companies as well.

Some researchers and positive psychologists utilize other terminology or related perspectives. For example, Simon Sinek in his landmark work, *Start with Why* (2009), suggests that the only way to truly have 20/20 foresight is to always begin a process with the understanding of why you do so—the aim being inspiration to deliver the best possible products, services, and so forth in line with your values, goals, and desires. As noted by Sinek (2009, p. 21): "For those who are inspired, the motivation to act is deeply personal." In other words, as emphasized by Sinek, it is crucial to attempt to focus on inspiration to influence human behavior, rather than on manipulations. He gives an example of American vs. Japanese car engineering and design, going back a few decades, where American cars often needed doors to be hammered into place after the body of the car and door had been created. In contrast, he notes that Japanese car doors were always designed from the beginning to fit in place without requiring this step because the design and what Toyota has coined as the "Total Production Concept" aims at no post-hoc manipulation being required.

So, should we wait around to be inspired as entrepreneurs, sitting on our preexisting "potential" in terms of psychosocial traits and our known passions, hoping for the best in terms of a good opportunity coming along which matches that potential?

The answer is no! Rather, we believe that entrepreneurs need to go through an initial process to be "proactively inspired." Seek, and ye shall find (Matthew 7:7). Striving to logically figure out what you desire, whether based on a lifelong passion, newfound inspiration, or strong skills you already possess or wish to develop, is an excellent place to start.

In order to help you get started on your entrepreneurial journey, we provide Worksheet 1, which aims to help you elucidate three key areas of passion and interests to serve as a basis for thinking about the ideas and worksheets provided in the remaining chapters of this book.

Worksheet 1: Declaring Your Passions and Interests

The objective of this worksheet is to clearly elucidate 3 key areas of passion and interest that will serve as a basis for further elaboration and active networking and may help with looking for complementary partners and advisors. Your assessment of your own interests and areas of passion, which you can start outlining using this worksheet, is the first key step in this process. Have fun with this!

For each of your 3 selected areas of passion/interest, outline the following points:

1. **General subject/topic area #1 of interest is:________________________**

2. Why is this important to you:
   a. importance to you:___________________________________
   b. importance to society_________________________________
   c. need/gap that you perceive may exist:___________________

3. Why is this of interest to you:
   a. previous personal involvements with the subject:__________
   b. mentors/role model influence:__________________________
   c. an idea you may have:________________________________
   d. something that motivates you and why:__________________

4. How the area fits with:
   i) your personality/motivations:___________________________
   ii) your values:____
   iii) your skills:____
   iv) any current goals you may have:_________________________

© Susan E. Reid and Charles B. Crawford, August 14, 2020.

3

1. **General subject/topic area #2 of interest is:____________________________**

2. Why is this important to you:

   a. importance to you: ____

   b. importance to society:______________________________________

   c. need/gap that you perceive may exist:__________________________

3. Why is this of interest to you:

   a. previous personal involvements with the subject:________________

   b. mentors/role model influence__________________________________

   c. an idea you may have:______________________________________

   d. something that motivates you and why:_________________________

4. How the area fits with:

   i) your personality/motivations:____________________________________

   ii) your values:____

   iii) your skills:____

   iv) any current goals you may have:_________________________________

© Susan E. Reid and Charles B. Crawford, August 14, 2020.

1. **General subject/topic area #3 of interest is:________________________**

2. Why is this important to you:
   a. importance to you: ______________________________
   b. importance to society:____________________________
   c. need/gap that you perceive may exist:____________________

3. Why is this of interest to you:
   a. previous personal involvements with the subject:____________
   b. mentors/role model influence:________________________
   c. an idea you may have:_____________________________
   d. something that motivates you and why:__________________

4. How the area fits with:
   i) your personality/motivations:__________________________
   ii) your values:____________________________________
   iii) your skills:___________________________________
   iv) any current goals you may have:______________________

© Susan E. Reid and Charles B. Crawford, August 14, 2020.

3

In his book, *True Purpose*, Tim Kelley (2009) describes the importance of finding your purpose as a concept similar to seeking to be proactively inspired. He describes a series of methods for finding one's purpose and frames them using "direct access methods" (Kelley, 2009, p. 71) such as asking good questions like "What is my mission?" (Kelley, 2009, p. 78) and "indirect access methods" (Kelley, 2009, p. 25) such as journaling or self-reflecting on questions such as "When are the times in your life when you've felt most passionate?" or "When are the times when you've felt most aligned?" (Kelley, 2009, p. 31). Often the answers are linked with the activities you turn to when you have free time, as was demonstrated when the Wright Brothers spent their free time building a flying machine as a hobby (◘ Fig. 3.4) while running their bicycle manufacturing business, The Wright Cycle Company. According to Roberge (2011, p. 118), "We all have a deep desire to make a meaningful contribution in life. Living a purposeful life leads to true and lasting fulfilment and flow in everyday life. And following your passion often leads you to your purpose. However, there is an opportunity to understand and live your purpose at a much more meaningful level." In other words, passion is just a starting place for proactive inspiration and, ultimately, long-term purpose.

In sum, tapping into and understanding your desires (passions and interests) and skills, in addition to understanding your motivations, whether intrinsic, extrinsic, or hybrid, moves you forward to the possibility of being proactively inspired through opportunity search and pattern recognition. Over a longer period of time, it enables "living on purpose" (Kelley, 2009) and fulfillment both at the individual

◘ **Fig. 3.4** First successful flight of the Wright Flyer, by the Wright brothers, December 17, 1903. The machine traveled 120 ft (36.6 m) in 12 seconds at 10:35 a.m. at Kill Devil Hills, North Carolina. ► https://commons.wikimedia.org/wiki/File:First_flight2.jpg. (Credit: John T. Daniels. Downloaded via Wikimedia Commons on July 20, 2020. Public Domain)

■ **Fig. 3.5** Conceptual image to portray "Remember why you started." (Source: Image licensed and downloaded from Adobe Stock on April 21, 2020. Credit: by gustavofrazao/▶ stock.adobe.com. License Link: ▶ https://stock.adobe.com/ca/images/remember-why-you-started-written-on-desert--road/97034596?prev_url=detail)

level and in our day-to-day work environment. In other words, understanding why we set our goals in the first place helps remind us to keep moving forward in pursuit of our vision (■ Fig. 3.5). Also, given what we know about the importance of championing behavior for entrepreneurs and its importance for helping develop a solid vision, being inspired is mission-critical for success. As Carl Jung famously said (Jung, n.d.), "Your vision will become clear only when you can look into your own heart…who looks outside, dreams, who looks inside, awakes."

3.6 Values and Their Relationship to Motivation

Values are represented by general goals people strive for over a lifetime (Schwartz, 1992) which affect beliefs, behaviors, and the passions and interests people invest their time in. Stern and Dietz (1994, p. 67) suggest that "value orientations take shape during the socialization process and are fairly stable in adults." Stern and Dietz (1994, p. 68) additionally state that "values may also act as filters for information, influencing beliefs by leading people to accept information selectively when it seems consonant with their values."

We believe that the impact of values on entrepreneurial potential and motivation is very important, and, as such, in the next sections, we investigate three key foci around which we can develop a better understanding of values: culture

Fig. 3.6 Conceptual image to portray "core values." (Source: Image licensed and downloaded from Adobe Stock on August 1, 2020. Credit: by @frank peters/▶ stock.adobe.com. License Link: ▶ https://stock.adobe.com/ca/images/core-values/153575257?prev_url=detail)

(▶ Sect. 3.6.1), spirituality (▶ Sect. 3.6.2), and social entrepreneurship (▶ Sect. 3.6.3) (Fig. 3.6).

3.6.1 Culture

In the early stages of entrepreneurship research, pre-2000, several authors linked entrepreneurial motivation and values through a discussion of culture. Cultural context and cultural values play an essential role in the individual's ability to identify and respond to or create entrepreneurial opportunities (Dana, 1993, 1995; Basu, 1998; Basu & Altinay, 2002; Danes et al., 2008; Filion et al., 2007; Kolvereid, 1992). Further, institutional and economic contexts have a significant influence over entrepreneurship (Hayton et al., 2002). The most recent Global Report of the GEM group (Bosma et al., 2019/2020, p. 17) shows strong evidence of this with high levels of differential rates of entrepreneurial startups between countries. Some research suggests that cultural elements only moderate this higher-level relationship of institutional economic context and entrepreneurial potential (Tan, 2002). Regardless of whether culture or economic context exerts the more significant influence, there seems to be a consensus that motivation is a dynamic and multifaceted concept that must be studied using multiple variables, including culture, however narrowly or broadly defined (Lalonde, 2010, 2012). So, for example, a more narrow definition of culture might consider culture based at the family and friends level (Danes et al., 2008; Gibb & Ritchie, 1982) or at the organizational level (à la Hofstede, 1980) and a more broad definition might operate at the country level (à la Peabody, 1967).

For many years, Geert Hofstede worked for IBM and administered over 116,000 questionnaires (in 1968 and 1972) to employees in over 50 different countries (Hofstede, 1980). The results of this research led Hofstede (1980, 2nd edition, p. xix–xx) to determine four main organizational cultural factors based upon responses to questionnaire items:

"Power distance" ("the extent to which the less powerful members of organizations and institutions accept and expect that power is distributed unequally") and what Hofstede termed "masculinity" ("the distribution of emotional roles between the genders") have often been examined in cross-cultural and organizational contexts. The other two factors—"uncertainty avoidance" and "individualism"—represent values which can be seen to have the potential to influence the entrepreneurial process dramatically, and these 2 are defined as follows (Hofstede, 1980, 2nd edition, p. xix–xx):

Uncertainty Avoidance:
"the extent to which a culture programs its members to feel either uncomfortable or comfortable in unstructured situations. Unstructured situations are novel, unknown, surprising, different from usual."

Individualism:
"is the degree to which individuals are supposed to look after themselves or remain integrated into groups."

In the early days of a startup, entrepreneurs likely need to demonstrate some tolerance (even embracing) of uncertainty and a fair degree of individualism. Indeed, these values may positively influence the processes of adoption and diffusion of innovation. According to Rogers (2003, p. 48), "diffusion is the process in which an innovation is communicated through certain channels over time among the members of a social system. It is a special type of communication in that the messages are concerned with new ideas." The embracing of uncertainty and the lack of fear and not being concerned about criticism that can come with individualism both enable the type of information sharing required for such diffusion of innovation.

Later in the startup process, uncertainty avoidance and concern for the collective may become more desirable characteristics, as cross-functional involvement and team structures are vital in the implementation phases of innovation and building a new enterprise. As vision crystallizes and a team capitulates toward a specific end goal at launch, removal of ambiguity can be helpful in these later stages.

As such, it seems important that entrepreneurs who strike strong scores on individualism and who embrace ambiguity consider how best to build a strong team to balance out these tendencies for later in their journey.

At the broader country level, "cross-cultural research in psychology is the explicit, systematic comparison of psychological variables under different cultural conditions in order to specify the antecedents and processes that mediate the emergence of behavior differences" (Eckensberger, 1972, p. 100). For the purposes of comparing entrepreneurial product development processes across cultures or comparing the impact of individuals exhibiting different traits linked to country culture when starting an enterprise, keeping such a definition in mind is important. One key topic in social psychology involves the degree to which individuals adhere to group norms (Asch, 1956). According to Berry et al. (1992, p. 80), "there are general expectations in all societies that members will conform to societal norms." That said, Berry et al. (1992, p. 80) note that "there appears to be variation across cultures in the degree to which individuals are raised or trained to be independent and self-reliant." As such, while several cross-cultural studies have been conducted related to the conformity paradigm (e.g., Boldt, 1978; Chandra, 1973; Claeys, 1967; Matsuda, 1985; Huang & Harris, 1973; Meade & Barnard, 1973; Munroe & Munroe, 1975) indicating support for the prediction that conformity will correspond to the degree of sociocultural "tightness" in the society, it certainly does not preclude the ability for creative, open-to-anomaly individuals to emerge in such societies.

An even broader way to consider "culture" has been defined by Berry et al. (1992, p. 1) as "the shared way of life of a group." This definition allows us to conceive of culture not only at the country or organizational level but across any group with shared values. For example, the term "pop culture" evokes images of famous singers from Madonna to Bruno Mars; given their unique take and influence on consumers interested in pop music, it can be argued that such icons are cultural ambassadors for pop music.

3.6.2 Spirituality

Spirituality is a "reconnection to the inner self; a search for universal values that lifts the individual above egocentric strivings; deep empathy with all living beings; and finally, a desire to keep in touch with the source of life (whatever name we give it). In other words, spirituality is a search for inner identity, connectedness, and transcendence" (Bouckaert & Zsolnai, 2012, p. 490).

In entrepreneurship, the introduction of the concept of spirituality allows for the emergence of new business models based on the values of entrepreneurs (King-Kauanui et al., 2005, 2010). Therefore, spirituality-based values may become associated with brands representing "the search for meaning, values, transcendence hope and connection in modern societies" (Raco & Tanod, 2014, p. 43). According to this view, the brand promise, when based on spiritual values, is about connection, joy, and fulfillment. Spirituality can therefore be seen as a possible way of achieving success for entrepreneurs, both in the realization of a spiritual vision and for their personal fulfillment (King-Kauanui et al., 2005, 2010).

The understanding of the importance of spirituality as a prime values-based motivational factor, while not prevalent in academic research, is certainly alluded to often in the business world. For example, according to Gerber (2001, Forward xiii–xiv), author of the *E-Myth*:

> "The greatest businesspeople I've met are determined to get it right no matter what the cost. And by getting it right, I'm not just talking about the business. I mean that there is something uplifting, some vision, some higher-end insight that 'getting it right' would serve."

There are many excellent entrepreneurial businesses which have stemmed from the spiritual space. Take Headspace, for instance. An app dedicated to achieving well-being through meditation, it teaches users to become more mindful by sticking close to the company's overarching mission: "To improve the health and happiness of the world" (Headspace, 2020). Not only does the company incorporate spirituality directly into the meditation series available on the app, but it is also rooted in its founder Andy Puddicombe's personal journey, as he spent 10 years living as a Buddhist monk. The value he found in meditation eventually led Puddicombe to create the app, which is now available in 190 countries and serves millions through his vision of creating a more mindful, peaceful, and healthy world.

3.6.3 Social Entrepreneurship

Social entrepreneurship is related to spiritual values on some level and is essentially based on noneconomic factors (Grimes et al., 2013; Mahto & McDowell, 2018; Miller et al., 2012). Social entrepreneurship is a practice that consists of proposing business responses tailored to social issues. Social entrepreneurs are "motivated, mission-driven individuals who strive to change the world, their cities and communities by putting in place sustainable businesses that are designed to create social impact" (Germak & Robinson, 2014; pp. 5–6), and they often decide to engage even before considering which type of social enterprise to establish. Such entrepreneurs might be motivated by the desire for success and social proximity, the need for money, the desire to help society, concentration on the problems of others, and/or the proximity of the social problem, as well as personal fulfillment (Germak & Robinson, 2014). Since the focus is also on sustainable practices (which include social, economic, and environmental foci according to a three-legged stool sustainability approach with origins generally attributed to the United Nations), environmental entrepreneurship is often related to this perspective.

Several literatures have contributed to the growing body of research in the field of social entrepreneurship. Three schools of thought with accompanying measurement techniques have sprung up. The first school has focused mostly on social values. For example, the "VALS" method ("Values and Life Style") (Mitchell, 1983) provides vivid imagery around the values of innovators, experiencers, and

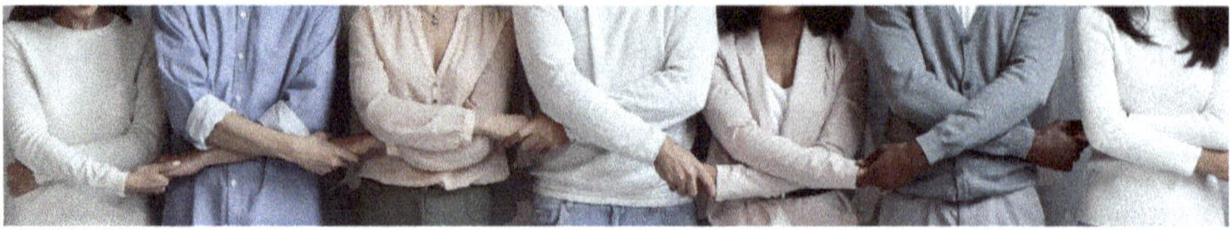

3

■ **Fig. 3.7** Conceptual image to portray "Warm Relationships with Others." (Source: Image licensed and downloaded from Adobe Stock on July 23, 2020. Credit: by @Prostock-studio/► stock.adobe.com. License Link: ► https://stock.adobe.com/ca/321825091)

strivers in consumer contexts, based on Maslow's (1954) "hierarchy of needs" and also utilizing the concept of "social character" (Riesman et al., 1950). A second methodology used with social values is the "LOV" ("List of Values") scale, which stemmed from the University of Michigan Survey Research Center and the work reported by Kahle (1983), based on Feather (1975), Maslow (1954), and Rokeach (1973). Some of the values included in the LOV scale (Kahle, 1983), for example, are "Warm Relationships with Others" (■ Fig. 3.7), "Being Well-Respected," and "Self-Respect."

A second school of thought focuses primarily on environmental or "biospheric" values, such as those developed in the work of Stern and Dietz (1994).

The third school puts social and environmental values together in order to provide a more complete view on sustainability-based values (Bouman et al., 2018; Schwartz, 1992) which are related to social entrepreneurship.

There are a growing number of successful, sustainability-focused businesses which have stemmed from this movement. On the social side, for example, Toms is a manufacturer of canvas shoes which notably donates one pair of shoes for every one pair purchased in support of developing economies. On the environmental side, green energy has gained a toehold across the world, with entrepreneurs developing everything from Tesla in the USA with Elon Musk at the helm, to Bullfrog Power in Canada, which sells excess energy production back to the grid.

3.7 Cognitive Styles and Their Relationship to Motivation

While passions and values can direct certain entrepreneurial decisions, such as the industry one hopes to zero in on, cognitive style and mindset shape the ways in which individuals interact with these interests and ideals. As mentioned in the introduction of this chapter, while the interests of an entrepreneur provide the "what," an entrepreneur's cognitive style is based on "how" they digest new information from the environment. For instance, potential interest in a new gap in the market within their field of interest is impacted by whether and how they process such information.

Messick (1996, p. 359) defines "cognitive style," as "characteristic modes of perception, memory, thought, and judgment reflective of information-processing regularities." In other words, cognitive style involves consistent preferred ways individuals have for organizing and processing information (Reid & de Brentani, 2015). For Sternberg and Grigorenko (1997) "cognitive style" offers a "bridge" between cognition and personality and therefore offers insights into how individuals process information.

Cognitive style represents one way to view how individuals go about processing information (i.e., perceiving, thinking, remembering, problem-solving, information sharing). Therefore, cognitive style, skills, and abilities should additionally be considered in a full account of entrepreneurial motivation (Shane et al., 2003), as cognition acts as an important filtering and focusing mechanism for other psychosocial traits and values. This research offers opportunities for more development. Research conducted by the authors and colleagues (Reid & de Brentani, 2015) aims at developing a better understanding of the key aspects of cognitive style related to vision success and mainly through the lens of how it relates to visioning capability given specific cues from the environment.

3.7.1 Divergent Thinking and Convergent Thinking

To understand the cognitive style which best lends itself to new problem-solving approaches, such as those typically encountered during the beginning stages of entrepreneurial startups, we need to understand the way in which information flows in the environment. Most notably, "incremental and discontinuous innovations differ extensively in the way in which problems are structured and in which information searches are initiated at the fuzzy front end of new product development" (Reid & de Brentani, 2004, p. 176). Incremental innovations reinforce established ways of understanding and relating product concepts, cultural regimes, and customer habits. On the other hand, more radical types of innovation (i.e., discontinuous innovations) force entrepreneurs to use new approaches to problem-solving to develop new technical skills and/or commercial skills, ideas, and products (Burns & Stalker, 1961; Ettlie et al., 1984; Garcia & Calantone, 2002; Hage, 1980; Reid & de Brentani, 2004; Tushman & Anderson, 1986). Essentially, as detailed in research investigating information flows and innovation (Alam, 2003; De Brentani & Reid, 2012), whether innovation is incremental or discontinuous, the most important input to innovation is new information from the environment. However, in the case of incremental innovation, problems can be structured in a top-down way by entrepreneurs and their teams and usually the pieces of the market and technical puzzle are fairly well understood. In the case of more new-to-the-world innovation, however, market and technical contexts may not exist yet (i.e., they are low-market context situations), and it may take time for individuals to put together the pieces to begin to ask the right questions.

So, what do we mean by cognitively "putting the pieces together" in low-market context situations?

Effectively, what we will describe here is a process which most entrepreneurs will go through involving moving from "divergent thinking" (DT), where the individual is just "feeling the information coming from the environment" and perhaps sharing the information with a small number of people in a way that is still divergent, then moving at a time when it seems right to a more convergent thinking process (◘ Fig. 3.8) where the entrepreneur (and possibly their team) begins to contextualize the information. Divergent thinking is a good starting place for gen-

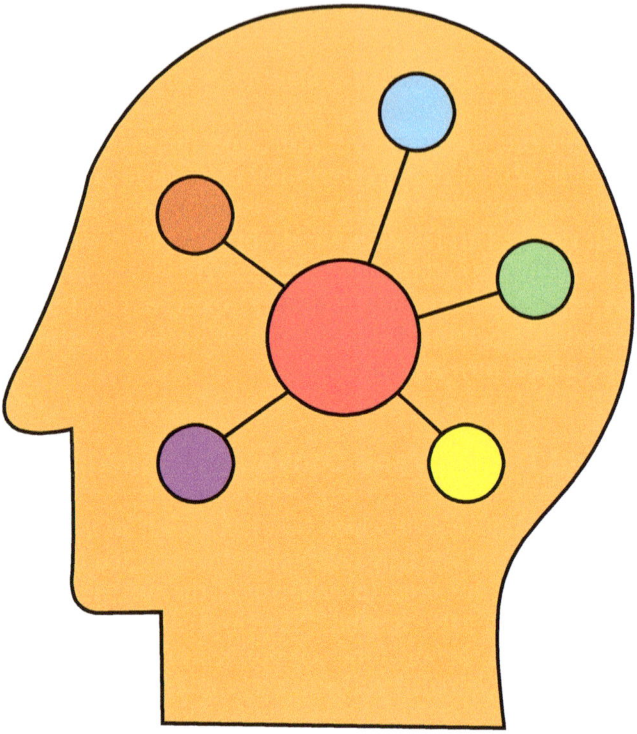

Fig. 3.8 Conceptual image to portray "convergent to divergent thinking." (Source: Image licensed and downloaded from Adobe Stock on April 21, 2020. Credit: by @alekseyvanin/▶ stock.adobe.com. License Link: ▶ https://stock.adobe.com/ca/images/mind-map-in-the-human-head-icon-line--glyph-and-filled-outline-colorful-version-creative-think-outline-and-filled-vector-sign-symbol-logo--illustration-different-style-icons-set-vector-graphics/265433799?prev_url=detail)

erating novel, unique, and sometimes ambiguous ideas and exploring many possible solutions (Guilford, 1967; Reid & de Brentani, 2012).

Divergent thinking processes related to a new product or service idea begin with what is commonly known as "intuition," which is described by Crossan et al. (1999, p. 525) as "a uniquely human attribute that organizations do not possess." As such, individual entrepreneurs, in theory, should always have a timing and exposure edge, compared to organizations, in their pursuit of new ideas (whether individuals can amass the necessary resources in time to respond as quickly as organizations is another question!).

The relationship between intuition and pattern recognition (Roos, 1996) is specified for radical innovations by Reid and de Brentani (2004, p. 179),[1] as follows:

1 Used with permission of John Wiley and Sons from (*The Journal of Product Innovation Management*, The Fuzzy Front-end of New Product Development for Discontinuous Innovations: A Theoretical Model, 21(3), p. 179); permission conveyed through Copyright Clearance Center, Inc. Rights Link.

> "Pattern recognition is a form of distinction making, which effectively allows individuals to separate potentially relevant from irrelevant background information…In the case of discontinuous innovation, we propose that it is the individual's ability to make a distinction regarding an unaddressed market need or a new technology path—due to some recurring elements in the environment—that is the starting point for building new organizational knowledge (either for themselves to use as an entrepreneur or to share within an organization as an 'intrapreneur'). That is, the individual recognizes patterns by perceiving new information in the environment, thereby marking its existence and attempting to determine and to classify the factual content of this information in relation to information already known (i.e. by contextualizing it)."

The critical point here is that the contextualization process itself requires visioning. Bunge (1962) breaks down the contextualization process into three core elements required for visioning which will therefore enable contextualization: "Perception" (i.e., quick identification, clear understanding, and interpretation ability), "Reconstruction" (i.e., representation ability, creative inference, synthesis), and "Classification" (evaluation). Further research (Reid & de Brentani, 2004, 2010, 2012, 2015) demonstrates that there are effectively two main stages in vision formation linked to the contextualization process.

The *first stage* of vision formation involves the set of resources that enable creating and developing radical ideas and entailing "divergent thinking" on the part of individuals. Divergent thinking deals with the ability to expand the boundaries of mental models and think creatively. It is required when "growing" a new vision, often in terms of entirely new frames of reference as we see in "low context" market and technology cases. The concept of "cognitive style" is, therefore, a useful basis for understanding a key filtering mechanism for motivational triggers en route to vision formation and entrepreneurial action. Divergent thinking cognitive styles, in particular "perception" and "reconstruction" à la Bunge (1962), are linked to better information processing skills which help when dealing with radical innovations. Related to this, divergent thinking can be expected to be a precursor to the Market Visioning Competence (MVC) components of networking and market learning skills/tools. Networking is a form of undirected social exploration which depends on variance-seeking learning processes and behaviors, as is the case with divergent thinking (McGrath, 2001). Similarly, Howell and Shea (2001) found that if individuals have an internal locus of control orientation (i.e., the "belief they have the ability to influence the direction of events," Howell & Shea, 2001, p. 18), it is positively related to individual-level environmental scanning which is actively engaged in the MVC processes of networking and market learning. Such activities are likely to lead to framing new information in the form of an opportunity.

In the *second stage*, moving from Market Visioning Competence (MVC) to Market Vision (MV) requires switching on "convergent thinking" skills, the type of thinking that focuses on eliminating ambiguity by coming up with a single answer to a problem (Cropley, 2006; Guilford, 1967) or "classification" according to Bunge (1962). Activating these skills is related to the MVC dimensions of "idea driving" (or championing) and "proactive market orientation." They allow for substantial risk

◘ **Fig. 3.9** Conceptual image to portray "convergence." (Source: Image licensed and downloaded from Adobe Stock on April 21, 2020. Credit: by @freshidea/▸ stock.adobe.com. License Link: ▸ https://stock.adobe.com/ca/images/unity-and-teamwork-concept/295371414?prev_url=detail)

reduction because of a focus on a less nebulous and uncertain future development and market space by moving to a clearer vision (concept represented in ◘ Fig. 3.9).

3.7.2 Mindset

"Mindset," according to the Cambridge English Dictionary (2020, online) is "a person's way of thinking and their opinions," related to their values and philosophy, which emerge in response to a stimulus or task (French, 2016). Mindset can act as a powerful motivator or tool, particularly if an individual has what is known as a "growth mindset." This term's first known use was by Carol Dweck, a psychology professor, and disseminated in her text, *Mindset: The New Psychology of Success* (2006). In short, a "fixed mindset" indicates that an individual believes that their basic abilities, intelligence, and so on are "set." On the flip side, a "growth mindset" individual will trust that they possess the capabilities to accomplish their goals or, if not, that they can develop what they require to get the job done, through efforts such as reading, access to good teachers and mentors, and persistence. This idea has taken root in several other fields from positive psychology to education. Dweck's original growth mindset scale has been tested most frequently with children and teens, and some work has been performed on adults, but there is every reason to hypothesize that it is also an applicable approach for entrepreneurs.

According to the Global Report from the GEM group (Bosma et al., 2019/2020, p. 16): "Self-belief and confidence in one's ability to succeed are indicators of one's readiness for entrepreneurship. In 36 of the 50 economies, more than half of the population considers that they have the skills, knowledge and experience to start their own business."

A related concept is that of "neuroplasticity." The term was first known to be used by neuroscientist Jerzy Konorski (1948) to describe observed changes in the neuronal structure of the brain. Positive and cognitive psychologists now utilize the term to describe this capability of the brain to be able to create new connections and reorganize them as the key to being able to change mindset and modes of thinking. One well-known example of this was a study (Maguire et al., 2000) conducted on London taxi drivers that examined their hippocampi, the part of the brain that holds spatial representation capacity. The results showed the hippocampi of taxi drivers to be measurably larger than bus drivers who were driving the same route every day. This means that the brain responds to the demands that we put on it. This is a fascinating concept when we consider an entrepreneur's potential to reduce fear by continually exposing themselves to new ideas, new challenges, and new opportunities.

There are numerous moving parts involved with understanding motivation, as described here in ▶ Chap. 3. It is, therefore, useful to consider, from the list of all potential motivators, what your primary motivators are as an entrepreneur to provide as much focus as possible out of the gates. To that end, the following ▶ Chap. 4 describes measures and provides worksheets aimed at gaining a better understanding of your primary motivators.

? Chapter Review Questions

1. What is the difference between intrinsic and extrinsic entrepreneurial motivation? Please give a specific example for each. How do values relate to motivation?
2. Take some time to identify some of your personal passions. How do you think these might influence your personal vision and "true purpose"?
3. Entrepreneurs often show strong tendency to traits of individualism and embracing ambiguity. What do you understand these terms to mean and why do these suggest the importance of early team formation in new ventures?
4. What is the difference between social entrepreneurship and other types of entrepreneurship?
5. How do divergent and convergent thinking work together in developing a clear vision? Please provide a concrete example.

References

Alam, I. (2003). Commercial innovations from consulting engineering firms: An empirical exploration of a novel source of new product ideas. *Journal of Product Innovation Management, 20*(4), 300–313.

Asch, S. E. (1956). Studies of independence and conformity: A minority of one against a unanimous majority. *Psychological Monographs, 70*(9, Whole No. 416), 1–70.

Basu, A. (1998). An exploration of entrepreneurial activity among Asian small businesses in Britain. *Small Business Economics, 10*(4), 313–326.

Basu, A., & Altinay, E. (2002). The interaction between culture and entrepreneurship in London's Immigrant Business. *International Small Business Journal, 20*(4), 371–393.

Baum, J. R., & Locke, E. A. (2004). The relationship of entrepreneurial traits, skill, and motivation to subsequent venture growth. *Journal of Applied Psychology, 89*(4), 587–598.
Berry, J. W., Poortinga, Y. H., Segall, M. H., & Dasen, P. R. (1992). *Cross-cultural psychology: Research and applications*. Cambridge University Press.
Boldt, E. D. (1978). Structural tightness and cross-cultural research. *Journal of Cross-Cultural Psychology, 9*(2), 151–165.
Bosma, N., Hill, S., Ionescu-Somers, A., Kelley, D., Levie, J., & Tamawa, A. (2020). *Global entrepreneurship monitor (GEM) 2019/2020 global report*. Global Entrepreneurship Research Association: London Business School.
Bouckaert, L., & Zsolnai, L. (2012). Spirituality and business: An inter-disciplinary overview. *Society and Economy, 34*(3), 489–514.
Bouman, T., Steg, L., & Kiers, H. A. L. (2018). Measuring values in environmental research: A test of an environmental portrait value questionnaire. *Frontiers in Psychology, 9*(564), 1–15.
Brockhaus, R. H. (1982). The psychology of the entrepreneur. In J. A. Hornaday, F. Tarpley Jr., J. A. Timmons, & K. H. Vesper (Eds.), *Encyclopedia of entrepreneurship* (pp. 39–56). Prentice Hall.
Bunge, M. (1962). *Intuition and science*. Prentice-Hall.
Burns, T., & Stalker, G. M. (1961). *The management of innovation*. Tavistock Publications.
Cambridge Dictionary. (2020, online). *Definition for "mindset"*. https://dictionary.cambridge.org/us/dictionary/english/mindset. Accessed on 31 Aug 2020.
Carsrud, A. L., & Brännback, M. (Eds.). (2009). *Understanding the entrepreneurial mind. Opening the black box*. Springer.
Carsrud, A. L., & Brännback, M. (2011). Entrepreneurial motivations: What do we still need to know? *Journal of Small Business Management, 49*(1), 9–26.
Chandra, S. (1973). The effects of group pressure in perception: A cross-cultural conformity study in Fiji. *International Journal of Psychology, 8*(1), 37–39.
Chell, E., Haworth, J., & Brearley, S. (1991). *The entrepreneurial personality: Concepts, cases, and categories*. Routledge.
Chen, X.-P., Yao, X., & Kotha, S. (2009). Entrepreneur passion and preparedness in business plan presentations: A persuasion analysis of venture capitalists' funding decisions. *The Academy of Management Journal, 52*(1), 199–214.
Claeys, W. (1967). Conflicting behavior and personality variables in Congolese students. *International Journal of Psychology, 2*(1), 13–24.
Crawford, C. (2018). *The net effect* (Dissertation). Athabasca University.
Cromie, S. (2000). Assessing entrepreneurial inclinations: Some approaches and empirical evidence. *European Journal of Work and Organizational Psychology, 9*(1), 7–30.
Cropley, A. (2006). In praise of convergent thinking. *Creativity Research Journal, 18*(3), 391–404.
Crossan, M. M., Lane, H. W., & White, R. E. (1999). An organizational learning framework: From intuition to institution. *The Academy of Management Review, 24*(3), 522–537.
Dana, L.-P. (1993). An inquiry into culture and entrepreneurship. *Journal of Small Business and Entrepreneurship, 10*(4), 16–31.
Dana, L.-P. (1995). Entrepreneurship in a remote sub-Arctic community. *Entrepreneurship Theory and Practice, 20*(1), 57–72.
Dandridge, T. C., & Ford, M. A. (1987). Use of a self-assessment profile to differentiate among professional groups on entrepreneurial characteristics. In N. C. Churchill, J. A. Hornaday, B. A. Kirchoff, O. J. Krasner, & K. H. Vesper (Eds.), *Frontiers of entrepreneurship research* (pp. 220–236). Babson College.
Danes, S. M., Lee, J., Stafford, K., & Heck, R. K. Z. (2008). The effects of ethnicity, families, and culture on entrepreneurial experience: An extension of sustainable family business theory. *Journal of Developmental Entrepreneurship, 13*(3), 229–268.
De Brentani, U., & Reid, S. E. (2012). The fuzzy front-end of discontinuous innovation: Insights for research and management. *The Journal of Product Innovation Management, 29*(1), 70–87.
Dweck, C. (2006). *Mindset: The new psychology of success*. (1st ed). New York: Random House.
Eccles, J. S., & Wigfield, A. (2002). Motivational beliefs, values, and goals. *Annual Review of Psychology, 53*(1), 109–132.

Eckensberger, L. H. (1972). The necessity of a theory for applied cross-cultural research. In L. H. Cronbach & P. J. D. Drenth (Eds.), *Mental tests and cultural adaptation* (pp. 99–107). The Hague.

Ettlie, J. E., Bridges, W. P., & O'Keefe, R. D. (1984). Organization strategy and structural differences for radical versus incremental innovation. *Management Science, 30*(6), 682–695.

Feather, N. (1975). *Values in education and society*. Free Press.

Filion, L.-J., Brenner, G., Dionne, L., & Menzies, T. V. (2007). L'identification d'une occasion d'affaires en contexte d'entrepreneuriat ethnique. *Revue Internationale PME, 20*(2), 33–57.

French, R. P. I. I. (2016). The fuzziness of mindsets: Divergent conceptualizations and characterizations of mindset theory and praxis. *International Journal of Organizational Analysis, 24*(4), 673–691.

Garcia, R., & Calantone, R. (2002). A critical look at technological innovation typology and innovativeness terminology: A literature review. *The Journal of Product Innovation Management, 19*(2), 110–132.

Gerber, M. E. (2001). *The E-myth revisited* (2nd ed.). Harper Business.

Germak, A. J., & Robinson, J. A. (2014). Exploring the motivation of nascent social entrepreneurs. *Journal of Social Entrepreneurship, 5*(1), 5–21.

Gibb, A., & Ritchie, J. (1982). Understanding the process of starting small businesses. *European Small Business Journal, 1*(1), 26–45.

Grimes, M. G., McMullen, J. S., Vogus, T. J., & Miller, T. L. (2013). Studying the origins of social entrepreneurship: Compassion and the role of embedded agency. *The Academy of Management Review, 38*(3), 460–463.

Guilford, J. P. (1967). *The nature of human intelligence*. McGraw-Hill.

Hage, J. (1980). *Theories of organization*. Wiley.

Hamdi-Kidar, L., & Vellera, C. (2012). *What drives lead users to become user entrepreneurs? An exploratory study of motivations*. 25 p. halshs-00851319, Cahier de Recherches No. 2012-01 E3.

Hayton, J. C., George, G., & Zahra, A. (2002). National culture and entrepreneurship: A review of behavioral research. *Entrepreneurship Theory and Practice, 26*(4), 33–52.

Headspace. (2020). *About headspace*. Retrieved August 10, 2020, from https://www.headspace.com/about-us?gclid=CjwKCAjw4MP5BRBtEiwASfwALxh8JNnwUDR1xXQyinPMYcpZgoY4X6fKOJWgqWIZOz3vNO9uJHYpTBoCfGkQAvD_BwE

Hofstede, G. (1980). *Culture's consequences: International differences in work-related values*. Sage.

Hornaday, J. A. (1982). Research about living entrepreneurs. In C. A. Kent, D. L. Sexton, et al. (Eds.), *Encyclopedia of entrepreneurship* (pp. 20–34). Prentice Hall.

Howell, J. M., & Shea, C. M. (2001). Individual differences, environmental scanning, innovation framing, and champion behavior: Key predictors of project performance. *The Journal of Product Innovation Management, 18*(1), 15–27.

Huang, L., & Harris, M. (1973). Conformity in Chinese and Americans: A field experiment. *Journal of Cross-Cultural Psychology, 4*(4), 427–434.

Jung, Carl Quotes. (n.d.). BrainyQuote.com. Retrieved August 26, 2020, from BrainyQuote.com Website: https://wwwbrainyquote.com/quotes/carl_jung_146686. Public Domain.

Kahle, L. R. (Ed.). (1983). *Social values and social change: Adaptation to life in America*. Praeger.

Kelley, T. (2009). *True purpose: 12 strategies for discovering the difference you are meant to make*. Transcendent Solutions Press.

King-Kauanui, S., Thomas, K. D., & Waters, G. R. (2005). Entrepreneurship and spirituality: Integration of spirituality into the workplace. *Journal of Management, Spirituality & Religion, 2*(2), 255–274.

King-Kauanui, S., Thomas, K. D., Rubens, A., & Sherman, C. L. (2010). Entrepreneurship and spirituality: A comparative analysis of entrepreneurs' motivation. *Journal of Small Business & Entrepreneurship, 23*(4), 621–635.

Kolvereid, L. (1992). Growth aspirations among Norwegian entrepreneurs. *Journal of Business Venturing, 7*(3), 209–222.

Konorski, J. (1948). *Conditioned reflexes and neuron organization*. Cambridge University Press.

Lalonde, J.-F. (2010). Culture and new venture creation: Links between anthropology and entrepreneurship. *Entrepreneurial Practice Review, 1*(2), 66–93.

3

Lalonde, J.-F. (2012). Cultural determinants of Arab entrepreneurship: An ethnographic perspective. *Journal of Enterprising Communities*. Accepté pour publication.
Lalonde, J.-F. & Reid, S.E. (2019/2020). Research proposal framework, .
Maguire, E., Gadian, D., Johnsrude, I., Good, C., Ashburner, J., Frackowiak, R., & Frith, C. D. (2000). Navigational structural change in the hippocampi of taxi drivers. *Proceedings of the National Academy of Science, 97*(8), 4398–4403.
Mahto, R. V., & McDowell, W. C. (2018). Entrepreneurial motivation: A non-entrepreneur's journey to become an entrepreneur. *International Entrepreneurship and Management Journal, 14*(3), 513–526.
Maslow, A. H. (1954). *Motivation and personality*. Harper.
Matsuda, N. (1985). Strong, quasi and weak conformity among Japanese in the modified Asch procedure. *Journal of Cross-Cultural Psychology, 16*(1), 83–97.
McClelland, D. (1961). *The achieving society*. Van Nostrand.
McGrath, R. (2001). Exploratory learning, innovative capacity, and managerial oversight. *Academy of Management Journal, 44*(1), 118–131.
Meade, R., & Barnard, W. (1973). Conformity and anti-conformity among Americans and Chinese. *Journal of Social Psychology, 89*(1), 15–24.
Messick, S. (1996). Bridging cognition and personality in education: The role of style in performance and development. *European Journal of Personality, 10*(5), 353–376.
Miller, T. L., Grimes, M., McMullen, J. S., & Vogus, T. J. (2012). Venturing for others with heart and head: How compassion encourages social entrepreneurship. *The Academy of Management Review, 37*(4), 616–640.
Mitchell, A. (1983). *The nice American lifestyles*. Macmillan Publishing Co., Inc.
Munroe, R. L., & Munroe, R. H. (1975). *Cross-cultural human development*. Brooks/Cole.
National Opinion Research Center (NORC) data enclave/Kauffman Foundation (1996 – ongoing). Survey of American entrepreneurs (Crawford, 2018, dissertation, The Net Effect, Athabasca University accessed data from 2004 to 2011, with permission).
Ott, T. (2020, online). (https://www.biography.com/news/jk-rowling-harry-potter-author-rags-to--riches-billionaire, original February 20, 2019; updated May 28, 2020). Accessed online 26 Aug 2020.
Peabody, D. (1967). Trait inferences: Evaluative and descriptive aspects. *Journal of Personality and Social Psychology Monographs, 7*(4p2), 1.
Pradhan, R. K., & Nath, P. (2012). Perception of entrepreneurial orientation and emotional intelligence: A study of India's future techno-managers. *Global Business Review, 13*(1), 89–108.
Raco, J., & Tanod, R. (2014). Understanding spirituality as experienced by Catholic entrepreneurs. World Review of Entrepreneurship, Management and Sustainable Development, 10(1), 40–51.
Riesman, D., Glazer, N., & Denny, R. (1950). *The lonely crowd: A study of the changing American character*. Yale University Press.
Reid, S. E., & de Brentani, U. (2004). The fuzzy front-end of new product development for discontinuous innovation: A theoretical model. *The Journal of Product Innovation Management, 21*(3), 170–184.
Reid, S. E., & de Brentani, U. (2010). Market vision and market visioning competence: Impacts on early performance for radically new high-tech products. *The Journal of Product Innovation Management, 27*(4), 500–518.
Reid, S. E., & de Brentani, U. (2012). Market vision and the front end of NPD for radical innovation: The impact of moderating effects. *The Journal of Product Innovation Management, 29*(S1, Dec), 124–139.
Reid, S. E., & de Brentani, U. (2015). Building a measurement model for market visioning competence and its' proposed antecedents: Organizational encouragement of divergent thinking, divergent thinking attitudes and ideational behavior. *The Journal of Product Innovation Management, 32*(2), 243–262.
Reid, S. E., Roberts, D. L., & Moore, K. (2015). Vision for technology-enabled radical innovation and its impact on early success. *The Journal Product Innovation Management, 32*(4), 593–609.
Roberge, J. (2011). 5 P's to make life-enhancing changes. In *Power to change* (pp. 112–120). Thrive Publishing.

Rogers, E. M. (2003). *Diffusion of innovations* (5th ed.). The Free Press.
Rogers, E. M., & Shoemaker, F. F. (1971). *Communication of innovations: A cross-cultural approach* (2nd ed.). The Free Press.
Rokeach, M. (1973). *The nature of human values*. Free Press.
Roos, J. (1996). Distinction making and pattern recognition in management. *European Management Journal, 14*(6), 590–595.
Schwartz, S. H. (1992). Universals in the content and structure of values: Theoretical advances and empirical tests in 20 countries. In M. Zanna (Ed.), *Advances in experimental social psycholog* (Vol. 25, pp. 1–65). Academic Press.
Shane, S., Locke, E. A., & Collins, C. J. (2003). Entrepreneurial motivation. *Human Resource Management Review, 13*(2), 257–279.
Sinek, S. (2009). *Start with why: How great leaders inspire everyone to take action*. The Penguin Group.
Stern, P. S., & Dietz, T. (1994). The value basis of environmental concern. *Journal of Social Issues, 50*(3), 65–84.
Sternberg, R. J., & Grigorenko, E. L. (1997). Are cognitive styles still in style? *American Psychologist, 52*(7), 700–712.
Tan, J. (2002). Culture, nation, and entrepreneurial strategic orientations: Implications for an emerging economy. *Entrepreneurship Theory and Practice, 26*(4), 95–111.
Tushman, M., & Anderson, P. (1986). Technological discontinuities and organizational environments. *Administrative Science Quarterly, 31*(3), 434–465.
Usunier, J.-C., & Valette-Florence, P. (2007). The time styles scale. *Time & Society, 16*(3), 333–366, Sage.
Vallerand, R. J., & Verner-Filion, J. (2013). Making people's life most worth living: On the importance of passion for positive psychology. *Terapia Psicologica, 31*(1), 35–48.
Vallerand, R. J., Blanchard, C., Mageau, G. A., Koestner, R., Ratelle, C., Léonard, M., Gagné, M., & Marsolais, J. (2003). Les passions de l'âme: On obsessive and harmonious passion. *Journal of Personality and Social Psychology, 85*(4), 756–767.

Measuring Entrepreneurial Motivation

Contents

© The Author(s), under exclusive license to Springer Nature Switzerland AG 2022

S. E. Reid, C. B. Crawford, *Entrepreneurial Vision*, Classroom Companion: Business,
https://doi.org/10.1007/978-3-030-77803-3_4

Learning Objectives

In this chapter, we describe and provide measures aimed at:

1. Gaining a better understanding of primary psychosocial characteristics and values related to entrepreneurial potential
2. Developing an understanding of cognitive style and the impact of a team's working environment on ideation.

4.1 Measuring General Personality Versus Entrepreneurial Potential

4.1.1 Measuring General Personality Traits

Personality tests such as the "Big 5" Inventory (Costa & McCrae, 1985) (■ Fig. 4.1), or the "Myers-Briggs Test" (Myers, 1962), have sometimes been used to see whether a given individual exhibits traits considered to be affiliated with entrepreneurship. Some components of these tests, for example, the "Openness to Experience" factor of the Big 5, have been shown to correlate with entrepreneurial potential in a variety of research, such as that conducted by Davis et al. (2015). Taken as a whole, however, such tests were not designed to specifically measure the traits of entrepreneurship. As such, they do not provide entrepreneurs with further insights on how to use the information regarding these traits. Additionally, a focus purely on psy-

■ **Fig. 4.1** Conceptual image to portray the constructs comprising the "Big 5." (Source: Image licensed and downloaded from Adobe Stock on July 23, 2020. Credit: by @Olivier Le Moal/▶ stock.adobe.com. License Link: ▶ https://stock.adobe.com/ca/images/psychology-model-big-five-personality-traits-ocean-model/356064897?prev_url=detail)

chological traits does not account for how these might interface with social and informational environments to provide further clarification of thinking about entrepreneurial potential.

4.1.2 Measuring Entrepreneurial Potential

Indeed, many researchers (Huefner et al., 1996; Brockhaus & Horwitz, 1986; Gartner, 1988; Leutner et al., 2014) have questioned some of the purer traits-based instruments for measuring entrepreneurial potential. As such, there has been a move towards using entrepreneurial motivation as a lens to focus in on and better understand entrepreneurial potential. Indeed, many adopters of this approach are focusing on the potential of the entrepreneur based on their existing psychological, social, and environmental characteristics. As a result, generic traits-based tests are being supplanted with more tailored scales examining the potential (◘ Fig. 4.2) of the entrepreneur and the specific qualities that might be related to such potential.

"Entrepreneurial potential" is defined by Santos et al. (2013, Abstract, p. 661) as "the main psychosocial aspects that contribute towards an individual's preparedness to engage in activities typically associated with entrepreneurship." By introducing social aspects (i.e., the impact of and response to the social environment) into their understanding of entrepreneurial potential, these researchers have enabled a hybrid approach to analysis which brings together individual factors with environmental factors.

In response to the move of researchers to focus on entrepreneurial potential, several measurement scales have recently been developed and tested for validity and reliability, including:

1. Ahmetoglu et al.'s 44-item "Measure of Entrepreneurial Tendencies and Abilities" (META) scale (2011).
2. Cuesta et al.'s 120-item "Eight Dimensions of Entrepreneurial Personality" (BEPE) scale (2018).
3. Santos et al.'s, (2013) "Entrepreneurial Potential Assessment Inventory" (EPAI) scale (70 items on their website).
4. Others have focused on "aptitude" or, as Cubico et al. (2010, p. 427) define it in their creation of the "TAI-Entrepreneurial Aptitude Test," "the potential toward creating and developing enterprise and self-employment."

The BEPE, EPAI, and TAI tests, along with a suggested inventory from Rausch and Frese (2007), have quite a few conceptual overlaps, in terms of the main factors they find as significant. In particular, "Need for Achievement," "Innovativeness," "Autonomy," and "Self-Efficacy" were found in these four tests of entrepreneurial potential as being significant indicators across the board, as noted in the abbreviated meta-analysis we have provided below (◘ Table 4.1).

While the BEPE scale items were not yet available, as of the time of this writing, the META and EPAI scales, which have been developed and tested for validity and

4

Fig. 4.2 Conceptual image to portray "potential." (Source: Image licensed and downloaded from Adobe Stock on July 23, 2020. Credit: by @freshidea/▶ stock.adobe.com. License Link: ▶ https://stock.adobe.com/ca/images/potential-success-concept/122453726?prev_url=detail)

reliability, are both available to the public through websites referring to the same names.

In Worksheet 2, we provide the original items from valid and reliable scales to measure the four constructs found to be significant across the board. These scales have been disseminated by their authors: Achievement Motivation, Ray (1979); Individual Innovativeness, Pallister and Foxall (1998); Autonomy, Bieling et al. (2000); and General Self-Efficacy, Chen et al. (2001)(see references for more details on their development)). As such, according to our abbreviated analysis, (▶ Sect. 4.1.2.1) "Achievement Motivation," (▶ Sect. 4.1.2.2) "Individual Innovativeness," (▶ Sect. 4.1.2.3) "Autonomy," and (▶ Sect. 4.1.2.4) "General Self-Efficacy" form a current consensus around the main psychosocial characteristics of entrepreneurial potential.

Table 4.1 An abbreviated meta-analysis of entrepreneurial potential research factors

Suggested factor	BEPE	EPAI	TAI	Rausch and Frese (2007)
Need for achievement[a]	X	X	X	X
Risk taking[b]	X			X
Innovativeness	X	X	X	X
Autonomy[c]	X	X	X	X
Internal locus of control[b]	X			X
Self-efficacy	X	X	X	X
Optimism		X		
Stress tolerance	X			
Goal orientation[d]		X	X	
Leadership		X	X	
Need for self-empowerment			X	
Flexibility			X	
Resource mobilization capacity		X		
Emotional intelligence		X		
Resilience[e]		X		
Communication/persuasion capacity		X		
Network development capacity		X		

Source: The authors
[a]Also referred to as achievement motivation in the BEPE and related to economic motivation in the EPAI
[b]Rausch and Frese (2007) found risk taking and internal locus of control, while significant, exhibited small effect sizes
[c]Also referred to as desire for independence in the EPAI
[d]Also referred to as vision in the EPAI
[e]Also referred to as tenacity and endurance by Rausch and Frese (2007)

4.1.2.1 Achievement Motivation

"Achievement Motivation", also referred to as "Need for Achievement", has a long litany of approaches and measurements related to its name, as well as multiple definitions. In order to simplify understanding, according to the site "iresearchnet.com" (2020, online), "achievement motivation may be defined as the energization and direction of competence-relevant behavior or why and how people strive toward competence (success) and away from incompetence (failure)." We use the 14-item scale developed by Ray (1979) to measure Achievement Motivation (Scale in Worksheet 2 permission granted by John Wiley and Sons on December 6, 2020, for reprint).

4.1.2.2 Individual Innovativeness

Hurt et al. (1977) defined "Innovativeness" (◘ Fig. 4.3) as "a normally distributed underlying personality construct, which may be interpreted as a willingness to change" (Pallister & Foxall, 1998, p. 663). In the context of entrepreneurship, innovativeness is related to willingness to adopt new information and ideas and act on them. We use the ten-item scale developed by Pallister and Foxall (1998) to measure "Individual Innovativeness" (Worksheet 2, STM guidelines "automatic process" with permission from Elsevier).

4.1.2.3 Autonomy

According to Beck (1983), "Autonomy" (◘ Fig. 4.4) may be described as "the person's investment in preserving and increasing his independence, mobility, and personal rights (Bieling et al., 2000, p. 272)." Entrepreneurship provides an excellent context for exercising these traits. We use the eight-item "Autonomy" scale for measurement developed by Bieling et al. (2000) (Scale in Worksheet 2 permission granted by Springer Nature on December 6, 2020, for reprint).

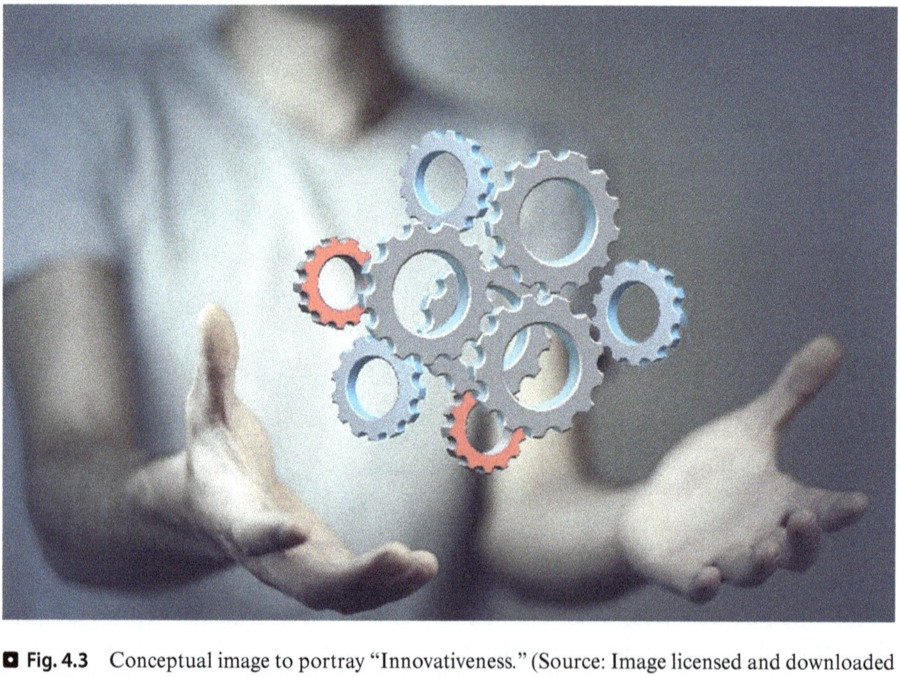

◘ **Fig. 4.3** Conceptual image to portray "Innovativeness." (Source: Image licensed and downloaded from Adobe Stock on July 23, 2020. Credit: by @tiko/▸ stock.adobe.com. License Link: ▸ https://stock.adobe.com/ca/images/close-up-of-businessman-holding-gears-in-palms/131566490?prev_url=detail)

Fig. 4.4 Conceptual image to portray "Autonomy." (Source: Image licensed and downloaded from Adobe Stock on July 23, 2020. Credit: by @fresh idea/► stock.adobe.com. License Link: ► https://stock.adobe.com/ca/images/charting-a-different-path/165453338?prev_url=detail)

4.1.2.4 General Self-Efficacy

According to Schwarzer and Jerusalem (1995), "Self-Efficacy" (Fig. 4.5) is a self-belief of how well an individual perceives him- or herself to be able to accomplish goals and come up with solutions to problems. They note that it is correlated to emotion, optimism, and work satisfaction. We use the eight-item scale developed by Chen et al. (2001) to measure Self-Efficacy (Worksheet 2, STM guidelines "automatic process" permission from Sage on December 7, 2020 for reprint).

4.2 Measuring Social and Environmental Values

To bring more validity to the overall measure of entrepreneurial potential, it may be beneficial to introduce both social values and environmental values into the equation, particularly given that enabling social justice and protection of the environment are two of the most important issues society faces today. As such, we include a scale from Bouman et al. (2018) to assess potential interest in sustainability-related social entrepreneurship (i.e., with a strong focus on social and environmen-

Fig. 4.5 Conceptual image to portray "Self-Efficacy." (Source: Image licensed and downloaded from Adobe Stock on July 23, 2020. Credit: y @kieferpix/► stock.adobe.com. License Link: ► https://stock.adobe.com/ca/151143696)

Fig. 4.6 Conceptual image to portray "Social-Altruistic Items." (Source: Image licensed and downloaded from Adobe Stock on July 23, 2020. Credit: by @JP Photography/► stock.adobe.com. License Link: ► https://stock.adobe.com/ca/168488349)

Fig. 4.7 Conceptual image to portray "Biospheric Items: Protecting the Environment." (Source: Image licensed and downloaded from Adobe Stock on July 23, 2020. Credit: by @Gajus/▶ stock.adobe.com. License Link: ▶ https://stock.adobe.com/ca/81717411)

tal values). Building on the earlier work of Rokeach (1968, 1973), Schwartz (1992), and Stern and Dietz (1994), Bouman et al. (2018) have provided a reliable and valid nine-item scale to measure *Social-Altruistic Values* (Fig. 4.6) and *Biospheric Values* (Fig. 4.7), as follows:

1. 5 "*Social-Altruistic Values*" items:
   Item 1 Equality
   Item 2 Taking Care
   Item 3 Social Justice
   Item 4 A World at Peace
   Item 5 Helpful
2. 4 "*Biospheric Values*" items:
   Item 1 Preventing Pollution
   Item 2 Protecting the Environment
   Item 3 Respecting the Earth
   Item 4 Unity with Nature

The Bouman 2018 scale is also incorporated in Worksheet 2 (Frontiers in Psychology, Open-Access Journal, CC-BY license).

In sum, to facilitate a base of measures for thinking about your primary motivators, Worksheet 2 incorporates each of the scales just described: the four psychosocial entrepreneurial potential scales as outlined in ▶ Sect. 4.1 and from ▶ Sect. 4.2 the nine-item "*Biospheric-Altruistic*" scale to measure social entrepreneurship.

4

Worksheet 2: What Motivates You Most

This worksheet is divided into 2 main parts: Section 1 is focused on Psychosocial Traits and Section 2 is focused on Values. In Section 2, the items highlight publicly diffused, short-form validated scales which tap into each of the 4 motivational areas of entrepreneurial behavior of interest from the research of a broad range of researchers. Section 2 provides a specific scale to test for interest in social entrepreneurship ('altruistic-biospheric' values).

Instructions:

While some of the scales provided here were originally developed using different scale lengths (for example, achievement motivation was originally scaled on a 1–3 scale), for our purposes, we will utilize a 7-point scale across the board for simplicity and to enable a little more differentiation between responses.

Please Note: For items marked "R", please reverse-score when you are writing down your scores so they are scaled in the same direction as all other items (e.g. "1" becomes "7"; "2" becomes "6"; "3" becomes "5" and the reverse) before you add them up to get the overall score on any given scale. In particular, this is the case in Parts I and IV of Section 1.

There are no right or wrong answers here; rather, your answers are meant to serve as a focal point for understanding the main factors underlying your general motivation. In order to best understand your primary motivators, simply add up your scores once finished on each scale and then divide by the number of items to come up with an average. Comparing your averages will give you a general sense of the emphasis each factor may play in your motivation set. Additionally, your answers will help you focus in the next chapters on appropriate ways to start your visioning activity/vision path.

© Susan E. Reid and Charles B. Crawford, August 14, 2020.

How do you score on the following scale from 1 to 7?

Definitely Not	**RATING**	**Definitely Yes**
Strongly DISAGREE	**Neutral**	**Strongly AGREE**

1-----------2-----------3-----------4-----------5-----------6-----------7

SECTION 1 PSYCHOSOCIAL TRAITS (INTRINSIC AND EXTRINSIC MOTIVATION)

PART I 14-Item Achievement Motivation Inventory (Ray)

The following items come from the 14-item short-form Achievement Motivation scale from the work of Ray (1979) (permission granted from Wiley on December 6, 2020).

1. Is being comfortable more important to you than getting ahead? "R"
2. Are you satisfied to be no better than most other people at your job? "R"
3. Do you like to make improvements to the way the organization you belong to functions?
4. Do you take trouble to cultivate people who may be useful to you in your career?
5. Do you get restless and annoyed when you feel you are wasting time?
6. Have you always worked hard in order to be among the best in your own line? (school, organization, profession).
7. Would you prefer to work with a congenial but incompetent partner rather than with a difficult but highly competent one? "R"
8. Do you tend to plan ahead for your job or career?
9. Is "getting on in life" important to you?
10. Are you an ambitious person?
11. Are you inclined to read of the successes of others rather than do the work of making yourself a success? "R"
12. Would you describe yourself as being lazy? "R"
13. Will days often go by without your having done a thing? "R"
14. Are you inclined to take life as it comes without much planning? "R"

© Susan E. Reid and Charles B. Crawford, August 14, 2020.

4

How do you score on the following scale from 1 to 7?

Definitely Not	**RATING**	**Definitely Yes**
Strongly DISAGREE	**Neutral**	**Strongly AGREE**

1-----------2-----------3-----------4-----------5-----------6-----------7

PART II 8-item General Self-Efficacy Scale (GSE) (Chen, Eden and Gully, 2001)

The following items come from the 8-item short-form new General Self-Efficacy scale from the work of Chen, Eden and Gully (2001) (STM Guidelines "automatic process" permission from Sage December 7, 2020).

1. I will be able to achieve most of the goals that I have set for myself.
2. When facing difficult tasks, I am certain that I will accomplish them.
3. In general, I think that I can obtain outcomes that are important to me.
4. I believe I can succeed at most any endeavor to which I set my mind.
5. I will be able to successfully overcome many challenges.
6. I am confident that I can perform effectively on many different tasks.
7. Compared to other people, I can do most tasks very well.
8. Even when things are tough, I can perform quite well.

PART III 8-item Autonomy Scale (Bieling, Beck and Brown, 2000)

The following items come from the 8-item Autonomy scale from the work Bieling, Beck and Brown (2000) (permission granted from Wiley on December 6, 2020).

1. If a goal is important to me, I will pursue it even if it may make other people uncomfortable.
2. The possibility of being rejected by others for standing up for my rights would not stop me.
3. I set my own standards and goals for myself rather than accepting those of other people.
4. If I think I am right about something, I feel comfortable expressing myself even if others don't like it.
5. It is more important to meet your own objectives on a task than to meet another person's objective.
6. When I achieve a goal, I get more satisfaction from reaching the goal than from any praise I might get.
7. It is more important that I know I've done a good job than having others know it.
8. I enjoy accomplishing things more than being given credit for them.

© Susan E. Reid and Charles B. Crawford, August 14, 2020.

How do you score on the following scale from 1 to 7?

Definitely Not	**RATING**	**Definitely Yes**
Strongly DISAGREE	**Neutral**	**Strongly AGREE**

1------------2------------3------------4------------5------------6------------7

PART IV 10-item Individual Innovativeness Scale (Pallister and Foxall, 1998)

The following items come from the 10-item Individual Innovativeness scale from the work of Pallister and Foxall (1998). (STM Guidelines "automatic process" permission from Elsevier).

1. I am generally cautious about accepting new ideas. R
2. I rarely trust new ideas until I can see whether the vast majority of people around me accept them. R
3. I am aware that I am usually one of the last people in my group to accept something new. R
4. I am reluctant about adopting new ways of doing things until I see them working for people around me. R
5. I find it stimulating to be original in my thinking and behavior.
6. I tend to feel that the old way of living and doing things is the best way. R
7. I am challenged (negative) by ambiguities and unsolved problems. R
8. I must see other people using new innovations before I will consider them. R
9. I am challenged by awkward questions. R
10. I often find myself skeptical of new ideas. R

© Susan E. Reid and Charles B. Crawford, August 14, 2020.

4

How do you score on the following scale from 1 to 7?

Definitely Not **RATING** **Definitely Yes**
Strongly DISAGREE **Neutral** **Strongly AGREE**
1-----------2-----------3-----------4-----------5-----------6-----------7

SECTION 2 VALUES

Please rate how strongly you value each of the following concepts. As with the other scales, there are no right or wrong answers. Rather, your answers are meant to serve as a focal point for understanding the main factors which are underlying your general motivation.

PART I 9-Item Altrusitic-Biospheric Scale (Bouman et al. 2018)

The following items come from the 9-item Altruistic-Biospheric scale from the work of Bouman *et al.*, (2018) (Frontiers in Psychology, Open-Access Journal. CC-BY license).

Biospheric Items

1. It is important to prevent environmental pollution.
2. It is important to protect the environment.
3. It is important to respect nature.
4. It is important to be in unity with nature.

Altruistic Items

1. It is important that every person has equal opportunities.
2. It is important to take care of those who are worse off.
3. It is important that every person is treated justly.
4. It is important that there is no war or conflict.
5. It is important to be helpful to others.

© Susan E. Reid and Charles B. Crawford, August 14, 2020.

Please keep in mind that with each of the tools provided in Worksheet 2, there are no right or wrong answers. The aim is to gain a subjective understanding of your own primary drivers in order to help better direct your visioning activities moving forward in a way that may provide the most ease, satisfaction, and benefit, given your unique combination of motivators.

4.3 Measuring Cognitive Style

Two sets of individual-level constructs are relevant to divergent thinking cognitive style: ► Sect. 4.3.1 "Divergent Thinking Attitudes" (Basadur & Hausdorf, 1996) and ► Sect. 4.3.2 "Ideational Behavior" (Runco et al., 2001). Building on this and other previous research, scales were developed and tested in a study conducted by Reid and de Brentani (2015), in a context specific to new innovations which is likely relevant for many entrepreneurs in their market visioning activities. The reasoning is detailed below.

4.3.1 Measuring Divergent Thinking Attitudes

"Divergent Thinking Attitudes" (Basadur & Hausdorf, 1996) deal with the predisposition of individuals to think in new and creative ways and, based on Reid and de Brentani (2015), involve two attitudinal styles of interest: (1) *Openness to New Ideas* (■ Fig. 4.8) and (2) *The Ability to Move Rapidly from a Mode of Divergent to Convergent Thinking* (■ Fig. 4.9).

1. Individuals with the first Divergent Thinking Attitudes factor, an attitude of *Openness to New Ideas*, are likely to display greater creativity (Williams, 2004) and resultant innovation (Miron & Naveh, 2004), and, based on McGrath (2001), the openness-creativity-innovation success relationship is likely to be facilitated by a greater tendency for exploration and information sharing in these open-minded individuals. As such, a positive association between openness and the Market Visioning Competence (MVC) components of networking, market learning, and idea driving can be expected. A three-item *Openness to New Ideas* scale was developed and tested by Reid and de Brentani (2015) in the radical innovation context for validity and reliability. Such a context is often linked to the case of entrepreneurial ventures. The Reid and de Brentani (2015) items for measuring *Openness to New Ideas* are provided in Worksheet 3 (Scale

■ **Fig. 4.8** Conceptual image to portray "Openness." (Source: Image licensed and downloaded from Adobe Stock on July 23, 2020. Credit: by @Delphotostock/► stock.adobe.com. License Link: ► https://stock.adobe.com/ca/26081235)

Fig. 4.9 Conceptual image to portray "Divergence to Convergence." (Source: Image licensed and downloaded from Adobe Stock on July 23, 2020. Credit: by @babamozi/▶ stock.adobe.com. License Link: ▶ https://stock.adobe.com/ca/51890332)

in Worksheet 3 permission granted by Wiley and Sons on December 17, 2020, for reprint).

2. The second Divergent Thinking Attitudes factor, *Efficient Divergent to Convergent Thinking*, deals with individuals' attitudes about reaching closure, that is, moving toward cutting off ideation in order to come to quality ideas more quickly (Basadur & Finkbeiner, 1985; Cropley, 2006). This can be linked to the Market Visioning Competence (MVC capability) of idea driving, which involves the championing of innovative and often risky ideas. Champions, while initially needing to have the ability to network and actively scan the external and internal environment on their own, at a later stage also need a skill set encompassing the ability to actively drive and sell one key vision of the market for a potential new product/technology. For this reason, the championing behavior affiliated with idea driving as part of MVC relies on the ability to move efficiently from divergent to convergent thinking to clearly communicate the idea that is being sold (Vandermerwe, 1987). The three items used to measure *Efficient Divergent to Convergent Thinking* were based on the 14-item Basadur and Finkbeiner (1985) *Preference for Ideation* scale and found to be valid and reliable in Reid and de Brentani in the case of radical innovation (2015). This three-item *Efficient Divergent to Convergent Thinking* scale is provided in Worksheet 3 (Scale in Worksheet 3 permission granted by Wiley and Sons on December 17, 2020, for reprint).

4.3.2 Measuring Ideational Behavior

"Ideational Behavior" (Runco et al., 2001) represents a second Divergent Thinking construct group with relevance to early entrepreneurial success. As pointed out by Runco et al. (2001, p. 394), "Divergent thinking reflects the individual's ability to be original, flexible and fluent with ideas." "Ideational Behavior" is measured in two ways: (1) through the *Ability to Generate New Ideas* and (2) through the *Need for Cognition*.

1. *The Ability to Generate New Ideas* means being proficient at and taking pleasure in involvement with new idea generation. This ability is seen as impacting the networking element of MVC, whereby individuals with strong ideational behavior display higher than normal levels of divergent thinking and thus are more likely to actively seek out higher levels of interaction with "nonredundant" network contacts (Burt, 1992). This enables a higher level of contact with new and different ideas. The *Ability to Generate New Ideas* scale was tested in Reid and de Brentani (2015) and found to be valid and reliable in the case of radical innovation using 3 items from the original 23-item scale developed by Runco et al. (2001). The three-item *Ability to Generate New Ideas* scale is provided in Worksheet 3 (Scale in Worksheet 3 permission granted by Wiley and Sons on December 17, 2020, for reprint).

2. Another Divergent Thinking skill (antecedent to Ideational Behavior) is *Need for Cognition*—that is, "the tendency for an individual to engage in and enjoy thinking" (Cacioppo & Petty, 1982, p.116 and Cacioppo et al., 1984, p. 306)—and the preference and need on the part of individuals for mental stimulation and complexity in problem-solving (Lord & Putrevu, 2006). According to Verplanken et al. (1992), there is a positive link between the *Need for Cognition* and *Length of Search Effort* scales for new information on the part of an individual. In other words, the higher the tendency of individuals to enjoy engagement in the actual process of thinking, the more likely it is that they will spend more time undertaking the search and problem-solving efforts linked to such activity. This suggests a potential slowdown in the ability to drive new ideas forward, a key dimension of MVC (Reid & Saad, 1999).

   On the other hand, *Need for Cognition* is also linked to thinking in ways that give a more detailed set of potential options or scenarios for consideration and thus to delivering a potentially better exploration outcome. As such, it is likely, overall, to be a positive antecedent of MVC, probably even more so in the case when technical innovation is involved. Based on the 34-item scale of Cacioppo and Petty (1982) and the 6-item scale by Lord and Putrevu (2006), Reid and de Brentani (2015) constructed a 5-item scale, found to be valid and reliable, for use in the case of radical innovation. The five-item scale for measuring *Need for*

Cognition is provided in Worksheet 3 (Scale in Worksheet 3 permission granted by Wiley and Sons on December 17, 2020, for reprint).

4.3.3 Measuring Team-Level Cognitive Environment

It was found in the 2015 Reid and de Brentani study that for intrapreneurs working in organizations, or entrepreneurs with startups, their team and organizational environments were important in allowing divergent thinking skills and attitudes to flourish. In particular, in terms of the best environment for the *Encouragement of Divergent Thinking*, (1) *Idea Freedom/Openness to New Ideas* and (2) *Encouraging Diversity* were found to be statistically significant. In terms of entrepreneurial startups, this means that the entrepreneur needs to focus on encouraging their team in certain ways. Two scales based primarily on interviews with experts, and developed and validated by Reid and de Brentani (2015), deal with the *Encouragement of Divergent Thinking* and capture the antecedent nature of the embedded behaviors and attitudes that impact MVC. Specifically *Idea Freedom* deals with how to encourage all types of ideas and promote access to a variety of information sources. It involves encouraging and supporting activities (e.g., conference attendance) of the individuals involved in the front end of innovation while at the same time providing a risk-free environment where ideas can be openly expressed. Also, *Encouraging Diversity* captures the mindset of the entire team about open communication and free access across functions and locations, as well as diversity in hiring practices. These two approaches to the *Encouragement of Divergent Thinking* have a clear role to play in setting the stage for the individual behaviors that are associated with networking and idea driving/championing. They also reflect the team's future orientation toward the use of market learning tools and the probing of latent customer needs.

In summary, building an effective vision is a two-stage process that requires entrepreneurs to first develop the ability to create and look at new radical ideas in diverse ways (i.e., Divergent Thinking skills), and then through Market Visioning Competence (MVC) come to a more focused and eventually specific, convergent view of the new technology/product and its potential in the marketplace—Market Vision (MV).

Worksheet 3 provides scales to test your cognitive style.

Worksheet 3: Cognitive Style Survey

This worksheet is divided into 3 sections. Section 1 looks at your cognitive tendencies in terms of divergent thinking attitudes. Section 2 looks at your ideational behavior. Sections 1 and 2 together are aimed at you understanding your 'cognitive style'. Section 3, where relevant for entrepreneurs who already have a startup organization, investigates your firm`s openness to new ideas and encouraging diversity. As described in Chapter 4, each of the question items has been tested in our previous research and has been found to be a statistically significantly reliable and valid indicator for the overall factor being examined in the context of new innovations.

It is suggested, as much as possible, to have each of your main team, partners or stakeholders participate in the survey. There are no right or wrong answers here; rather, your answers are meant to serve as a focal point for discussion around team members' different cognitive styles. You should try to identify one or two key areas where you/your team feel you have challenges/need external help, list potential ideas for improvement or resources you require, and then put together a plan with your team for obtaining these.

How do you score on the following scale from 1 to 7:

Definitely Not **RATING** **Definitely Yes**
Strongly DISAGREE **Neutral** **Strongly AGREE**
1-----------2-----------3-----------4-----------5-----------6-----------7

SECTION 1 DIVERGENT THINKING ATTITUDES FACTORS

PART I OPENNESS

Item 1: I think everyone should communicate his or her ideas, no matter how unusual. ——

Item 2: I feel that people ought to be encouraged to share all their ideas, because you will never know when a crazy-sounding one might turn out to be best. ——

Item 3: I feel that all ideas should be given equal time and be listened to with an open mind, regardless of how outside the norm they seem to be. ——

PART II ABILITY TO MOVE FROM DIVERGENT TO CONVERGENT THINKING EFFICIENTLY AND EFFECTIVELY

Item 1: Judgment is necessary during idea generation to ensure that only quality ideas are developed. ——

Item 2: Quality is a lot more important than quantity in generating ideas. ——

Item 3: We should cut off ideas when they get ridiculous and get on with it. ——

© Susan E. Reid and Charles B. Crawford, August 14, 2020.

4

Definitely Not **RATING** **Definitely Yes**
Strongly DISAGREE **Neutral** **Strongly AGREE**
1------------2------------3------------4------------5------------6------------7

SECTION 2 IDEATIONAL BEHAVIOR

PART I ABILITY TO GENERATE NEW IDEAS

Item 1: Friends ask me to help them think of ideas and solutions. _______
Item 2: I come up with a lot of ideas or solutions to problems. _______
Item 3: I am good at combining ideas in ways that others have not tried._______

PART II NEED FOR COGNITION

Item 1: I would rather do something that is sure to challenge my thinking abilities than something that requires little thought. _______
Item 2: I seek out situations where there is a likely chance that I will have to think in depth about something. _______
Item 3: I would prefer life to be filled with puzzles that I must solve. _______
Item 4: I prefer complex to simple problems. _______
Item 5: I like to have the responsibility of handling a situation. _______

SECTION 3 TEAM-LEVEL COGNITIVE ENVIRONMENT

PART I ORGANIZATIONAL ENCOURAGEMENT OF IDEATION

Item 1: My organization encourages a risk-free environment where ideas can be openly expressed. _______
Item 2: Employee freedom to generate ideas is valued in our organization._______
Item 3: We actively encourage our people to find external stimuli for idea generation, such as attending conferences or reading blogs. _______

PART II ORGANIZATIONAL ENCOURAGEMENT OF DIVERSITY

Item 1: We actively engage in cross-departmental product development practices. _______
Item 2: My organization openly promotes diversity in its hiring practices. _______
Item 3: A diverse workplace is important for having a variety of inputs into product development processes. _______
Item 4: Different departments in our organization work cooperatively together on product development. _______

© Susan E. Reid and Charles B. Crawford, August 14, 2020.

Not only will this worksheet aid you in knowing where in the entrepreneurial process your natural cognitive style will likely shine, but it will also help you identify areas where you may need to enlist more support from your network and teammates and establish how to build an encouraging work environment for your team.

4.4 Measuring Mindset

A starting point for measuring "mindset" is to determine whether you exhibit more of a "fixed mindset" or a "growth mindset" (Dweck, 2016). Dweck (2016) has developed a valid, reliable three-item, six-point scale (1 = strongly agree; 6 = strongly disagree) to see where you stand. This scale is available through the Stanford SPARQtools website (Growth Mindset Scale | SPARQtools). The idea here is that we can develop a growth mindset by acknowledging that it is a possibility. Dweck (2016) discusses the benefits of a growth mindset that include the ability to take on challenges and learn from them as well as learning how to deal with roadblocks. Further, by modeling growth mindset-related behaviors, this can positively influence the outcomes for others as well.

Angela Lee Duckworth (2013, online) gave a well-known 2013 TED Talk called *Grit: the power of passion and perseverance*, where she noted that "it's not enough to shift your mindset. You also need a good dose of 'grit' and 'resilience' to achieve short-term and long-term goals." According to Duckworth et al. (2007, p. 1087-1088): "Grit" is "defined as perseverance and passion for long-term goals. Grit entails working strenuously toward challenges, maintaining effort and interest over years despite failure, adversity, and plateaus in progress." It is therefore clearly linked to intense passion for a particular goal.

This brings us back to the importance of vision. If passion is a key component of vision, it makes sense that creating and developing a strong vision is the linchpin for moving the needle forward with neuroplasticity, mindset, persistence, and grit.

At the end of the day, economists and B-school professors hold many different perspectives on the "nature" vs. "nurture" entrepreneurial debate. Regardless of how much they are born with and how much they adapt to or learn, entrepreneurs all possess different sets of special traits, skills, and values, forged by life events and environmental circumstances. But, your current situation does not dictate your future potential. You need to give yourself permission to have that dream and then develop whatever the necessary skills and resources are to go after it. While some of these skills may be difficult to "learn" per se, all types of entrepreneur, whether they be solo, intrapreneur, co-preneur, business owner, or future entrepreneur, can learn some valuable managerial, financial, marketing/new product development, and people skills lessons to make their journey a little easier and, hopefully, a lot more fruitful. The remainder of this book focuses on meeting entrepreneurs at the current stage of their motivational and realized journey and then using an appropriate lens to help them create and realize their visions.

Chapter Review Questions

1. What are the four main traits that have generally been found by researchers to be indicators of entrepreneurial potential? Provide an example for each one.
2. Why is it important for would-be entrepreneurs to reflect on their social and environmental values?
3. How do divergent and convergent thinking relate to each other? How do these cognitive styles change in importance over the life of a startup?
4. What is the difference between a fixed and growth mindset? What ways do you think individuals can develop or enhance their growth mindset?
5. With regard to entrepreneurial potential, do you think it is more a result of nature or nurture? Do you believe there are ways to improve entrepreneurial potential? Please provide some examples.

References

Ahmetoglu, G., & Chamorro-Premuzic, T. (2011). EQ-nomics: Understanding the relationship between individual differences in trait emotional intelligence and entrepreneurship. *Personality Individual Differences, 51*(8), 1028–1033.

Basadur, M. S., & Finkbeiner, C. T. (1985). Measuring preference for ideation in creative problem-solving training. *Journal of Applied Behavioral Science, 21*(1), 37–49.

Basadur, M. S., & Hausdorf, P. A. (1996). Measuring divergent thinking attitudes related to creative problem solving and innovation management. *Creativity Research Journal, 9*(1), 21–32.

Beck, A. T. (1983). Cognitive therapy of depression: New perspectives. In P. J. Clayton & J. E. Barnett (Eds.), *Treatment of depression: Old controversies and new approaches* (pp. 205–290). Raven Press.

Bieling, P. J., Beck, A. T., & Brown, G. K. (2000). The Sociotropy-Autonomy Scale: Structure and implications. *Cognitive Therapy and Research, 24*(6), 763–780. https://doi.org/10.1023/A:1005599714224

Bouman, T., Steg, L., & Kiers, H. A. L. (2018). Measuring values in environmental research: A test of an environmental portrait value questionnaire. *Frontiers in Psychology, 9*(564), 1–15.

Brockhaus, R. H., & Horwitz, P. S. (1986). The psychology of the entrepreneur. In D. L. Sexton & R. W. Smilor (Eds.), *The art and science of entrepreneurship* (pp. 25–48). Ballinger.

Burt, R. S. (1992). *Structural holes: The social structure of competition*. Harvard University Press.

Cacioppo, J. T., & Petty, R. E. (1982). The need for cognition. *Journal of Personality and Social Psychology, 42*(1), 116–131.

Cacioppo, J. T., Petty, R. E., & Kao, C. F. (1984). The efficient assessment of need for cognition. *Journal of Personality Assessment, 48*(3), 306–307.

Chen, G., Gully, S. M., & Eden, D. (2001). Validation of a new general self-efficacy scale. *Organizational Research Methods, 4*(1), 62–83.

Costa, P. T., & McCrae, R. R. (1985). *The NEO personality inventory manual*. Psychological Assessment Resources.

Cropley, A. (2006). In praise of convergent thinking. *Creativity Research Journal, 18*(3), 391–404.

Cubico, S., Bortolani, E., Favretto, G., & Sartori, R. (2010). Describing the entrepreneurial profile: The entrepreneurial aptitude test (TAI). *International Journal of Entrepreneurship and Small Business, 11*(4), 424–435.

Cuesta, M., Suare-Alvarez, J., Lozano, L. M., Garcia-Cueto, E., & Muniz, J. (2018). Assessment of eight entrepreneurial personality dimensions: Validity evidence of the BEPE battery. *Frontiers in Psychology, 9*(2353), 1–10.

Davis, M. H., Hall, J. A., & Mayer, P. S. (2015, Oct 19). Developing a new measure of entrepreneurial mindset: Reliability, validity, and implications for practitioners. *Consulting Psychology Journal: Practice and Research*. Advance online publication. https://doi.org/10.1037/cpb0000045.

Duckworth, A. L., Peterson, C., Matthews, M. D., & Kelly, D. R. (2007). Grit: Perseverance and passion for long-term goals. *Journal of Personality and Social Psychology, 92*(6), 1087–1101.
Duckworth, A. L. (2013). *Grit: The power of passion and perseverance*, TED Talk online, May 9, 2013, https://www.bing.com/videos/search?q=Duckworth+2013+TED+talk+Grit&docid=608036553110716984&mid=52E3784A0FD900C3796E52E3784A0FD900C3796E&view=detail&FORM=VIRE. Accessed on 31 Aug 2020.
Dweck, C. (2016). *Mindset: The new psychology of success* (Updated ed. original 2006). Ballantine Books.
Gartner, W. B. (1988). "Who is an entrepreneur?" is the wrong question. *American Journal of Small Business, 12*(4), 11–32.
Huefner, J. C., Hunt, H. K., & Robinson, P. B. (1996). A comparison of four scales predicting entrepreneurship. *Academy of Entrepreneurship Journal, 1*(2), 56–80.
Hurt, H. T., Joseph, K., & Cook, C. D. (1977). Scales for the measurement of innovativeness. *Human Communication Research, 4*(1), 58–65.
Iresearchnet.com. (2020, online). http://psychology.iresearchnet.com/social-psychology/personality/achievement-motivation/, definition for "achievement motivation". Accessed on 25 Aug 2020.
Leutner, F., Ahmetoglu, G., Akhtar, R., & Chamorro-Premuzic, T. (2014). The relationship between the entrepreneurial personality and the Big Five personality traits. *Personality and Individual Differences, 63*(June), 58–63.
Lord, K. R., & Putrevu, S. (2006). Exploring the dimensionality of the need for cognition scale. *Psychology and Marketing, 23*(1), 11–34.
McGrath, R. (2001). Exploratory learning, innovative capacity, and managerial oversight. *Academy of Management Journal, 44*(1), 118–131.
Miron, E. M. E., & Naveh, E. (2004). Do personal characteristics and cultural values that promote innovation, quality and efficiency compete or complement each other? *Journal of Organizational Behavior, 25*(2), 175–199.
Myers, I. B. (1962). *The Myers-Briggs type indicator manual*. Educational Testing Service.
Pallister, J. G., & Foxall, G. R. (1998). Psychometric properties of the Hurt-Joseph-Cook scales for the measurement of innovativeness. *Technovation, 18*(11), 663–675.
Rausch, A., & Frese, M. (2007). Born to be an entrepreneur? Revisiting the personality approach to entrepreneurship. In J. R. Baum, M. Frese, & R. Baron (Eds.), *The psychology of entrepreneurship* (pp. 41–65). Lawrence Erlbaum Associates.
Ray, J. J. (1979). A quick measure of achievement motivation – Validated in Australia and reliance in Britain and South Africa. *Australian Psychologist, 14*(3), 337–344.
Reid, S. E., & de Brentani, U. (2015). Building a measurement model for Market Visioning Competence and its' proposed antecedents: Organizational encouragement of divergent thinking, divergent thinking attitudes and ideational behavior. *Journal of Product Innovation Management, 32*(2), 243–262.
Reid, S. E., & Saad, G. (1999). *The roots of innovation*, ASAC Marketing Proceedings, St. John, NB, Canada.
Rokeach, M. (1968). *Beliefs, attitudes, and values: A theory of organization and change*. Jossey-Bass.
Rokeach, M. (1973). *The nature of human values*. Free Press.
Runco, M. A., Plucker, J. A., & Lim, W. (2001). Development and psychometric integrity of a measure of ideational behavior. *Creativity Research Journal, 13*(3–4), 393–400.
Santos, S. C., Caetano, A. N., & Curral, L. (2013). Psychosocial aspects of entrepreneurial potential. *Journal of Small Business and Entrepreneurship, 26*(6), 661–685.
Schwarzer, R., & Jerusalem, M. (1995). Generalized self-efficacy scale. In J. Weinman, S. Wright, & M. Johnston (Eds.), *Measures in health psychology: A user's portfolio* (Causal and control beliefs) (pp. 35–37). NFER – Nelson.
Schwartz, S. H. (1992). Universals in the content and structure of values: Theoretical advances and empirical tests in 20 countries. In M. Zanna (Ed.), *Advances in experimental social psychology* (Vol. 25, pp. 1–65). Academic Press.
Stern, P. S., & Dietz, T. (1994). The value basis of environmental concern. *Journal of Social Issues, 50*(3), 65–84.

Vandermerwe, S. (1987). Diffusing new ideas in-house. *Journal of Product Innovation Management, 4*(4), 256–264.

Verplanken, B., Hazenberg, P. T., & Palenewen, G. R. (1992). Need for cognition and external information search effort. *Journal of Research in Personality, 26*(2), 128–136.

Williams, S. D. (2004). Personality, attitude, and leader influences on divergent thinking and creative organizations. *European Journal of Innovation Management, 7*(3), 187–204.

Vision Frameworks Based on Motivation

Contents

© The Author(s), under exclusive license to Springer Nature Switzerland AG 2022
S. E. Reid, C. B. Crawford, *Entrepreneurial Vision*, Classroom Companion: Business,
https://doi.org/10.1007/978-3-030-77803-3_5

Learning Objectives

In this chapter, we begin by building an understanding of where aspiring entrepreneurs might start with their vision development. We suggest looking back at your primary motivations from ▶ Chaps. 3 and 4 and potentially using these as a springboard for deciding on one of five generic frameworks, we present in this chapter, as a basis for early vision construction.

In this chapter, we aim to:

1. Discuss the importance of preparing to meet opportunity.
2. Explain the two main types of opportunities: innovation-driven and socioeconomic-driven.
3. Describe five types of vision formation approaches and potential motivation matchups.

5.1 Preparation Meets Opportunity

From our perspective, one of the biggest mistakes any entrepreneur can make is to move forward with a new idea without thinking about the larger, longer-term picture and its implications. Often, people will say things like, "Well, come on now, there are lots of examples of entrepreneurs who were successful by doing just that—jumping right in without a thought," or "what about that guy who bought and flipped several real estate holdings and made a short-term killing and it happened without much planning?" More likely, much passion and planning went into such success stories.

The thing is—we don't believe in shortcuts. For an entrepreneurial success that looks like it "just happened" out of the blue, if you dig deeper, chances are that the entrepreneur and their team were preparing all along. As one example, Tito's Handmade Vodka has been described as an "overnight success," but the brand, founded in Texas in 1995, was growing over an approximate 6-year period when it skyrocketed in terms of company sales and winning competitions.

On closer examination, entrepreneurial success stories often embody Louis Pasteur's famous quote (1854, lecture): "Dans les champs de l'observation le hasard ne favorise que les esprits prepares," and the truncated translation to English, "Chance favours the prepared mind," which many philosophers have iterated throughout history. In other words, it's difficult to jump into a new project without having done any groundwork beforehand. What may look to be an overnight success is often the result of long-term preparation, so that when the "right" opportunity comes along, the prepared entrepreneur is ready to take advantage of it.

A great example of this is the famous tale of the discovery of the theory of buoyancy by Archimedes (◘ Fig. 5.1). The local ruler of Syracuse during the fourth century BC, Hiero II, had given Archimedes the task of figuring out whether a gold crown had been adulterated by blending gold with silver. To the eye, such an alteration would likely not be detectable but would have saved the goldsmith quite a bit of money. Archimedes, the local polymath, was working on the question for quite some time before the famous incident where he apparently was in the bath

Fig. 5.1 Archimedes. (Source: Image licensed and downloaded from Shutterstock on May 3, 2020. Credit: by Natata/► Shutterstock.com. License Link: ► https://www.shutterstock.com/image-vector/archimedes-famous-vector-sketch-portrait-1266622978)

and figured out that a certain sized object dropped into water would displace the water to a certain level regardless of its weight. Therefore, an adulterated crown would weigh approximately the same, but the alloy of gold and silver would cause the size of the crown to be slightly larger and therefore cause slightly more water to be displaced. His famous "ah-ha" moment led to him apparently running down the street in his birthday suit shouting "Eureka!" or, as Biello (2006) notes, translates to "I've found it." Biello also notes (2006, p. 1) "The oldest authority for the naked-Archimedes eureka story is Vitruvius, a Roman writer, who included the tale in his introduction to his ninth book of architecture some time in the first century B.C. Because this was nearly 200 years after the event is presumed to have taken place, the story may have been improved in the telling." The main point here is that Archimedes had been studying math much of his life and had been long pondering the question before his Eureka moment. So, in the end, he was very prepared when the right circumstances for realization and pattern recognition occurred. What might look like luck is more often a case of preparation meeting opportunity, through hard work and determination.

So, we can probably agree on the importance of being careful when talking about luck creating success directly. Yes, luck is a factor in terms of opportunities presenting themselves at certain times; however, as much as possible, we need to prepare ourselves to proactively go after and envision the future based on opportunities which resonate with who we are. Actively reviewing our decisions as to whether we are 'picking a good path' or whether we are just 'picking any old path' is likely a good practice. Sure, opportunities get put in our path, and sometimes we jump for lack of a better idea or opportunity; however, that does not necessarily mean that an opportunity is right for us.

If you already have an entrepreneurial idea in mind or if you have an opportunity that has recently been put in front of you, an excellent first place to start might be a quick litmus test. Close your eyes for a moment and try to picture yourself 5–10 years, in the future, if you were to spend a good deal of your time and energy on this pursuit. Does the idea of it draw you in? Do you feel passionate about it, even in the projected future? Do you think you would be in a good flow state if you were working on this every day for the foreseeable future? Do you have a good feeling about being involved, possibly for a long time, with this pursuit? If you were at a dinner party, is it something you would be proud of talking about? Would it harmonize with your core values and primary motivators we identified in the last chapters? If the answers are still pretty much "yes" then, by all means, continue forward. That said, however, if you have a bad feeling in the core of your stomach and can't piece together your underlying motivation with the opportunity in any meaningful way, then perhaps it's time to take a pass and reconsider—or at least consider—how you might be able to reframe the opportunity in a way that does resonate with your skills and motivators.

You may have heard stories about people who spent years on a project only to be disappointed. Maybe it wasn't aligned with their skills or interests properly. Maybe they didn't do the litmus test. Maybe the timing wasn't right. Maybe the money ran out, and they didn't have the skills or network to figure out how to right the ship. Maybe they didn't execute well in terms of making good market or channel decisions. Maybe unforeseen circumstances such as a recession transpired.

To at least better leverage/hedge our chances from the get-go, it's essential to consider what we can control and what we can't. Without a doubt, luck and timing of evolving opportunities in the environment are sometimes out of our control. But there is a lot that we can still control. We can actively think about how new opportunities mesh with our underlying motivations and skills. We can also do our homework researching the opportunity, related markets, and channels as much as possible. We can make decisions to seek advice through our networks, advisors, and experts in the field as well as working closely with our customers to develop the best products and services possible.

From our experience, however, probably the most important starting point is thinking with clarity about the vision one has of oneself as an entrepreneur and the vision one has for involvement with one's nascent and growing ideas. From there, it is key to modify and clarify our vision as we move forward along the path toward it once we have determined it to be our North Star. We believe there are seven major steps for moving along a vision's development path once you have decided you want to move forward, as follows:

1. Linking your primary motivation drivers to potential frameworks for vision formation
2. Deep diving into industry and market opportunities to understand how your core competencies and motivators, including your "purpose," might align with potential broad opportunities of interest and to work toward proactive inspiration for an early vision
3. Refining these ideas with input from various types of partners
4. Creating a very early version of your market vision and technology vision (where relevant)
5. Developing, communicating and testing the vision with an appropriate niche market and channel members
6. Developing a vision for the financial side of your business
7. Using test markets to refine and/or pivot your vision

In the rest of this chapter, we will focus on matching your primary motivations to potential general vision frameworks for moving forward.

5.2 Two Main Types of Opportunities

Entrepreneurship is a path-dependent process. It evolves through a process of building self-awareness in combination with laying the foundation for the early stages of opportunity identification. Therefore, it's important to spend time thinking about the context within which you enable opportunity identification and how you will incorporate chosen opportunities into your vision. What you know about your own motivational triggers from your work in ▶ Chaps. 3 and 4, should help you to gain a better idea about how to move toward opportunity identification. In general, there are two very broad views about opportunity goals: some opportunities are driven by growth objectives and others emerge through the need for social change.

5.2.1 Opportunity Driven by Growth Objectives

On the one hand, the pursuit of some opportunities may be related to their potential for growth and profit. This may be achieved through developing innovations (◘ Fig. 5.2), anticipating and/or responding to demographic/social changes and/or new technological opportunities.

Schumpeter (1934) identified five profit growth opportunity types, generally related to for-profit activities, and these include creation of new goods/services, types of organization, means of production and/or new markets, as well as controlling raw materials/supplies.

■ **Fig. 5.2** Conceptual image to portray "growth opportunities". (Source: Image licensed and downloaded from Shutterstock, on Oct 22, 2018. Credit: by Monster Ztudio/► Shutterstock.com. License Link: ► https://www.shutterstock.com/image-photo/business-development-success-growing-growth-concept-748617433)

5.2.2 Opportunity Through the Need for Change

On the other hand, the pursuit of some opportunities may be more focused on responding to social or environmental need for change (■ Fig. 5.3).

These two major philosophies, in terms of where the pursuit of opportunities and the innovations related to them stems from—growth motive or need for change motive—can help to provide us with some guidance in terms of our upfront approaches to visioning activity. Specifically, you may want to look to your values to see whether spirituality, cultural, and/or biospheric (environmental)/social (altruistic) values are highly important to you. Visions based on such values may be based on profit or not-for-profit philosophies, but whichever model is chosen should be consciously considered from the get-go as a critical component of your overall vision framing. Additionally, even if you decide to go for a not-for-profit model, it does not negate the importance of running a business in a fiscally responsible fashion (i.e., including considering how you will support yourself and your team in the running of such a business). It just means that your approach to visioning may come from a different way of framing your long-term goals.

With this broad-brush understanding of two main perspectives related to opportunity formation, let's drill down into five specific approaches that can be utilized for vision framing and formation.

Fig. 5.3 Mohandas K. Gandhi. (Source: ▶ https://commons.wikimedia.org/wiki/File:Portrait_Gandhi.jpg. Photographer unknown. Downloaded via Wikimedia Commons on July 26, 2020. Public Domain)

5.3 Matching Motivation with Vision Formation Approach

We suggest looking back at the work you have already done in ▶ Chaps. 3 and 4 to develop a better understanding of your primary motivations and using these as a springboard to consider five potential generic frameworks for vision construction. The frameworks include the following:

5.3.1 Target-based vision
5.3.2 Innovation-based vision
5.3.3 Benchmark-based vision
5.3.4 Positioning-based vision
5.3.5 Values-based vision

We provide specific examples so you can get a feel for the overall approach to each type of vision formation. In the next chapters, we will be providing more detailed approaches to creating your own vision, once you have done more of the upfront homework needed to get to that stage.

5.3.1 Target-Based Vision

5

Target-based vision uses a specific and clear outcome goal to drive passion and interest around making the goal happen. A targeted approach is a natural pairing for aspiring entrepreneurs who are motivated by achievement and/or self-efficacy. It works well for those who like to know they are reaching a specific milestone in order to help pace themselves and make better managerial decisions and especially those who love achieving these goals based on their own actions. In many ways, this is the easiest type of vision formation approach and, as such, can easily be linked with setting a clear financial vision, one of the most often used methods, particularly by large companies, in their vision-setting exercises.

Target outcome goals may be of several types including, but not limited to, the following.

5.3.1.1 Growth Targets

i. Revenue or Profit Growth Goals

Revenue-or profit-based growth goals are perhaps two of the simplest mechanisms for target-based vision setting because they use specific and clear outcome goals to quickly achieve understanding of the vision.

► Example: "We Want to Make $25 Million by 2025!"

This is a fictional example however, we used this mechanism for vision framing with our own family business. Using this form of visioning was particularly useful in helping to reframe the revenue goal directly into budget and market targets aligned with the revenue we were aiming at generating within a certain timeframe. ◄

► Example: Cooper Tire & Rubber Co.

Cooper Tire has long been in the business of manufacturing tires for cars (including racing tires), motorcycles, and trucks. Their vision, "to earn money for its shareholders and increase the value of their investment" (Mission Statements website, 2020), is driven by keeping an eye on their shareholder value, and they do this by "growing the company, controlling assets and properly structuring the balance sheet, thereby increasing EPS, cash flow, and return on investment capital" (Mission Statements website, 2020). ◄

ii. Target for Number of Customers (an Increase)

Target-based vision can be achieved in many ways beyond just focusing on the balance sheet. One of these ways is to focus on achieving a target number of customers for growth. This can be a beneficial approach for NGOs but can also be used by for-profit companies.

► Example: Government of India's Ministry of Power's e-Mobility Target for 2030

The Indian "government's target of achieving 30% e-mobility by 2030" (Energy Efficiency Services Limited India website, 2020) (◘ Fig. 5.4). ◄

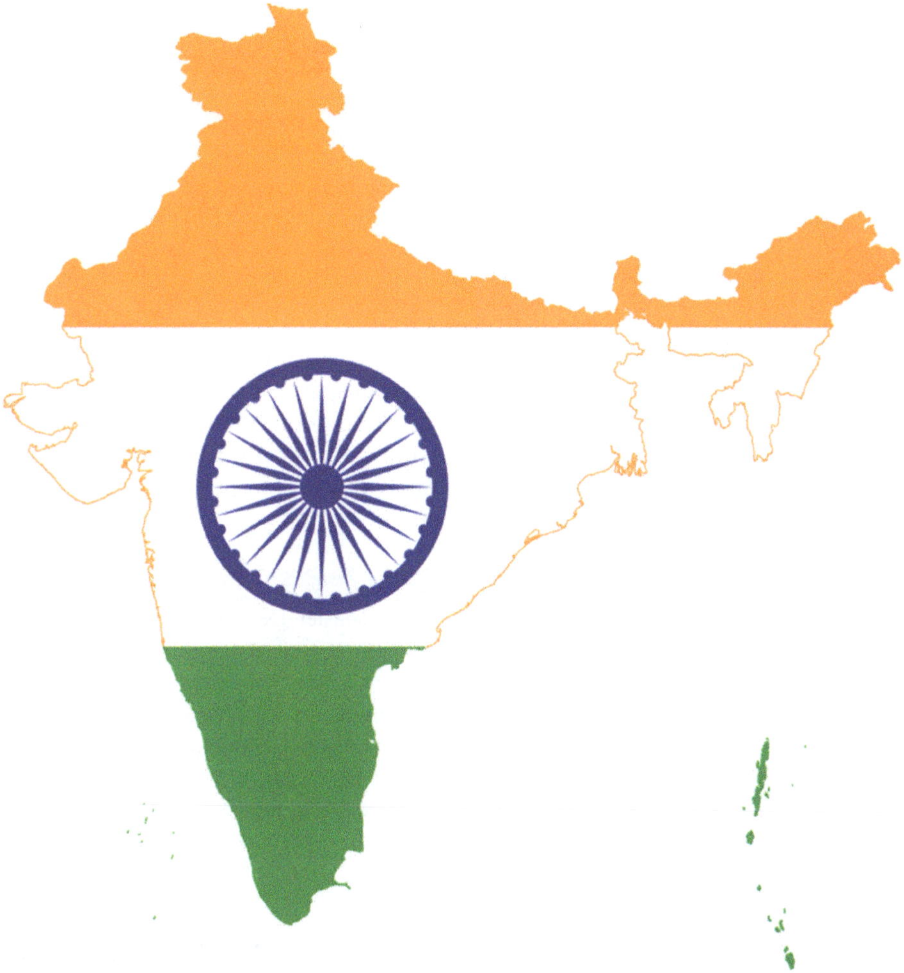

◘ **Fig. 5.4** Map of India with Indian flag superimposed. (Source: ► https://commons.wikimedia.org/wiki/File:Flag-map_of_India_(de-facto).svg. By Stasyan117/CC BY-SA (► https://creativecommons.org/licenses/by-sa/4.0). Downloaded via Wikimedia Commons on July 13, 2020)

iii. Target for Number of Customers (a Decrease)

While focusing on a decrease in the number of customers is a much less common approach than focusing on an increase, it can be a very successful approach for NGOs and NFPs focusing on reduction in numbers of those, for example, with, a specific disease or in terms of eliminating undesirable conditions such as in the case of climate change.

► Example: Alzheimer's Association

The Alzheimer's Association is an example of targeting where their aim is to decrease their number of clients to zero.

» "A world without Alzheimer's and all other dementia (Alzheimer's Association website, 2020)." ◄

5.3.1.2 Physical Size or Scale Target

Another target type related to the growth target idea is the concept of building or scaling based on physical size, either by aiming at superior size/scale (as in the Burg Khalifa example below) or by aiming for reduction in rates or outcomes (as in the European Commission example below). Visions of this form have the potential to be very magnetic and inspiring and therefore may appeal to those with substantial achievement or self-efficacy motivations.

► Example: Burg Khalifa (◘ Fig. 5.5)

The Burj Khalifa, built in Dubai, UAE, by the Master Developer Emaar Properties PJSC, began construction starting in 2004 and was completed in 2009. There is a very clear vision for the city of Dubai and part of the urban vision and plan was to construct the tallest building in the world. According to the Burj Khalifa website (2020), Emaar (Properties) "had but one inspiration, the unflagging enthusiasm set in motion by His Highness Sheikh Mohammed Bin Rashid Al Maktoum, Vice President and Prime Minister of the UAE and Ruler of Dubai, who inspires us to reach for the stars."

» "The world's tallest building. A living wonder. A stunning work of art. An incomparable feat of engineering (Emaar website, 2020)." ◄

► Example: European Commission for 2030

The European Union, as part of an ongoing fight against global climate crisis, has on an ongoing basis set ambitious targets for reductions, including for greenhouse gas emissions (GHGs).

» "to cut emissions in the EU by at least 40% below 1990 levels by 2030 (European Commission website, 2020)." ◄

Fig. 5.5 The Burj Khalifa. (Source: The authors. Photo taken March 4, 2020)

5.3.1.3 Geographic Market Target

Target-based vision can also move to a different type of target beyond pure numbers or scale by focusing on the movement of a business idea to a new geographic market sometimes with a new twist.

► Example: Blue Ribbon Sports (Eventually Nike) (Fig. 5.6)

Phil Knight's original vision for Blue Ribbon Sports (born out of a Stanford MBA business plan) involved importing and distributing the high-quality, low-cost Japanese "Onitsuka Tiger" brand running shoe to the USA (Knight, 2016). ◄

5.3.1.4 Physical Quality Target

Target-based vision can also include a focus on physical qualities based around various product or process attributes such as "smoothest," "best taste," "softest," "lightest," and "fastest." Such vision strategies are often employed by consumer-packaged goods companies such as those in the food and beverage industry, the cosmetics industry, the apparel industry, the sporting goods industry, and so on.

Fig. 5.6 University of Oregon Track Team, including Phil Knight (back row, second from left) and coach Bill Bowerman (back row, center). (Source: Bill Bowerman papers, UA 003/PH 339, Special Collections & University Archives, The University of Oregon Libraries. Permission granted from the University of Oregon Libraries Special Collections and University Archives on December 16, 2020)

► Example: Casper

Casper, founded in 2014 by Philip Krim (an amalgamation of three previous online bedding companies), is a public e-commerce company with select retail locations in the USA. The company vision is based on high physical quality mattresses available online.

» "Great sleep, made simple (Rampton, 2019)." ◄

5.3.1.5 Emotional Target

A type of targeting also utilized extensively by the consumer-packaged goods and retail sectors, emotional targeting, is a way to focus on the emotional aspects of customer-targeted visioning.

◘ **Fig. 5.7** A Gymboree retail store. (Source: ► https://commons.wikimedia.org/wiki/File:A_Gymboree_retail_store.tif. By Ina Huang/CC BY-SA (► https://creativecommons.org/licenses/by-sa/3.0). Downloaded via Wikimedia Commons on July 13, 2020)

► Example: Gymboree (◘ Fig. 5.7)

Gymboree, in the business of retailing children's clothing since 1976, has focused on fun, simple designs available in a beautiful and well laid-out retail store at a value-based price point. Despite a clear vision, the sector was highly competitive, and the company relaunched the brand in February 2020 through Children's Place.

> "We aim to make shopping and getting dressed easy and fun (Gymboree website, 2020)." ◄

5.3.1.6 Date Target

► Example: President J.F. Kennedy's 1961 Vision (◘ Fig. 5.8)

Another highly effective form of targeted visioning is through the use of a specific date by which a given vision will be achieved. The following example of target visioning is described in the work of Collins and Porras (1991, p. 42): "The NASA moon mission, as articulated by President Kennedy in 1961, provides a good example of the concept":

> "Achieving the goal, before this decade is out, of landing a man on the moon and returning him safely to earth (Boorstin, 1974)." ◄

5

Fig. 5.8 John F. Kennedy, 1961. (Source: ▶ https://commons.wikimedia.org/wiki/John_F._Kennedy#/media/File:Kennedy_Giving_Historic_Speech_to_Congress_-_GPN-2000-001658.jpg Downloaded via Wikimedia Commons on May 1, 2013. Public Domain)

5.3.2 Innovation-Based Vision

Innovation-based vision is a great match for those who are highly motivated by their own ability to innovate and/or are divergent thinkers in terms of their own cognitive style. This type of framing enables very out-of-the-box, broad-based, long-range thinking and enabling around new solutions. The result may be an ability to build new conceptual frameworks and tools in order to solve current problems and approach incoming opportunities in very different ways. Divergent thinking enables moving around the current way of doing things to come up with new approaches.

Innovation-based vision is usually linked to more radical forms of innovation through new products/processes, new design, new organizational form, or new concept.

5.3.2.1 Solving Known Market Needs Through New Products or Processes (High-Market Context)

▶ Example: Genentech (◘ Fig. 5.9)

Genentech was founded in the USA in 1976 by UC San Francisco professor Herbert Boyer and venture capitalist Robert Swanson, to commercialize the discoveries related to the new field of recombinant DNA made by Boyer and Cohen. According to Niosi and Reid (2007, p. 427), "Between the time of its foundation and their first IPO, in 1980, Genen-tech produced a first human protein in bacteria and cloned human insulin and human growth hormone. Since then, over 5000 dedicated biotechnology firms (DBFs) have been created in the world."

> "Genentech is a biotechnology company dedicated to pursuing ground-breaking science to discover and develop medicines for people with serious and life-threatening diseases (Genentech website, 2020)." ◀

◘ Fig. 5.9 A pedestrian crossing painted to resemble a DNA strand on the Genentech head-quarter campus in South San Francisco, California. (Source: ▶ https://commons.wikimedia.org/wiki/File:Genentech_HQ_pedestrian_crossing.JPG. BrokenSphere/CC BY-SA (▶ https://creativecommons.org/licenses/by-sa/3.0). Downloaded via Wikimedia Commons on July 13, 2020)

5.3.2.2 Developing Radically New Technological Solutions as a Platform for New Products or Processes (with No Market or Low-Market Context)

► Example: Father of Nanotechnology 1950s Richard Feynman

"Nanotechnology involves the intentional manufacture of large-scale objects whose discrete components are less than a few hundred nanometers wide" (Niosi & Reid, 2007, p. 432). According to Reid et al. (2014, p. 2), "The vision of early proponents of nanotechnology, such as Richard P. Feynman, Ralph Merkle, and K. Eric Drexler, was to provide inexpensive 'bottom-up' manufacturing technology," through the use of nanoscale organisms, such as nanobots or flagellated bacteria to move around the human body to treat disease. Ultimately, this is a very long-term vision which may play out over the next century or more.

5

» There's Plenty of Room at the Bottom (Feynman, 1959). ◄

5.3.2.3 Creation of New Design (i.e., Product, Inputs, Process, Packaging, or Distribution System) (High-Market Context)

► Example: L'eggs

In the 1970s a product called L'eggs, launched by the nylon hose, sock, and t-shirt manufacturer Hanes, took the dated and mature women's pantyhose market by storm. Since time immemorial, until the advent of the L'eggs product, pantyhose had mostly been sold in department stores, and the manufacture of pantyhose was dominated by large players like DuPont who made other nylon products. As such, the distribution channels were sewn up. For a new product entry, it was difficult to break in. In such cases, the vision for new entrants or existing players with new products needs to focus on how to gain distribution in new channels which have not been utilized yet. L'eggs was a small new brand player (owned by Hanes) which looked at their female target market to see whether there were places other than department stores where women were shopping on a relatively frequent basis. They discovered that the working woman of the 1970s was not always able to go to the department store during the week, especially if they had a pantyhose run emergency. As such, Hanes had the vision to target grocery stores and pharmacies, places where a working woman of the time was likely to make a quick pit stop on their way to or from work. In order to appeal to this target and get buy-in from smaller retailers, where shelf space was at a premium, they not only created packaging to jump off the shelves in little "egg containers"; they also created a small tree where the egg containers would nest, and it would be relatively easy for the salesperson to bring their own display unit to fill an end of aisle space and restock as needed. The retailer literally did not need to create anything new, except for a small space, to house the new player. ◄

5.3.2.4 Creation of New Organizational Form

► Example: DoorDash

Food delivery by car or bike has existed for a long time, particularly for single-restaurant or single-food style companies like pizza where speedy delivery is of importance. The latest addition to this idea has come from companies like DoorDash and Uber Eats, which provide delivery from multiple sources all under one (car) roof. Particularly during the time of the COVID-19 pandemic, such companies became increasingly prevalent as demand for in-home delivery skyrocketed. ◄

5.3.2.5 Creation of a New Concept to Serve the Same Market in a Radically New Way or "What's Old Is New Again!" (Reid, 2017)

► Example: Cirque du Soleil

The concept of providing entertainment for the masses has been around for a long time and serviced through a variety of experiences, including the circus. In 1984, Montreal-based Guy Laliberté and Gilles Ste-Croix updated the "circus" concept with the creation of Cirque du Soleil and re-introduced the concept with a radically new twist whereby rather than the circus moving from place to place, it became a destination experience. ◄

5.3.3 Benchmark-Based Vision

Benchmark-based vision has several potential faces, including comparisons based on the competition, based on role modeling, and also based on a second but-better strategy. Convergent thinkers will like using this type of strategy as it holds up an already convergent solution of success to mirror the activity or walk away from it. It provides a ready-made solution on which to build another ready-made solution.

5.3.3.1 Benchmarking Based on the Competition

One form of benchmark-based vision is based on a competitive mentality. There are several famous examples of this type of visioning. While competition-based benchmarking can be a powerful motivator and unifier, it may be best used as a shorter-range vision strategy, since over a longer run, there will always be another competitor around the corner. Most strategy pundits agree it's likely a better strategy in the long-run to focus on what you do best and distinguish yourself through unique advantage.

► Example: Honda in the 1970s

This type of competitive benchmark visioning was first suggested in the work of Collins and Porras (1991, p. 44):

Honda: "Yamaha wo tsubusu! (We will crush, squash, slaughter Yamaha!)" (Stalk Jr, 1988). ◄

5.3.3.2 Benchmarking Based on Role Modeling

The second form of benchmark-based vision includes setting a high bar using role modeling.

► Example: Jim Gentes, Giro Sport Design (◘ Fig. 5.10)

"The vision of Jim Gentes, the founder of cycling-focused Giro Sport Design, was, as noted by Collins and Porras (1991, p. 45), "To be a great company by the year 2000–to be to the cycling industry what Nike is to athletic shoes and Apple is to computers"." ◄

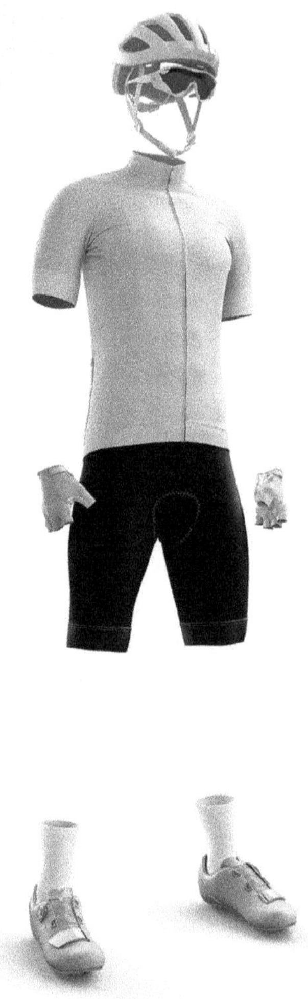

◘ **Fig. 5.10** Giro d'Italia, 2019 clothing in 3D illustration. (Source: Image licensed and downloaded from Shutterstock on July 14, 2020. Credit: by Box Lab/► Shutterstock.com. License Link: ► https://www.shutterstock.com/image-illustration/giro-ditalia-2019-clothing-3d-illustration-1335403760)

5.3.3.3 Benchmarking Based on a Second-but-try-to-be-Better Strategy

The third type of benchmark, a second-but-try-to-be-better strategy can fit the bill for players in the same industry which have used a role model which was first to market and put a new, or what may be perceived as "better," spin on the original idea or product. For example, Starbucks took the barista concept from Italy and made it scalable.

► Example: The Pepsi Challenge (◘ Fig. 5.11)

In 1975, Pepsi created a new marketing campaign known as "The Pepsi Challenge," a blind taste test which compared preferences for their brand with Coke. Interestingly, while the vision of Pepsi today has a global focus, we still see remnants of the old competitive streak with reference to "winning":

> "Be the global leader in convenient foods and beverages by winning with purpose (Pepsi website, 2020)." ◄

◘ Fig. 5.11 Pepsi Challenge promotional can from the early 1980s. (Source: ► https://commons.wikimedia.org/wiki/File:Pepsi_Challenge.jpg. Attribution: TeemPlayer/CC BY-SA (► http://creativecommons.org/licenses/by-sa/3.0/). Downloaded via Wikimedia Commons on July 14, 2020)

5.3.4 Positioning-Based Vision

Startup entrepreneurs who are strongly motivated by the need for autonomy, self-efficacy, and/or achievement motivation may gravitate toward this type of vision framework because it enables them to be unique and set themselves apart from the rest. That said, when your vision is based on a position goal, it is critical to distinguish extremely clearly what the position is, why it is important, and how it sets you apart from the rest.

5.3.4.1 Position to Be the Best/#1

Simply put, the "to be the best"-based vision is all about being the number one or premier product or service in the business. While this can be a very effective strategy, the "we want to be #1" approach needs to be couched in meaningful terms, so it creates a clear visual. If not, it can make it difficult for you and your employees to set meaningful parameters for achievement related to the vision. So, for example, when McDonald's uses this strategy with their vision to say they want to be the best, they still clearly explain what this means for them - to be the best family restaurant experience ever. Moreover, if the vision is stated without any clear basis for positioning, even if it is true based on sales, market share, or being the pioneer, it is easy for competitors to refute or counter. A famous example of this was Hertz rental car's campaign "We're #1," which Avis countered with "When you're only No. 2, you try harder" (Stevenson, 2013).

► Example: McDonald's

To provide "the best family restaurant experience, ever" (McDonald's website, 2020). ◄

5.3.4.2 Position as the Most Upmarket

Positioning as the most upmarket brand is a great place to be; however, it needs to be authentic to customers based on unique history, unique story, price point, or highest quality products or retail outlets, to name a few strategies. Of course, there will always be several players competing to be perceived as the highest-end brand, so while the vision is commendable, it can be a tough place to achieve and maintain occupancy as there will always be others trying to steal your crown.

► Example: Harry Winston (◘ Fig. 5.12)

Harry Winston, long considered to be one of the most prestigious jewelers in the world, is an excellent example of just how tough it is to use this type of visioning strategy. They legitimately are one claimant to the space, primarily because of their long-term and global legacy, however, there have been many challengers to this title over the years. ◄

◘ **Fig. 5.12** Front doors of Harry Winston, NYC. (Source: ► https://commons.wikimedia.org/wiki/File:Harry_Winston,_Manhattan.JPG. Credit: Elisa.rolle/CC BY-SA (► https://creativecommons.org/licenses/by-sa/4.0). Uploaded on August 10, 2014. Downloaded via Wikimedia Commons on July 15, 2020)

5.3.4.3 Position as the Price Leader/Lowest-Cost Player (Economies of Scale)

Since the 1950s, Walmart has held the position of being the price leader in general merchandising and is still the #1 retailer in the world with an enviable low-cost structure related to its size.

► Example: Dollarama (◘ Fig. 5.13)

5 Much as is the case with luxury positioning, the top-dog position for price leadership is often under siege by the competition. For example, in the general merchandise category, stores such as Dollarama in Canada and Family Dollar and Dollar General in the USA are attempting to claim some of the price leadership territory in this space. ◄

◘ **Fig. 5.13** Dollarama storefront. (Source: ► https://commons.wikimedia.org/wiki/File:DollaramaSouthEdmontonCommon.jpg. Credit: Rowanlovescars/CC BY-SA (► https://creativecommons.org/licenses/by-sa/4.0). Uploaded on May 11, 2020. Downloaded via Wikimedia Commons on July 15, 2020)

5.3.4.4 Position for Vertical Integration

► Example: Lipman's Tomatoes

In the low-margin game of selling tomatoes, one strategy for success comes through achieving economies of scale. Some players achieve this by moving both upstream and downstream to achieve economies in their channels. Lipman's (tomatoes and other produce), based in Florida, is a great example of such a player, whose vision was to achieve scale and survive in a tough market. They are the largest growers of tomatoes for use in the fresh value chain in North America (Alvarez & Knoop, 2016) and also have come to dominate both upstream unique seed stock production and the downstream market with well-known cultivars at the retail level such as the Crimson Queen and grape tomatoes (◘ Fig. 5.14). ◄

◘ **Fig. 5.14** Grape tomatoes. (Source: Image licensed and downloaded from Shutterstock on July 15, 2020. Credit: by @Videowokart/► Shutterstock.com. License Link: ► https://www.shutterstock.com/image-photo/fresh-tomatoes-plants-305329874)

5.3.5 Values-Based Vision

Values-based visions are linked to the notions of value that underlie them. Broadly speaking, for those motivated primarily by social values, it makes sense to highlight the specific social values of focus with the enterprise whether it be social justice, poverty, hunger, access to water, disease, or peace. Likewise, for those motivated primarily by environmental values, the focus of the vision should be related to the environmental issue at hand. In both cases, the main idea for resolution or solution should also be incorporated as part of the vision, whether it be through technology, solution, intervention, or aid.

5.3.5.1 Social Vision

Those with broad overarching goals directed toward one culminated social vision might require utilizing a broad-brushed approach, as with the Oxfam approach to achieve: "A just world without poverty." Such an approach may need to incorporate a multi-pronged approach to solutions.

► Example: Oxfam (◘ Fig. 5.15)

» "A Just World Without Poverty (Oxfam website, 2020)." ◄

◘ Fig. 5.15 Oxfam, Market Place, Knaresborough, North Yorkshire. (Source: ► https://commons.wikimedia.org/wiki/File:Oxfam,_Market_Place,_Knaresborough_(24th_August_2019).jpg. Credit: Mtaylor848/CC BY-SA (► https://creativecommons.org/licenses/by-sa/4.0). Downloaded via Wikimedia Commons on July 26, 2020)

5.3.5.2 Environmental Vision

A clear example of a company which has had a strong environmental vision from the beginning is Patagonia, an American company with quality products using environmentally acceptable and socially aware solutions to create, manufacture, and distribute their products.

► **Example: Patagonia**

» "Build the best product, cause no unnecessary harm, use business to inspire and implement solutions to the environmental crisis (Patagonia website, 2020)." ◄

In sum, the key to starting the visioning process is building an understanding of your chief motivators and using these to bridge to appropriate frameworks to begin the vision construction process, as will be the focus of the remaining chapters.

Chapter Review Questions

1. Why is it so important to spend time developing a clear vision rather than jumping into a business or opportunity?
2. What are the five types of vision framework? Provide one concrete example for each that is not from the text.
3. Do you think one type of vision framework is more powerful than the others? Please discuss.
4. What is the difference between innovation- and positioning-based vision?
5. Do you think a values-based vision can work for a for-profit business? If so, please provide an example.

References

Alvarez, J. B., & Knoop, C.-I. (2016). Lipman: Vertical integration in fresh tomatoes. *Harvard Business School Case,* 9-516-053.

Alzheimer's Association website. (2020). https://www.alz.org/about/strategicplan. Accessed on 31 Aug 2020

Biello, D. (2006, December 8th). *Fact or fiction? Archimedes coined the term "Eureka!" in the bath.* ScientificAmerican.com, 2 pp, downloaded on November 12, 2020. https://www.scientificamerican.com/article/fact-or-fiction-archimede/

Boorstin, D. (1974). *The Americans: The democratic experience*. Vintage Books.

Collins, J. C., & Porras, J. I. (1991). Organizational vision and visionary organizations. *California Management Review, 34*(1), 30–52.

EESL India website. (2020). https://www.eeslindia.org/content/raj/eesl/en/Programmes/EV-Charging-Infrastructure/About-EV-Charging-Infrastructure1.html. Accessed on 31 Aug 2020.

Emaar website. (2020). (Burj Khalifa). https://www.burjkhalifa.ae/en/thetower/vision/#:~:text=A%20Stunning%20work%20of%20art,Burj%20Khalifa%20has%20no%20peer. Accessed on 31 Aug 2020.

European Commission '2030 climate and energy framework' website. (2020). https://ec.europa.eu/clima/policies/strategies/2030_en./. Accessed on 31 Aug 2020.

Feynman, R. (1959). "There's plenty of room at the bottom", lecture, *American Physical Society Annual Meeting*, Caltech, CA, December 29, 1959 (later published in *Caltech Engineering and Science* 23(5): 22–36, February, 1960).

Genentech website. (2020). https://www.gene.com/about-us. Accessed on 31 Aug 2020.

Gymboree website. (2020). https://www.comparably.com/companies/gymboree/mission. Accessed on 31 Aug 2020.

Knight, P. (2016). *Shoe dog: A memoir by the creator of Nike*. Scribner.

McDonald's website. (2020). https://www.mcdonalds.com.sg/careers/themcdonalds-experience/. Accessed on 31 Aug 2020.

Mission Statements website. (2020). https://www.missionstatements.com/fortune_500_mission_statements.html. Accessed on 31 Aug 2020.

Niosi, J., & Reid, S. (2007). Biotechnology and nanotechnology: Science-based technologies as windows of opportunity for LDC's? *World Development, 35*(3), 426–438.

Oxfam website. (2020). https://www.oxfamamerica.org/explore/stories/achieving-just-world-without-poverty/. Accessed on 31 Aug 2020.

5 Pasteur, L. (1854). Quote: "Chance favors only the prepared mind", lecture, University of Lille, December 7, 1854, accessed from https://en.wikiquote.org/wiki/Louis_Pasteur, August 25, 2020.

Patagonia website. (2020). https://www.patagonia.com.au/pages/our-businessand-climate-change. Accessed on 31 Aug 2020.

Pepsi website. (2020). https://www.pepsico.com/about/mission-and-vision. Accessed on 31 Aug 2020.

Rampton, J. (2019). https://www.entrepreneur.com/article/327447#:~:text=For%20example%2C%20the%20mission%20statement%20of%20Casper%2C%20the,associates%3B%20and%20a%20business%20that%20achieves%20financial%20success.%22. Accessed on 31 Aug 2020.

Reid, S. E. (2017). "The Power of Entrepreneurial Vision", Keynote Speaker, Katalysis 2017, (coordinated by l'espace, Sherbrooke startup incubator), Sherbrooke, September, 2017.

Reid, S. E., Coronini, R., & Ramani, S. V. (2014). Evolution of nanotechnology: The science and the industry. In S. V. Ramani (Ed.), *Nanotechnology and development: What's in it for emerging countries?* (pp. 3–36). Cambridge University Press.

Schumpeter, J.A. (1934). *The theory of economic development*. (Translated from the German 1911 version), Cambridge, MA: Harvard University Press.

Stalk, G., Jr. (1988). Time – The next source of competitive advantage. *Harvard Business Review, 66*(4), 41–51.

Stevenson, S. (2013). *We're no. 2! We're no. 2!* https://slate.com/business/2013/08/hertz-vs-avis-advertising-wars-how-an-ad-firm-made-a-virtue-out-of-second-place.html. Accessed on 31 Aug 2020.

Creating Vision Context Through Networks: The Role of Early Advisors

Contents

© The Author(s), under exclusive license to Springer Nature Switzerland AG 2022
S. E. Reid, C. B. Crawford, *Entrepreneurial Vision*, Classroom Companion: Business,
https://doi.org/10.1007/978-3-030-77803-3_6

Learning Objectives

In this chapter, we describe what vision context means and why it plays a major role in the selection of early advisors, as follows:

1. What vision context means and why it is important
2. The importance of developing your network to set vision context
3. Vision context setting: the concepts of network centrality, broad networks, and diverse networks as critical components of developing your Market Visioning Competence
4. Vision context setting: the factors impacting efficiency and efficacy of new idea recognition and sharing
5. The vital role of early advisors, including mentors and experts, and how to initiate networking with them

6.1 What Vision Context Means and Why It's Important

The Oxford Dictionary (2020, online) defines the word "context" as: "The circumstances that form the setting for an event, statement, or idea, and in terms of which it can be fully understood and assessed." Therefore, vision context means the circumstances surrounding vision development (◘ Fig. 6.1).

Specifically, *vision context involves the network for gathering, sharing, and developing new information and ideas, and the psychosocial and environmental factors impacting access to that information*. As such, we can see that during visioning and related idea formation, the environment or context in which the vision is being created counts. Furthermore, with vision formation specifically, not only does the temporal environment count due to its impact on the trajectory of the vision, but in turn this will also impact the future environment.

This link between environmental context and vision output is why it's essential to start making conscious decisions about whom you will network and partner with, as early on in your entrepreneurial journey as possible, because this will create part of the early context for visioning. Later context will include the industry and markets of focus. However, early context is mostly about your close network—i.e., mentors, advisors, and, eventually, your entrepreneurial team (the focus of ► Chap. 7)—during the early days of starting up and how you actively decide to grow this initial network and interface with them to work on early ideas (◘ Fig. 6.2).

Context development through the creation of your initial personal network, and how you decide to actively grow it, is one of the most important things for entrepreneurs to focus on, regardless of whether you are "closer to" or "further from" commercialization in terms of future vision realization. It is also imperative to realize that, while your network may not include the captains of industry you would like to know in the early days, it is still important to visualize how you would like to actively grow your network to incorporate the right people to help realize your goals, and this is an ongoing process. Your network is not equal to the current list of names in your contact file, and it is certainly not an endpoint—it is just the beginning. Indeed, it is better to think of your network as organic and, like your

6

Fig. 6.1 Zebra on a striped background. Conceptual image to portray "vision context." (Source: Image licensed and downloaded from Shutterstock on July 25, 2020. Credit: by Sirtravelalot/Shutterstock.com. License Link: ▶ https://www.shutterstock.com/image-photo/zebra-against-background-black-white-stripes-207465979)

vision, as an ever-growing mental map which you want to continually be thinking about in terms of what you would like it to become and how you might fill the holes which currently exist with the best contacts possible (Fig. 6.3).

In a large-scale quantitative study of early-stage new ventures in Spain, it was concluded that early-stage "resource ties" were strongly correlated with both speed and growth of new ventures (Capelleras & Greene, 2008). The authors state (p. 321) that there is "a general recognition that ventures are, themselves, path dependent; in essence, those with particular resources at the start of the venture are more likely to receive better outcomes than those without appropriate resources." The research strongly confirmed that entrepreneurs who were able to use their personal networks to identify and build formal and informal ties with advisors, experts, important suppliers, and customers, as well as finding financing sources, had created an essential set of starting resources that provided significantly better conditions for a path to success.

6.2 The Importance of Actively Developing Your Network

It is not surprising that networking is key to building a strong Market Visioning Competence. This is related to the fact that networking involves individuals drawing on both their "strong ties" and "weak ties" to gain access to new information

■ **Fig. 6.2** Conceptual image to portray a team working on the birth of an early-stage creative idea. (Source: Image licensed and downloaded from Shutterstock on July 25, 2020. Credit: by Viktoria Kurpas/Shutterstock.com. License Link: ▶ https://www.shutterstock.com/image-vector/vector-illustration-people-grow-potted-plants-1048863869)

and combining information in new ways (Granovetter, 1973, 1983). "Strong ties," on the one hand, include those trusted individuals with whom the entrepreneur has close relationships and where there is repeated and strong contact. "Weak ties," on the other hand, according to Granovetter (1983, p. 201/2), "are less likely to be socially involved with one another than our close friends (strong ties)." Weak ties provide their own form of "strength" in terms of providing access to different and nonredundant contacts and ideas, a concept well described in the work of Granovetter (1973, 1983). As noted by Granovetter (1983, p. 202), "It follows, then, that individuals with few weak ties will be deprived of information from distant parts of the social system and will be confined to the provincial news and views of their close friends."

According to Reid (2005), the best networks for entrepreneurs are those combinations where:

1. The entrepreneur is central in their networks (i.e., has many strong ties).
2. The network of the entrepreneur is widespread and broad with numerous contacts (i.e., has many weak and strong ties).

Fig. 6.3 Conceptual image to portray a team bringing their different ideas together. (Source: Image licensed and downloaded from Shutterstock on July 25, 2020. Credit: by Rido/Shutterstock.com. License Link: ▸ https://www.shutterstock.com/image-photo/closeup-businessman-woman-jigsaw-puzzle-pieces-261293111)

3. The network is diverse in terms of touching many different unique networks in order to access novel, non-repetitive information (i.e., high network variety with many weak ties).

6.2.1 The Importance of Network Centrality

Granovetter (1973, p. 1361) notes: "The strength of a tie is a (probably linear) combination of the amount of time, the emotional intensity, the intimacy (mutual confiding), and the reciprocal services which characterize the tie." Strong ties lead to a higher level of helping behavior and are usually more readily available (than weak ties) (Granovetter, 1983). For example, the helping behavior that stems from strong ties may be useful in building a dialogue within a community capable of furthering the understanding, dissemination, and adoption of a given idea or innovation. This finding is related to the fact that "the benefit of adopting a new idea, product or technology varies directly with the number of others who adopt it (Herbig et al., 1995; Hunt & Morgan, 1996; Katz & Shapiro, 1985; Redmond, 1991)" (Reid & de Brentani, 2004, p. 173). Thus, new products or ideas which are first out of the gates may be able to corner the market for innovators or early adopters, with competitors becoming locked out and the winners gaining what are known as "increasing

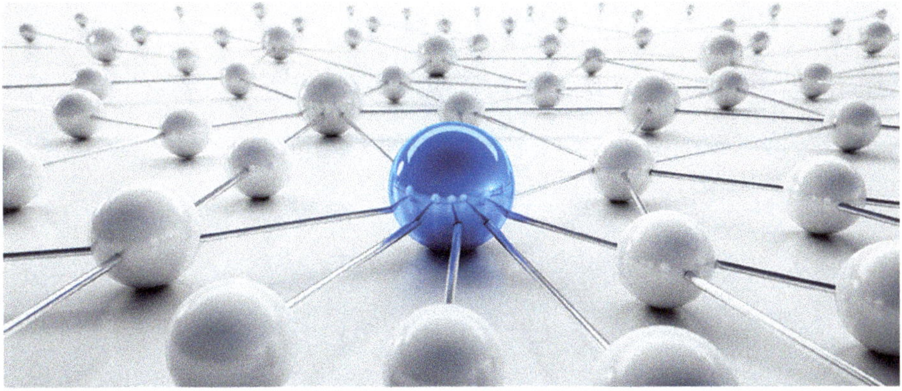

■ **Fig. 6.4** Conceptual image to portray "network centrality." (Source: Image downloaded and licensed from Adobe Stock on August 12, 2020. Credit: by peterscheiber.media/▶ stock.adobe.com. License Link: ▶ https://stock.adobe.com/ca/images/concept-of-teamwork-people-and-icons/70268405)

returns to adoption" (Arthur, 1989). The underlying structure of such a process is based on "network effects" (Berkowitz, 1982; Burt, 1992; Scott, 1990). Network effects mean that, as noted by Reid and de Brentani (2004, p. 173), "decision-makers react to decisions of other decision-makers," and as noted by Burt (1992), such choices may turn to their advantage if the technology turns out to be a winner. Given this, for large networks with high levels of adoption of a given idea, there should be an inherent advantage to being part of the network. In particular, there should be benefits to being a central part of such a network (■ Fig. 6.4).

6.2.2 The Importance of Broad Networks

The literature on innovation strongly supports the notion that the environment is the primary source of new ideas for entrepreneurs and firms alike (Alam, 2003; Allen, 1977; Burgelman & Sayles, 1986; Crossan et al., 1999; Ettlie, 1976; Macdonald & Williams, 1994; Roos, 1996). Of specific importance is the idea that individuals gain access to environmental information through their networks. In turn, the broader the network of such individuals (■ Fig. 6.5), the greater the potential level of new information they can attain (Quinn, 1985). Gratuitous interactions between entrepreneurs and their networks may provide the fodder of ideas for new combinations of old elements (Usher, 1929) where an individual combines one or more ideas or technologies, which previously were unrelated in an important way (Burgelman & Sayles, 1986; Hargardon & Sutton, 1997). As such, this means that it is advantageous to be a central (i.e., early and influential) player in a broad network (Berkowitz, 1982; Scott, 1990).

6

Fig. 6.5 Conceptual image to portray "broad networks." (Source: Image downloaded and licensed from Shutterstock on May 7, 2013 2018. Credit: by Sashkin/Shutterstock.com. License Link: ▸ https://www.shutterstock.com/image-illustration/group-people-leader-63644902)

6.2.3 The Importance of Varied/Diverse Networks

Utterback (1994) notes that variety in an individual's network (Fig. 6.6) creates a scenario where there is a greater likelihood of unusual combinations resulting in what Reid and de Brentani (2004, p. 174) call "new-to-the-world type products that expand the market." This idea builds on the "strength of weak ties" idea put forward by Granovetter (1973) and the work on "structural holes" of Burt (1992).

These arguments assert that acquaintances (i.e., weak tie connections in a person's network) will likely be less involved socially than in the case of close friends (Granovetter, 1973), and, therefore, more nonredundant information and hence more novel ideas are likely to result from the interaction of such weak-tie contacts. Additionally, weak ties often provide earlier access to information, knowledge, and resources than might be provided by close friends and strong-tie networks, due to their nonredundant information provision.

Fig. 6.6 Conceptual image to portray "varied/diverse networks." (Source: Image downloaded and licensed from Shutterstock on July 29, 2020. Credit: by Lightspring/Shutterstock.com. License Link: ► https://www.shutterstock.com/image-photo/central-connection-business-concept-group-diverse-402281074)

The case of "structural holes" (Burt, 1992) (Fig. 6.7) occurs when two people or networks have never been affiliated, thereby providing a situation with potential for developing beneficial network ties. If two such people, companies, or entire networks come together, bridged by a person or company operating as a connection (often due to chance) across the structural hole (sometimes as a result of "technology brokering," Hargadon & Sutton, 1997), it provides the opportunity for a highly potent combinatorial experience capable of providing brand-new combinations drawing on technologies and markets which have not been affiliated before.

Based on these insights, we see that networks are the social facilitators of diffusion and adoption of new ideas and innovation. In sum, networks are particularly effective when they are broad and varied and when the key individuals are central in their networks.

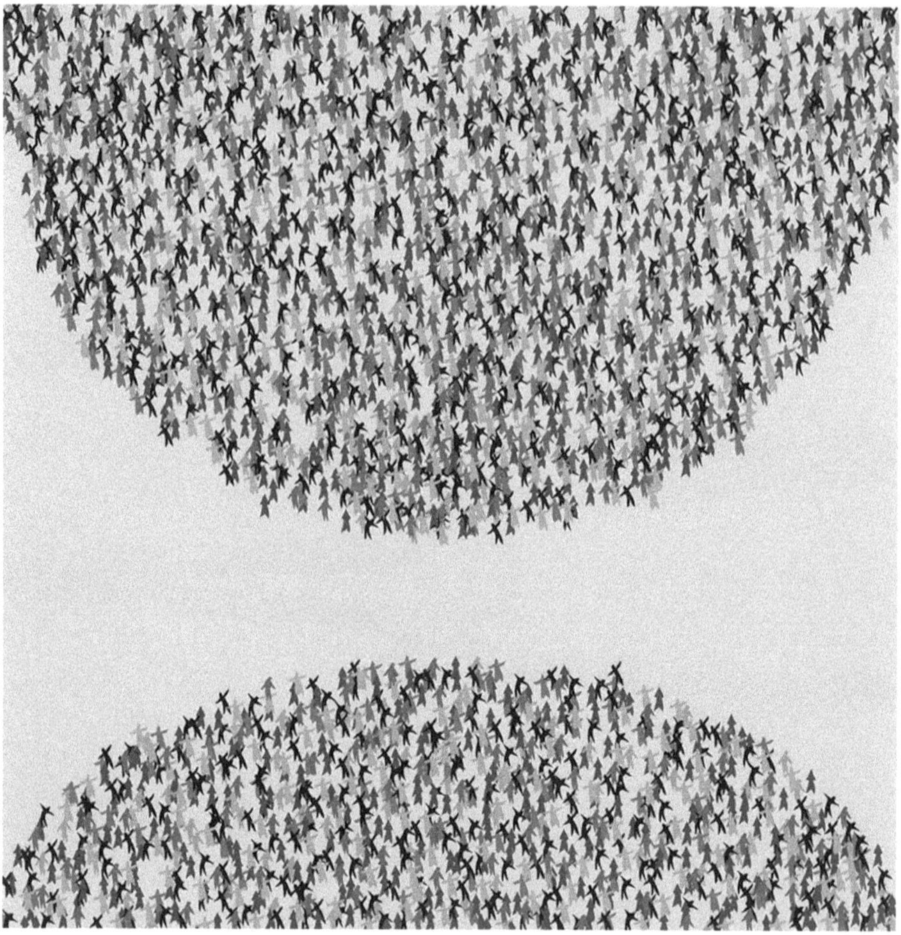

Fig. 6.7 Conceptual image to portray "a structural hole." (Source: Image downloaded and licensed from Shutterstock on July 29, 2020. Credit: by Tanya Zima/Shutterstock.com. License Link: ► https://www.shutterstock.com/image-vector/abstract-background-colorful-silhouettes-people-men-368239940)

6.3 Factors Impacting Efficiency and Efficacy of Information Recognition and Sharing

In ► Chap. 3, we introduced the concept of the importance of new ideas and information from the environment as a key propellant of innovation for entrepreneurs.

The movement of information through what is known as the "fuzzy front end," or very early and often unclear stage, of new product development ("NPD") (Reid & de Brentani, 2004) can be captured by an idea known as the "NPD vector," which comprises two key dimensions: the “efficiency” and “efficacy” of movement of information from the environment to individuals (see as well de Brentani and Reid (2012) for more detailed discussions on this topic). Efficiency, or speed, increases the chances of attaining early-mover advantage. Efficacy, through the best possible access to and sharing of information from and to the network (i.e., taking into consideration the best network sources; types of information, with whom information is shared; and so on), has a cumulative impact on the ability to make good decisions.

The speed and quality of information sharing depend on three key variables (de Brentani & Reid, 2012):

1. The attributes of the innovation itself
2. The people the entrepreneur interacts with from their position in their networks
3. The entrepreneur’s cognitive style

6.3.1 The Impact of Innovation Attributes on Information Recognition and Sharing Effectiveness

When information has a high level of novelty and complexity, it will typically be more challenging to understand the benefits of the innovation, particularly if it is difficult to observe or try out (Rogers, 1983). Additionally, high perceived costs, uncertainty, and risk may slow down involvement with an innovation (Gatignon & Robertson, 1991). According to de Brentani and Reid (2012, p. 75), “Information flow from the environment tends to be sequential (i.e., a bit at a time),” and, as noted by Schmalhofer et al. (1986), such flow is often uneven from the environment, as well as somewhat ad hoc (Macdonald & Williams, 1994). As such, entrepreneurs often need to make several “trips to the environment” to interact with network contacts. One mitigating factor is if a technology is perceived to have a strong relative advantage or social value. In this case, entrepreneurs and their teams may have a greater incentive to gather more information about it and do so more quickly. Therefore, attributes of innovation impact the speed at which individuals recognize new opportunities, the quality of information collected, and the timing of sharing (◘ Fig. 6.8).

6.3.2 The Impact of Network Position on Information Recognition and Sharing Effectiveness

An entrepreneur’s position in their network will also impact the rate of adoption/diffusion of new information related to an innovation. Given that there is a strong probability that important sources of new information (i.e., nonredundant contacts) may be far away, hard to find or unknown (Goodman & Lawless, 1994; Mowery & Rosenberg, 1998), and/or difficult to access or engage with (Birkinshaw et al., 2007), access may vary depending on an individual's network position. As such, an entrepreneur with a position situated at the center of a broad, diverse, nonredundant network has a better chance at securing useful information in a timely manner and being able to relay it to others ahead of the competition (◘ Fig. 6.9).

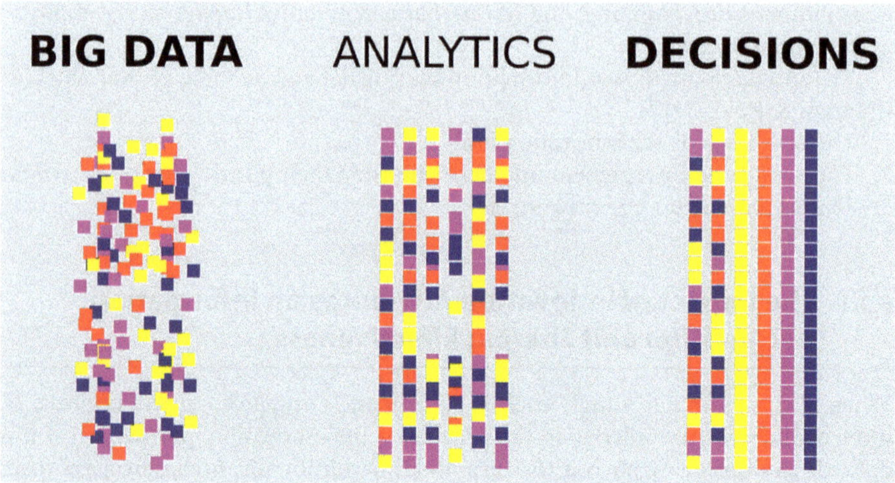

◘ **Fig. 6.8** Conceptual image to portray "impact of innovation attributes on information recognition and sharing effectiveness." (Source: Image downloaded and licensed from Shutterstock on July 29, 2020. Credit: by Cyber Kristanyan/Shutterstock.com. License Link: ► https://www.shutterstock.com/image-vector/big-data-transformed-through-analytics-into-398469061)

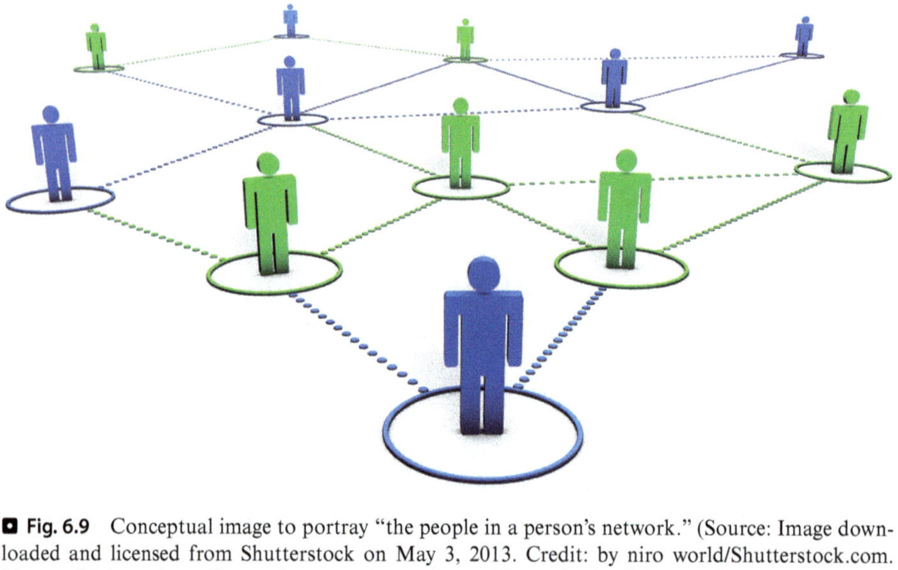

◘ **Fig. 6.9** Conceptual image to portray "the people in a person's network." (Source: Image downloaded and licensed from Shutterstock on May 3, 2013. Credit: by niro world/Shutterstock.com. License Link: ► https://www.shutterstock.com/image-illustration/social-network-concept-team-3d-people-113103937)

6.3.3 The Impact of the Individual's Cognitive Style on Information Recognition and Sharing Effectiveness

An individual's cognitive style also impacts the rate of diffusion of an innovation. As noted in Reid and de Brentani (2002), Kuhn (1962) suggests that pattern recognition, sometimes referred to as "intuition" (Roos, 1996), involves both "that something is" (a perceptual element) and "what it is" (a cognitive element)." So, for those individuals working in networks with new information, their ability to move quickly through the processes of perception and cognition, related to the emergence of new markets and technologies, offers potential for competitive advantage. As noted in ► Chap. 3, one study on the topic found that there is a positive relationship between "need for cognition" (scale provided in ► Chap. 4) and "length of search effort" (Verplanken et al., 1992). Another study (Sauter, 1999) suggests that "left-brain style," a more analytical approach to cognition, predicts a tendency for longer search times but with the potential to elicit more detailed information. Other research in this stream has focused on the number of ideas that an individual can bring into awareness at one time related to, in some instances, the need for integrating technologies from more than one field of expertise (Griffin & Hauser,

Fig. 6.10 Conceptual image to portray "individual cognitive style." (Source: Image downloaded and licensed from Shutterstock on September 24, 2018. Credit: by leolintang/Shutterstock.com. License Link: ► https://www.shutterstock.com/image-photo/puzzle-head-brain-concept-human-profile-289107095)

1996; Meyer & Utterback, 1995). Therefore, the ability of individuals to deal with such complexity played against the sometimes accompanying desire for longer searches for information will impact how much information can be integrated and how quickly this can be done and then shared with others (◘ Fig. 6.10).

6.4 The Role of Early Advisors

In our dog-eared copy of Napoleon Hill's *Think and Grow Rich* (1960/1937), Hill describes Dale Carnegie's "Master Mind" principle. The "Master Mind," as defined by Napoleon Hill (1960, p.449) is: "Coordination of knowledge and effort, in a spirit of harmony, between two or more people, for the attainment of a definite purpose. No individual may have great power without availing himself of the 'Master Mind'."

One of the best ways to create the kind of network advantages Hill refers to is with a team of advisors. In fact, building a team of advisors is particularly important early in the new venture formation process (Ozcan & Eisenhardt, 2009). As early as possible, entrepreneurs should call upon informal business advisors through the creation of a personal board of directors (PBOD), as well as networking with experts (i.e., accountants, lawyers, financial advisors, technical experts) in order to start getting advice about how to move forward, even at an early stage of entrepreneurship (Smeltzer et al., 1991). This team of advisors should not only have depth of experience and expertise but also the ability to be honest, critical, balanced, and growth-oriented.

In this chapter, we focus on building relationships with and creating a "team" of early external advisors: your mentors (i.e., PBOD) and experts.

In this way, at the earliest stages of new venture creation, the entrepreneur creates the fundamental building block of the new venture: a team, which includes both external advisors (informal advisors such as on your PBOD, professional experts, and later, board members) (Crawford, 2018) and partners and employees (the focus of ► Chap. 7).

6.4.1 Mentors (Also Known as Your "Personal Board of Directors" or "PBOD")

What is a personal board of directors (PBOD)? As noted in Reid (2015, online), "They are peers and influencers who have specific mentoring capabilities; a dynamic group of people with close ties to you. They are those whom you respect and consider extremely important in terms of your circle of influence – that which goes well beyond your business interests and objectives. They have a strong positive influence on your life because they know you well, understand your interests, and most importantly, have your interests at heart."

A typical roster for building your PBOD might include some, or all, of the following:

- Family members
- A few close friends
- Influential teachers
- Financial advisors
- Community leaders
- Trusted current and former bosses and colleagues

Some of the outside skills and expertise you should be actively searching for in your PBOD include the abilities to:

- Keep you on point in terms of your passion and core competencies/skills.
- Challenge you to ask the right questions and help you to re-formulate your strategic thinking when required.
- Push your idea championing skills.
- Assist you with networking and offering expertise with your new ventures.

With these goals in mind for creating a PBOD, we direct you to Worksheet 4, where you will be led through an exercise to identify first potential members for your PBOD. From there, you will conduct a focus group with them so they can act as a sounding board for the exercises you performed in Worksheets 1–3 to get a better sense of your key motivators, passions/interests, and style.

6

Worksheet 4: Focus Group with your 'PBOD'

The objective of this worksheet is to first, clearly elucidate the 3 key areas of interest that were chosen as potential areas for further study in Worksheet 1 and then combine these with your primary motivators and cognitive style from Worksheets 2 and 3. This will form a snapshot of your overall interests and 'style'. Second, you will subject these to a litmus test with a group of personal mentors, as described below.

The objective of forming the 'Personal Board of Directors' (PBOD) is to create a 'circle of influence' with 3 people who already exist in your personal network. The 3 people you select for this exercise should be those who you feel have had a strong and positive influence on your life to date because they know you well, understand your interests and style, have your interests at heart and, importantly, are those who you are motivated by. These individuals would likely be people you would refer to as 'mentors' if you were to describe them to someone else. Ultimately, these 3 individuals would be people who you would want to carry forward on your 'Personal Board of Directors' throughout your life. You might consider the following types of individuals in terms of the role they have played in your life to fill a position on this board (in our incubator course, we suggest that they must be 18 years or older). Provide the first names that come to mind and the key reason why you think they should be on your PBOD:

- A close lifelong friend:

  Name: ______________ should be on my PBOD because ______________________
- An influential teacher or counselor (it should not be a current teacher of this course):

  Name: ______________ should be on my PBOD because ______________________
- A spiritual advisor:

  Name: ______________ should be on my PBOD because ______________________
- A financial advisor:

  Name: ______________ should be on my PBOD because ______________________
- A business leader:

  Name: ______________ should be on my PBOD because ______________________
- A community leader:

  Name: ______________ should be on my PBOD because ______________________
- A volunteer:

  Name: ______________ should be on my PBOD because ______________________

© Susan E. Reid and Charles B. Crawford, August 14, 2020.

Based on your final selection and availability, work with 3 of these individuals to complete the exercise, as follows.

Prior to performing the focus group, you should get some initial 'undirected input' from your PBOD related to how they perceive your interests and style before showing them your 3 key areas of interest from Worksheet 1. Five suggested questions to get them thinking include the following:

1. What are 3 things I do very well?

2. What are 3 things I don't do that well?

3. Based on what you know about me, what job or experience do you perceive I have liked the best in the past?

4. Based on what you know about me, what job or experience have I liked the least in the past?

5. What are 3 things you can imagine me doing in the future?

Following this initial request, the focus group exercise itself requires that you present a summary of your key passions/interests and motivations (1-page max) from Worksheets 1, 2, and 3 to your PBOD and then document the ensuing discussion using an open-ended questionnaire format. The questionnaire should include at least 5 key questions, which you design, to best tap into what your PBOD thinks of this summary snapshot of your interests and motivators given what they know about you (either using a recording device or by taking notes). It is recommended that you give the board members at least one week to reflect on your summary description. It is suggested that you use one of two formats for this exercise: either one 1.5-hour focus group with all three board members at the same time or three half-hour interviews each completed separately. Personal availability will likely dictate the format. While face-to-face interviews are always best, a virtual format also suffices if necessary.

The summary should include the questions you asked the PBOD (including those asked for the initial undirected input), and a summary of the key points they made during the focus group or interviews; the points should focus on how they perceive that your primary motivations and style might best mesh with some of the opportunities which might potentially be available in your areas of interest, as well as any that they may suggest. It should end with a paragraph describing any key recommendations that were made or ideas that were brought forward and importantly, a final prioritization list of the 3 areas of interest for moving forward, based on your reflections.

© Susan E. Reid and Charles B. Crawford, August 14, 2020.

The role of the PBOD does not end here, though. This is a group of people who may act as advisors for you throughout your career and life, as is possible. With that in mind, once you have completed the worksheets in this book, which lead to the identification of a market opportunity and potential visions to address it, we suggest revisiting your PBOD as a litmus test before moving forward with deciding on a final Market Vision (► Chap. 11) and, if relevant, a Technology Vision (► Chap. 12). Some questions to keep in mind to ask your PBOD related to potential market opportunities (► Chap. 9) will include:

- What would I like about (____________________)?
- What would I find limiting about (____________________)?
- How could I incorporate my (____________________) interests into (____________________)?
- What do you think this might lead to for me?

6.4.2 Expert Advisors

In addition to building a core group of mentors through your PBOD strong ties to act as your personal advisors, another group of potential advisors exists who will likely come from your weak-tie networks. This group of "expert advisors" will be able to help you identify very early industry opportunities that exist in your area of interest and potential market opportunities within these. Additionally, from this pool of your PBOD and expert advisors, you may be able to select people to be part of your advisory board later.

At this early stage, you may not know anyone with a high level of expertise in your area(s) of interest, so your homework related to this will be to start building a list of potential contacts who might be willing to speak with you given your early stage of interest and involvement. To get you started with this, we provide Worksheet 5 (Charting Your Network Strategy).

Worksheet 5: Charting Your Network Strategy

Thinking about your areas of passion and interest given your primary motivators, please complete the following to help with further developing your network:

STRONG TIES
List 5 people you know well who you think might make good potential partners and list why:

1 ____________________
2 ____________________
3 ____________________
4 ____________________
5 ____________________

List 5 people you know well who you think might make good business advisors and why:

1 ____________________
2 ____________________
3 ____________________
4 ____________________
5 ____________________

WEAK TIES
Now list 5 more people you have met but do not know very well, but whom you think would be valuable contacts to get to know better, potentially as partners, experts, or advisors.

1 ____________________
2 ____________________
3 ____________________
4 ____________________
5 ____________________

NEW TIES
List 5 people (potential partners, experts, or advisors) you would like to meet to be able to discuss your business ideas with. If you do not have the person's name, you can simply list their job title and company, for example.

1 ____________________
2 ____________________
3 ____________________
4 ____________________
5 ____________________

NETWORKING ACTIVITY
List specific tools (e.g. social media), events, or introductions that can be used to enhance your list and/or ability to contact potentially important weak ties and to meet the new ties on your list.

- Tools:
- Events:
- Introductions:

© Susan E. Reid and Charles B. Crawford, August 14, 2020.

Once you have gone through the exercises provided in Worksheets 4 and 5, you will be in a good position to move forward toward deciding on key partners for your entrepreneurial team (if you decide to move that way) and, in time, employees.

In addition to thinking about the early contacts whom you would like to meet and include in your network as experts, you also need to build a plan for how to contact them. Three potential ways to meet experts in your field, to get you started, include the following:

- Join a group on LinkedIn or another professional networking site specific to your area of interest and ask the administrative group leader or manager if they can make three suggestions of people you could speak with to gain more industry insights to see whether it is a good fit for you.
- Join a local mentoring organization—for example, in Montreal, Charles was the President of an organization called Youth Employment Services (YES), which sponsors and helps young entrepreneurs in various ways, including the provision of industry knowledge through mentoring, workshops, and conferences.
- Attend a local conference on a subject/industry topic which you are passionate about: attend workshops of interest, chat with people in attendance, and ask questions of conference presenters directly after their presentations; ask the conference organizers if they have discounted rates for students.

In the case of expert advisors who have critical insights and who resonate well with you, it may be beneficial, if possible, to secure their involvement on your advisory board as they will be able to provide you with industry- and technology-specific advice very quickly. Even if you are unable to get them to commit to joining your advisory board, if they are a key person in the field (and you should shoot for contacts as high up the ladder as possible), it is still important to have them in your network and keep them up to date on your progress.

By recruiting experts in your field of interest, they will be in a good position to help ratify and validate your burgeoning vision. Tapping into their power as "Master Minds" (Hill, 1960) will help you enter and navigate the, sometimes, fickle world of business.

Chapter Review Questions

1. What is meant by vision context, and why is it important in the visioning process?
2. Why are networking and network ties so important for entrepreneurs, and how do they help build Market Visioning Competence?
3. What is the difference between strong and weak ties? Why are weak ties particularly important?
4. As an aspiring entrepreneur, list three new ways you would go about building your network as you are developing a vision for a new business.

References

Alam, I. (2003). Commercial innovations from consulting engineering firms: An empirical exploration of a novel source of new product ideas. *Journal of Product Innovation Management, 20*(4), 300–313.

Allen, T. (1977). *Managing the flow of technology*. MIT Press.

Arthur, B. W. (1989). Competing technologies and lock-in by historical small events. *Economic Journal, 99*(394), 116–131.

Berkowitz, S. D. (1982). *An introduction to structural analysis: The network approach to social research*. Butterworths.

Birkinshaw, J., Bessant, J., & Delbridge, R. (2007). Finding, forming, and performing: Creating networks for discontinuous innovation. *California Management Review, 49*(3), 67–84.

Burgelman, R. A., & Sayles, L. R. (1986). *Inside corporate innovation*. Macmillan.

Burt, R. S. (1992). *Structural holes: The social structure of competition*. Harvard University Press.

Capelleras, J.-L., & Greene, F. J. (2008). The determinants and implications of venture creation speed. *Entrepreneurship and Regional Development, 20*(4), 317–343.

Crawford, C. B. (2018). *The net effect: The impact of entrepreneurial alliance networks on new venture performance*. D.B.A. Dissertation, Athabasca University.

Crossan, M. M., Lane, H. W., & White, R. E. (1999). An organizational learning framework: From intuition to institution. *The Academy of Management Review, 24*(3), 522–537.

de Brentani, U., & Reid, S. E. (2012). The fuzzy front-end of discontinuous innovation: Insights for management. *The Journal of Product Innovation Management, 29*(1), 70–87.

Ettlie, J. E. (1976). The timing and sources of information for the adoption and implementation of product innovations. *IEEE Transactions on Engineering Management, 23*(1), 62–68.

Gatignon, H., & Robertson, T. S. (1991). Innovative decision processes. In T. S. Robertson & H. H. Kassarjian (Eds.), *Handbook of consumer behavior*. Prentice-Hall.

Goodman, R. A., & Lawless, M. W. (1994). *Technology and strategy: Conceptual models and diagnostics*. Oxford University Press.

Granovetter, M. (1973). The strength of weak ties. *American Journal of Sociology, 78*(6), 1360–1380.

Granovetter, M. (1983). The strength of weak ties: A network theory revisited. *Sociological Theory, 1*, 201–233.

Griffin, A., & Hauser, J. R. (1996). Integrating R&D and marketing: A review and analysis of the literature. *The Journal of Product Innovation Management, 13*(3), 191–215.

Hargadon, A., & Sutton, R. I. (1997). Technology brokering and innovation in a product development firm. *Administrative Science Quarterly, 42*(4), 716–749.

Herbig, P. A., Howard, C. A., & Kramer, H. E. (1995). The installed base effect: Implications for the management of innovation. *Journal of Marketing Management, 11(5)*, 387–401.

Hill, N. (1960). *Think and grow rich* (Updated ed.). Fawcett Crest.

Hunt, S. D., & Morgan, R. M. (1996). The resource-advantage theory of competition: Dynamics, path dependencies and evolutionary dimensions. *Journal of Marketing, 60*(4), 107–114.

Katz, M. L., & Shapiro, C. (1985). Network externalities, competition, and compatibility. *American Economic Review, 75*(3), 424–440.

Kuhn, T. (1962). *The structure of scientific revolutions* (1st ed.). University of Chicago Press.

Macdonald, S., & Williams, C. (1994). The survival of the gatekeeper. *Research Policy, 23*(2), 123–132.

Meyer, M. H., & Utterback, J. M. (1995). Product development cycle time and commercial success. *IEEE Transactions on Engineering Management, 42*(4), 297–304.

Mowery, D. C., & Rosenberg, N. (1998). *Paths of innovation: Technological change in 20th-century America*. Cambridge University Press.

Oxford Dictionary. (2020, online). Definition for "context". www.lexico.com/definition/context. Accessed 5 May 2020.

Ozcan, P., & Eisenhardt, K. M. (2009). Origin of alliance portfolios: Entrepreneurs, network strategies, and firm performance. *Academy of Management Journal, 52(2)*, 246–279.

Quinn, J. B. (1985). Managing innovation: Controlled chaos. *Harvard Business Review, 63*(3), 73–84.

Redmond, W. H. (1991). When technologies compete: The role of externalities on nonlinear market response. *The Journal of Product Innovation Management, 8*(3), 170–183.
Reid, S. E. (2005). *Market Vision for radically new, high-tech products.* Ph.D. Thesis, John Molson School of Business, Concordia University.
Reid, S. (2015). Give your new venture liftoff: Recruit a Personal Board of Directors. Give your New Venture Liftoff: Recruit a Personal Board of Directors (forbes.com), November 11, 2015.
Reid, S. E., & de Brentani, U. (2002). *The fuzzy front-end: Insights for managing discontinuous innovation.* Proceedings of the European Marketing Academy Conference, Braga, Portugal, June 2002.
Reid, S. E., & de Brentani, U. (2004). The fuzzy front end of new product development for discontinuous innovations: A theoretical model. *The Journal of Product Innovation Management, 21*(3), 170–184.
Rogers, E. M. (1983). *Diffusion of innovations* (3rd ed.). The Free Press.
Roos, J. (1996). Distinction making and pattern recognition in management. *European Management Journal, 14*(6), 590–595.
Sauter, V. L. (1999). Intuitive decision-making. *Association for Computing Machinery: Communications of the ACM, 42*(6), 109–115.
6
Schmalhofer, F., Albert, D., Aschenbrenner, K. M., & Gertzen, H. (1986). Process traces of binary choices: Evidence for selective and adaptive decision heuristics. *Quarterly Journal of Experimental Psychology, 38*(A), 59–76.
Scott, J. (1990). *Network analysis.* Sage.
Smeltzer, L. R., Van Hook, B. L., & Hutt, R. W. (1991). Analysis of the use of advisors as information sources in venture startup. *Journal of Small Business Management, 29*(3), 10–21.
Usher, A. P. (1929). *A history of mechanical inventions.* Harvard University Press.
Utterback, J. M. (1994). *Mastering the dynamics of innovation: How companies can seize opportunities in the face of technological change.* Harvard Business School Press.
Verplanken, B., Hazenberg, P. T., & Palenewen, G. R. (1992). Need for cognition and external information search effort. *Journal of Research in Personality, 26*(2), 128–136.

Creating Vision Context Through Networks: Building the Entrepreneurial Team

Contents

© The Author(s), under exclusive license to Springer Nature Switzerland AG 2022
S. E. Reid, C. B. Crawford, *Entrepreneurial Vision*, Classroom Companion: Business,
https://doi.org/10.1007/978-3-030-77803-3_7

Learning Objectives

In this chapter, we describe a process for building a better understanding of your situational context, in terms of how well developed the market and your idea are, as well as whether you have partners yet (or not). Given an understanding of various potential contexts, this will enable you to make early decisions about your network related to building an appropriate entrepreneurial team to best prepare for and execute your future vision.

The learning objectives of this chapter include developing an understanding of how to proceed in the case of:

1. The high-context scenario
2. The low-context scenario
3. The lone wolf or the entrepreneurial team

With that in mind, let's look at some potential initial contextual scenarios and some ways to actively grow your team, given your particular situation.

7.1 The High-Context Scenario

In the high-context scenario, an idea for a product/service will likely be closer to commercialization because a market already exists. It is more often the case that entrepreneurial innovation begins here than in the low-context situation. So, let's understand how to recognize and prepare for two potential types of high-context scenario.

7.1.1 High-Context Scenario #1: Developing an Idea on Your Own for an Existing Market

Recognition of a new idea for a high-context market may stem from various situations. You may have been working in a certain field for a long time and have recognized an opportunity in your field, ahead of the curve, and want to act on it. You may see an opportunity that is already being exploited but think you can do a better job of addressing it than others already have—either through product/service improvements or through cost reductions. In other words, you may have some ideas for potential market opportunities that already exist, but feel you can provide a new take or a second-but-better version or a variation on the theme that has not yet been capitalized upon. With the high-context case, since the overall market opportunity is usually somewhat defined, once you have decided whether to get involved with the idea or not, one of the main jobs at hand involves deciding on the specific niche market to go after. Narrowing the vision scope should be based on your own motivations (interests, values, skills, etc.), the timing, effort and level of resources available and/or willingness to devote to the opportunity, as well as access and proximity to the market. Also, you will need to think about whether you want to have a partner or team moving forward and, if so, who to approach. Finding a partner in this case is very similar to that presented in ▶ Sect. 7.2, potential situation #1, described under the low-context scenario case.

7.1.2 High-Context Scenario #2: The Case of Opportunity Knocks

Perhaps you were not looking for an opportunity, and one just happened along. Opportunity may visit in different ways. A friend might call with an idea that they think you might be interested in working with them on, or that they believe ideal for you to work on yourself. You may have been approached within your firm to work on a new intrapreneurial opportunity. Whatever the case, the place for getting started in this externally motivated case is quite different from that of looking actively for inspiration or recognizing an opportunity on your own.

In the high-context situation, the starting point in effect has been delivered to you. The challenge in this case is whether, or not, to accept the "gift" of the opportunity that is in front of you. In either case, an active decision needs to be taken as to whether, or not, to move forward with the potential interest/opportunity space that is opening up before you. If you need to make a speedy decision, you might want to take a quick litmus test, as suggested in ▶ Chap. 5. If you have a little more time, looking at your primary motivators, as presented in ▶ Chap. 3 (Worksheet 1) and ▶ Chap. 4 (Worksheets 2 and 3), is a good place to start to ensure a good fit with your entrepreneurial style. Another test of fit can be performed using a personal SWOT (Strengths, Weaknesses, Opportunities, and Threats) analysis based on your individual strengths and weaknesses (as well as your interest level), vis-à-vis the opportunities and threats of the potential product/service idea.

7.2 The Low-Context Scenario

In the case where the market context may be extremely low or underdeveloped, the job of market creation, which is one part of context creation, often lies in the hands of the entrepreneurs and other actors involved in developing the sector in the early going. Therefore, it is vital to understand the potential paths for going through this process and how to best focus your efforts. The low-context case will require more development and iterations to understand existing opportunities and/or to establish/develop Market Vision around potential market opportunities. This is usually a much longer process than in the high-context case and requires more steps, as will be outlined in later chapters of this book.

The case of low context is challenging because not only can it take time to develop, find, or decide upon an appropriate market context in which to nurture your interests, skills, values, and ideas, but you may also be flying solo. Furthermore, depending on the level of difficulty or complexity associated with developing the idea or technology, it may be challenging or perhaps even undesirable to find people to share your ideas with on the topic, particularly if there are concerns about intellectual property (IP) protection. So, it is important to give due consideration to whom and how you "share" your early ideas.

That said, sharing your interests and ideas with others, who may become part of your team, to develop a language and context around and about your emerging ideas can be an incredibly valuable thing to do. In the long run, entrepreneurial teams are critical, not only to put together as many great ideas as quickly as possible, but also, because being part of a team helps to diffuse and share risk. Therefore, developing a team of partners and mentors, whether in situ or virtually, is paramount, as is an advisory board (please note this is not the same thing as your "corporate board"—an advisory board is a "friendly," usually unpaid, group of expert/contacts who are willing to give you very early-stage advice for free). Team development and networking are crucial considerations for all beginning entrepreneurs, but they are of particular importance for those operating in the low-context scenario, due it being an inherently longer, riskier process. In terms of any IP concerns, there are some simple solutions for engaging partners and board members, including the use of boiler-plate nondisclosure agreements, early in the process, to protect early ideas.

You may also be working within an organization and therefore you may need to make a tough decision as to whether to leave and go it alone or to stay. This involves taking into consideration pre-existing contractual obligations and, also, whether you would have the resources required for development on your own. If your situation precludes leaving and going it alone, and you remain with the firm to develop your idea as an intrapreneur, you need to consider how best to be supported from within the organizational context.

7.2.1 Low-Context Scenario #1: Developing an Idea on Your Own for a New Market

From our perspective, this is one of the most fun (albeit most challenging) scenarios. You are on your own to do as you like in terms of creative direction, market shaping, and choosing your co-creators and/or partners. The sky is also the limit in terms of setting an off-the-charts vision and completely stamping your own set of values, skills, and personality on it.

There are multiple potential situations you may be in as an individual starting up in a low-context scenario, as follows:

- Potential Situation #1: You already have an idea based on your interests, skills, or experience, but there is no extant market, so you need to go about finding or developing a strong market or potential customers for your idea.

In this case, there is every chance that there are like-minded people out there on the "idea" and/or "passion" side, but there are likely far fewer people in a low-context situation who have much information about the newly developing market landscape, particularly if the market doesn't exist yet. As such, this scenario is inherently more complex in terms of getting others on board. Nevertheless, it is crucial to find partners who can balance out your weaknesses in order to increase your chances of success. For instance, if marketing is not your forté, it may be a good idea to identify a partner who is a strong marketer. If marketing is, in fact, a strength for you, then you may need balance on the technological, financial, or operational side. Also, given that you already have an idea, in this situation, potential partners need to be open to working with your idea in the stage you are already at, and depending on the stage of development they may even need to be open to having less of a stake in the idea from the get-go. The challenge then is how to find your counterpart(s). You might leave it to chance, but our advice would be to proactively start building a team ASAP. But who to choose as partner #1?

Often, the most natural place to look for your first partner is someone you already know well (i.e., a network "strong-tie"), such as someone you work closely with and trust, your life partner, or a very close friend. This may work well because trust is very important to the success and longevity of partnerships—provided that the potential partner balances out your skillset rather than duplicating it. So, for example, if you are a techie with a technical idea, make sure your potential partner has some marketing, sales, or finance strength. For a good example of a successful dynamic duo, think Steve Jobs and Steve Wozniak. As described in Isaacson's work (2011), both co-founders were passionate about computers, but Jobs was the dreamer, the designer, the marketer; Wozniak was the technical genius. It's key to try to balance out your team in terms of skills as early as possible and that begins with your first partner. Your partner should also share your passion/interest, at least to a certain extent.

> Potential Situation #2: You have done the work of finding what you are passionate about but do not have a specific idea yet.

In this case, you are coming at things from a little behind situation #1, but in some ways, it may be easier to find potential partners here. This may be because you are not yet "locked in" to a particular idea where it may be more difficult to find partners who share not only your passion but also your specific idea. Additionally, you may be able to divide you and your partners' involvement more evenly in the beginning as neither has put prior IP or investment into a specific idea. As such, you may be better set up for partnerships earlier on in the process, allowing for a potentially stronger early ideation process. You are well set up for co-creation to find people with similar areas of passion working toward new ideas and/or a new market. Co-creation (as will be described in ▶ Chap. 9) is essentially a way to work on a shared platform with others with mutual interests to create something really great. This scenario also enables working virtually with partners more easily out of the gates. This is a particularly good approach if you don't mind sharing the rewards with others or if you don't expect any rewards at all for your contributions, in the case, for example, of a "greater good for the community" type of project. If you want to take more time to think things through on your own initially, however, and/or are more driven to own the ideas yourself, then you might consider starting with a deep dive into your key areas of interest on your own before building a team.

> Potential Situation #3: You don't have an idea yet, and you need to do some self-reflection to think about what really motivates you and, in particular, what you are passionate about and what your skills are.

If you are in this situation, take heart. In Susan's entrepreneurial incubator class at the undergraduate level, fewer than 10% of the students come into the class with an idea they already want to work on. The vast majority are also in the situation where they are still trying to figure out what motivates them most and how best to focus their energies. In order to help you get started with this self-reflection, if you haven't already, you may want to go through ▶ Chaps. 3 (Worksheet 1) and ▶ 4 (Worksheets 2 and 3).

7.2.2 Low-Context Scenario #2: Developing an Idea Within an Organization (for Intrapreneurs)

While the main focus of this book is on entrepreneurs who are starting up their own businesses, it bears mentioning that according to a recent University of Phoenix study, approximately 37%, or more than one third, of all US adults working within an organizational context consider themselves to be intrapreneurs, and a whopping 56% believe their firms enable them to use an entrepreneurial mindset (The Harris Poll on behalf of The University of Phoenix, 2015).

One reality about starting from an organizational context, beyond the obvious advantage of better resource access, is that the team may already be ready-made. This may be an unchangeable situation, or perhaps the intrapreneur is able to influence the team selection. If there is some ability to influence team selection, in many ways, some of the same considerations given to the importance of key partnerships for entrepreneurs starting out also apply to the construction of intrapreneurially led organizational teams.

Whether for an entrepreneur or intrapreneur, it is important to consider how networks and the various factors which affect their effectiveness and efficiency interact with new environmental information.

7.3 The Myth of the Lone Entrepreneur Without a Network

As we can see from the previous discussion, regardless of the context, a key question during the early days of a startup for the first founding entrepreneur is whether to partner or not. Certainly, there are some apparent "lone wolfs" out there in terms of not having one key partner (e.g., Ray Kroc, McDonald's); and this may be particularly true in the case of self-employment and small businesses, but this concept of the lone figure battling the storms (◘ Fig. 7.1) can never really be accurate, as even "small-e" entrepreneurs need to have a team, whether internal to the startup or firm, or external through their network. Truly, this is one of the "greatest myths" of entrepreneurship (Cooney, 2005; Gerber, 2001).

While it is possible that a founder starts a company largely on their own, as the saying goes, "no (wo)man is an island" (Donne, 1572-1631). In other words, even when someone runs the show themselves, they still require advisors, suppliers, and

7

Fig. 7.1 Conceptual image to portray "the concept of the lone figure battling the storm." (Source: Image licensed and downloaded from Shutterstock on September 24, 2018. Credit: by robuart/Shutterstock.com. License Link: ▶ https://www.shutterstock.com/image-vector/bad-stormy-weather-vector-concept-flat-500144302)

customers to make things happen and they do so in an ecological context involving governments, banks, and so forth. Further, if such entrepreneurs decide to grow the business, the need to add employees is inevitable.

7.4 Developing Your Entrepreneurial Team: Idea Driving/Championing

As we have just described, context development is important whether you are far from commercialization where the market context may be extremely low or closer to commercialization where you may have a better idea of potential market opportunities but need to narrow down the scope. Taking context development to the next step is challenging because this is where you begin to overlay your interests with those of your startup partner(s) and/or team (as relevant) with potential industry options (in ▶ Chap. 8, next) and market opportunities (in upcoming ▶ Chap. 9) in a way that can potentially create value, and in most people's cases, without having specific product/service ideas yet. So, where to begin?

Sharing your interests and ideas with others can help to develop a language around and about your emerging ideas as well as keeping you on point in terms of your vision and being true to who you are in the process.

◘ Fig. 7.2 Conceptual image to portray the concept of "idea championing." (Source: Image licensed and downloaded from Adobe Stock on April 24, 2020. Credit: by peshkov/7 stock.adobe.com. License Link: ▸ https://stock.adobe.com/ca/images/innovation-concept/163008971)

"Champions," and their importance in promoting radical innovations, were first described by Schon (1963). It is well recognized that "champions" and their ability to drive new ideas (◘ Fig. 7.2) are required, as described by Howell and Higgins (1990, p. 40), "to make a decisive contribution to the innovation process by actively and enthusiastically promoting innovation, building support, overcoming resistance, and ensuring that the innovation is implemented."

7.4.1 Developing Your Early Internal Team: Partners

Now that you are in the mode of considering who your partners might be (or you may have already decided whom you are teaming up with), it is a good idea to consider in detail how your skills and interests might intersect. As such, we provide the next worksheet, Worksheet #6.

One important place to start is to see how well your existing team, or the "virtual team" you are considering, is matched up on core competencies. "Core competencies" can be defined as "a harmonized combination of multiple resources and skills that distinguish a firm in the marketplace" (Schilling, 2016, p. 119) and therefore are the foundation of companies' competitiveness. It may be that you find that your existing or virtual team may be able to accomplish achieving their vision together without adding more people or skills. More likely, you may find that additional people are needed to plug holes in the team or to think constructively around how to develop and/or overcome weaker skill areas.

Worksheet #6 aims at maximizing your core interests, areas of inspiration, and potentially, areas of core competence with others while minimizing overlap in terms of your overall skill set so that you are working in a complementary fashion. It can also be used to examine levels of complementarity and divergence with potential investors, advisors, or other stakeholders. The aim of this exercise is for your team or virtual team to create a "joint core competence map." Using the previous Worksheets 1–3, which each team member should complete on their own first, the team can put together this combined worksheet, #6, showing where they have overlap in interests, skills, and personality traits and where/how they differ from each other. The entrepreneurial team should give themselves as much time as possible for this assignment as it sets the trajectory for the rest of their journey together.

We suggest aiming at a three-page note from this worksheet: effectively, two pages for completing the questions on the competence mapping worksheet itself, and the final page should attempt to create a visual map of your findings from the worksheet (i.e., how far apart your team members are in terms of your divergent skills; how close together your team members are in terms of your overlapping skills and interests). Worksheet 6 provides a visual suggestion to help you do this.

Worksheet 6: Joint Core Competencies Map

1. For each team member (based on Worksheet 1), list 3 general areas of interest that you each might like to pursue. After thinking about your responses to the worksheet, have each person prioritize these in terms of overall interest using a 3-point scale (#1 most favorite = 3 points; #2 = 2 points; #3 = 1 point; for an interest area someone else lists which you did not = 0). Now tally up the total points for every potential interest brought up by the group. (See the example provided in Chapter 7 of the text). Discuss the results.

____

____

____

____

____

____

____

____

____

2. List the top overlaps in interests and passions which might serve as a basis for beginning to look at potential industry and marketplace opportunities of interest. Have a discussion with your team to see if there is a clear winner and/or whether there might be some interesting potential for bridging between interest areas.

____

____

____

____

____

____

____

© Susan E. Reid and Charles B. Crawford, August 14, 2020.

3. For each team member (based on Worksheets 2 and 3), list the most important strength(s) that you feel you can offer the team in terms of motivations, values, cognitive style, or other skills.

4. Based on overlapping strengths, list the strongest capabilities your team seems to have taken together as a unit. While you may not have worked together yet, if you had to make an educated guess, what would you list as your team's core capabilities moving forward?

© Susan E. Reid and Charles B. Crawford, August 14, 2020.

5. If you were, right now based on this exercise, to assign each person in your team a theoretical organizational role, who might occupy these roles (for example, VP Human Resources, VP Marketing, VP Sales, VP Operations, VP Finance)? In order to help you think about this, again use a 3-point scale with #1 being highest (#1 = 3 points; #2 = 2 points; #3 = 1 point for how you would self-score your interest/potential capability on each of these skills). Once you have done this, you can use Excel (or other spreadsheet software) to plug each person with their scores into a spreadsheet and then use the commands 'Insert', then 'Other Charts', then 'Radar' (Excel method) to capture the data visually and create a spider web diagram (see example below) of how your skill sets overlap/converge and diverge. In the example provided below, you can see that there is a very good balance across the skill sets and a core competence leaning slightly towards Marketing. It points to one person who has strong Finance skills and one who is highly skilled at Marketing, but no one person with a high skill in HR, although two people rated themselves as good at this. This may mean you want to consider how to account for this as a team, or given the focus of your interests, this may be sufficient for now while still a startup. You can do the same thing with your passions and interests to see points of divergence and convergence. The key is to have divergence on enough skills for balance and overlaps on key areas of passion/interest and on key core competencies where you think you may be able to build a core advantage.

Example: (format and idea for skill mapping provided with permission from 2017 Bishop's University student team: Ashton Glenn, Owen Martel and Brady Van der Well)

Person	Skill 1 Finance	Skill 2 Marketing	Skill 3 HR
Person 1	1	3	2
Person 2	1	2	2
Person 3	3	1	1

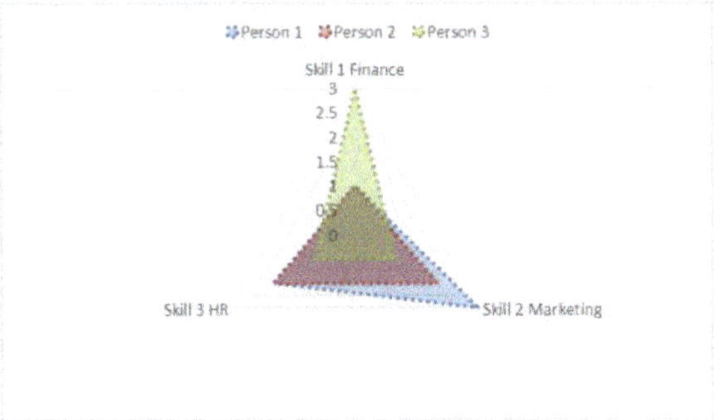

© Susan E. Reid and Charles B. Crawford, August 14, 2020.

As an example, say you are three people considering working together, and you have each prioritized your areas of interest. The combined number of interest areas between the three people is 5: skiing, hiking, cooking, travel and reading. For each person, their #1 choice gets three points, choice #2 gets two points, and choice #3 gets one point. If you did not overlap on an interest area mentioned by another person, you score a zero for that interest area.

Listed activity	Person 1	Person 2	Person 3	Total
Skiing	3 points	2 points	0 points	5
Hiking	2 points	0 points	3 points	5
Cooking	0 points	3 points	2 points	5
Travel	1 point	0 points	0 points	1
Reading	0 points	1 point	1 point	1

7

The top three areas of intersection each received five points and were skiing, hiking, and cooking, and the overlaps occurred across all three people at least twice and with one other person at least once. This seems like a reasonable place to start, but you would want to explore further to see if you feel if some blend of the activities/interests could be of enough interest to all of you, or whether it might work better if you brought in one or two other people.

To drill down you can see whether you have overlap in terms of values and primary motivators but divergence in terms of skills and thinking styles. For example, if all three of the above people scored strongly on environmental values and/or autonomy in addition to overlapping interests in skiing and hiking, there might be something good to work with there as a team: a core competence related to love of outdoors and environmental values. It would also be beneficial if these people were divergent in terms of their skill sets and cognitive styles. You might consider skill sets linked to basic functions of a business such as operations management, HR, marketing and sales, finance, etc. to see if there is enough divergence there to get good coverage in abilities out of your initial partners. In sum, if it looks like you have overlaps in passion and values but divergence in skills, then you have good potential "fit" as a team. If not, don't panic, you just need to think very strategically whether it makes sense to still work together and, if so, how to balance things out, possibly by bringing other people on board. In terms of your areas of passion, this analysis could also provide some attractive potential opportunities by mixing fields in a way that has not been done before.

7.4.2 Developing Your Early External Team: Sponsors

One key aspect of idea driving is the ability to hook in with people with resources that can help further the cause. In an existing firm, for intrapreneurs, this might involve getting a senior VP or the CEO on board. For entrepreneurs, this might, early on, involve advisors, attracting angel or VC investors, support of key suppliers, channel members, policymakers, market mavens, and lead users.

These influencers and deciders are collectively known as "sponsors" (Cooper and Kleinschmidt, 1995). It is important to get their buy-in as early as possible in the life of a new idea so that they can help rally additional resources toward it. The competition for resources in developing industries and markets involves contests among entrepreneurs because different people are motivated by different self-interests and preferences as they strive to acquire, manage, and control resources. Also, the more innovative the idea, the more people stand to gain or lose as a result of getting involved or not getting involved. There is also the problem that when the stakes are higher, people tend to not want to discuss things and only reveal what they really think and feel in informal settings behind closed doors by engaging in personal politicking. In any case, regardless of the need to protect early ideas, information, and innovation, there is a need to drive ideas forward with key stakeholders in order to gain their support early on. If the entrepreneur is not willing to drive new ideas forward, even in nascent stages while the Market Vision is still forming, even with the best ideas, it may be very difficult to gain traction later on.

Chapter Review Questions

1. What is the difference between a high-context and low-context scenario for potential entrepreneurial ventures?
2. Why do you think it is important to start to build your network as early as possible in the new venture planning process?
3. What is an advisory board, and why is it so valuable for nascent and established entrepreneurs?
4. What is a Joint Core Competency Map, and why should you consider using this tool when looking at potential partners?
5. What is a sponsor, and what are the advantages of finding one in your area of interest? Provide a concrete example to illustrate.

References

Cooney, T. M. (2005). What is an entrepreneurial team? (editorial and introduction to special issue on 'Entrepreneurial Teams'). *International Small Business Journal, 23*(3), 226–235.

Cooper, R. G., & Kleinschmidt, E. J. (1995). Benchmarking the firm's critical success factors in new product development. *The Journal of Product Innovation Management, 12*(5), 374–391.

Donne, J. (1572-1631). *Devotions XVII.* From "The Classic Quotes Collection", Laura Monur, www.quotationspage.com/collections.html#classic. Accessed online August 25, 2020.

Gerber, M. E. (2001). *The E-myth revisited* (2nd ed.). Harper Business.

Howell, J. M., & Higgins, C. A. (1990). Champions of change: Identifying, understanding, and supporting champions of technological innovations. *Organizational Dynamics, 19*(1), 40–55.

Isaacson, W. (2011). *Steve Jobs*. Simon & Schuster Paperbacks.

Schilling, M. (2016). *Strategic management of technological innovation* (5th ed.). McGraw Hill.

Schon, D. A. (1963). Champions for radical new inventions. *Harvard Business Review, 41*(2), 77–86.

The Harris Poll on behalf of The University of Phoenix. (2015). *The Working Adult Survey*, 2015.

Creating Vision Context Through Market Insights: Deep Diving an Industry

Contents

© The Author(s), under exclusive license to Springer Nature Switzerland AG 2022
S. E. Reid, C. B. Crawford, *Entrepreneurial Vision*, Classroom Companion: Business,
https://doi.org/10.1007/978-3-030-77803-3_8

Learning Objectives

In ► Chaps. 6 and 7, we focused on how to create vision context through network development. We now begin to swing our focus to the market in order to continue building a meaningful context for vision creation.

In this chapter, we seek to:

1. Explain a method for conducting a "deep dive" of industry(ies) of interest to the entrepreneurial team.
2. Explain how to match your team's core competencies with identified broad industry opportunities.
3. Select one broad industrial opportunity for potential further development through the visioning exercises provided in the rest of this textbook.
4. Learn the differences between constructionist, realist, and hybrid approaches to market opportunity management.
5. Provide an introduction to understanding how market learning works under various innovation scenarios.

8.1 Upfront Industry Homework

One of the key factors identified as crucial to increasing success in the early stages of market opportunity identification is doing your "upfront homework" (Cooper, 1996). In other words, before diving into the ideation, development, and testing phases of any new project, it is important to get as complete a picture, as is possible, of the relevant industry(ies) upfront.

In ► Chap. 3, we spoke about the importance of keeping options open and using divergent thinking skills during the early processes of opportunity seeking. As such, we suggest at this stage, with your first partners, based on knowledge of how your interests and passions intersect, that this is a good time to look at as many opportunities for your potential joint future as possible. We recommend not just looking at one industry/field of interest, but as many as seem important to explore in the timeframe, you have available to you. For those people on your team with more "convergent thinking" tendencies, the urge to move forward with the first opportunity of interest, without looking at further options, may be irrepressible. As such, it is a good time for your team's "divergent thinkers" to play an important role here in terms of keeping the team openly focused on as many potential options as possible for investigation at this stage. Depending on the amount of time you have available to you, you need to at least look at the most pressing area of joint team interest in detail—i.e., do your homework upfront—but, if time and circumstances permit, it would be potentially beneficial to additionally look at least at one or two other industries of joint interest.

A great place to start doing your homework is by looking at the big picture. To do this, we recommend looking up as many existing industry analyses as possible, to get some snapshots of your field(s) of interest. This does not preclude performing a much more in-depth analysis, but examining existing industry reports provides a good starting point and usually will direct you toward other references to continue your data hunt. One tool for forecasting industrial and technological trends is known as the "roadmap" (Barker & Smith, 1995; Kostoff & Schaller, 2000; Simonse, 2018). This tool is often the first place where industry players share their research and insights vis-à-vis potential new technology and market developments. Roadmaps help industry players to get a forecast of future opportunities. It is then up to each individual organization to see how they might focus their own efforts given their position in the industry. For example, in the early days of the semiconductor industry, a consortium of industry players including government bodies, academics, and corporations such as Sandia joined together to work on a roadmap, *The National Technology Association Roadmap for Semiconductors* (USA), for their industry association. This roadmap has continued to evolve and is now the responsibility of the International Roadmap for Devices and Systems through the Institute of Electrical and Electronics Engineers ("IEEE"). While such roadmaps are used extensively for understanding new technology fields and related industries, they can, equally, be used to understand consumer goods and services industries and other less tech-driven fields. Where such roadmaps exist, they can provide a plethora of information including the key players and experts in the field (institutions, universities, governments, key companies, key venture capitalists, and banks that are interested in the industry).

As an example, in 2014, Susan co-authored the introductory chapter in a book on the emerging field of nanoscience and nanotechnology (Reid et al., 2014), because this industry had been the context focus of her research on vision with radical innovation. She went through this exercise of doing homework on the global field before moving forward with her own more specific research focus. In this case, one of the first starting points to gaining an understanding of the industry, globally, was to see which countries were involved in developing the field through various initiatives, how much they had committed to their efforts financially, in which sectors of focus, and whether roadmaps had been created by any of these countries. An illustration of this research is provided in ◘ Table 8.1 (from Reid et al., 2014). This tabulation provided a first cut of the data to gain an overall understanding of the relative efforts being put forward by various countries/regions and which specific areas they were focused on in the field of nanotechnology. The roadmaps themselves also provided clues as to where to dig for more information by country. Certain data sources are strongly recommended for building knowledge of such developments. Just as one example, statistics from the Organisation for Economic Co-operation and Development (OECD) are globally focused and often free from the OECD website and, as such, may offer a good starting point for such research.

Moving from developing a solid industry overview as a first starting point (Activity 1), any industrial "deep dive" should then focus on at least three additional key areas (Activities 2, 3, and 4), as follows:

Table 8.1 Government R&D spending in nanotechnology (with a focus on select leading countries) Source: Reid et al. (2014), permission granted on December 4, 2020, from Cambridge University Press for reprint

Country	Population 2009 mid-year[d] ('000)	Govt. spending in nanotech R&D 2007–2012 stats (US$mill)	Sig Coop Agreements with other countries	Govt. initiatives	Industry roadmaps
USA[a]	307,212	2100 for 2012[e] (began 2000)	Yes—Numerous	NNI (National Nanotechnology Initiative) (2001)	Yes "NNI Strategic Plan, Dec 2007"
Japan[a]	127,079	890 in 2009 (began 2001); MEXT program annually investing 600[e]	No	3rd Science and Technology Basic Plan (2006)	Yes "Nanotechnology business creation initiative"
Germany[a,f]	82,330	547 in 2009 (began investing in 1998)	Yes—With EU and ISO members	Nano-Initiative Action Plan 2010 (2006 started planning for 2008-2013)	BMBF Forschungsunion and BMWi branch dialogues
France[e]	65,821	640 during 2008–2012	Yes—With other EU members	Nano 2012 Programme	Yes
China[b]	1,338,613	240 during 2003–2007; 200 during 2008–2009	No	National Center for Nanoscience and Technology (2002)	Yes
Russia[a]	140,041	100 in 2009 (began 2007); 890 to be invested between 2008 and 2011[e]	Yes—EU	Strategy for Nanoindustry development (since 2007)	Yes "Developing of nanoindustry infrastructure in Russian Federation 2008–2010"

(continued)

Table 8.1 (continued)

Country	Population 2009 mid-year[d] ('000)	Govt. spending in nanotech R&D 2007–2012 stats (US$mill)	Sig Coop Agreements with other countries	Govt. initiatives	Industry roadmaps
India[c]	1,156,898	15 million for smart material development and DST funding is ten million from 2007 to 2010	No	Department of Science and Technology has launched a National Nanotechnology Program (2007)	No
Brazil[c]	198,739	35 between 2004 and 2007; approximately 6 in 2009[e]	Yes—Argentina	National Program of Nanotechnology (2007) consolidating other efforts since 2000 (The Millennium Institutes and other co-op networks involving >40 institutes) and Rede BrasilNano	No

[a] OECD Working Party on Nanotechnology, Committee for Scientific and Technological Policy, Inventory of National Science, Technology and Innovation Policies for Nanotechnology (2008)

[b] Chen Wang, Presentation of the National Center for Nanoscience and Technology, Beijing, China

[c] Niosi and Reid (2007), Kay and Shapira (2009)

[d] U.S. Census Bureau, International Database (▸ www.census.gov/ipc/www/idb/country)

[e] OECD 2012 Working Party on Nanotechnology Report

[f] Germany and France were the only European countries highlighted here, but it should be noted that 3.5 billion euros are to be invested in the Framework Programme 7 between 2007 and 2013 as noted in the OECD 2012 Working Party Report on Nanotechnology

8

- *Activity 1*: A global overview of key nations or trading areas involved in the industry and how much they have committed to the new area in relation to each other and whether any technology or market roadmaps exist from these regions.
- *Activity 2*: An industrial overview with an assessment of critical opportunities and issues for the industry.
- *Activity 3*: A market analysis of industry demand by segment and projected short- and long-term market trends.
- *Activity 4*: A competitive analysis including company profiles of the major and upcoming players and their positioning strategies.

Worksheet 7 provides suggested statistics and information to research within your "area of interest" industry(ies) to develop a sound understanding of the key opportunities, issues, markets, trends, and competitive positioning of key players.

Worksheet 7: Deep Dive: Industry ("Area of Interest") Analysis

1. Global Overview:
   a. List of Key Countries
   b. Population by Key Country
   c. Government Spending on R&D or $ Spent on Developments/Initiatives in the Sector
   d. Significant Co-operative Agreements with other Countries in the Sector
   e. Government Initiatives
   f. Extant Industry Roadmaps by Country
   g. Key Associations by Country
   h. Key Experts by Country

2. Industry Overview:
   a. Major Segments of the Industry (products, services, etc.)
   b. Total Number of Companies (U.S., Canada, worldwide)
   c. # of Employees (U.S., Canada, worldwide)
   d. Annual Sales (U.S., Canada, worldwide)
   e. Distribution of Companies by Size of Organization
   f. Key Industry Success Drivers
   g. Business Trends and Key Opportunities for the Future
   h. Nature of the Distribution System
   i. Typical Cost Structures
   j. Technological Advances in the Industry and Projected Impact
   k. Social, Political, Legal, Economic, and Regulatory Influences
   l. Special Issues (export/import, government policies, etc.)

3. Market Analysis (Industry Demand):
   a. Current Market Sizes by Segment
   b. Customer Characteristics by Segment
   c. Key Factors that Drive Demand by Segment
   d. Short-Term Projected Market Trends
   e. Long-Term Projected Market Trends
   f. Summary of the Market

4. Competitive Analysis:
   a. Company Profiles broken down by:
      i. Market share geographically
      ii. Market share by product
      iii. Positioning strategies of direct and indirect competitors

5. Summary of Critical Issues for the Industry

© Susan E. Reid and Charles B. Crawford, August 14, 2020.

As part of your deep-dive assessment, we suggest additionally contacting industry experts (some of whom you may have identified in ▶ Chap. 6, Worksheet 5), in order to interview them to get their take on potential opportunities and challenges in the industry.

Worksheet 8 provides a set of questions to help get you started with your expert interviews. The focus should be a combination of getting to know the person and performing an initial scan of the big picture of the industry.

Worksheet 8:
Industry Expert Interview
(Suggested Initial Questions)

The objective is to conduct an 'initial scan' with 2 experts, who are willing to work with you (and your team) as advisors. The advantage of doing this is, not only, to collect information as an early signal of potential opportunities in your field of interest, but to also start building your advisory network.

Here is a list of interview questions you might consider asking:

1. Can you tell me a little about your background and how you got interested in this area?
2. As you see it, what are the key opportunities available to new entrants/entrepreneurs?
3. Are there key associations I can join or conferences I can attend to learn more?
4. What publications should I read?
5. What new technologies or demographic changes might influence future opportunities? In other words, what are the most important trends to consider in this field?
6. What are some of the key challenges right now in the field?
7. Who are the most important people in the industry and why?
8. Would you be willing to suggest other contacts in the field and provide an introduction (if not would it be ok to use their name when introducing yourself)? If relevant, you might ask if they know any alumni or professors from your college/university from the field of interest to connect with.
9. Would you consider being on my (our) advisory board?

© Susan E. Reid and Charles B. Crawford, August 14, 2020.

8.2 Matching Team Core Competencies with Broad Industry Opportunities

Once you have completed Worksheets 7 and 8, the next step which will be outlined in ► Chap. 9 is to pull together your entrepreneurial team's interests, passions, and skills with the most salient and relevant information you culled from your industrial deep dive. Again, if you have time to do this exercise with more than one industry, it could pay off. Not only will you be able to see which industry will be a better fit for your overall team, but you may even be able to see if there are some thought-provoking intersections between multiple industries of interest which other people have not thought of before. These types of opportunities are along the lines of those described by Burt (1992) and Hargadon and Sutton (1997) in terms of their theories relating to brokering across structural holes in networks.

Worksheet 9 will serve as a basis for using the deep-dive industry assessment to pull together the key issues of interest to the team for moving forward with developing a Market Vision (and Technology Vision where relevant). This worksheet should help the team best understand how they can utilize their core competencies as a group to position themselves in a specific industry field/area of joint mutual interest. It might point them in the direction of certain technologies or markets related to the industry which appeal to them or toward opportunities that are crystallizing in the environment.

For example, if a government decides to offer incentives for technology developments of a certain type, this might open doors for opportunity which had not previously existed or been considered. So, if that specific technical field is of interest to a would-be entrepreneur, such incentives might be enough to encourage entry into that specific arena. Hegde & Mowery (2008) discuss the impact of the US government deciding to wage a "war on cancer," in response to a massive public outcry and lobbying related to the issue during the 1960s and 1970s. The response was the direction of massive levels of funding to academia and industry in support of this decision. The result was unprecedented levels of research in the biosciences leading to a surge in new biopharma developments and growth in the numbers of biotech IPOs in the 1980s and 1990s.

While the idea behind the next section is to start moving toward developing a market vision for a specific opportunity later on, it is important at this stage that the team not get too specifically market-focused or product- or idea-oriented just yet. Try to keep the opportunity level "high" and "broad" at this stage without the need to converge to any specific market or product ideas.

Here is a hypothetical example, we created, to illustrate what we mean:

> "Based on the matching joint core competencies exercise in Worksheet 6, our team's overlapping interests are in the areas of (1) services, (2) housing aesthetics/design, and (3) time optimization. As such, we have a team interest in jointly developing an opportunity in the field of home cleaning solutions. This is the industry we have investigated in detail in Worksheets 7 and 8. As a result, we see multiple potential opportunities related to the industry, such as new cleaning products and materials, robotics solutions, or opportunities to offer highly customized services. In putting these together with our own interests and skills, using Worksheet 9, we have deter-

mined that we would like to specifically focus in on the opportunity of home cleaning service solutions using robotics and AI. These areas seem to hold a lot of potential for the future of home cleaning solutions and resonate well with our team's core competencies and interests related to technology development."

We suggest writing a report for Worksheet 9 of approximately two pages of text maximum: effectively, one page which describes your broad joint opportunity area of interest, and one page which explains how it maps onto your core competencies as a team.

Worksheet 9
Industrial Opportunity Identification
(...and how opportunities might be differentiators for the team)

1. Summarize (where relevant) the most important new technologies in the industry of interest to your team and why

____
____
____
____
____

2. Summarize social and/or demographic changes occurring in the industry of interest to your team and why

____
____
____
____
____

3. Summarize under-utilized resources or new resources available in the industry

____
____
____
____

© Susan E. Reid and Charles B. Crawford, August 14, 2020.

4. Gap analysis - what would you need to do to fill in the blanks from where you are now to address key opportunities of interest either in terms of technology or consumers/demographics (i.e., file for a patent? gain technical expertise? find out more about regulations/government information?)

____

____

____

____

____

5. Who are the key players in the industry operating in the specific opportunity space? Are any lead users or experts identifiable? Do they represent a certain demographic? Who might you contact to find out more?

____

____

____

____

____

6. List at least 3 potential opportunities for differentiation which may be of interest to your team and why

____

____

____

____

____

© Susan E. Reid and Charles B. Crawford, August 14, 2020.

Potential approaches for developing specific solution options for these broad opportunities will be described in the next chapters of this book. Of course, ideas may pop up as you move forward through these worksheets, so make sure to keep a journal to document this flow and the discussions that ensue.

8.3 Using Market Learning to Decide on the Market Opportunity

You have decided on the industry(ies) you are going to delve into. You have also started building your entrepreneurial team and advisors. Based on the homework you have done in the last section, you are now building in-depth knowledge of your industry(ies) and have a sense of which opportunities are of interest, technologically and in the market. As well, you may possibly even have a sense of how your team's core competence might speak to certain specific opportunities and potential differentiation hot points, which may already exist, based on feedback from your advisors and experts. Now it is time to decide on which of the identified opportunities you want to pursue and which gap you wish to resolve. In effect, you are looking to come up with a first cut of your team's value proposition for a specific opportunity of interest within your industry of interest.

Before we cut to the chase, let's first take a step back and think about what "opportunity" actually means. The Merriam-Webster Dictionary (2020, online) defines it as "a favorable juncture of circumstances." When discussing opportunity, there are two perspectives we can use to better understand it: the realist perspective and the constructionist perspective.

8.3.1 The Realist Perspective: Opportunity as an Objective Phenomenon

According to Karlesky (2015), a realist perspective views opportunities as "objective phenomena" in that they occur independently of individual action. The basic underlying premise is that opportunities result from imperfections in the marketplace because individuals in a given market possess asymmetric information about new technologies or societal, demographic, or political change. This perspective has been espoused by many researchers, including Kaish and Gilad (1991), who propose that opportunities result from disequilibrium in the market. According to this perspective, some people possess more relative advantage than others depending on the timing of their information access related to "the opportunity" (◘ Fig. 8.1).

A good example of a primarily objective opportunity occurs when a government agency posts funding available by year for each area of public policy or science (◘ Fig. 8.2). We assume that the government has conducted research to identify new technology growth areas, as well as listening to various lobbyists and experts to establish the interests and needs of society and the expected impact of anticipated demographic changes to determine funding priorities.

Universities, for example, may use such government funding allocation information as a primary indicator of how to direct their own efforts toward gaining available funding (◘ Fig. 8.3). Governments and universities which access and act on such information the most quickly will stand to gain the most benefit from the signaled opportunities.

Fig. 8.1 Conceptual image to portray "relative advantage based on differences in timing exposure and asymmetric information." (Source: Image licensed and downloaded from Shutterstock on October 22, 2018. Credit: by Palto/► Shutterstock.com. License Link: ► https://www.shutterstock.com/image-illustration/different-people-leaders-3d-illustration-446090578)

	Requested	Awarded	Funding rate	Applied	Awarded	Success rate	Average requested	Average awarded
Genes, cells and molecules (RTI)	$13,298,575	$3,757,979	28.3%	114	31	27.2%	$116,654	$121,225
Biological system and functions (RTI)	$17,732,235	$5,107,495	28.8%	151	43	28.5%	$117,372	$118,779
Evolution and ecology (RTI)	$3,535,278	$1,022,161	28.9%	36	10	27.8%	$98,202	$102,216
Chemistry (RTI)	$13,512,875	$3,763,527	27.9%	108	30	27.8%	$125,119	$125,451
Physics (RTI)	$9,887,906	$2,865,328	29.0%	73	22	30.1%	$135,451	$130,242
Geosciences (RTI)	$7,433,024	$2,091,838	28.1%	70	20	28.6%	$106,186	$104,592
Computer, mathematical and statistical sciences (RTI)	$2,488,269	$776,731	31.2%	25	7	28.0%	$99,531	$110,962
Civil, Industrial and systems engineering (RTI)	$6,972,454	$2,058,799	29.5%	58	17	29.3%	$120,215	$121,106
Electrical and computer engineering (RTI)	$7,813,690	$2,222,612	28.4%	64	16	25.0%	$122,089	$138,913
Materials and chemical engineering (RT)	$13,372,560	$3,867,621	28.9%	105	29	27.6%	$127,358	$133,366
Mechanical engineering (RTI)	$11,105,064	$3,190,982	28.7%	88	24	27.3%	$126,194	$132,958
Grand total	**$107,142,93**	**$30,725,073**	**28.7%**	**892**	**249**	**27.9%**	**$120,115**	**$123,394**

Fig. 8.2 Canadian government funding for discovery grants by scientific discipline for research tools and instruments. 2020 Competition results by selection committee. (Downloaded from ► https://www.nserc-crsng.gc.ca/_doc/DGP2020_e.pdf on June 11, 2020. Public Domain)

8.3.2 The Constructionist Perspective: Opportunity as a Subjective Phenomenon

In contrast to the objective realist perspective, the constructionist perspective views opportunities as constructed by individuals (Jackson & Dutton, 1988). This is a more subjective perspective in that opportunities are co-created through an "enactment" process (Karlesky, 2015), which results from the interpretation of information and/or opportunities from the environment by the entrepreneur and the ways in which they use this information.

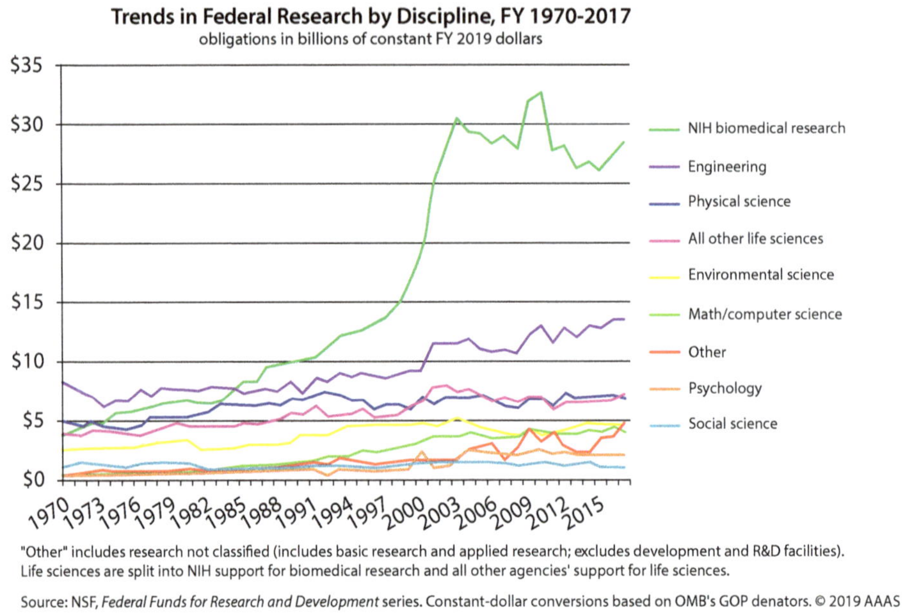

Fig. 8.3 Federal Funds for Research and Development (USA) by Discipline. (Source: National Science Foundation (▶ https://www.aaas.org/programs/r-d-budget-and-policy/historical-trends-federal-rd). Permission granted on December 10, 2020, from the American Association for the Advancement of Science for reprint)

A great example of an entrepreneur who interpreted a specific environmental opportunity in a certain way, and decided to do something about it, is illustrated by Phil Knight of Nike in his book *Shoe Dog* (Knight, 2016). On a trip to Japan in 1962, he enticed the owners of Onitsuka (now part of Asics) to allow him to represent "Tiger brand" shoes in the USA. His basic idea was to bring good quality Japanese shoes to the USA at a lower cost.

The constructionist perspective extends along a spectrum. At the one end, the entrepreneur looks at the existing opportunities that present themselves and decides whether they believe they will be able to exploit them with what they have on hand. At the other end of the spectrum, the entrepreneur, regardless of resources under controlled, believes they will adapt to and do or get what it takes, including constructing new ideas, to be able to take advantage of the opportunity.

The concept of "opportunity beliefs," or, as described by Grégoire et al. (2010, p. 118), the degree of "certainty that a 'venture idea' represents an opportunity" aligns with this second part of the spectrum when it relates to a particularly strong belief in the opportunity. For example, such high belief is illustrated in the statement by Stevenson and Jarillo (1990, p. 23) noting "the essence of entrepreneurship is the willingness to pursue opportunities, regardless of resources under control." The idea here is that an individual will utilize their mindset to get the job done no matter what—or, in other words, make the best of what you've got and then some (Fig. 8.4)!

Fig. 8.4 Conceptual image to portray "opportunity beliefs based on mindset." (Image licensed and downloaded from Shutterstock on October 22, 2018. Credit: by tomertu/Shutterstock. License Link: ► https://www.shutterstock.com/image-photo/top-view-image-table-open-notebook-1116708380)

When the context is high with little uncertainty, then opportunities may be more concrete and possible to approach from a realist's objective perspective. However, under higher levels of uncertainty, a more subjective approach may be required, or what has been coined by Sarasvathy (2001) as "effectuation." As Sarasvathy explains, there are opportunities that may be recognized by exploiting existing markets, or those with lower uncertainty (i.e., through lower cost structures, services, promotions, awareness, better distribution, etc.). For most entrepreneurs, as Sarasvathy's data suggests, there is usually some level of uncertainty, particularly in the early days, and therefore opportunities must be created on some level (Fig. 8.5). Indeed, in Sarasvathy's research, 89% of expert entrepreneurs (45 interviewed) used effectuation more often than causation.

8.3.3 A Hybrid Perspective: Combining Opportunity Search with Psychological Construction

At the ends of the realist(objective)-constructionist(subjective) spectrum, therefore, the emergence of opportunity may be thought of as either a result of cultural/social/environmental/political/technological change causing disequilibrium, i.e., "objective change" in the environment, or as a result of psychological construction

Fig. 8.5 Conceptual image to portray "uncertainty." (Source: Image licensed and downloaded from Shutterstock on October 22, 2018. Credit: by Carlos G. Lopez/Shutterstock. License Link: ► https://www.shutterstock.com/image-photo/girl-wearing-woolly-hat-wellington-boots-517562086)

creating "subjective change" related to how an individual sees the current and future potential resources and situation in the environment.

In this book, we use a two-step hybrid process, embracing both perspectives. We believe this is important to getting the most out of one's understanding of the environment and potential opportunities therein (step 1), while at the same time putting one's own spin on things (step 2).

Step 1. Finding opportunities related to disequilibrium or objective phenomena is about doing your homework and looking "outside" for new information. This involves an active knowledge search, both domain-specific and cross-boundary, based on where your interests take you. The focus of this chapter has been on performing the homework to see the potential broad opportunities which exist "out there" (Fig. 8.6). This homework phase, in reality, is never truly complete. It is important for all businesspeople to maintain an eye on their external environment to remain aware of newly evolving opportunities, environmental information, and competition.

Step 2. Psychological construction is more subjective and emergent. It often looks to create both new supply and demand through processes of creativity and vision-driven action (Fig. 8.7). This is what we will be focusing on moving forward with the remainder of this book!

Fig. 8.6 Conceptual image to portray "searching for opportunities which exist." (Source: Image licensed and downloaded from Shutterstock on October 22, 2018. Credit: by fran_kies/▶ Shutterstock.com. License Link: ▶ https://www.shutterstock.com/image-photo/business-man-on-top-tower-watching-1159933027)

8.4 Introduction to Market Learning

Now that a broad joint opportunity area of interest to your entrepreneurial team has been established (using Worksheet 9), it is important to start learning as much as possible about any current markets that may exist in the opportunity area and how those markets might potentially be developed moving forward. We accomplish this through actively learning about markets we would like to investigate and understand in more detail. This process is known as "market learning."

"Market learning" is defined by Colarelli O'Connor and Veryzer (2001, p. 232) as "the manner by which a direction and sense of the market opportunity are infused into the innovation process." A key question related to market learning involves when and how consumers should be involved in the new product or service development (NPD) process.

One principle, which has been shown to influence customer involvement in the NPD process, is the level of innovativeness. According to Colarelli O'Connor (1998), the "technology voice" tends to be louder when a technology is new or young and still needs a lot of development. In contrast, the "customer voice" tends to be louder later in the technology life cycle when the level of innovativeness has

Fig. 8.7 Conceptual image to portray "psychological construction." (Image licensed and downloaded from Shutterstock on October 22, 2018. Credit: by Lightspring/▶ Shutterstock.com. License Link: ▶ https://www.shutterstock.com/image-illustration/training-development-business-education-concept-hand-195037466)

8

become more incremental. These processes are related to what is sometimes referred to as "technology push" and "market pull."

An example of a "technology push" innovation was the invention of the touch screen technology developed by Royal Radar Establishment in the 1960s. This technology was further "pushed" by Hewlett Packard in the 1980s through their launch of the touch screen computer. Over the years, this technology has become increasingly advanced in devices such as phones, tablets, and cameras.

An example of a "market pull" innovation is the demand for space travel (Fig. 8.8). It may seem that this is a logical place for technology push inventions, and of course, there are many push inventions in this field, but the original impetus for space travel was initiated from the market. Space travel has been envisaged by writers, futurists, movie producers, explorers, and scientists for centuries, long before it ever became a technical reality. After years of the market dreaming about what might be possible, Russia's Sputnik program in the 1950s spurred the USA to follow suit with the NASA space program in the 1960s, which led to the moon landing of 1969.

Fig. 8.8 Conceptual image to portray "space travel." (Source: Image licensed and downloaded from Shutterstock on January 13, 2019. Credit: by galacticus/▶ Shutterstock.com. License Link: ▶ https://www.shutterstock.com/image-vector/baby-astronaut-sits-on-saturn-welcomes-695705065)

An interesting study which illustrates this proposition was published by Langrish et al. (1972) in *Wealth from Knowledge.* Mowery and Rosenberg (1979) describe the Langrish et al. research, based on case studies of 84 innovations that received the Queen's Award for technological innovation in 1966/1967. All of these innovations were considered to have been commercially successful. For major (i.e., radical) innovations, 14.4% were of the technology push type, and this was found to be more important than demand-pull through need identification (6.1%). This finding was reversed for what they called "minor" innovations (i.e., incremental innovations), where need identification was responsible for 18.3% of the innovations and the discovery factor related to technology push was responsible for only 5%.

Since radical innovations tend to occur earlier on in a technology's life cycle, this means that technology push processes tend to be more prevalent with radical innovations. As such, while still desirable when it is possible, it is more challenging to bring the "voice of the customer" (Griffin & Hauser, 1993) into play for existing markets which are not yet familiar with a radical (or major) new technology early in its development or for future markets which don't exist yet.

Given this information, in combination with the fact that the ability to envision and understand future markets is clearly an essential component of Market Visioning Competence, an important question involves whether and, if so, how it may be possible to incorporate the voice of the customer in the development of radical technologies and products for those markets.

First, let's look at how the voice of the customer has been demonstrated in the case of incremental innovation. Second, let's consider why it is challenging to hear the voice of the customer in the case of more radical innovation. Finally, some suggestions are made as to how to listen to the voice of the customer for future markets with radical innovations and thereby improve Market Visioning Competence.

8.4.1 How the Voice of the Customer Works in the Case of Incremental Types of Innovation

The customer's voice can be incorporated very early on in the case of incremental types of innovation through the use of many traditional market research methodologies including interviewing, focus groups, surveys, observation, and the use of customer feedback, to name a few. Consumer involvement is undeniably important to new product development in the case of incremental or continuous innovations because *the most consistent findings in success/failure studies have been that unique product/service advantage in the eyes of the consumer is significantly correlated with success* (Balachandra & Friar, 1997; Biolos, 1996; Booz & Hamilton, 1982; Cooper, 1979; Cooper, 1981; Cooper, 1985; Cooper & de Brentani, 1984; de Brentani, 1989, 1991; de Brentani & Dröge, 1988; Lilien & Yoon, 1989; Mahajan & Wind, 1992; Maidique & Zirger, 1984; Rubenstein et al., 1976; Sowrey, 1989).

8.4.2 Why Is It Challenging to Hear the Voice of the Customer in the Radical Innovation Situation?

In the case of radical innovation, which occurs mostly during the early stages of a technological trajectory, markets (particularly of the low-context sort) are difficult to assess using the more conventional marketing tools for opportunity identification, idea sourcing, and idea generation used with more incremental innovations (de Brentani, 2001; Lynn, 1993; Song & Montoya-Weiss, 1998; Veryzer Jr., 1998). Customer needs, which usually form the basis for market targeting and segmentation, are often unarticulated or unknown by the customers themselves under the more radical innovation scenario (Moriarty & Kosnik, 1989). Potential market applications for disruptive technologies are often unknown or unknowable at the time of a disruptive technology's development. As well, under conditions of high technological uncertainty, potential manufacturers may not yet have rallied around a dominant design (Abernathy & Utterback, 1978). Furthermore, entrepreneurial teams may still be playing with prototypes often under conditions of limited resources and partial information from the environment. The implication is that many of the ways in which companies and entrepreneurs typically manage market learning for more incremental innovations are irrelevant in the case of disruptive technologies. In fact, applying inappropriate marketing, financial, and management processes may even be counterproductive in the case of radical innovation (de Brentani, 2001; Song & Montoya-Weiss, 1998; Veryzer Jr., 1998). Related to these ideas, Christensen (1997, p. 98) suggests that "listening carefully to customers may lead established firms to reject disruptive technologies which they should in fact be embracing."

8.4.3 Are There Ways to Successfully Listen to the Voice of the Customer with Radical Innovation?

If we shouldn't focus on listening to customers' expressed needs, in the case of radical innovation, then where should we begin? Research suggests (1) listening empathetically with current customers in order to develop a proper understanding of their latent needs (i.e., the work of Leonard & Rayport, 1997) or (2) listening with the right potential customers and working with them as potential partners in developing new products and markets together (i.e., the work of von Hippel on "Lead Users": Von Hippel, 1986; Von Hippel, 1988).

Most entrepreneurs, marketers, and businesspeople have been schooled extensively in the art of listening to customers. Few, however, have theoretical or practical experience dealing with how to discover new markets alongside potential customers who may not be able to express their needs or those who want to work hard to learn how to serve their own needs better. Perhaps, then, the art lies in (1) developing a more "proactive market orientation" (Narver & Slater, 1990) either by collaborating with current customers empathetically through attempting to discover latent needs or by collaborating with lead users when working with current customers is not possible, and (2) by developing "market learning tools" (Reid & de Brentani, 2010) which allow entrepreneurs to work with more than one market or scenario at the same time to push different potential futures forward and see how they unfold.

In the next chapters, we take a closer look at methods and examples of (1) proactive market orientation (► Chap. 9) and (2) market learning tools (► Chap. 10).

Chapter Review Questions

1. When doing an industry deep dive, what are the key areas one should be analyzing?
2. Why is it important to map team core competencies against industry opportunities?
3. What is the difference between constructive and realist approaches to managing market opportunities? What is a hybrid approach?
4. What is an opportunity belief? What does effectuation mean?
5. Explain what technology push means and why it is more often a driver of radical innovation than market pull.

6. Why is listening to current customers not always effective in the case of developments based on radical innovation?
7. What is the most consistent finding in studies of success/failure with new product development?

References

Abernathy, W. J., & Utterback, J. M. (1978). Patterns of industrial innovation. In R. Burgelman & M. Modesto (Eds.), *Strategic management of technology and innovation* (pp. 141–148). Irwin, 1988.

Balachandra, R., & Friar, J. H. (1997). Factors for success in R&D projects and new product innovation: A contextual framework. *IEEE Transactions on Engineering Management, 44*(3), 276–287.

Barker, D., & Smith, D. J. H. (1995). Technology foresight using roadmaps. *Long Range Planning, 28*(2), 21–28.

Biolos, J. (1996). *Managing the process of innovation. Harvard management update*. Harvard Business School Publishing.

Booz, A., & Hamilton, I. (1982). *New product management for the 1980's*. Booz, Allen & Hamilton.

Burt, R. S. (1992). *Structural holes: The social structure of competition*. Harvard University Press.

Christensen, C. M. (1997). *The innovator's dilemma*. Harvard Business School Press.

Colarelli O'Connor, G. (1998). Market learning and radical innovation: A cross case comparison of eight radical innovation projects. *The Journal of Product Innovation Management, 15*(2), 151–166.

Colarelli O'Connor, G., & Veryzer, R. (2001). The nature of market visioning for technology-based radical innovation. *The Journal of Product Innovation Management, 18*(4), 231–246.

Cooper, R. G. (1979). The dimensions of industrial new product success and failure. *Journal of Marketing, 43*(1), 93–103.

Cooper, R. G. (1981). An empirically derived new product project selection model. *IEEE Transactions on Engineering Management, 28*(3), 54–61.

Cooper, R. G. (1985). Selecting winning new product projects: Using the NewProd system. *The Journal of Product Innovation Management, 2*(1), 34–44.

Cooper, R. G. (1996). Overhauling the new product process. *Industrial Marketing Management, 25*(6), 465–482.

Cooper, R. G., & de Brentani, U. (1984). Criteria for screening new industrial products. *Industrial Marketing Management, 13*(3), 149–156.

de Brentani, U. (1989). Success and failure in new industrial services. *The Journal of Product Innovation Management, 6*(4), 239–258.

de Brentani, U. (1991). Success factors in developing new services. *European Journal of Marketing, 25*(2), 33–59.

de Brentani, U. (2001). Innovative versus incremental new business services: Different keys for achieving success. *The Journal of Product Innovation Management, 18*(3), 169–187.

de Brentani, U., & Dröge, C. (1988). Determinants of the new product screening decision: A structural model analysis. *International Journal of Research in Marketing, 5*(3), 91–110.

Grégoire, D. A., Shepherd, D. A., & Lambert, L. S. (2010). Measuring opportunity-recognition beliefs: Illustrating and validating an experimental approach. *Organizational Research Methods, 13*(1), 114–145.

Griffin, A., & Hauser, J. (1993). The voice of the customer. *Management Science, 12*(1), 1–27.

Hargadon, A., & Sutton, R. I. (1997). Technology brokering and innovation in a product development firm. *Administrative Science Quarterly, 42*(4), 716–749.

Hegde, D., & Mowery, D. C. (2008). Politics and funding in the U.S. public biomedical R&D system. *Science, 322*(5909), 1797–1798.

Jackson, S. E., & Dutton, J. E. (1988). Discerning threats and opportunities. *Administrative & Science Quarterly, 33*(3), 370–387.

Kaish, S., & Gilad, B. (1991). Characteristics of opportunities search of entrepreneurs versus executives: Sources, interests, general alertness. *Journal of Business Venturing, 6*(1), 45–61.

Karlesky, M. J. (2015). *Identifying entrepreneurial opportunities: Cognition and categorization in nascent entrepreneurs.* Ph.D. Dissertation, University of Michigan.

Kay, L., & Shapira, P. (2009). Developing nanotechnology in Latin America. *Journal of Nanoparticle Research, 11*(2), 259–278.

Knight, P. (2016). *Shoe dog: A memoir by the creator of Nike*. Scribner.

Kostoff, R. N., & Schaller, R. R. (2000). Science and technology roadmaps. *IEEE Transactions on Engineering Management, 48*(2), 132–143.

Langrish, J. M., Gibbons, M., Evans, W. G., & Jevons, F. R. (1972). *Wealth from knowledge*. Macmillan.

Leonard, D., & Rayport, J. F. (1997). Spark innovation through empathic design. *Harvard Business Review, 75*(6), 102–113.

Lilien, G. L., & Yoon, E. (1989). Determinants of new industrial product performance: A strategic re-examination of the empirical literature. *IEEE Transactions on Engineering Management, 36*(1), 3–10.

Lynn, G. (1993). Understanding products and markets for radical innovation. Ph.D. Dissertation, Faculty of the Graduate School of Rensselaer Polytechnic Institute. *UMI Proquest Digital Dissertations*.

Mahajan, V., & Wind, Y. (1992). New product models: Practices, shortcomings, and desired improvements. *The Journal of Product Innovation Management, 9*(2), 128–139.

Maidique, M. A., & Zirger, B. J. (1984). A study of success and failure in product innovation: The case of the U.S. electronics industry. *IEEE Transactions on Engineering Management, 31*(4), 192–203.

Merriam-Webster Dictionary. (2020, online). Definition for "opportunity", https://www.merriam-webster.com/dictionary/opportunity, accessed on September 1, 2020.

Moriarty, R. T., & Kosnik, T. J. (1989). High-tech concepts, continuity, and change. *IEEE Engineering Management Review, 3*(1), 25–35.

Mowery, D., & Rosenberg, N. (1979). The influence of market demand upon innovation: A critical review of some recent empirical studies. *Research Policy, 8*(2), 102–153.

Narver, J. C., & Slater, S. F. (1990). The effect of market orientation on business profitability. *Journal of Marketing, 54*(4), 20–35.

Niosi, J., & Reid, S. E. (2007). Biotechnology and nanotechnology: Science-based enabling technologies as windows of opportunity for LDCs? *World Development, 35*(3), 426–438.

OECD Working Party on Nanotechnology, Committee for Scientific and Technological Policy: *Inventory of National Science, Technology, and Innovation Policies for Nanotechnology*, 2008; *International Symposium on Assessing the Economic Impact of Nanotechnology*, 2012. www.oecd.org.

Reid, S. E., Coronini, R., & Ramani, S. V. (2014). "Evolution of nanotechnology: The science and the industry", pp. 3–36, introductory chapter. In S. V. Ramani (Ed.), *Nanotechnology and development: What's in it for emerging countries?* Cambridge University Press.

Reid, S. E., & de Brentani, U. (2010). Market vision and market visioning competence: Impact on early performance for radically new, high-tech products. *The Journal of Product Innovation Management, 27*(4), 500–518.

Rubenstein, A. H., Chakrabati, A. K., O'Keefe, R. D., Souder, W. E., & Young, H. C. (1976). Factors influencing innovation success at the project level. *Research Management, 19*(3), 15–20.

Sarasvathy, S. D. (2001). Causation and effectuation: Toward a theoretical shift from economic inevitability to entrepreneurial contingency. *Academy of Management Review, 26*(2), 243–263.

Simonse, L. (2018). *Design roadmapping: Guidebook for future foresight techniques*. BIS Publishers.

Song, M. X., & Montoya-Weiss, M. M. (1998). Critical development activities for really new versus incremental products. *The Journal of Product Innovation Management, 15*(2), 124–135.

Sowrey, T. (1989). Idea generation: Identifying the most useful techniques. *European Journal of Marketing, 24*(5), 20–29.

Stevenson, H. H., & Jarillo, J. C. (1990). A paradigm of entrepreneurship: Entrepreneurial management. *Strategic Management Journal, 11*(5), 17–27.

U.S. Census Bureau., International Database (www.census.gov/ipc/www/idb/country).

Veryzer, R. W., Jr. (1998). Discontinuous innovation and the new product development process. *The Journal of Product Innovation Management, 15*(4), 304–321.

Von Hippel, E. (1986). Lead users: A source of novel product concepts. *Management Science, 32*(7), 791–805.

Von Hippel, E. (1988). *The sources of innovation*. Oxford University Press.

Creating Vision Context: Proactive Market Orientation

Contents

© The Author(s), under exclusive license to Springer Nature Switzerland AG 2022
S. E. Reid, C. B. Crawford, *Entrepreneurial Vision*, Classroom Companion: Business,
https://doi.org/10.1007/978-3-030-77803-3_9

Learning Objectives

In ► Chap. 8, we focused on how to map out a broad industry-level opportunity for an entrepreneurial team. Now, it is time to learn more about potential markets given an entrepreneurial team's opportunity area of interest. We facilitate market learning by utilizing the two proactive market orientation (PMO) techniques introduced in the last chapter, empathic research with current customers and interviews with lead users and experts. As such, our learning objectives in this chapter are to focus on proactive market orientation and how it works, including:

1. Understanding empathic research.
2. Understanding lead users.
3. Co-creating with lead users and experts.

9.1 Proactive Market Orientation

Being proactive towards markets enables entrepreneurs to move beyond consumers' expressed needs, which, according to Christensen (1997), can sometimes be misleading. Rather than focusing on what customers can tell you, "proactive market orientation" ("PMO") (Narver et al., 2000) instead focuses either on (1) customers' latent, unarticulated needs or on (2) discovering/creating new needs. Understanding how to develop a PMO is key to understanding meaningful gaps in the market in terms of potential products and services.

The original research on "market orientation" (Deshpande & Farley, 1998; Narver & Slater, 1990), conducted with organizations, focused on three behaviors needed to lean toward markets to better understand and serve them. These behaviors included "customer orientation" (◘ Fig. 9.1), "competitor orientation," and "inter-functional coordination" (i.e., between different departments to ensure good communication around consumer needs).

While a market orientation is vital to ensuring customer satisfaction and loyalty, it tends to focus on the needs which customers express to companies related to their current products and, therefore, represents a reactive form of behavior on the part of manufacturers (Christensen & Bower, 1996; Frosch, 1996; Reid & de Brentani, 2010).

Expressed needs and solutions are those which a customer is aware of and can express. A simple example would be a person needing to purchase a warm ski suit in an alpine sports store because they are on a ski trip. The problem is that this type of need and related solution can be anticipated easily by all companies in the marketplace, and, therefore, firms working on solutions for expressed needs tend to offer similar benefits to a set of customers and, as such, offer only limited competitive advantage, if any at all.

To advance marketers' ability to be more focused on the future, Narver et al. (2000) put forth a new construct, which they labeled "proactive market orientation." Based on its focus on customers' latent needs, proactive market orientation is a better tool for developing Market Visioning Competence in the case of new innovations which consumers may not have experience with or understanding of (Reid & de Brentani, 2010), as is the case for many startups.

■ **Fig. 9.1** Conceptual image to portray "customer orientation." (Source: Image licensed and downloaded from Adobe Stock on August 4, 2020. Credit: by Martin Barraud/KOTO/▸ stock.adobe.com. License Link: ▸ https://stock.adobe.com/ca/images/businesswoman-listening-to-headphones-at-desk/357278458)

PMO may involve two main methods:

1. Conducting empathic research to understand customers' latent needs.
2. Conducting research with lead users and experts to discover/create new needs.

9.1.1 Empathic Research with Current Customers

We can utilize certain tools to get at what are described above as the "latent needs" of consumers, or in other words, those needs which they are sometimes unaware of. Many consumer goods companies such as 3M and design companies such as IDEO have benefited from using a variety of techniques to understand latent needs. In *Designing Interactions* (2007), Bill Moggridge of IDEO (with contributions from Jane Fulton Suri and Duane Bray) describes the importance of the process of bringing together multidisciplinary teams which include psychologists, sociologists, ethnographers, and designers, in order to uncover underlying latent needs requiring a solution.

Some researchers have referred to this type of research as "empathic research" (Leonard & Rayport, 1997). In the design realm, much of the groundwork for this field of human-centered approaches to design was developed by Jane Fulton Suri, whose background was in psychology and architecture. She is now (as of the writing of this text) a creative director and managing partner at IDEO. Through using

Fig. 9.2 Conceptual image to portray "observation." (Source: Image licensed and downloaded from Adobe Stock on August 4, 2020. Credit: by Axel Bueckert/▸ stock.adobe.com. License Link: ▸ https://stock.adobe.com/ca/228352681)

empathic techniques such as re-enactments, discourse, and direct observation (Fig. 9.2), she has discovered many user issues requiring solutions. These include finding answers to questions such as why there are so many accidents with lawnmowers or why a portable defibrillator could be a life-saving device for so many people (Fulton Suri, 2000).

Finding current customers from a given market to contact and observe during product use may be a straightforward exercise for a company already serving those customers. That said, the work of approaching and working with current customers to conduct experimental research is still challenging. The basic idea behind empathic research is that we need to listen and probe for latent needs, rather than simply work with expressed needs. This takes skill, patience, time, and often, several reiterations to revisit and observe subjects to fill in gaps for understanding their latent needs. See Verplank et al. (1993) for a useful tutorial guide on *Observation and Invention*.

According to the Merriam-Webster dictionary (2020, online), "latent" means "present and capable of emerging or developing but not now visible, obvious, active, or, symptomatic." As such, latent needs in a marketing context involve potential customer needs which are not yet visible, obvious, or active. Latent needs, therefore, may be subdivided further into two types:

1. Those needs which the customer is completely unaware of.
2. The customer may be aware of certain problems, but there is no current apparent way to resolve them.

9.1.1.1 Discovering Latent Needs Through Observation (What Do you Need/Want?)

One good example of empathic design in the case of customers being unaware of their needs comes from an interview with Smart Design co-founder Davin Stowell, conducted by Warren Berger and described in his book *Glimmer* (Berger, 2009). One of the projects Stowell worked on was initiated by an entrepreneur who, in response to watching his wife struggle with using a potato peeler had developed a better understanding of the challenges of those who, like her, deal with arthritis. After having visited the local arthritis foundation to observe and speak with more people, they designed the OXO Good Grips peeler (◘ Fig. 9.3). Doing this enabled them to create a new design that was significantly more functional and that, as Stowell said in the interview (Berger, 2009, p. 114), "as soon as you looked at it, you just wanted to squeeze it."

An example of customers being aware of existing challenges (◘ Fig. 9.4), sometimes with improved solutions from one generation to the next, is in the household cleaning products industry. There is always a question, however, as to what genuinely optimal household cleaning solutions might look like where housework might

◘ **Fig. 9.3** OXO Good Grips peelers. (Source: Image licensed and downloaded from Adobe Stock on April 24, 2020. Credit: by kurizo/► stock.adobe.com. License Link: ► https://stock.adobe.com/ca/297154888)

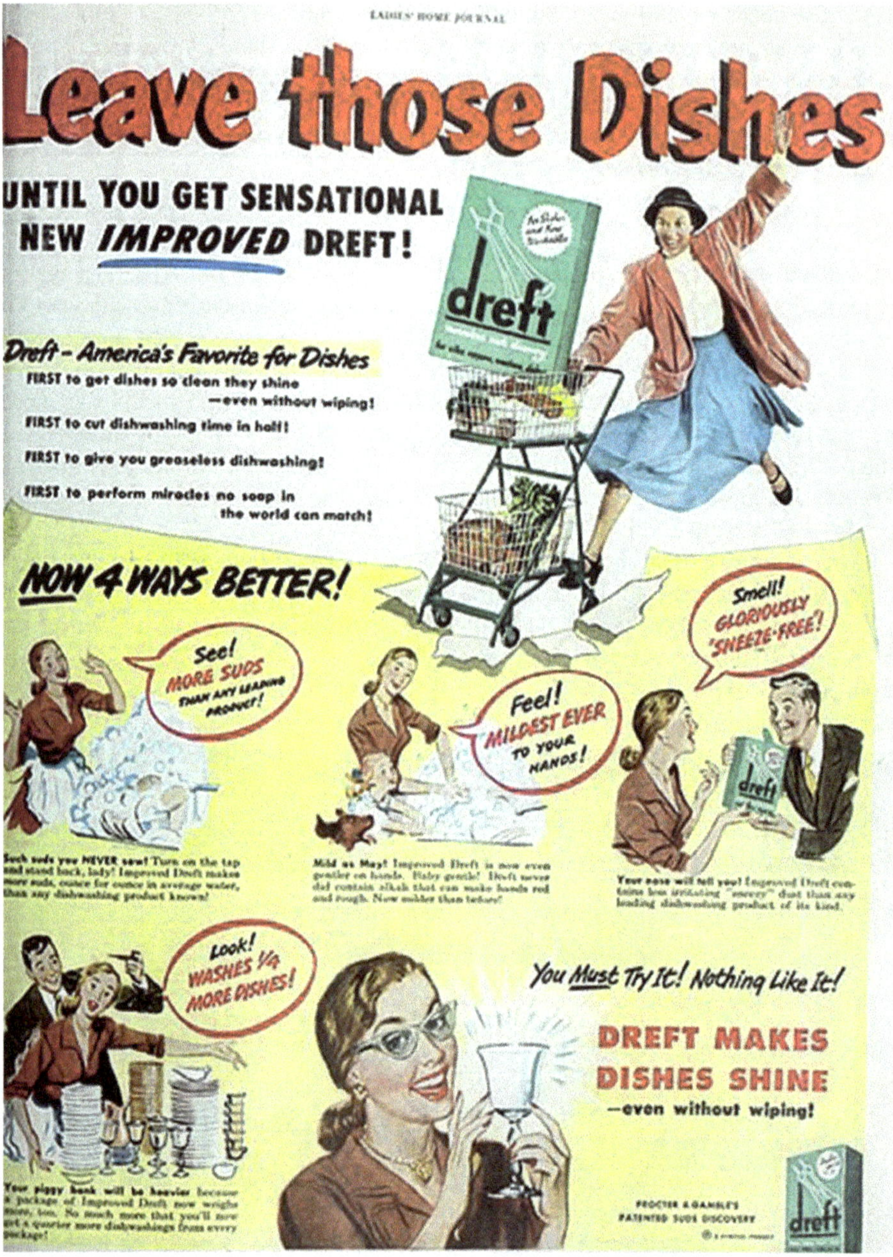

■ **Fig. 9.4** Dreft print commercial. (Source: ► https://commons.wikimedia.org/wiki/File:The_Ladies%27_home_journal_(1948)_(14766679855).jpg. Downloaded via Wikimedia Commons on August 4, 2020. Public Domain)

be accomplished exponentially faster and more easily. According to a *Wall Street Journal* article (Nelson, 2001), in order to understand their customers better, P&G visited approximately 80 households and filmed their behavior over a period of time. This allowed the P&G team to better understand a variety of issues faced by participants during cleaning and other household activities, particularly those which a focus group might not readily consider relevant or salient enough to bring up during an interview removed from the activities involved with household chores.

9.1.1.2 Discovering Latent Needs by Monitoring Complaints and Through Suggestion Boxes (What's Wrong? Or What Could Be Improved?)

Another way to find latent needs, in the case where problems are understood by consumers, is to look at complaints or suggestions on social media or in reviews. These can reveal knowledge about ease of use (or lack thereof) or even suggestions that customers make directly about their problems or what they would like to see changed or added to in a product. It's amazing to look online at the discussion feeds of user groups (which may or may not be linked to the corporate website they are discussing).

Just as one example, Strava is an app used by running (and other sports) enthusiasts to log activities and interact with other members of the community. Over time, discussions emerge between community members which sometimes become fodder for new ideas. For example, ideas which have been incorporated and have evolved over time include having local segments on which runners can record how they do over time, on both speed and frequency—and related to that, honoring local legends based on frequency. Site stickiness can be enhanced by adding suggestions made by customers. As such, companies can benefit from paying attention to such discussion threads and feedback.

9.1.1.3 Discovering Latent Needs by Working with Customers Operating Ahead of the Curve (Where Do You Hope to Go?)

With some customers, instead of asking "what do you want?" or "what could be improved?", perhaps a better question may be "where do you hope to go?" This helps you to figure out what some of the possibilities might be and then to develop products accordingly. Zeroing in on details such as when someone appears to be paying a lot of attention to one specific thing and spending more time on a task or is apparently frustrated or excited by something can lead to interesting insights.

Research on leading customers sometimes focuses on key influencers such as "market mavens" who have the potential to influence others' buying behavior. Feick and Price (1987, p. 83) emphasize that the difference between "market mavens" and other types of influencers like opinion leaders and early adopters is that their influence is not explicitly based on product expertise, "but rather on more general knowledge and experience with markets." They call these types of influencers "market mavens" and define them (Feick & Price, 1987, p. 85) as "individuals who have information about many kinds of products, places to shop, and other facets of markets, and initiate discussion with consumers and respond to requests from consumers for market information."

By focusing on market mavens, companies can reap the advantages of network effects by observing, listening to, and asking clever, probing questions of these types of customers.

In some cases, individuals experiencing needs ahead of the curve decide to actively develop solutions through their own efforts. These individuals are referred to as "lead users" (von Hippel, 1986), and they may either attempt to commercialize the fruits of their efforts or use their own solutions without necessarily looking to commercialize them.

As one example, Kim Cole started the company, Gleener (makers of smart fabric care and laundry solutions), out of her own frustrations with buying sweaters. Typically, a more expensive clothing item, sweaters quickly "pill," get covered in pet fur, and/or not look nearly as nice as when first purchased. To resolve this issue, Cole developed "The Gleener" (◘ Fig. 9.5), the "Ultimate Fuzz Remover," a lightweight, environmentally friendly device (i.e., no batteries or electricity required!) for quickly "gleening" a sweater so that it would look nearly new again. The product was a runaway success and resonated with people everywhere, gaining distribution from Bed Bath & Beyond through to the Home Shopping Channel.

9.1.2 Working with Lead Users

MIT's Eric von Hippel (1986) has focused on identifying "lead users" to discover and create new needs hand in hand with consumers/users themselves. These lead

◘ **Fig. 9.5** "The Gleener." (Source: downloaded from company website on August 4, 2020. Permission granted for use by business owner, Kim Cole, on December 2, 2020)

users are individuals who work as a kind of lightning rod for understanding the needs that are likely to develop for others like them in the future. What puts them in the lead is that they, for whatever reason, expect to receive important benefits (not necessarily of the monetary sort) in some way by helping to develop a new idea, technology, product, or service. As a result, as noted in von Hippel et al. (1999), these individuals experience and/or understand needs well ahead of the majority of other potential customers/users (◘ Fig. 9.6).

Not only do lead users understand needs ahead of the curve, but they also lead with respect to using, and/or developing, trailblazing usages of novel technologies, products, and/or services, often far ahead of adoption by the mass market. For example, a lead user for new ski equipment might be a skier on a college racing team (◘ Fig. 9.7).

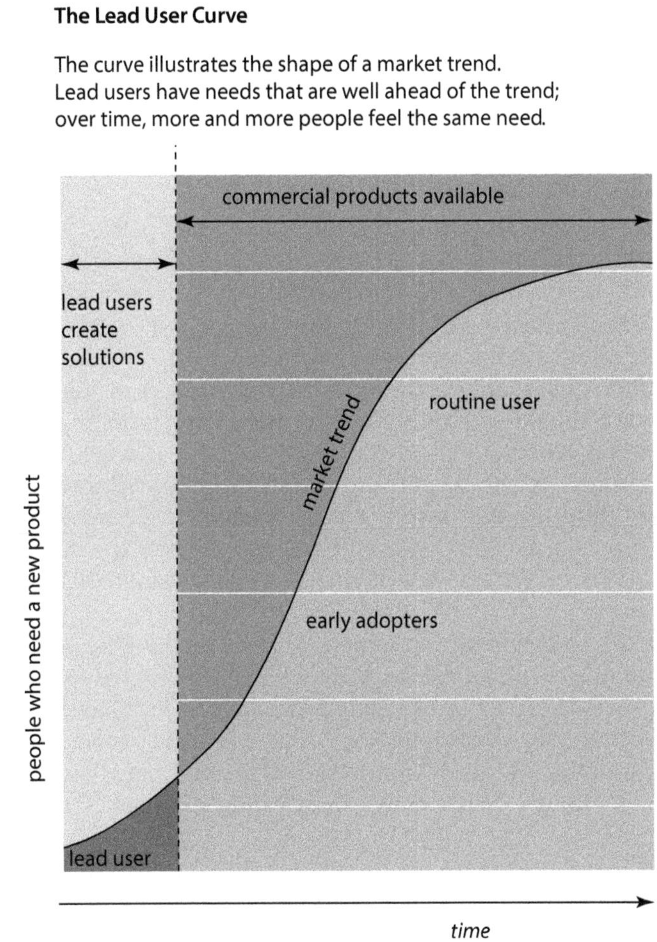

◘ **Fig. 9.6** The lead user curve. (Reprinted by permission of Harvard Business Review. (Exhibit) From "Creating Breakthroughs at 3M" by Eric von Hippel, Stefan Thomke, and Mary Sonnack, September–October 1999. Copyright ©1999 by Harvard Business Publishing; all rights reserved)

Fig. 9.7 Conceptual image to portray a "ski racer." (Source: Licensed and downloaded from Adobe Stock on January 20, 2019. Credit: by kapona/▶ stock.adobe.com. License Link: ▶ https://stock.adobe.com/ca/232819101)

Indeed, as noted in Henkel and von Hippel (2004, p. 75), "Urban and von Hippel (1988) found that 82% of the lead-user cluster in their sample had developed their own version of or had modified the specific type of industrial product they employed while only 1% of the non-lead users had done this," and these lead user activities resulted in major functional improvements for those in their study. Since many industrial markets consist of a small number of high volume firms, special attention should be given to the needs of these types of users under the industrial market context. This also illustrates that it is important to consider that lead users may not only be individuals, but they could also be corporate buyers/consumers from the B2B sector. As an example, in *Creating Breakthroughs at 3M* (von Hippel et al., 1999), the authors describe how if a car manufacturer wanted a new braking system, they might ask a racing team to help with its development.

An example of a company that went out to not just look for lead users, but to "create" them, was Nike's global soccer business. Nike wanted to create a unique competitive advantage in terms of selling soccer-related merchandise (Fig. 9.8). In order to do this, they created the "SQUAD," a global community of teen football/soccer fans. Over 100 teens from 10 countries co-created with Nike's global marketing team through the company Sense Worldwide to help shape the future of soccer.

As an example of setting the bar by working with internal corporate lead users, when asked about the launch of the iPad, Steve Jobs said "Apple never holds focus groups. It doesn't ask people what they want; it tells them what they're going to want next" (Fry, 2010a). In Fry's 2010 interview with Jonathan Ive (Fry, 2010b),

Fig. 9.8 Nike soccer ball. (Source: ▶ https://commons.wikimedia.org/wiki/File:2020_Nike_Merlin_CBF.jpg Attribution: Ik ben groot/CC BY-SA (▶ https://creativecommons.org/licenses/by-sa/4.0). Created on February 4, 2020. Downloaded via Wikimedia Commons on May 28, 2020)

who then was leading design on the iPad, he further espoused the Apple perspective that "It's not for us to predict what others will do…we have to concentrate on what we think is right and offer it up."

So, not only do lead users (including those working within companies) provide access to richer ideas and information on emerging customer needs in a given market, but they may also be able to help develop better products and service concepts than traditional market research, and do so ahead of the competition (von Hippel, 1986).

One significant question people often ask is "how to identify lead users?" Churchill et al. (2009, p. 9, Creative Commons License 3.0), in their *Lead User Project Handbook: A Practical Guide for Lead User Project Teams*, distinguish three main types of "lead users" which include those (1) "lead users in the *applica-*

tion and target market," (2) "lead users of similar applications in advanced 'analog' markets," and (3) "lead users with respect to important *attributes* of problems faced by users in the target market."

9.1.2.1 "Lead Users in the *Application* and Target Market" (Churchill et al., 2009, p. 9)

The first type of lead user belongs in the target application which includes those users/consumers who may have experimented with developing their own prototypes and products.

An example of this type of lead user, which experiments and creates their own prototypes, is the founder of the product Olio Lusso, Linda Rodin. Rodin created a self-named line of skincare oils (◘ Fig. 9.9). As a former model, she was aware of the industry, had apparently always been "into oils," and wanted to experiment and make some skincare oils for herself, initially (Into the Gloss, 2010), until they became a success in the marketplace.

In other words, lead users sometimes innovate on their own. For example, according to von Hippel (1988), 20% of mountain bikers modify their own equipment (◘ Fig. 9.10) and 18% of university-based surgeons modify their tools and equipment.

◘ **Fig. 9.9** Conceptual image to portray "experimenting with oil-based natural skincare solutions." (Source: Image licensed and downloaded from Adobe Stock on August 14, 2020. Credit: by paulynn/▶ stock.adobe.com. License Link: ▶ https://stock.adobe.com/ca/187290417)

◘ Fig. 9.10 Mountain biking. (Source: ▸ https://commons.wikimedia.org/wiki/File:MountainBiking_MtHoodNF.jpg. Attribution: Jim Semlor/Public domain. Downloaded via Wikimedia Commons on May 28, 2020)

9.1.2.2 "Lead Users of Similar Applications in Advanced 'Analog' Markets" (Churchill et al., 2009, p. 9)

The second type of lead user is comprised of users and developers/manufacturers in analogous markets, i.e., in fields with similar applications.

For example, the primary attribute of computer servers (◘ Fig. 9.11) and air conditioners (◘ Fig. 9.12) is their cooling system technology, and therefore, producers in both sectors can likely help one another with similar technological problems.

Another excellent example of this is provided by Keinz and Prügl (2010), developers of the "Intelligent Search for Additional Applications Method", in their description of working with the company RallyPoint, an MIT startup. They worked together to come up with a first application for a glove as part of an overall sensor system for military personnel. The main benefit was that users wearing the

Fig. 9.11 Computer server storage room. (Source: Image licensed and downloaded from Adobe Stock on August 5, 2020. Credit: by senticus/▶ stock.adobe.com. License Link: ▶ https://stock.adobe.com/ca/26807738)

glove could perform tasks such as driving a car or carrying a weapon without having to remove their hands and could at the same time issue tactical commands using simple hand and arm gestures. Through traditional brainstorming, two additional markets outside the military field with analogous needs were identified: firefighters and police officers. Just like military personnel, they tend to get into situations where they need to speak into a microphone/radio while their hands are occupied with other devices. According to Keinz and Prügl (2010), abstract problem descriptions were posted in 37 online communities related to analogous markets which had been identified by experts (using a "pyramiding search technique" of von Hippel et al., 2009). Their search resulted in 32 valid applications for RallyPoint's technology, from fields as diverse as welding and underwater photography to maintenance of high-voltage power lines to virtual rehabilitation.

9.1.2.3 "Lead Users with Respect to Important Attributes of Problems Faced by Users in the Target Market" (Churchill et al., 2009, p. 9)

This type of lead user stems from the greater community interested in developing solutions for users and may include users themselves, designers, fabricators, engineers, and enthusiasts, as well as people from associations, suppliers, retailers, and so on.

The main thing is that in this case, from a more global perspective on solutions development, this broader range of lead users (i.e., beyond users in the target mar-

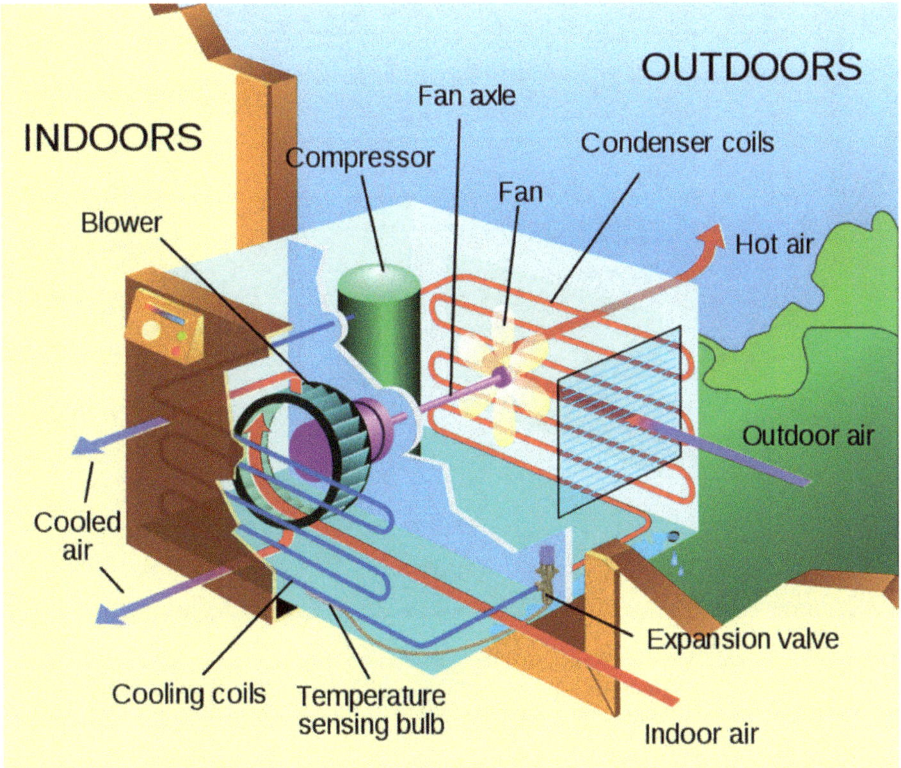

Fig. 9.12 Air-conditioning cooling system technology. (Source: ► https://commons.wikimedia.org/wiki/File:Air_conditioning_unit-en.svg. Attribution: Pbroks13 / CC BY (► https://creativecommons.org/licenses/by/3.0). Created November 14, 2008. Downloaded via Wikimedia Commons on May 28, 2020)

ket) understand and are involved with the more salient attributes of opportunities and/or problems faced by early consumers in the target market (Burgelman et al., 2004; von Hippel, 1986).

An excellent example of this is Local Motors' Rally Fighter (Fig. 9.13), initially launched in 2009. The car is a four-speed automatic which was the first car to be developed using co-creation design utilizing votes from the community interested in developing and producing rally cars which would be "street legal." According to the blog, Bless This Stuff (2020, website), the exterior design was submitted by Sangho Kim who won the most community votes.

Such examples point to the fact that there are "user innovation communities" (von Hippel, 2001) filled with lead users. Not only do they bring their expertise, keen interest, and ideas to the community, but they often develop collaborative toolkits for products. Shah (2000), Franke and Shah (2001), and von Hippel (2001) have described the example of kitesurfing (or "high-performance windsurfing") as a strong user innovation community (Fig. 9.14), where users have actively shared their designs since the incarnation of the sport.

Fig. 9.13 Local Motors' Rally Fighter. (Source: ▸ https://commons.wikimedia.org/wiki/File:Rally_Fighter_Local_Motors_1.jpg. Attribution: ▸ https://www.flickr.com/photos/markus941// CC BY (▸ https://creativecommons.org/licenses/by/2.0). Created on August 9, 2011. Downloaded via Wikimedia Commons on January 21, 2018)

The reason for having many people collaborate and co-create in this fashion is that everyone has a different perspective. With a larger group of potential solutions and ideas, you have a greater chance of solving major problems, even potentially "wicked problems"—i.e., those which are extremely difficult (and potentially impossible) to solve, such as world hunger. The distributed lead user solution model has much better odds of solving difficult problems than more traditional manufacturer-based solutions due to the much larger number of potential solutions and perspectives that can be brought into play. As mentioned in previous chapters, the broader your network—especially if it consists of weak ties—the higher your chances of stumbling upon unprecedented ideas by combining your different experiences.

9.2 Co-Creation

The idea of co-creation platforms to help user innovation communities has also really taken off, driven by both companies looking to co-create with users and, also, by creators and users themselves. If you think about it, in the past, companies used many types of loyalty programs and structural ties (e.g., charging lower price to volume customers, adding service, dedicated use of customer relationship management (CRM), and long-term contracts) in order to attract and retain custom-

Fig. 9.14 Kitesurfing. (Source: ▶ https://commons.wikimedia.org/wiki/File:Kitesurfing_near_Prasonisi._Rhodes,_Greece.jpg Attribution: Ввласенко / CC BY-SA (▶ https://creativecommons.org/licenses/by-sa/3.0). Created on September 17, 2013. Downloaded via Wikimedia Commons on May 28, 2020)

ers. A major advantage of co-creation platforms is that they enable prospective consumers to voluntarily participate in early product design, and in this way, partnerships and advocacy can occur before a person or company even becomes a customer.

"Co-creation" (Fig. 9.15) as it is now known (Prahalad & Ramaswamy, 2000) has been referred to over time using many names and is related to many concepts including "co-production," "value constellations" (Normann & Ramírez, 1993), "mass customization" or "customerization" (Fuart Firat et al., 1995), "open innovation" (Chesbrough, 2003), and "mass collaboration" (Tapscott & Williams, 2006).

9.2.1 Co-Creation Facilitated through an Intermediary

One example of co-creation exists when a company or an individual entrepreneur looks to work with designers, users, experts, or other interested parties to solicit input for creative aspects of new product development, and does so using a platform operated by an intermediary. The intermediary creates such a co-creation platform based on crowdsourcing. In other words, the creative input may come from anyone from professional to novice, and it is up to the buyer to decide on the ideas which they receive through the process.

Fig. 9.15 Conceptual image to portray "co-creation." (Source: Image licensed and downloaded from Shutterstock on May 5, 2013. Credit: by sommthink/▸ Shutterstock.com. License Link: ▸ https://www.shutterstock.com/image-illustration/well-coordinated-work-51871312)

The aforementioned type of platform includes companies such as "eYeka" (▸ https://en.eyeka.com/) or "99designs" (▸ http://99designs.ca/). Input might include anything from ideation for product or service concepts to designs for packaging and marketing campaigns. There is usually a creative design aspect with the potential for a high level of variability in input. A progressive selection mechanism is used, including a culling process with the ability to send the early design options out to focus groups or friends to get votes on the design. Once a designer is selected for moving forward with for finalization, options for output in terms of size and format may be selected (e.g., banners, labels, posters, business cards, etc. might be desired output from a creative branding exercise).

9.2.2 Co-Creation Directly between Company and Customers

Sometimes, a company will start the co-creation process directly with lead users and customers (rather than using an intermediary platform). For example, Lego has used this technique for many years with their fan clubs of innovators. Several years ago, Lego launched Lego Mindstorms. From there, Lego Moonbase (◘ Fig. 9.16) was launched, a collaborative social activity sponsored by Lego.

9.2.3 Co-Creation with Experts

In this situation, experts often need to meet specific participation criteria, and there are sometimes technical issues to be resolved. The company or individual decides on the experts whom they will work with to come up with solutions to their problems or new product development work. This form of co-creation is particularly suitable for complex situations involving standards development or roadmaps for technologies where the cost of development is too high for any one player to sustain. For example, 3M, long a proponent of lead user techniques, often looks to work in partnership with such experts to create next-level innovations.

◘ **Fig. 9.16** Lego Moonbase. (Source: ► https://commons.wikimedia.org/wiki/File:Lego_Completed_Moonbase_-_BrickCon_2008_-_Seattle_Center_Exhibition_Hall_-_Seattle,_Washington.jpg. Attribution: B Mauro/CC BY (► https://creativecommons.org/licenses/by/2.0). Created on October 4, 2008. Downloaded via Wikimedia Commons on May 29, 2020)

9.3 How to Cold Call Lead Users and Experts

Now that you have some idea of where to start looking for potential lead user and expert contacts, the next step is to create a list of questions that you would like to ask them once you make contact in order to perform in-depth interviews. The objective of contacting lead users and experts is to obtain a better understanding of the most salient needs of potential future customers in a potential target market (i.e., needs which the lead user will be experiencing ahead of the curve or that the expert may be anticipating). As described, lead users and experts have specific qualities that make them good early market contacts. Essentially, this step serves as a deep dive into the most urgent needs being experienced by the lead users or anticipated by experts in your area of interest.

You should contact as many lead users and experts as you are able to identify and have time to interview and then document the ensuing discussions. It is also recommended that you give the lead users and experts at least 1 week prior to interviews to reflect on explanations of your early ideas. After the interviews, make sure to write up a summary of the key points made by the lead users and experts during the interviews. This should include benefits they consider necessary to achieve a minimum viable product/service (MVP) for future customers.

If you or your team members are fortunate enough to already have a "warm introduction" to speak with key lead users or experts, perhaps through your personal board of directors or advisory board, then the task is, on some level, less intimidating. However, in many cases, you will need to start by making the dreaded "cold call."

In follow-up surveys with students who have taken our entrepreneurship courses, we found that one of the most challenging aspects for students is making that first cold call. After they had done it once, though, they found that the task became more manageable. The interesting thing was that while many found the task very intimidating, they also found that the information provided during such interviews was some of the most salient information they received during the course of their research activities. The students found that it enhanced their knowledge around their industry of interest, as well as heightening awareness related to potential key benefits for potential consumers.

So, given its importance, but also considering the challenges people experience when making such calls, we have put together Worksheet 10, with some suggested prompt questions for your first lead user/expert interviews to make it slightly less daunting. While it is sometimes challenging to get people's attention upfront due to their daily time pressures and demands for their attention, if they say yes, people are usually very helpful and will generally provide further suggestions for other people to speak to.

Worksheet 10: Prompt Questions for Lead User Interviews

Types of questions to consider including

1. Warm-up Discussion and Your Background/Interest
    a. Thank you for coming and introductions.
    b. Brief explanation of what you hope to achieve with the interview including a brief explanation about your context (i.e., you are conducting the interview as part of an entrepreneurship course, as a networking exercise, to start a business, etc.) and the 3 potential industry/market opportunities for differentiation you have identified.
    c. Give them a bit of a background on how/why you got interested in the field and why the particular opportunity areas you have chosen are of interest to examine further.
2. Background Questions:
    a. "Can you tell us a bit about your story and how you got involved in this area?"
    b. "If you are working in this field, how long have you been working and in which capacities?"
    c. "We consider you to be a lead user in our field of interest because….; are we on the right track with our assessment?"
3. Industry/Field-Specific Questions:
    a. "What do you consider to be the most important developments in the last 5 years in this area/in the next 5-10 years?"
    b. "What are the most important new technologies in the area?" (if not discussed already)
    c. "Are there any demographic or social changes expected to impact the future landscape?"
    d. "Are there any important government initiatives which I/we should be aware of?"
    e. "What challenges do you experience in this field where you would like to see some new solutions developed? Are many other people experiencing this issue? What types?
    f. "Are you trying to work on any solutions yourself related to this challenge?"
    g. "Who do you consider to be the most important people in the industry and why?"
    h. "What areas would you suggest a startup like us/entrepreneurs focus on?"
4. Other Questions:
    a. "Which publications, books, conferences, and associations in the field do you feel are the best to read/join?"
    b. "Is there anyone else you suggest we speak with about our interests? Would you be willing to provide an introduction (if they know the person) or, would it be ok to use your name when introducing ourselves?"
    c. "Would we be able to contact you in future with further questions?"

© Susan E. Reid and Charles B. Crawford, August 14,2020.

While preparing for lead user interviews, here are 11 suggestions to help:

1. If possible, use a formal letter to make first contact; this gives you something specific to refer to when you make the first cold call.
2. Try very hard to meet people face to face; it makes a world of difference to how well they will remember you and the nature of the information you are able to elicit.
3. Make sure you are prepared for your interviews! You do not want to waste anyone's time.
4. Keep the appointment as brief as possible while still getting the job done (1-hour max).
5. Decide what information you want to find out from the interview and design questions that will specifically draw out this information.
6. Use a recording device if your interviewee does not mind; you will be better able to focus on the discussion at hand, rather than taking notes.
7. If the contact has questions for you that you cannot answer, promise to get back to them with an answer and follow up!
8. People are looking for benefits for themselves in all situations; actively listen for opportunities to be able to provide your interviewee with ideas or contacts they may not have; look for mutual points of interest and direct the conversation accordingly.
9. Don't try to ask too many questions.
10. Let people talk and listen!
11. Always follow up with a proper thank-you note (i.e., hard copy in the mail—which means you need to ask for an address to which you can send a follow-up). This is one of the best pieces of advice our mothers ever gave us (thank you mom)!

Chapter Review Questions

1. What are customer *latent needs* and why are they important to understand?
2. List three ways to assess customers' latent needs. Provide an example for each.
3. What is meant by *lead users*? Give a concrete example to describe what a lead user might be in a specific industry.
4. Explain in your own words the three main different types of lead users.
5. Provide an example of a user innovation community and provide details of the nature of some of the innovations which have come about as a result of developments from the community.
6. List the three types of co-creation described and give your own example for each of the three types.

References

Berger, W. (2009). *Glimmer: How design can transform your life and maybe even the world*. Random House Canada.

Bless This Stuff. (2020, website). https://www.blessthisstuff.com/stuff/vehicles/cars/rally-fighter/.

Burgelman, R. A., Christensen, C., & Wheelwright, S. C. (2004). *Strategic management of technology and innovation* (4th ed.). McGraw-Hill Education.

Chesbrough, H. (2003). *Open innovation: The new imperative for creating and profiting from technology*. Harvard Business School Press.

Christensen, C. M. (1997). *The innovator's dilemma*. Harvard Business School Press.

Christensen, C. M., & Bower, J. (1996). Customer power, strategic investment, and the failure of leading firms. *Strategic Management Journal, 17*(3), 197–218.

Churchill, J., von Hippel, E., & Sonnack, M. (2009). *Lead user project handbook: A practical guide for lead user project teams* (pp. 1–162). Creative Commons License 3.0 (and derivatives). Downloaded through SCRIBD.

Deshpande, R., & Farley, J. (1998). Measuring market orientation: Generalization and synthesis. *Journal of Market-Focused Management, 2*(3), 213–232.

Feick, L. F., & Price, L. L. (1987). The market maven: A diffuser of marketplace information. *Journal of Marketing, 51*(1), 83–97.

Franke, N., & Shah, S. (2001). How community matters for user innovation: The "open source" of sports innovation. *MIT Sloan Working Paper* #4164, April 2001.

Frosch, R. (1996). The customer for R&D is always wrong! *Research-Technology Management, 39*(6), 22–27.

Fry, S. (2010a). The iPad Launch: Can Steve Jobs do it again? Time.com, Thursday, April 1, 2010.

Fry, S. (2010b). On the mothership. *Time Magazine, 175*(14), 40–43.

Fuart Firat, A., Dholakia, N., & Venkatesh, A. (1995). Marketing in a postmodern world. *European Journal of Marketing, 29*(1), 40–56.

Fulton Suri, J. (2000). Saving lives through design. *Ergonomics in Design: The Quarterly of Human Factors Applications, 8*(3), 4–12.

Henkel, J., & von Hippel, E. (2004). Welfare implications of user innovation. *The Journal of Technology Transfer, 20*(1), 78–87.

Into the Gloss (2010). Linda Rodin – Olio Lusso, Linda Russo interview as told to ITG, https://intothegloss.com/2010/11/linda-rodin-olio-lusso, downloaded on August 14, 2020.

Keinz, P., & Prügl, R. (2010). A user community-based approach to leveraging technological competences: An exploratory case study of a technology start-up at MIT. *Creativity and Innovation Management Journal, 19*(3), 269–289.

Leonard, D., & Rayport, J. F. (1997). Spark innovation through empathic design. *Harvard Business Review, 75*(6), 102–113.

Merriam-Webster Dictionary (2020, online). Definition for 'latent needs', retrieved on August 21, 2020, https://www.merriam-webster.com/dictionary/latent.

Moggridge, B. (2007). *Designing interactions*. MIT Press.

Narver, J. C., & Slater, S. F. (1990). The effect of market orientation on business profitability. *Journal of Marketing, 54*(4), 20–35.

Narver, J.C., Slater, S.F., & MacLachlan, D.L. (2000). Total market orientation, business performance and innovation. *Marketing Science Institute Working Paper* No. 00-116.

Nelson, E. (2001). P&G plans to visit people's homes to record (almost) all their habits. *The Wall Street Journal* (online), May 17, 2001 (updated): https://www.wsj.com/articles/SB990052006887981055.

Normann, R., & Ramírez, R. (1993). From value chain to value constellation: Designing interactive strategy. *Harvard Business Review, 71*(4), 65–77.

Prahalad, C. K., & Ramaswamy, V. (2000). Co-opting customer competence. *Harvard Business Review, 78*(1), 79–90.

Reid, S. E., & de Brentani, U. (2010). Market vision and market visioning competence: Impact on early performance for radically new, high-tech products. *Journal of Product Innovation Management, 27*(4), 500–518.

Shah, S. (2000). Sources and patterns of innovation in a consumer products field: Innovations in sporting equipment. *MIT Sloan Working Paper* #4105.

Tapscott, D., & Williams, A. D. (2006). *Wikinomics: How mass collaboration changes everything*. Portfolio.

Urban, G. L., & von Hippel, E. (1988). Lead user analyses for the development of new industrial products. *Management Science, 34*(5), 569–582.

Verplank, B., Fulton, J., Black, A., & Moggridge, B. (1993). *Observation and invention: Use of scenarios in interaction design.* Tutorial Notes from INTERCHI'93 (pp. 1–80), Amsterdam, Monday April 26, 1993.

von Hippel, E. (1986). Lead users: A source of novel product concepts. *Management Science, 32*(7), 791–805.

von Hippel, E. (1988). *The sources of innovation*. Oxford University Press.

von Hippel, E. (2001). Innovation by user communities: Learning from open-source software. *MIT Sloan Management Review, 42*(4), 82–86.

von Hippel, E., Franke, N., & Prügl, R. (2009). Pyramiding: Efficient search for rare subjects. *Research Policy, 38*(9), 1397–1406.

von Hippel, E., Thomke, S., & Sonnack, M. (1999). Creating breakthroughs at 3M. *Harvard Business Review, 77*(5), 47–57.

Creating Vision Context: Using Market Learning Tools

Contents

© The Author(s), under exclusive license to Springer Nature Switzerland AG 2022

S. E. Reid, C. B. Crawford, *Entrepreneurial Vision*, Classroom Companion: Business, https://doi.org/10.1007/978-3-030-77803-3_10

Learning Objectives

In ► Chap. 9, we learned about how to facilitate market learning by using proactive market orientation techniques such as empathic research with current customers and interviews with lead users and experts. Sometimes, however, in-depth interaction with existing customers or with lead users is challenging to achieve, especially in the case where market context is low and/or technology development is involved. Here in ► Chap. 10, we examine market learning tools for these scenarios.

Our aims in this chapter are to:

1. Explain why there are some scenarios where it is difficult to learn about customer needs.
2. Gain an understanding of alternative market learning tools available.
3. Learn about three primary forms of ideation.
4. Focus in on morphological analysis as one form of ideation and learn how it works.
5. Learn about the importance of "attributes" and "determinant attributes."

10.1 Market Learning Tools

10 In many cases, potential new technologies and/or markets are in such early stages of development that deep interaction with customers, even of the empathic sort, may not be a possibility and, as a result, forecasting may seem a little like using a crystal ball (◘ Fig. 10.1). As noted in Reid and de Brentani (2010, p. 507): "Other techniques for market learning need to be employed" in such cases.

The main reasons why it is sometimes challenging to learn about latent customer needs are because the technologies are being developed for the business-to-business ("B2B") sector, the technologies are in a very early stage of development, or the needs don't exist yet in the marketplace. While it might be theoretically possible to project the development of a market for an early-stage technology or to see how a current market might be better served, it is often more about the "hopes and dreams" of the technology visionary than about latent needs requiring a solution. In this case, it is possible that lead users may be identified, although this may only come after a period of technological development.

Several key steps typically occur in the technology community as a discontinuous innovation starts to make its way to an unknown marketplace:

1. A language is developed among the early developers and users of the technology as pattern recognition is taking place so that ideas can be shared in a meaningful way.
2. There is usually some recognition of the various roles to be played in the emerging new sector by material makers/suppliers, toolmakers, device makers, service providers, and so on.
3. An ecosystem will begin to develop and coalesce, made up of universities, financial institutions, V.C.s, governments, and the public that will support and be a part of the developing sector.

Fig. 10.1 Conceptual image to portray "forecasting using a crystal ball." (Source: Image licensed and downloaded from Shutterstock on April 24, 2020. Credit: by wavebreakmedia/▸ Shutterstock.com. License Link: ▸ https://www.shutterstock.com/image-photo/businessman-forecasting-crystal-ball-office-303688010)

As such, the need to share meaningful information, among this growing community, requires rallying around shared concepts, and one of the challenges with doing this is building concepts about what the potential market spaces might be for the developing technology.

Several researchers (e.g., Hamel & Prahalad, 1994; Leifer et al., 2000) point out that the combinatorial thinking behind developing a "techno-market insight" comes from both the technical characterization of the problem and the ability to identify the compelling benefits of that technology and characterize them from the perspective of a market that may not yet exist, or for which early insights are just starting to emerge (Reid & de Brentani, 2010). Similarly, in the case of market- or service-based innovations, it is necessary to develop market insight where market context is low. In the case where there is an absence of focus on technology, the flash of market-related understanding often comes down to how attributes can match with potential benefits (through new design, new configurations, etc.), and so, in this case, we can call it the "attribute-market insight."

We like to refer to such a market, at this stage, as the "proto-market," meaning the earliest version of the market. Not only is there the case where the market does not yet exist for a given technology/product, but also, your spin on what will be delivered will decide which existing market(s) might respond to it. So, in other words, there may be a large number of people or companies out there potentially interested by the broad early concept or set of attributes, but this early market is technically a proto-market. The set of attributes or product concepts have not yet been refined and defined into a specific value proposition, and therefore we do not yet know what the final market(s) will be.

Jolly (1997) calls the ability to link technology or products to such a proto-market, "marketing flair." This vital ability, and the process underlying it, is what drives the creation of a product/market vision. Hamel and Prahalad (1994) refer to the process as "visioning" the future market and Colarelli O'Connor and Veryzer (2001, p. 231) refer to it as "market visioning competence." In other words, by playing with a technology and, particularly, if you are a potential consumer/user of the technology as well as the entrepreneur, developing a more robust understanding of market context may be a result of close interaction between the user-developer and the early prototypes of the product or technology (Reid & de Brentani, 2010).

In the next sections of this chapter, we investigate specific market learning tools to help us develop a better sense of brand-new proto-markets and how to use what we learn to build our vision.

Part of the key to vision building is the early identification of what are known as "compelling attributes" (e.g., Hamel & Prahalad, 1994; Leifer et al., 2000) or, in other words, potential determinant attributes of technology(ies)/product ideas. It is essential to characterize these in terms of the proto-market so that some market directionality can be infused into the process. In the next section, we investigate market learning techniques designed to help us key into the potential determinant attributes for the proto-market.

10.2 Key Techniques for Market Learning

10.2.1 Learning by Using

Reid and de Brentani (2010) point out that techniques for market learning under radical innovation scenarios sometimes involve what is known as "learning by using" (Rosenberg, 1982). This technique is precisely what it suggests and can be utilized both when developing new technologies as well as with low-tech or no-tech new products and services. We learn about the potentiality of the technology, product, or service while we are testing it out and at the same time get a sense of potential determinant attributes which, if included in the design, might direct the product toward specific market spaces. Several techniques may be employed in order to enable learning by using, and we explore two of them here: prototyping and the use of patsy markets.

10.2.1.1 Prototyping

Defining a radical product opportunity with a future market, as described by Veryzer (1998), is primarily governed by the development of prototypes with different markets, so these become an important focus in the study of Market Visioning Competence. This is true, partly because prototypes allow not only for technical experimentation but also for experimentation with different markets to

Fig. 10.2 Sneaker made using a 3D printer to enable rapid prototyping. (Source: Image licensed and downloaded from Shutterstock on May 21, 2020. Credit: by RonaldL/► Shutterstock.com. License Link: ► https://www.shutterstock.com/image-photo/3d-printed-shoe-printing-technology-1346694518)

see which techno-market interface, or combination, works best (Lynn, 1993; Lynn et al., 1996). For example, early and rapid prototyping, such as that which can be facilitated through the use of 3D printers (Fig. 10.2), allows firms to potentially discover insights more quickly than the competition and also inherently increases the rate of experimentation through learning by using (Hamel & Prahalad, 1994; Jolly, 1997; Leifer et al., 2000; Leonard-Barton, 1995; Rosenberg, 1982; Shanklin & Ryans, 1984; Veryzer, 1998). Rather than launching one final version of the product after one round of test marketing, risk and learning are built into the process as it evolves by adapting the product slightly with information gleaned from each iteration with a test market or focus group. This usually means less time on the market for each extension but more success with emergent "dominant designs" (i.e., those which become the industry standard) (Utterback & Abernathy, 1975).

10.2.1.2 Patsy Markets

Lynn (1993) suggests that intentional use of "patsy markets," a type of "probe and learn" technique (Lynn et al., 1996), is a good learning-by-using method for developing and trying out various potential market networks and applications before deciding upon one given market. Patsy markets are those which are not necessarily the intended end markets for the product or service, but rather serve as an intermediate tool for developing knowledge regarding the capabilities of the product and how to improve on the first mach version. This strategy has lower risk than immediately launching into one target market. Experience with a patsy market may also provide ideas for additional markets that were not originally considered.

Sometimes it is the case that a company quickly pivots after launch to a different but better market based on what they learned from dealing with their first target market. This type of probe and learn situation may not be as intentional as the use of a patsy market; however, it can be just as useful. As an example, a Montreal-based B2B eyewear and gear manufacturer, for end-users working under high-risk environmental scenarios, began by selling eyewear through shopping channels to B2C consumers. After testing their products with the B2C market initially, they found that their high-end lenses were a much better match for users who would benefit more from the high range of attributes offered by the product (i.e., anti-glare, anti-fog, high protection from external damage, etc.). As a result, the company moved on to a more lucrative and better fitting market, selling to B2B markets such as buyers for the military (Anecdote used with permission from Jonathan Blanshay, December 7, 2020).

10.2.2 Expert Mapping Techniques (Plotting from a Starting Point to an Endpoint)

Several expert mapping techniques exist for predicting the manifestations of advanced technologies in the marketplace including the "Scenario Planning Method" (Schoemaker, 1995), "Technology Opportunities Analysis" (TOA) (Porter, 1994), and "Technology Scenarios" (Ettlie, 2000) such as "Science and Technology Roadmapping" (Willyard & McClees, 1987). Other techniques that can be applied in the case of radical innovations, but do not necessarily have a heavy technology development base, include "core driver mapping" (Wheelwright & Clark, 1992) and "The Delphi Method" (Linstone & Turoff, 1974a, 1995). These techniques are all considered to be useful tools for readying new product developers and entrepreneurs preparing for the future.

10.2.2.1 The "Scenario Planning Method"

The "Scenario Planning Method" (Schoemaker, 1995) involves constructing "what if" scenarios and examining these logically in terms of their potential impact on the business and environment to see whether they enable the firm to meet its objectives and vision with a reasonable level of certainty. The firms that are most successful with their market visioning skills incorporate this tactic of building out more than one option and pursuing multiple potential opportunities for a period of time before crystallizing the options into one superior strategy. This method may be boosted by delineating possible future outcomes based on forecasted trends with degrees of confidence (Colarelli O'Connor & Veryzer, 2001). ◘ Table 10.1 provides an example of a "STEEP" analysis related to the current COVID-19 scenario.

Table 10.1 Summary STEEP analysis—COVID-19

Environmental dimension	Factor	Impact	Uncertainty over time
Social	Reduction in social activities	High	Med
	Reduction in travel activities	Med	High
	Reduced work hours	High	Med
	Children at home	High	Low
	Social distancing, masks, gloves	High	Med
	Increased exercise for some; decreased for	Low/Med	Low
	others esp. in cities	High	High
	Racism and xenophobia	High	Med
	Travel fear	Med	High
	Remote work	High	High
	Emotional distress and mental illness		
Technological	More dependence on broadband	High	Low
	Increased online education	High	Med/High
	Distance tech providers—Zoom, etc.	Med	Low
	Exploration for vaccines, other drugs,	High	High
	more P.P.E.		
Economic	Delivery services skyrocket	High	Med
	Canadian emergency response benefit	Med	Low
	(CERB)	High	High
	Potential recession	High	High
	S.M.E. bankruptcies	Med	High
	Large businesses	High	High
	Stock market	High	High
	Layoffs		
Environmental	Environmental resurgence due to lack of	Med/High	High
	travel	Med/High	Med
	Reduction in carbon emissions	High	High
	Increase in medical waste		
Political	Political backlash for inaction	Med	Med
	Highly polarized political groups	Med	Med
	Contraction of internationalization	High	High
	Dissolution of trade blocks	High	High
	Reduced trust in the WHO	Med	High

Source: Created by the authors as an example

10.2.2.2 The "Technology Opportunities Analysis" (TOA)

The "Technology Opportunities Analysis" (TOA) technique (Porter, 1994) involves environmental scanning to see potential options for new technologies and blends monitoring, forecasting, and assessment (much like the Scenario Planning Method of Schoemaker, 1995, described above).

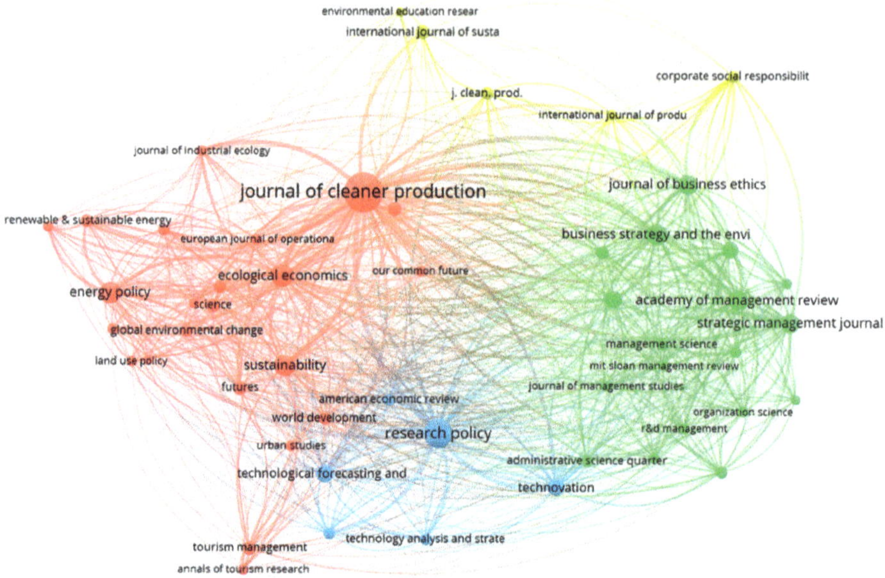

Fig. 10.3 Bibliometric analysis example from the field of sustainable development. (From Vatananan-Thesenvitz et al. (2019))

Several new techniques for TOA include (1) bibliometrics using journal citations (Vatananan-Thesenvitz et al., 2019, Fig. 10.3), (2) data visualization techniques (Holloway, 2007, Fig. 10.4), and (3) online surveys of expert opinion (e.g., ► https://answerthepublic.com) to generate the data for use in such analyses.

10.2.2.3 Technology Scenarios

"Technology Scenarios" (Bers et al., 1997; Ettlie, 2000; Hartmann & Lakatos, 1998; Henriksen, 1997) are often developed as a result of monitoring and assessment exercises. Several of the techniques suggested by Ettlie (2000) ("the nominal group method," "correlation analysis," "analytical hierarchies," "systems dynamics," "cross-impact analysis," and "relevance trees") are aimed at generating scenarios on which such analyses can be performed. Based on the ability to tap into several potential futures simultaneously, scenario analysis exhibits the characteristics of an appropriate tool for assessing and comparing the potential of emerging technologies or markets.

One scenario analysis technique, which seems to be gaining in popularity, is the *roadmapping* technique introduced in ► Chap. 8 (Barker & Smith, 1995; Kostoff & Schaller, 2000; Simonse, 2018; Willyard & McClees, 1987). "A S & T (science and technology) roadmap provides a consensus view or vision of the future S & T landscape available to decision-makers. The roadmapping process provides a way to identify, evaluate, and select strategic alternatives that can be used to achieve a desired S & T objective" (Kostoff & Schaller, 2000, p. 132). While roadmaps are often prepared by industry associations or governments, they may also be prepared

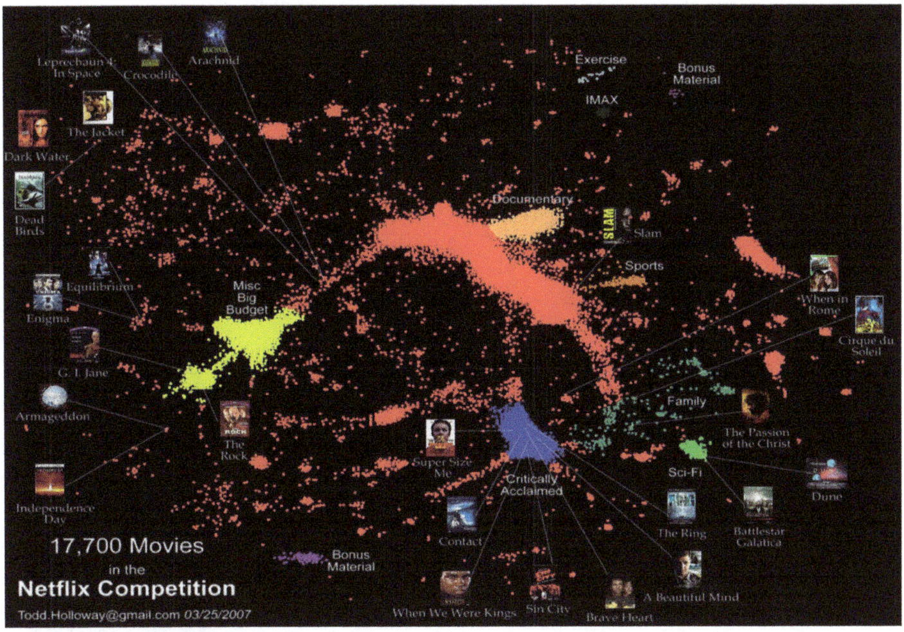

Fig. 10.4 Data visualization: "17,700 movies in the Netflix competition." (Source: Google Image: ► http://abeautifulwww.com/. Permission granted by Todd Holloway on December 6, 2020, for reprint (Created 03/25/2007))

by organizations and entrepreneurs. Regardless of the origin of preparation, they can provide an important view of potential technology scenarios available.

10.2.2.4 The Delphi Method

Additionally, special expert forecasting methods have been suggested for learning about potential markets and technologies, including "The Delphi Method." According to Linstone and Turoff (1974b, 2002, p. 10), and based on previous work of Dalkey and Helmer (1963), "Project Delphi was the name given to an Air Force-sponsored Rand Corporation study, starting in the early 1950s, concerning the use of expert opinion." As outlined in Linstone and Turoff (1995), Rand was consulting with the US Air Force on how to use expert opinion to build consensus about how Soviet military might target the US industrial complex and how many atomic bombs would be needed to have an impact on US military capability. The project was coined "Project Delphi" from the ability of the Oracle of Delphi in Ancient Greece to divine the future (Fig. 10.5). The Delphi Method allows a group of experts to work autonomously and anonomously together as a forecasting panel, to come up with a consensus solution to a complex problem. After a first round of gathering forecast opinions from the experts, the set of potential solutions to the complex problem are fed back to the experts, again without being ascribed to particular people, and this continues in a series of rounds each time including each other's anonymous comments as to why they deviated from others' opinions on the previous rounds, in an attempt to reach consensus.

Fig. 10.5 The Oracle of Delphi. (Source: Image licensed and downloaded from Adobe Stock on May 21, 2020. Credit: by Studio Trebuchet/► stock.adobe.com. License Link: ► https://stock.adobe.com/ca/30992053)

10.2.3 Visioning and Backcasting (Plotting from an Envisioned Endpoint Back to the Beginning)

A popular phrase among various motivational educators and business leaders is "begin with the end in mind." Hamel and Prahalad (1994) have described this process as "visioning," and Colarelli O'Connor and Veryzer (2001) have described using vision to "backcast." This means starting with a mental model of the future goal, which is worked back to the activities that must take place and resources required to enact that desired version of the future (Davis, 1987; Noori et al., 1999). These approaches differ from scenario analysis in that they do not define future scenarios using the probability of occurrence of events, but instead focus on end states as desired goals (Davis, 1987; Godet, 1986; Weick, 1969) and work toward constructing that future.

10.2.4 Combining Forecasting Methods

Meade and Islam (1998) suggest that forecasting methods that offer a combination of techniques tend to outperform individual approaches. This finding suggests that techniques such as Porter's "Technology Opportunities Assessment" or combining some of the above methods together may be more robust methods for forecasting than those relying on singular techniques on their own, particularly in situations where uncertainty is very high, as often exists for entrepreneurs.

As such, the market learning tools described build on learning by using because of their ability to tap into several potential futures simultaneously, and therefore, prove useful when learning about or developing markets for new products for the future.

10.3 Ideation

Opportunity identification usually involves some element of psychological construction on the part of individuals, and, as a result, cognitive effort is involved to match development of technologies and products with perceived opportunities in the marketplace. In other words, once you have done an initial deep dive into your industry(ies) of interest, combined with market learning tools, you can start playing with your own conceptions of how things might go together in a new way.

The act of doing this is known as "ideation" (◘ Fig. 10.6). We accomplish this through active psychological construction to advance the visioning process. The final output is the creation of new products and services in line with a defined vision.

◘ **Fig. 10.6** Conceptual image to portray "ideation." (Source: Image licensed and downloaded from Shutterstock on October 22, 2018. Credit: by magic pictures/► Shutterstock.com. License Link: ► https://www.shutterstock.com/image-vector/vector-illustration-colorful-keyholes-matching-keys-1108222646)

While we want to draw your attention to some overall types of ideation related to cognitive efforts, so much has already been written on the topic of how to come up with new ideas that we do not want to recreate the wheel. Instead, we want to emphasize that the kinds of cognitive efforts that are required for psychological construction are not passive. They require action to make them happen—which is the element we want to help you with specifically—and, importantly, cognitive effort needs to be paired with your own proactive inspiration (based on the various motivational triggers discussed in ▶ Chaps. 3 and 4 and very early vision frameworks as discussed in ▶ Chap. 5). As well, it is a good idea to spend as much time as possible on the ideation phase because it is usually less expensive than later in the process when developing, testing, and marketing your ideas.

Karlesky (2015) suggests three types of cognitive processes to move forward with ideation: (1) "analogistic thinking," (2) "recombination," and (3) "distinction making."

10.3.1 Analogistic Thinking

> » "Great conquerors, we read, have been both animated, and, also in a great measure, formed by reading the exploits of former conquerors. Why may not the same effect be expected from the history of philosophy to philosophers? May not, even more, be expected in this case? The wars of many of those conquerors, who received this advantage from history, had no proper connection with former wars: they were only analogous to them. Whereas the whole business of philosophy, diversified as it is, is but one; it being one and the same great scheme, that all philosophers, of all ages and nations, have been conducting, from the beginning of the world; so that the work being the same, the labours of one are not only analogous to those of another, but in an immediate manner subservient to them; and one philosopher succeeds another in the same field; as one Roman proconsul succeeded another in carrying on the same war, and pursuing the same conquests, in the same country. In this case, an intimate knowledge of what has been done before us cannot but greatly facilitate our future progress, if it be not absolutely necessary to it. Joseph Priestley (1767)"

Merriam-Webster (2020, online) defines "analogy" as "a comparison of two otherwise unlike things based on resemblance of a particular aspect." Every individual's mind is a "mental construct" which they carry around with them about the way the world works. A variety of concepts combine to make the mental construct. Concepts are bundles of specific examples clustered around a common conceptual core. For example, when you meet another person, if they say a word that you don't recognize, your brain will search for an "analogy," or an example, which you already possess in your mental construct and that might apply to the word. If it seems to apply, the new term will be stored with the analogy as another example of the overall concept.

Analogies are, therefore, helpful to the ideation process because they help us to create, categorize, and process brand-new information and ideas. Using this idea, a person might actively search for external inspiration for an analogy to be able to

■ **Fig. 10.7** Title: Antonio Bonet, Juan Kurchan, and Jorge Ferrari Hardoy: B.K.F. Chair commonly referred to as butterfly chair or Hardoy chair designed in 1938/1940, steel frame and one-piece leather seat. (Credit: Kippelboy. This file is licensed under the ▶ Creative Commons ▶ Attribution--Share Alike 3.0 Unported license. No changes made except scaling to size for printing. Uploaded on April 11, 2012. Downloaded via Wikimedia Commons on May 24, 2020. License Link: ▶ https://commons.wikimedia.org/wiki/File:BKF_Chair.jpg)

apply it to their ideation process in their field of interest. For example, a designer might look to nature for an analogous form of inspiration. Doing so, therefore, would be an act of proactive inspiration.

An example is given by the "butterfly chair" created by Antonio Bonet, Juan Kurchan, and Jorge Ferrari Hardoy or the B.K.F. Chair designed in 1938/1940 (■ Fig. 10.7).

10.3.2 Recombination

Recombination may be used to match up existing skills, technologies, markets, products, ideas, or information in new ways. Recombination is a proactive undertaking of looking to see what exists "out there" and mixing things up in a new way to see what could potentially exist using a new combination of old elements. Recombination techniques include (1) patent search, (2) re-engineering and analysis of competitive products, and (3) morphological combinations and determinant attributes, each of which is described with an example below.

10.3.2.1 Patent Search

Patent and trademark offices (e.g., the USPTO, USA; CIPO, Canada; and EPO, Europe) provide a wealth of information about the current state of the art in specific industries, domains, and technology, product, and process areas. There are five requirements for patent applications to be considered for acceptance: the subject matter must be patentable, the patent must be new and must be regarded as inventive to a skilled person in the field, it must be useful, and it must not have been used previously by the inventor. So, when a patent application is made, the applicant must include an abstract, a field of classification, a list of related art and prior art and citation documents, a detailed description of specifications often accompanied by images (which may be downloaded), a list of claims, and the scope. The great thing about this is that not only are you able to have access to the detailed reference list of prior art leading to the invention (thereby helping with your upfront homework), but you will also see the list of claims and the scope. These will usually give some clues as to the market applications which are being considered by the inventor. So, perhaps there are other markets which the idea can be applied to in a new and creative way that the inventor has not thought of or is not interested in, or you might have ideas for the next generation of the technology, product, or process. Let's be clear here—the idea is not to copy what other people do, but to be inspired to create the next generation of ideas or bring ideas about in new and different ways. As such, by performing a simple patent or trademark search a country's patent office website (or on Google Patents), it is possible to see how key technologies or products in your field have been developed based on the "state of the art" techniques and ideas in order to see how these, in turn, might be improved with your own ideas.

10

A good example is provided by the patent for a novel handheld billiards bridge (▶ www.uspto.gov Patent# **10625143 B1)** (◘ Fig. 10.8, Page 1 of the patent). In a search of this reasonably short patent, you will see each of the elements clearly laid out including a diagram of the bridge from several angles. For anyone who has ever played billiards, it's a great idea! And for any historians, inventors, and designers among you, the old patents going back to 1790 are fantastic. As an example, check out the original patent for the billiard ball (Patent #**50359**) (◘ Fig. 10.9).

10.3.2.2 Re-Engineering and Analysis of Competitive Products

Re-engineering takes constructed products, deconstructs them into components by removing the current interfacing mechanisms, and then reconstructs new products using new interfaces.

According to Computer World (Schwartz, 2001), Phoenix Technologies Ltd. provides an excellent example of re-engineering without copyright infringement using a "clean-room approach." In the 1980s, the company produced a BIOS

US010625143B1

(12) **United States Patent**
Kirk

(10) **Patent No.:** **US 10,625,143 B1**
(45) **Date of Patent:** **Apr. 21, 2020**

(54) **HANDHELD BILLIARDS BRIDGE**

(71) Applicant: **Judith Ann Kirk**, Kihei, HI (US)

(72) Inventor: **Judith Ann Kirk**, Kihei, HI (US)

(*) Notice: Subject to any disclaimer, the term of this patent is extended or adjusted under 35 U.S.C. 154(b) by 0 days.

(21) Appl. No.: **16/350,651**

(22) Filed: **Dec. 12, 2018**

(51) **Int. Cl.**
A63D 15/10 (2006.01)

(52) **U.S. Cl.**
CPC ***A63D 15/105*** (2013.01)

(58) **Field of Classification Search**
CPC A63D 15/105
See application file for complete search history.

(56) **References Cited**

U.S. PATENT DOCUMENTS

570,459 A * 11/1896 Cronin A63D 15/105 473/43
774,621 A * 11/1904 Van Setres A63D 15/105 473/43
4,149,718 A * 4/1979 Russo A63D 15/105 473/42
4,210,325 A * 7/1980 McCann A63D 15/105 473/43
4,629,187 A * 12/1986 Mirowski A63D 15/105 473/43
7,611,416 B1 * 11/2009 Mattina A63D 15/105 473/2
2016/0296831 A1 * 10/2016 Bartolomucci A63D 15/105

* cited by examiner

Primary Examiner — Jeffrey S Vanderveen

(57) **ABSTRACT**

Invention comprises a hand held device for controlling and assisting with the striking of billiard balls. A user of the device slides the device over his or her knuckles on their bridge hand and the device, rather than the user's fingers, controls and directs the movement of the cue stick. The devices consists of a rigid thermoplastic or similar material with four apertures, into which the user the inserts his or her fingers, and various protrusions creating semi-circular guides through and against which the user slides the pool cue. The guides through which the tapered fore part of the cue stick is placed are located above and adjacent to the finger holes. In certain circumstances, the user can use one of the finger holes for directing the cue stick. Additionally, certain embodiments of the device may have fully circular (enclosed) guides for the cue stick.

5 Claims, 4 Drawing Sheets

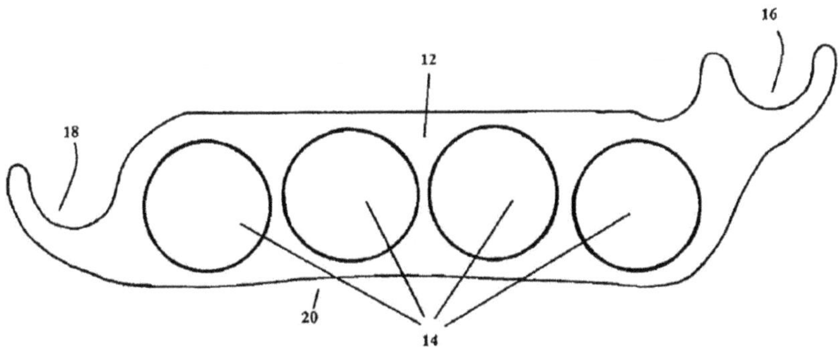

◘ Fig. 10.8 The handheld billiards bridge, inventor Judith Ann Kirk, filed on December 12, 2018. (Source: The United States Patent and Trademark Office (USPTO). Website: ▶ http://patft.uspto.gov/netacgi/nph-Parser?Sect1=PTO2&Sect2=HITOFF&p=1&u=%2Fnetahtml%2FPTO%2Fsearch-bool.html&r=1&f=G&l=50&co1=AND&d=PTXT&s1=%22Handheld+Billiards+Bridge%22.TI.&s2=10625143.PN.&OS=TTL/, accessed August 28, 2020. Full text and image available. Public Domain)

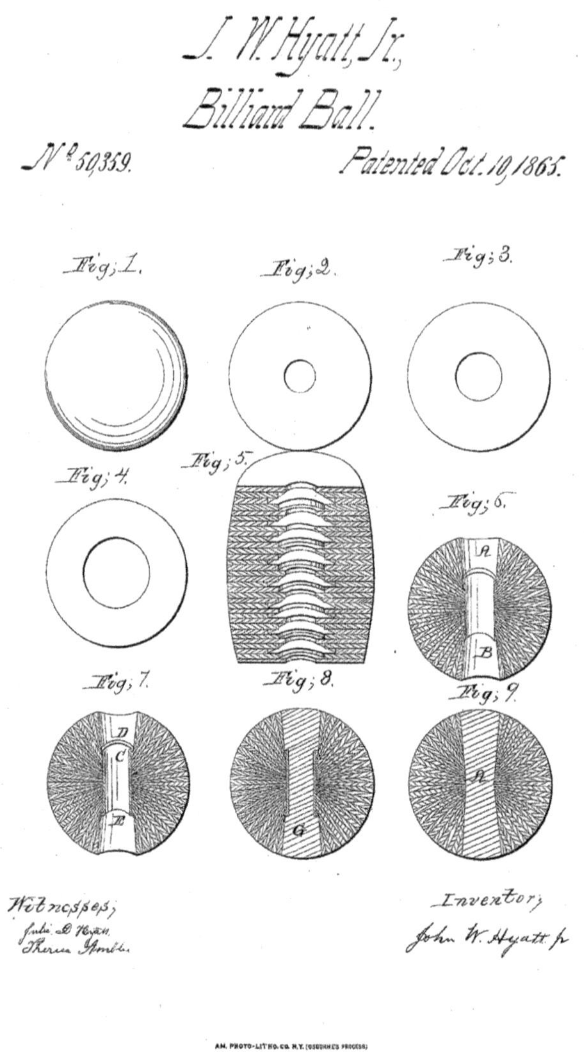

◻ Fig. 10.9 Example of an early patent design for the Billiard Ball, inventor J.W. Hyatt Jr., patented on October 10, 1865. (Source: The United States Patent and Trademark Office (USPTO). Website: ► https://pdfpiw.uspto.gov/.piw?Docid=50359&idkey=NONE&homeurl=http%3A%252F%252Fpatft.uspto.gov%252Fnetahtml%252FPTO%252Fpatimg.htm, accessed August 28, 2020. Full text and image available. Public Domain)

(◻ Fig. 10.10—a basic input/output system—the program runs when a computer starts) compatible with I.B.M. PC. To do this, their engineering team examined the I.B.M. BIOS describing everything it did without using any of the original code. Afterward, a group of programmers worked with the first team's specifications to create the new system without prior knowledge of the original code. According to

Fig. 10.10 PhoenixBios chip. (Source: ▶ https://commons.wikimedia.org/wiki/File:Bios_chip-Phoenix_1998.jpg. Credit: by Adrianot at Polish Wikipedia/CC BY-SA (▶ https://creativecommons.org/licenses/by-sa/3.0). Uploaded on November 16, 2007. Downloaded via Wikimedia Commons on May 25, 2020)

Schwartz (2001, online), "the resulting Phoenix BIOS was different from the I.B.M. code, but for all intents and purposes, it operated identically."

10.3.2.3 Morphological Combinations and Determinant Attributes

The basic concept behind using morphological combinations to create new concepts has been around for a long time—likely even before it was formally called that. One of the first known academics to use the term was Zwicky (1966, 1969) in his research on the use of "morphological boxes" as creativity tools. The approach

Table 10.2 Hypothetical invention based on morphological combinations and determinant attributes

Shape	Color	Material(s)	Writing/ink source
Square	Black	Metal/plastic	No cartridge
Rounded	***Wood***	***Wood***	Paper
Flexible	Green	Glass	Ink
Sculptured	Silver	Paper	Vegetable dye
Small loom	White	***Linen-cotton***	***Woven***

Hypothetical invention: an environmentally friendly wooden loom printer imprinting on soft material like linen-cotton with woven writing. Source: Created by the authors as an example.

is detailed in Tom Ritchey's, 2002 book, *General Morphological Analysis*. Essentially, the idea is to take any system (a technology, a product or tool, a service, a user system, etc.), break it into as many smaller units as you can think of which combine to make up the system (sometimes referred to as "means" or "attributes"), and create a matrix of all of the possible ways you can think of to deliver each attribute. Once this is done, you can investigate the various potential combinations that might be possible.

So, if we, for example, wanted to create a new environmentally friendly printer, we might first break down a typical printing system into some of the key attributes which typically exist in a printer: shape, color, the material of the printer, the material you are printing on, and cartridge ink source. From there, we would be able to create a matrix enabling us to see all of the theoretical combinations of these key attributes based on as many ideas as we could think of for each attribute. So, in the printing example we provide in Table 10.2, we have $5^4 = 625$ possible morphological combinations based on 4 printer characteristics with 5 options for each characteristic.

To think through how to generate innovative concepts and solutions from this matrix, a further tool exists known as TRIZ (invented by Genrich Altshuller and colleagues, beginning circa 1946, while working in "Inventions Inspection" for the Soviet Navy), which is useful in this regard. The first journal publication of the work was in 1956: Altshuller and Shapiro (1956).

Basically, there are 40 TRIZ principles. These are presented in a handy schematic created by "FotoSceptyk" and made available through a Creative Commons license on Wikimedia (Fig. 10.11). The principles basically ask the question "what if?" and then apply an action to attributes of interest. So, for example, "What would happen to two attributes if they were merged?", i.e., using TRIZ principle #5.

There are some limitations to this method, including the fact that depending on the complexity of the original system, there can be a very high number of potential combinations. Therefore, going through all the possibilities can be extremely

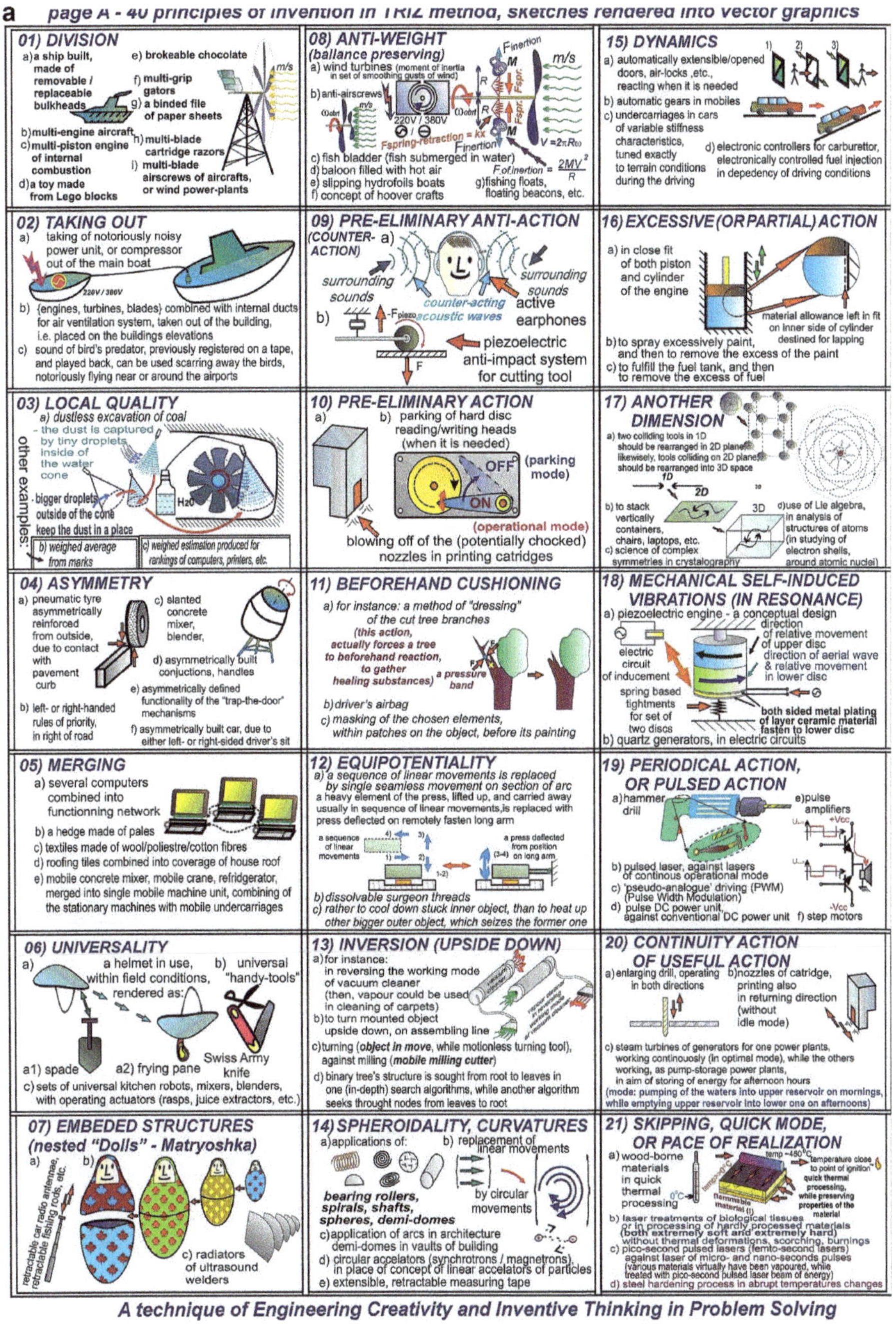

Fig. 10.11 40 principles of invention in TRIZ method. (Source: ▶ https://commons.wikimedia.org/w/index.php?curid=45719323. Attribution: By FotoSceptyk - Own work, CC BY-SA 4.0. Downloaded via Wikimedia Commons on May 25, 2020)

10

b

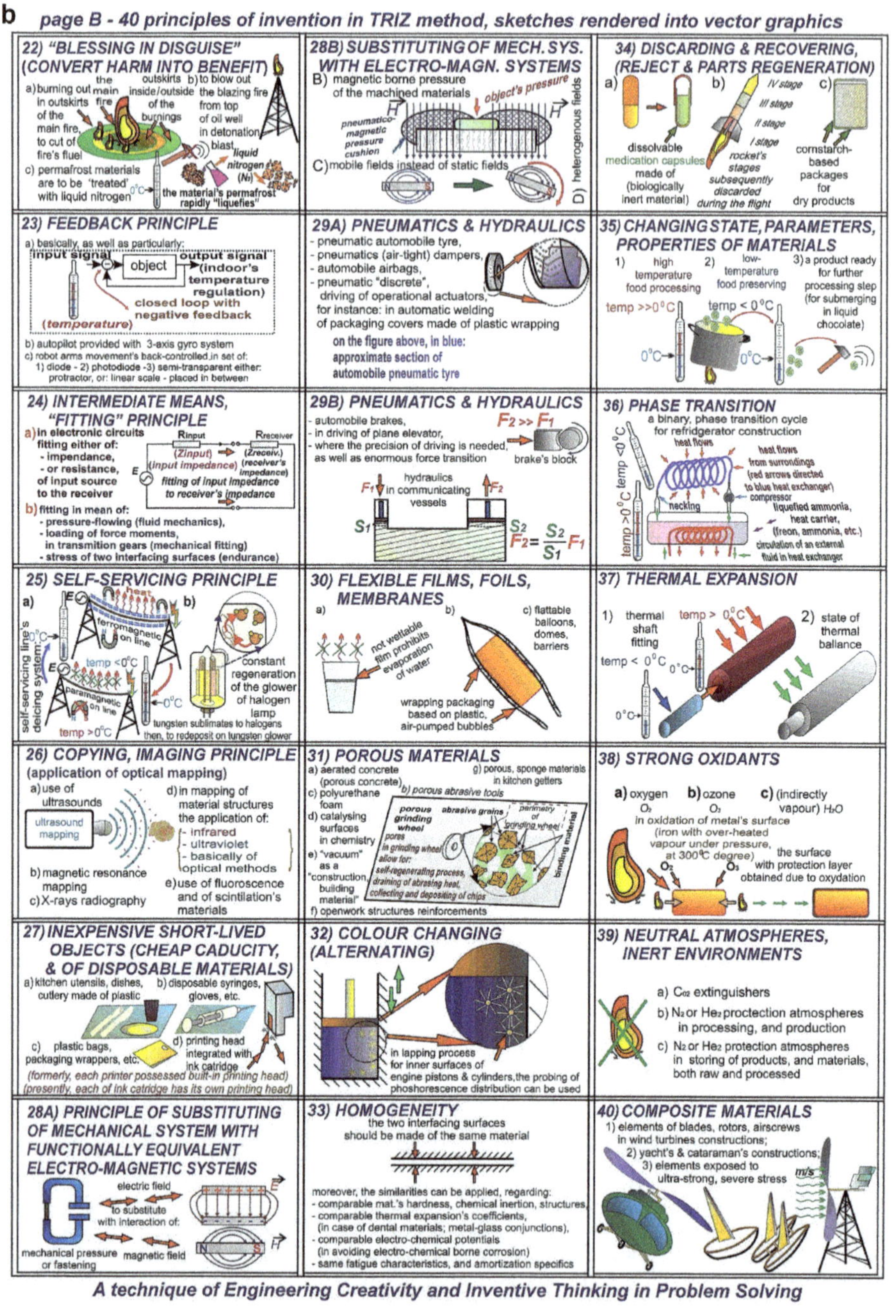

Fig. 10.11 (continued)

labor-intensive, and some may not even be possible to apply. Due to this factor, it is a good idea to do a first scan of the TRIZ principles to see which might have the best chances of success given your objectives and preferences.

As we can see, the basic "unit" of morphological analysis is the "attribute," and we must be sure to carefully generate a meaningful series of attributes, which can take some time and effort, before engaging in combining them. An attribute can be a property or characteristic such as a benefit, function, and feature such as size, color, components, etc. Basically, a product or service is a sum of its attributes—and these are not necessarily physical. Attributes may be emotional, psychological, or functional in terms of making use easier or increasing speed, for example. The central importance of attributes lies in the fact that bundled together in combination, they create the value-add of an offering directed toward a potential consumer.

"Determinant attributes" are essentially those attributes which consumers use to distinguish between service or product offerings. They are not necessarily the most important attributes in terms of the functionality of the product, but they are undoubtedly those which are considered the most unique or important from the consumer's perspective and are therefore used to compare and possibly choose between competitive offerings. As noted by Alpert (1971, p. 184), "those attributes projected by the product's image which lead to the choice of that product may be called *determinant*, since they determine preference and purchase behaviour."

10.3.3 Distinction Making

"Distinction making" (Langer, 1989; Weick & Sutcliffe, 2006), according to Karlesky (2015, p. 45), "involves the process of creating and refining new categories of information, objects and events" and was the most prevalent form of cognitive thinking in Karlesky's research on entrepreneurial opportunity identification. The basic idea behind distinction making is that it looks at the current state of understanding in a specific domain, and then it starts to drill down to uncover answers to questions that exist at a more granular level of understanding in the field. For example, an intermediate tennis player may be able, after some instruction, observation, and a few tips, to put a topspin on a forehand swing, but an expert will understand the mechanics behind it and why and how they work, which should ultimately lead to progress and consistency over time. Cognitive categories exist for any field of interest in terms of the level of knowledge and information that exists. Most nonexperts will have a surface level of cognitive category understanding entailing the social and technical landscape of any given field; experts will understand the limits of current knowledge and what the key questions are that exist in that field.

According to Karlesky (2015), distinction making either actively recategorizes information or creates more categories of information. He also proposes that this activity enables the production of larger sets of new attributes, as input for potential conceptual combinations. This is great for entrepreneurs who already have expertise in a field or who know customers in the field, but for new entrepreneurs, it may require doing homework with experts. Analogical thinking and various

Fig. 10.12 Conceptual image to portray "distinction making." (Source: Image licensed and downloaded from Shutterstock on October 22, 2018. Credit: by chinnapong/▶ Shutterstock.com. License Link: ▶ https://www.shutterstock.com/image-photo/lifehealth-insurance-protection-business-financial-leadership-407193883)

forms of recombination may be easier places to start, particularly for nascent non-expert entrepreneurs just beginning their ideation process. Once a base of ideas has been established using other techniques, a focus on distinction making will help to further the ideation process (Fig. 10.12).

We suggest, as much as possible, playing in all three creative sandboxes during your ideation phase. While some of the specific recombination techniques are more tech-focused in nature (e.g., patent search, re-engineering), the others – analogy, determinant attributes/morphology, and distinction making – can all be used together to generate novel ideas for less tech-focussed products and services.

Here is an example from one of our former students, Rebecca Yates (anecdote used with permission from graduate B.U. student and alumna, Rebecca Yates, December 2, 2020), who had a startup idea for bringing Gaelic football to Canada for kids. It represents the use of a combination of analogy, morphological combinations and determinant attributes, as well as distinction making. The overall idea was to apply an existing game (Gaelic football) to a new market (Canadian youth) using an analogy (looking at the game of rugby to see how it had been adapted for younger players). In so doing, the idea was to examine the attributes of rugby, which had needed to be adapted for kids, to understand what might be similarly applied to the new market for kids playing Gaelic football. Doing so helped in understanding which attributes needed to be applied in a new way for the new youth market. The new market also provided brand-new opportunities, meaning that entirely new attributes could be developed for the new market as well. So, for example, the questions Rebecca asked were along the lines of whether there were opportunities to switch things up to make Gaelic football "easier to play" at a younger age (taking into consideration attributes such as smaller fields, smaller equipment, shorter playtime).

By creating a good understanding of common attributes between two somewhat similar sports (i.e., the analogies between Gaelic football and rugby), you can then get the new target segment to help you co-create a new set of attributes (i.e., morphological combinations) and make it specific for them by going more in-depth with specific questions with lead users from the new market (i.e., distinction making). In other words, how can you switch it up for a new market, a new demographic, or a new geographical market to put your stamp on it?

In sum, the starting point for creating an interesting group of questions stemmed **from first finding an analogy** from an existing and somewhat similar adult game which had been applied to kids already. The next step was **then examining the attributes and determinant attributes in the first system to see which new combination** made sense to apply to the second system. **Finally, the last stage involved coming up with additional new attributes through distinction making** to respond specifically to the second opportunity and shaking and baking until a unique and exciting new combination resulted.

As you can see from looking at the above main forms of action-based ideation, the end goal of these processes is to come up with a very in-depth understanding of all potential attributes and possible interactions these can have in a given system, and to focus in on those which are desired by lead users and potential customers (i.e., they possess "determinant attributes"). The final task is coming up with a winning new combination of these attributes which, based on your own competencies and interests, you desire to implement into a Market Vision.

Chapter Review Questions

1. Define "learning by using" and "expert mapping techniques." Of each of the techniques described list one which you think might be most helpful to you (and your team) given your area of interest and how you might be able to apply it.
2. What are the three main forms of ideation? Give an example of each type.
3. Explain the idea behind morphological analysis. Create an example for a hypothetical product or service using a 3x3 matrix.
4. What is an attribute?
5. What is a compelling or determinant attribute? Why are determinant attributes so important for entrepreneurs to understand?

References

Alpert, M. I. (1971). Identification of determinant attributes: A comparison of methods. *Journal of Marketing Research, 8*(2), 184–191.

Altshuller, G. S., & Shapiro, R. B. (1956). О Психологии изобретательского творчества (On the psychology of inventive creation). *Вопросы Психологии (The Psychological Issues) (in Russian), 6*, 37–39.

Barker, D., & Smith, D. J. H. (1995). Technology foresight using roadmaps. *Long Range Planning, 28*(2), 21–28.

Bers, J. A., Lynn, G. S., & Spurling, C. (1997). A venerable tool for a new application: Using scenario analysis for formulating strategies for emerging technologies in emerging markets. *Engineering Management Journal, 9*(2), 33–40.

Colarelli O'Connor, G., & Veryzer, R. (2001). The nature of market visioning for technology-based radical innovation. *The Journal of Product Innovation Management, 18*(4), 231–246.

Dalkey, N., & Helmer, O. (1963). An experimental application of the Delphi Method to the use of experts. *Management Science, 9*(3), 458.

Davis, S. M. (1987). *Future perfect*. Addison-Wesley.

Ettlie, J. E. (2000). *Managing technological innovation*. Wiley.

Godet, M. (1986). Introduction to la prospective. *Futures, 18*(2), 134–157.

Hamel, G., & Prahalad, C. K. (1994). *Competing for the future*. Harvard Business School Press.

Hartmann, G. C., & Lakatos, A. L. (1998). Assessing technology risk – A case study. *Research-Technology Management, 41*(2), 32–38.

Henriksen, A. D. (1997). A technology assessment primer for management of technology. *International Journal of Technology Management, 13*(5/6), 615–638.

Holloway, T. (2007). 17,700 movies in the Netflix competition. Google Image: http://abeautifulwww.com/, created 03/25/2007. Permission granted by Todd Holloway on December 6, 2020, for reprint.

Jolly, V. K. (1997). *Commercializing new technologies*. Harvard Business School Press.

Karlesky, M. J. (2015). *Identifying entrepreneurial opportunities: Cognition and categorization in nascent entrepreneurs*. Ph.D. Dissertation, University of Michigan.

Kostoff, R. N., & Schaller, R. R. (2000). Science and technology roadmaps. *IEEE Transactions on Engineering Management, 48*(2), 132–143.

Langer, E. J. (1989). *Mindfulness*. Addison-Wesley/Addison Wesley Longman.

10 Leifer, R., McDermott, C. M., Colarelli O'Connor, G., Peters, L. S., Rice, M., & Veryzer, R. W. (2000). *Radical innovation: How mature companies can outsmart upstarts*. Harvard Business School Press.

Leonard-Barton, D. (1995). *Wellsprings of knowledge*. Harvard Business School Press.

Linstone, H., & Turoff, M. (1974a). The Delphi Method: Techniques and applications. *Journal of Marketing Research, 13*(3), 317–318.

Linstone, H., & Turoff, M. (1974b). *The Delphi Method: Techniques and applications* (pp. 1–116). Addison-Wesley.

Linstone, H., & Turoff, M. (Eds.). (1995). *The Delphi Method: Techniques and applications*. Addison-Wesley.

Linstone, H., & Turoff, M. (Eds.). (2002). *The Delphi Method*. Shared by editors open access on ResearchGate. Accessed March 20, 2022.

Lynn, G. (1993). *Understanding products and markets for radical innovation*. Ph.D. Dissertation, Faculty of the Graduate School of Rensselaer Polytechnic Institute. U.M.I. Proquest Digital Dissertations.

Lynn, G. S., Morone, J. G., & Paulson, A. S. (1996). Marketing discontinuous innovation: The probe and learn process. *California Management Review, 38*(3), 8–37.

Meade, N., & Islam, T. (1998). Technological forecasting – Model selection, model stability, and combining models. *Management Science, 44*(8), 1115–1130.

Merriam-Webster Dictionary. (2020, online). Definition for the word "analogy" downloaded on December 19, 2020 (Analogy | Definition of Analogy by Merriam-Webster (merriam-webster.com).

Noori, H., Munro, H., Deszsca, G., & McWilliams, B. (1999). Developing the "right" breakthrough product/service: An umbrella methodology, Part A. *International Journal of Technology Management, 17*(5), 544–562.

Porter, A. (1994). Technological opportunities analysis: Integrating technology monitoring, forecasting and assessment with strategic planning. *S.R.A. Journal, 26*(2), 21–31.

Priestley, J. (1767). *The history and present state of electricity.* Source: https://quotepark.com/authors/josephpriestley/, accessed on September 1, 2020.

Reid, S. E., & de Brentani, U. (2010). Market vision and market visioning competence: Impact on early performance for radically new, high-tech products. *The Journal of Product Innovation Management, 27*(4), 500–518.
Ritchey, T. (2002). *General morphological analysis: A general method for non-quantified modelling*. Swedish Morphological Society.
Rosenberg, N. (1982). *Inside the black box: Technology and economics*. Cambridge University Press.
Schoemaker, P. J. H. (1995). Scenario planning: A tool for strategic planning. *Sloan Management Review, 36*, 25–40.
Schwartz, M. (2001). How to reverse-engineering. *Computer World*, November 12, 2001, https://www.computerworld.com/article/2585652/reverse-engineering.html, accessed online from Computer World, May 25, 2020.
Shanklin, W. L., & Ryans, J. K., Jr. (1984). *Essentials of marketing high technology*. Lexington Books.
Simonse, L. (2018). *Design roadmapping: Guidebook for future foresight techniques*. BIS Publishers.
Utterback, J. M., & Abernathy, W. J. (1975). A dynamic model of process and product innovation. *The International Journal of Management Science, 3*(6), 639–656.
Vatananan-Thesenvitz, R., Schaller, A. A., & Shannon, R. (2019). A bibliometric review of the knowledge base for innovation in sustainable development. *Sustainability, 11*(2), Article Number 5783, Figure 7 Journal co-citation network of the I.S.D. literature, https://www.mdpi.com/2071-1050/11/20/5783. Downloaded on December 9, 2020, via MDPI online, open access, Creative Commons CC-BY license. https://doi.org/10.3390/su11205783
Veryzer, R. W., Jr. (1998). Discontinuous innovation and the new product development process. *Journal of Product Innovation Management, 15*(4), 304–321.
Weick, K. E. (1969). *The social psychology of organizing* (1st ed.). Addison-Wesley Publications.
Weick, K. E., & Sutcliffe, K. M. (2006). Mindfulness and the quality of organizational attention. *Organization Science, 17*(4), 514–524.
Wheelwright, S. C., & Clark, K. B. (1992). *Revolutionizing product development: Quantum leaps in speed, efficiency and quality*. The Free Press.
Willyard, C., & McClees, C. (1987). Motorola's technology roadmap process. *Research Management, 13*(9), 13–19.
Zwicky, F. (1966). *Entdecken, Erfinden, Forschen im Morpholologischen Weltbild*. Droemer Knaur.
Zwicky, F. (1969). *Discovery, invention, research – Through the morphological approach*. The Macmillan Company.

Market Vision Creation

Contents

© The Author(s), under exclusive license to Springer Nature Switzerland AG 2022

S. E. Reid, C. B. Crawford, *Entrepreneurial Vision*, Classroom Companion: Business,
https://doi.org/10.1007/978-3-030-77803-3_11

Learning Objectives

The first half of this book has been focused on understanding why you should and how you can have an impact on the marketplace, no matter where you sit on the entrepreneurial spectrum and developing the most relevant, opportunistic context and highly-differentiated, impactful ideas through which to achieve this. Now, we are ready to start operationalizing this.

Our aims for the following chapter are to:

1. Build an understanding around what a mind map is and why/how it can be helpful in constructing a Product/Market Vision.
2. Build up the Market Vision construct by developing granularity of focus through the aspects of Form, Scope, Magnetism, Clarity, and Specificity.
3. Help assess the strength and structure of your initial vision construct, which is the outcome of your efforts from moving through the exercises and theory provided thus far in this book.

Whether you have already started the ideation process, or you are just beginning, the aim here is to create a mind map with the new combinations of attributes you have been building in the previous chapters. Gaining a clear understanding of your Market Vision construct will help you move toward creating a first vision statement later in ► Chap. 13.

11

11.1 Let's Create a Mind Map

If you have not created one before, a mind map is a visual representation of a concept that you have in your head and the various categories of information and ideas which you use to relate to it with specific words. Mind maps are meant to be an individual's conceptual representation of knowledge but can also be shared or created with teams and others to build ideas out further.

Tony Buzan was the first person credited with the use of the specific term "mind map" (Buzan, 1974), but the idea has been around for centuries. For example, according to Schwendimann (2014), Porphyry of Tyre (third century A.D.) constructed "node-map diagrams", a form of mind map, to illustrate the concepts of Aristotle. The work of philosopher Ramon Llull (1232–1316) in his *Arbor Scientiae* (1515) has also been illustrated using the basic technique of mind mapping (◘ Fig. 11.1).

As we shall see later in the chapter on communicating your vision (► Chap. 19), the ability to build imagery around the core components of your vision can act as a key ingredient in transforming a mediocre vision statement into a truly great one. Imagery does so through its ability to elicit emotion and, as such, facilitates a smooth transfer of understanding between people about the underlying meaning of the vision. The process of mind mapping helps to focus on such imagery that can become a core aspect of a refined vision statement later on.

Fig. 11.1 *Arbor scientiae*. (Source: By Ramón Llull (1232–1316?) Fecha 1515, BNE – Biblioteca Nacional de España, CC BY-SA 4.0, ► https://commons.wikimedia.org/w/index.php?curid=57509449. Downloaded via Wikimedia Commons on November 12, 2020. Public Domain)

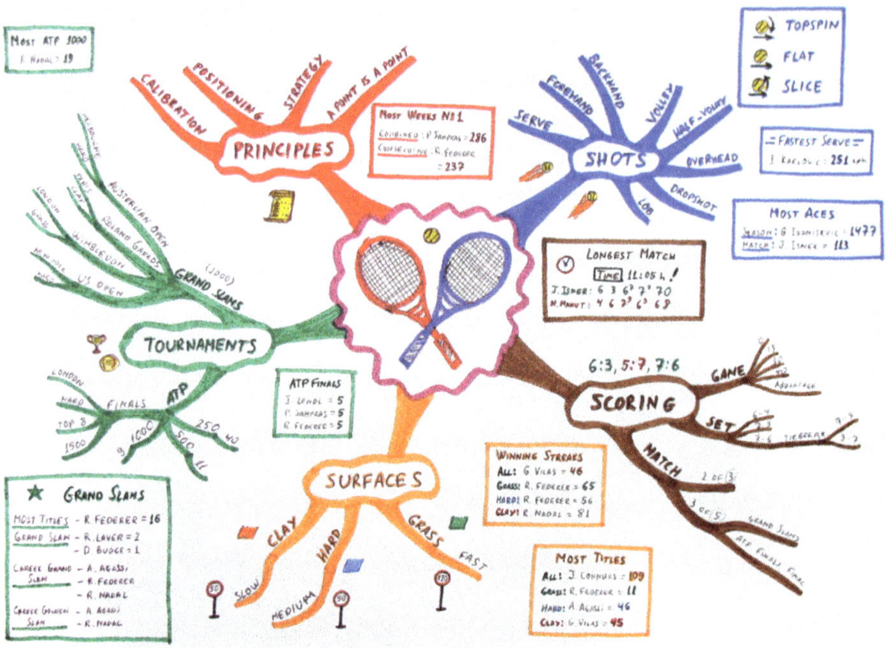

◘ Fig. 11.2 Tennis mind map. (Source: ► https://commons.wikimedia.org/wiki/File:Tennis-mindmap.png. ► http://mindmapping.bg / CC BY-SA (► https://creativecommons.org/licenses/by-sa/2.5). Created August 24, 2013. Downloaded via Wikimedia Commons on May 25, 2020)

Essentially, a mind map usually focuses on one core concept and then draws a relationship to sub-concepts (also called "dimensions" or "attributes") as defined in ► Chap. 10 previously, which are related to the central concept. These attributes may be further fleshed out in terms of aspects, qualities, characteristics, or values that the attributes may take on or be comprised of.

◘ Figure 11.2 provides an example of a tennis mind map which was shared through creative commons on Wikimedia. In this example, the core concept is the game of tennis. The attributes are elements like "surfaces" or "scoring," and the aspects of each attribute may include characteristics like "clay," "hard," and "grass," as in the case of the surfaces attribute.

The wonderful thing about the mind map is that it provides a sort of petri dish in which to start thinking about and listing attributes which you believe may be helpful in the creation of your vision. As we mentioned in ▶ Chap. 10, our goal is to create a laundry list of attributes and then cull it down to figure out our "determinant attributes" that will provide value-add to potential customers. To prepare for this, we recommend pulling together the work you have done to this point with Worksheets 6–10 as follows:

- Revisit your team's passions and strengths/core competencies and your responses to Worksheet 6.
- Revisit the significant opportunities identified in your industry(ies) of interest from Worksheets 7–9.
- Revisit the main hot point challenges/areas where a problem requires a solution identified by your lead user and expert interviews from Worksheet 10 and where you and your team can shine given your team passions and strengths and where you are currently not aware of competition or where competition is limited or focused on other targets or other facets of value-add.
- Based on your market learning and ideation exercises from ▶ Chaps. 9 and 10, did you identify any other potential differentiation hot points which might be of value for both your team and lead users/potential customers?
- Now, think about what each of those potential differentiation hot points might look like in terms of a possible product or service interaction with potential consumers.
- Now you are ready to move on to Worksheet 11 (mind mapping) and Worksheet 12 (creating three potential Market Vision constructs).

One point which is essential to keep in mind at this stage: it is important to do something that is as different as possible from what everyone else is trying to do to answer a need, resolve a problem, or create benefits for customers. As Billie Holiday famously said (Holiday & Dufty, 1956, p. 53): "No two people on earth are alike, and it's got to be that way in music or it isn't music."

Worksheet 11 aims to help you create a mind map which will enable you to build up your attributes to create your value-add for customers. Then you will be in an excellent position to move toward creating a Market Vision.

Worksheet: 11
Mind Mapping to Elaborate 3 Differentiated Hot Points

1. What is the central concept you want to explore? (e.g., improved airport experience)

   ____

   ____

2. Based on your research thus far, start by reflecting on all the potential attributes that might be relevant when thinking about this concept. List as many as you can for both the product side and the service side of the concept (e.g., safety, accessibility, cleanliness, speedy time from parking to security to gate, parking, hotel, something for kids while waiting, food, etc.).

   ____

   ____

   ____

3. Now, list any potential sub-dimensions to each attribute (e.g., airport cleanliness might be related to locations like bathrooms, open spaces, mirrors and doors, elevators and escalators, handrails, restaurants, security, gate, seating at gate, ticket taking, plane etc.)

11

   1. ______________________________
   2. ______________________________
   3. ______________________________
   4. ______________________________
   5. ______________________________
   6. ______________________________
   7. ______________________________
   8. ______________________________

© Susan E. Reid and Charles B. Crawford, August 14, 2020.

4. Once Q1-Q3 are complete, quickly sketch out a preliminary mind map of your attributes using the tennis example provided in the text or the example provided on the last page of this worksheet. It does not need to be perfect, but rather it is to be used as a tool for soliciting input from others for the next stages.

5. Build on this list by asking for input from your network including PBOD, advisors, experts, and where possible, lead users. Ask them to suggest (prior to showing them your list) their perceptions of what the key underlying activities, components, dimensions (or in other words, attributes) and sub-dimensions are for the central concept. Try to get people to just start adding keywords without too much probing or contemplation – you want people to think creatively here. Once they have provided their ideas around the central concept, show them your list and preliminary mind map to facilitate more discussion.

© Susan E. Reid and Charles B. Crawford, August 14, 2020.

6. With your team, continue building on the understanding of the sum of the attributes collected and how they might lead to potential customer benefits. You might try to think of a cluster as a set of benefits related to the attributes. For example, which potential attributes relate to which of the following types of benefits (both functional and emotional):

    a. Functionality (design, components, interfaces, technologies)
    b. Functional Benefits (ease of use, ease of understanding, increased speed, increased satisfaction)
    c. Enhanced Product/Service (packaging, aesthetics, services and experiences, warranties loyalty)
    d. Environmental System (complementary products and services, neighboring products or markets, suppliers, distribution channel)
    e. Scope (market, resource requirements)
    f. Health, Emotional, and Psychological Benefits
    g. Cost Attributes

7. Cluster together those attributes, sub-attributes, and benefits that seem similar or related and come up with a summary description for each cluster (sometimes a typical category header will be an attribute that comes to mind for more than one person). At this point, you may want to rework your team mind map to reflect the new clusters.

© Susan E. Reid and Charles B. Crawford, August 14, 2020.

8. List the clusters/key attributes in order of importance to your team as potential areas of focus moving forward (ex. (1) Safety, (2) Cleanliness, and (3) Speedy Time through Security).

____

____

____

____

9. List any known competitors and how they compete based on value proposition in any of the spaces noted above as priorities for your team.

____

____

____

____

10. For the attributes you listed as of most importance to your team, either by just focusing on the first priority or by combining 2 or 3 of them in some way, list 3 potential 'hot points' you would like to potentially focus on in order to differentiate an offering (include lead user or consumer feedback in your decision, if relevant).

____

____

____

____

11. How might the 3 early differentiated ideas you have listed clearly distinguish you from the current competition?

12. List the 3 'hot points' addressing the overall opportunity in prioritized order:
    1. (like the most) ____________________________
    2. (like) ____________________________
    3. (like) ____________________________

© Susan E. Reid and Charles B. Crawford, August 14, 2020.

Hypothetical example for the airport experience used in Table 11.1.
(Mind map created by Gillian Regnier, Research Assistant to the authors)

© Susan E. Reid and Charles B. Crawford, August 14, 2020.

11

▣ Table 11.1 provides an analogy we have created which you can use to get your thought process started. The questions are also listed in Worksheet #11 in a slightly more elaborated form, and provides space for your answers.

The following order of operations may be helpful in getting you started, with ingredients to put in your "petri dish" for "growing" your list of attributes:

1. Starter Yeast: First, we provide an hypothetical analogical example by giving you a set of questions to map your own ideas onto (in ◘ Table 11.1 and illustrated in Worksheet 11).
2. Gestation Period: Then, you can start filling in attributes which may be helpful and interesting around your own core ideas. Make sure to give yourself the time you need to flesh these out as fully as possible.
3. Clustering Colonies: Your mind map will allow you to cluster together "colonies" of attributes which share underlying qualities and speak to the basic value-add for your potential customers.

◘ Table 11.1 Questions to provide attributes for clustering into three differentiator hot point ideas

	Question	Example
Q1	What is the central concept/opportunity you want to explore?	Improved airport experience
Q2	Based on your research thus far, think about all of the potential attributes and benefits that might be relevant when thinking about this concept. List as many as you can for both the product and service side of the concept	Safety Accessibility Cleanliness Speedy time to gate through security Parking Hotel Something for kids while waiting Restaurants Washrooms Device charging and use Entertainment
Q3	List any potential subdimensions to each attribute	Ex. airport cleanliness might include a focus on bathrooms, open spaces, mirrors and doors, elevators and escalators and handrails, floors, restaurants, security, gate and seating at the gate, ticket taking, plane, etc.
Q4	Once Q1–Q3 are complete, quickly sketch out a mind map of your attributes using the mind map example for the airport experience provided in Worksheet 11. It does not need to be perfect, but rather should be used as a tool for soliciting input for the next stages	See example in Worksheet 11
Q5	Build on this list by soliciting input from your network. Ask them for new attributes and sub-attributes	Perhaps a key lead user looks at your list and mentions that the bins at the security check are a real harbinger of disease and need to both be and appear to be sterile

(continued)

Table 11.1 (continued)

	Question	Example
Q6	How might the attributes and clusters lead to potential customer benefits? Can you think of benefits linked to the attributes? See examples. (a) Functionality of benefits (ease of use, ease of understanding, increased satisfaction, etc.) (b) Enhanced product/service (packaging, loyalty). (c) Environmental impact. (d) Scope and ability to have an important impact. (e) Health, emotional, and psychological benefits. (f) Cost attributes.	Ex. health and psychological benefits: COVID-free environment at the airport related to cleanliness and safety attributes in all areas of the airport
Q7	Cluster together the ideas, attributes, and benefits which seem most important and related to your interests. Give a category header to each if possible	Ex. based on the location: Bathroom cleanliness attributes, screening area cleanliness attributes, restaurant area cleanliness attributes, gate cleanliness attributes, etc.
Q8	List the clusters/key attributes in order of importance to your team	(1) Safety, (2) cleanliness, and (3) speedy time through security.
Q9	List any known competitors and how they compete on their value proposition in spaces noted as priorities for your team	1. ABM industries "Enhanced-Clean". 2. ISS world airport cleaning services. 3. Infax smart restroom technology for airports.
Q10	For the attributes you listed as of highest importance to your team, either by just focusing on the first or by combining them in some way, list three key "hot points" you would like to focus on in order to differentiate an offering (include lead user or consumer feedback if relevant to your decision)	1. Create a new, secure way to get through security check in a way that people are not concerned about potential contamination from diseases such as Covid (i.e., due to re-use of bins, being in close contact with others, etc.). 2. Make a faster way to go through security check without having to line up. 3. Redesign the customer experience right from the parking area to avoid the need for check-in or airport security altogether.
Q11	How might the three early differentiated ideas you have listed clearly distinguish you from the competition?	The security check process is still a challenge for most consumers and compelling solutions are limited.

Source: Created by the authors as an example of clustering attributes into potential "hot point" differentiators

11

Once you have created this initial mind map, which will bulk together attributes sharing certain qualities, you can test these "attribute clusters" by revisiting your lead users and experts to get a sense of which determinant attributes or clusters jump out as most important from your initial mind map bank of details. Finally, you can use distinction making to refine your ideas by creating continued levels of granularity among the key attribute clusters identified as priority steps for moving forward with the aim of elaborating as many differentiable "hot point" ideas as possible (we suggest aiming at least at three).

You are going to utilize your answers from Worksheet #11 and the three nascent hot point differentiation ideas you have listed and elaborated (i.e., Q10 from ◘ Table 11.1) along with the supporting information that helped you build to these ideas. You will do this in order to prepare three potential strategic options or avenues of focus for moving forward. In effect, you are going to use this information to create three possible early Market Vision constructs before choosing one to move forward with and develop further into a full Market Vision statement.

11.2 Making the Components of Market Vision Clear

Based on Reid (2005, dissertation) and further detailed in Reid and de Brentani (2010) and Reid (2015), the elements of Market Vision have been empirically tested, and five dimensions were found to comprise Market Vision:

1. Market Vision Form.
2. Market Vision Scope.
3. Market Vision Magnetism.
4. Market Vision Clarity.
5. Market Vision Specificity.

Just a reminder that both Market Vision Form and Market Vision Scope are related to the overall dimension of Market Vision Goals. Also, to simplify things for our purposes, we combine Market Vision Clarity and Market Vision Specificity into one dimension here. ► Chap. 2 outlines the definitions for each of these and provides examples.

Specific Market Vision components and related questions for consideration were described in Reid (2005) and detailed in Reid (2015) (they are outlined here with permission granted on December 3, 2020, from Springer Nature for reprint with adaptations). These details will help you start constructing some "meat" on the key attributes which you had decided to move forward with based upon your answers in Worksheet #11.

11.2.1 Market Vision Form

Market Vision Form is what the mental image of the Market Vision actually looks like in the visionary's mind. The image relates to how the product, possibly within a product system, might be utilized by consumers (see ◘ Fig. 11.3 for an example of a well-developed design concept by Forrest Fulton for the future of "big box agriculture"). In order to aid in constructing such an image, the following types of questions might be considered in the construction of the form of the vision:

- **Product/Service Concept:**
  - What is the relationship between anticipated product/service features (form or technology) and consumer benefits?
  - What does the interface look like between product/service and consumer?
  - What does the consumer look like when they are using the product or service? How are they experiencing the value you are delivering?

- **Overall System of Use:**
  - What does the overall system of use look like?
  - What else needs to happen or be present for the system to work?
  - What complementary products need to be in place for it to work?
  - What complementary services need to be in place for it to work?
  - What is the usage environment? Where does it need to happen?

◘ **Fig. 11.3** Big-box agriculture: a productive suburb by Forrest Fulton, from Dwell article by Sarah Rich, August 19, 2009. (Source: ▶ www.dwell.com/article/reburbia-winners-announced-11e0f4a3, downloaded on August 28, 2020)

- **Timing of Use:**
  - What is the timing of use? When during the day, week, year, etc. is it used?
  - By when does it need to happen, or do you want it to happen?
  - Is there a specific launch date you are aiming for?

- **Product Design:**
  - What are the components of the service or product?
  - What are the key or distinctive components capable of eliciting advantage?
  - How do the components need to be interfaced?
  - Does the design offer the potential for standardizing or leveraging the idea or vision (ripple effect)?

11.2.2 Market Vision Scope

Market Vision Scope relates specifically to the size or grandiosity of the market goal as well as the potential for impacting people. As such, Market Vision Scope has two main components which need to be considered: Target Magnitude and the Target Market itself. Target Magnitude involves the scope of the envisioned market. The Target Market provides the direction for the development path. To aid in understanding the Scope, the following types of questions need to be considered:

- **Target Magnitude:**
  - To what extent does it have the potential to help society or enhance the future for society?
  - How many people or companies could it potentially apply to long term?
  - What is the potential for profit or to create value from the vision?

- **Target Market:**
  - Who does the vision apply to in the marketplace (i.e., What are the potential target markets? What are the potential niche markets?)?
  - How many people or companies will it apply to for each target or niche (at the beginning and longer term)?
  - What end-user groups and activities will be affected downstream from your immediate target? How many people or companies will be affected in the channel?

11.2.3 Market Vision Magnetism

Market Vision Magnetism (◘ Fig. 11.4) is essential in that the Market Vision needs to have a certain level of magnetism (attraction) and/or inspiration (desirability) in order to be proactively compelling. This motivation will push the vision holders to move toward enacting the vision and breaking the inertia around that movement (i.e., it needs to be something they are truly passionate about). Key questions the visionary should reflect on relate to themselves, potential teammates/advisors, potential customers, and potential investors:

How desirable/attractive is the vision (for you, your teammates, advisors, potential customers, and potential investors)—i.e., how much do you want/like it?

- This particular market vision is desirable/attractive to the team/advisors because….
- This particular market vision will be desirable/attractive to customers because….
- This particular market vision will be desirable/attractive to potential investors because….

11

◘ **Fig. 11.4** Conceptual image to portray "Magnetism." (Source: Image licensed and downloaded from Shutterstock on May 5, 2013. Credit: by Oleksiy Mark/▸ Shutterstock.com. License Link: ▸ https://www.shutterstock.com/image-illustration/social-engineering-concept-horseshoe-magnet-capturing-105928628)

How important is the vision (for you, your teammates, advisors, potential customers, and potential investors)?

- This particular market vision is important to the team/advisors because....
- This particular market vision will be important to customers because....
- This particular market vision will be important to potential investors because....

11.2.4 Market Vision Clarity and Specificity

Market Vision Clarity and Specificity speak to understanding in a very well-articulated way (◘ Fig. 11.5) the who, what, why, and by when underlying the vision. The specifics of the "how" or the "action plan" can be built in after the vision itself is clearly understood. In other words, what are the specific building blocks that are required to build the vision? The clearer the vision, the more quickly we can see how to build a path toward it. In order for a vision to be clear, it needs to be tangible, and this requires something known as "specificity." Specificity can occur when a vision is operationally meaningful or contextualized and has a tangible form.

1. Using the details from the previous answers, as clearly as possible, state the who, what, why, and by when behind the vision. How tangible are each of these current elements? Is it possible to make them more tangible? Is it possible to use

◘ **Fig. 11.5** Conceptual image to portray a vision being "crystal clear." (Source: Image licensed and downloaded from Shutterstock on May 2, 2013. Credit: by 123dartist/► Shutterstock.com. License Link: ► https://www.shutterstock.com/image-illustration/luxury-diamond-isolated-on-white-background-119434465)

high imagery wording to connote these ideas? List strategies for gaining a higher level of tangibility.
2. What are the most important building blocks and key differentiators that will impact the ability to be successful with this vision? Highlight these as key elements to try to incorporate into the vision statement.
3. Is the current level of understanding of these building blocks capable of being operationalizable in a meaningful way?
4. Are there elements which still lack clarity? If so, highlight these and try to gather more information to help build more clarity.
5. Given all of your answers thus far, how well do you understand the context for enacting your vision in terms of the current and potential market, current and potential investors, and current and potential network (i.e., supply chain, downstream distribution, alliance partners)? What do you need to do to create a more explicit context for vision enactment?

11.3 Creating an Early Market Vision Construct

In Worksheet 11, the aim is to create at least three differentiable hot points to potentially move forward with and prioritize them. Worksheet 12 invites you to flesh out three Market Vision constructs. To do this, you might use either three target market variations with the same basic hot point idea or three different hot point ideas to get at the same target market. Finally, you will choose the best one for your team, based on where you feel you can provide the best value-add as a
11 team. It is a good idea to maintain the other target market variation and hot points ideas of interest, in case the first one does not pan out during future concept testing and refinement or during development or scale-up.

To illustrate, we will provide one example of how to begin creating such an early Market Vision construct using Worksheet 11 based on the #1 priority chosen from our hypothetical example. In ◘ Table 11.1, priority/hot point #1 was: make a cleaner and more secure way to go through the security check at the airport in a way that relieves travelers of worries about contamination from COVID-19 or other diseases.

So, let's think about some potential elements of the Market Vision that might help us do just that.

Market Vision Form: The above hot point idea combines all three of the key attributes which we prioritized: (1) safety, (2) cleanliness, and (3) speedy time through security. It also addresses a key benefit for consumers we are interested in addressing: health and psychological benefits—COVID-free environment at the airport. The basic concept we want to introduce to address these attributes and benefits is a "sterile envelope." Specifically, we envision a clean, soft pouch with a drawstring which is inserted by a masked and gloved security employee into a sterilized bin. This pouch has been sterilized using a UV treatment and will act as a sort of "mask" for our goods from the time they go through the safety detection devices at security, through to the overhead bin in the airplane. Once we deplane, we can leave the pouch in a set location at the next airport for recycling. A recycling and cleaning system will need to be part of the service element of the offering. Given the COVID-19 threat, there is an urgency on the part of airports to find solutions to this and the installation of such an hypothetical system might be a type of idea to build upon.

Market Vision Scope: The magnitude is large scale given that there are X# of travelers in North America and globally per year and at least X% of the population travels by plane each year. It has important implications for enhancing the future of society by making travel much safer both for business and pleasure travelers (targets) and airport employees (government buyer).

Market Vision Magnetism: Such a system is highly motivating because the visionary is also a frequent traveler and interested in traveler safety and cleanliness.

Market Vision Clarity and Specificity:

Who: Government (buyers for airport security systems).

By when: 2021.

Why: Very important given current COVID-19 situation and the continuing threat of new viruses.

What: See description under Market Vision Form.

You are now going to use the information from your Worksheet 11 to create three potential early Market Vision constructs before deciding on one to move forward with developing further. Worksheet 12 will help you to do this by building up the core aspects of each Market Vision and in so doing will help you to make a preliminary recommendation for moving forward with one of the three options.

Worksheet 12: Create 3 Potential Market Vision Statements

From Worksheet 11, you should now have a favorite hot point for the area of opportunity you would like to address (along with 2 backup hot points). Based on this, list 3 potential target markets you might go after with the hot point differentiator OR list 3 variant ideas to address the hot point. The next step is to now take these and start working towards building a clear market vision statement for each of the 3 ideas. Trying to elucidate each idea more clearly will help you to determine which vision of the 3 is going to be the best for you to focus your attention on for potential development moving forward.

Differentiator Concept #1 ______________________________

____

Differentiator Concept #2 ______________________________

____

Differentiator Concept #3 ______________________________

____

For each of the following Market Vision aspects, how does **Concept #1** incorporate or address each of the following:

Market Vision Form #1:

a) Product Concept: What is the relationship between anticipated product features and consumer benefits? What does the interface look like between products and consumers? What does the consumer look like when using the product?

b) Overall System of Use: What does the overall system of use look like? What else needs to happen or be present for it to work? What complementary products or services need to be in place for it to work? What is the use environment?

c) Timing of Use: What is the timing of the use or application? When during the day, week, year etc. is it used? By when does it need to happen or do you want it to happen? Is there a specific launch date you are aiming at?

d) Design: Components of service or product? How do they need to be interfaced? What is the potential for standardizing or leveraging the idea – ripple effect?

____

____

____

____

____

© Susan E. Reid and Charles B. Crawford, August 14, 2020.

11

Market Vision Scope #1:

a) Potential to help society or enhance future for society?
b) How many people or companies could the idea apply to long-term?
c) What is the potential for profit or to create value from the vision?
d) Who does the vision apply to? (list of target markets or niche markets). How many people or companies will it apply to for each target or niche? (in the beginning and longer term).
e) What end user groups and activities will be affected downstream from your immediate target? How many people or companies will be affected?

____

____

____

____

____

____

Market Vision Magnetism #1:

a) This particular market vision is desirable or attractive to the team because…
b) This particular market vision will be desirable or attractive to customers because…
c) This particular market vision will be desirable or attractive to potential investors because…
d) This particular market vision is important to the team because…
e) This particular market vision will be important to customers because…
f) This particular market vision will be important to potential investors because…
g) Did you feel joy as you worked on filling out the various ideas underlying this vision (as outlined in the form and scope)?

____

____

____

____

____

____

© Susan E. Reid and Charles B. Crawford, August 14, 2020.

Market Vision Clarity and Specificity #1:

a) Using the details from the previous answers, as clearly as possible state the Who? What? Why? and When? behind the vision. How tangible are each of these current elements? Is it possible to make them more tangible?

b) What are the most important building blocks which will impact the ability to be successful with this vision? Highlight these as key elements to try to incorporate into the vision statement.

c) Is the current level of understanding of these building blocks capable of being operationalizable (i.e. put into action) in a meaningful way?

d) Are there elements which still lack clarity? If so, highlight and list these. Develop a plan for gathering more information to seek more clarity on these elements (Who is responsible? What do they need to collect? Who do they need to contact? How should they go about it? By when will it be done?).

e) Given all of your answers thus far, how well do you understand the context for enacting your vision in terms of current and potential market, current and potential investors, current and potential network (i.e. supply chain, downstream distribution, alliance partners)? What do you need to do to create a more clear context?

How/how much is Market Vision #1 in line with your team Core Competence and Capabilities?

11

Does Market Vision #1 pass the following tests?

- Is it gut grabbing?
- Are you excited and driven by it? Do you think customers would be?
- Is it very clear?

© Susan E. Reid and Charles B. Crawford, August 14, 2020.

- Does it specifically tie in (at least intuitively) with a specific product and market and how they intersect?

____

- Is it able to address both the present and the future? Which direction does it tend to lean to?

____

- Are you addressing an existing market or one you understand? Can the MV help you to learn more about a new market?

____

____

Using all of this information, construct a one sentence market vision statement for Concept #1:

____

____

For each of the following Market Vision aspects, how does **Concept #2** incorporate or address each of the following:

Market Vision Form #2:

a) Product Concept: What is the relationship between anticipated product features and consumer benefits? What does the interface look like between products and consumers? What does the consumer look like when using the product?
b) Overall System of Use: What does the overall system of use look like? What else needs to happen or be present for it to work? What complementary products or services need to be in place for it to work? What is the use environment?
c) Timing of Use: What is the timing of the use or application? When during the day, week, year etc. is it used? By when does it need to happen or do you want it to happen? Is there a specific launch date you are aiming at?
d) Design: Components of service or product? How do they need to be interfaced? What is the potential for standardizing or leveraging the idea – ripple effect?

____

____

____

____

____

© Susan E. Reid and Charles B. Crawford, August 14, 2020.

Market Vision Scope #2:
a) Potential to help society or enhance future for society?
b) How many people or companies could the idea apply to long-term?
c) What is the potential for profit or to create value from the vision?
d) Who does the vision apply to? (list of target markets or niche markets). How many people or companies will it apply to for each target or niche? (in the beginning and longer term).
e) What end user groups and activities will be affected downstream from your immediate target? How many people or companies will be affected?

Market Vision Magnetism #2:
a) This particular market vision is desirable or attractive to the team because…
b) This particular market vision will be desirable or attractive to customers because…
c) This particular market vision will be desirable or attractive to potential investors because…
d) This particular market vision is important to the team because…
e) This particular market vision will be important to customers because…
f) This particular market vision will be important to potential investors because…
g) Did you feel joy as you worked on filling out the various ideas underlying this vision (as outlined in the form and scope)?

11

Market Vision Clarity and Specificity #2:
a) Using the details from the previous answers, as clearly as possible state the Who? What? Why? and When? behind the vision. How tangible are each of these current elements? Is it possible to make them more tangible?
b) What are the most important building blocks which will impact the ability to be successful with this vision? Highlight these as key elements to try to incorporate into the vision statement.
c) Is the current level of understanding of these building blocks capable of being operationalizable (i.e., put into action) in a meaningful way?
d) Are there elements which still lack clarity? If so, highlight and list these. Develop a plan for gathering more information to seek more clarity on these elements (Who is responsible? What do they need to collect? Who do they need to contact? How should they go about it? By when will it be done?).

© Susan E. Reid and Charles B. Crawford, August 14, 2020.

e) Given all of your answers thus far, how well do you understand the context for enacting your vision in terms of current and potential market, current and potential investors, current and potential network (i.e., supply chain, downstream distribution, alliance partners)? What do you need to do to create a more clear context?

How/how much is Market Vision #2 in line with your team Core Competence and Capabilities?

Does Market Vision #2 pass the following tests?

- Is it gut grabbing?
- Are you excited and driven by it? Do you think customers would be?
- Is it very clear?
- Does it specifically tie in, at least intuitively, with a specific product and market and how they intersect?
- Is it able to address both the present and the future? Which direction does it tend to lean to?
- Are you addressing an existing market or one you understand? Can the MV help you to learn more about a new market?

Using all of this information, construct a one sentence market vision statement for Product/Service idea #2:

© Susan E. Reid and Charles B. Crawford, August 14, 2020.

For each of the following Market Vision aspects, how does **Concept #3** incorporate or address each of the following:

Market Vision Form #3:

a) Product Concept: What is the relationship between anticipated product features and consumer benefits? What does the interface look like between products and consumers? What does the consumer look like when using the product?

b) Overall System of Use: What does the overall system of use look like? What else needs to happen or be present for it to work? What complementary products or services need to be in place for it to work? What is the use environment?

c) Timing of Use: What is the timing of the use or application? When during the day, week, year etc. is it used? By when does it need to happen or do you want it to happen? Is there a specific launch date you are aiming at?

d) Design: Components of service or product? How do they need to be interfaced? What is the potential for standardizing or leveraging the idea – ripple effect?

Market Vision Scope #3:

a) Potential to help society or enhance future for society?

b) How many people or companies could the idea apply to long-term?

c) What is the potential for profit or to create value from the vision?

11 d) Who does the vision apply to? (list of target markets or niche markets). How many people or companies will it apply to for each target or niche? (in the beginning and longer term).

e) What end user groups and activities will be affected downstream from your immediate target? How many people or companies will be affected?

© Susan E. Reid and Charles B. Crawford, August 14, 2020.

Market Vision Magnetism #3:
a) This particular market vision is desirable or attractive to the team because…
b) This particular market vision will be desirable or attractive to customers because…
c) This particular market vision will be desirable or attractive to potential investors because…
d) This particular market vision is important to the team because…
e) This particular market vision will be important to customers because…
f) This particular market vision will be important to potential investors because…
g) Did you feel joy as you worked on filling out the various ideas underlying this vision (as outlined in the form and scope)?

___

___

___

___

Market Vision Clarity and Specificity #3:
a) Using the details from the previous answers, as clearly as possible state the Who? What? Why? and When? behind the vision. How tangible are each of these current elements? Is it possible to make them more tangible?
b) What are the most important building blocks which will impact the ability to be successful with this vision? Highlight these as key elements to try to incorporate into the vision statement.
c) Is the current level of understanding of these building blocks capable of being operationalizable (i.e., put into action) in a meaningful way?
d) Are there elements which still lack clarity? If so, highlight and list these. Develop a plan for gathering more information to seek more clarity on these elements (Who is responsible? What do they need to collect? Who do they need to contact? How should they go about it? By when will it be done?).
e) Given all of your answers thus far, how well do you understand the context for enacting your vision in terms of current and potential market, current and potential investors, current and potential network (i.e., supply chain, downstream distribution, alliance partners)? What do you need to do to create a more clear context?

___

___

___

___

How/how much is Market Vision #3 in line with your team Core Competence and Capabilities?

___

© Susan E. Reid and Charles B. Crawford, August 14, 2020.

Does Market Vision #3 pass the following tests?

- Is it gut grabbing?

  ____

- Are you excited and driven by it? Do you think customers would be?

  ____

- Is it very clear?

  ____

- Does it specifically tie in, at least intuitively, with a specific product and market and how they intersect?

  ____

- Is it able to address both the present and the future? Which direction does it tend to lean to?

  ____

- Are you addressing an existing market or one you understand? Can the MV help you to learn more about a new market?

  ____

  ____

Using all of this information, construct a one sentence market vision statement for Product/Service idea #3:

____

11

After having done this exercise, which Market Vision for your team elicits the most excitement and feels most 'right' to move forward with?*

____

***Test with your Advisory Board (PBOD, Experts, Lead Users, etc. using Worksheet 13 prior to moving forward with your #1 choice).**

© Susan E. Reid and Charles B. Crawford, August 14, 2020.

The end goal of Worksheet 12 is to provide some clarity as to which of the three potential early Market Vision constructs you and your team feel most motivated to work toward.

We suggest doing a quick check-in with your advisory board at this stage (PBOD, and key experts and lead users), to get their feedback prior to making a final call as to which Market Vision to put forward. In order to help you do this, we have constructed a short questionnaire to share with your advisors in Worksheet 13.

Worksheet 13: Testing 3 Potential Market Visions with your Advisory Board (PBOD, Key Experts and Lead Users)

Types of Questions to Consider:

1. Warm-up Discussion
   a. Thank you for coming and introductions
   b. Give them a bit of a background on how/why you got interested in these specific ideas.
   c. "Have you had a chance to look over the 3 initial potential market vision concepts/statements we sent you (Worksheet 12)?"
   d. "Do you understand the general concepts?" (if not, spend some time describing in a little more detail, possibly using your mind map if you think it might be helpful)

2. Background Questions:
   a. "Have you ever seen or heard something similar to these concepts before reading what we sent you? Are you aware of other companies or people who are working on anything similar? If not, have you ever wondered why the idea hasn't been pursued before?"
3. Product/Service Specific Questions:
   a. "What do you like most about the ideas?"
   b. "What do you like least about the ideas?"
   c. "Is there anything you would change about the basic ideas?"
   d. "Are we missing anything from your perspective?"

4. Concept Preference:
   a. "Which concept would deliver the most value for you specifically? Why?"
   b. "Which aspects of our favorite idea do you like the most? Would you add anything to the basic concept to make it more appealing to consumers?"
5. Competition-Specific Questions for the concept you like best:
   a. "What products/services do you currently use to fill similar needs?"
   b. "What aspects of the ideas do you think might be easily copied? By whom?"
   c. "Which idea do you think has the most potential for us to be able to differentiate ourselves from the competition? Do you also like this idea the best?"

6. Other Questions:
   a. "Are there any publications, books, conferences, associations in the field we should be investigating to get even more information about these concepts?"
   b. "Is there anyone else you think we should discuss about the concept you liked best?"

© Susan E. Reid and Charles B. Crawford, August 14, 2020.

Given the results from Worksheets 11 and 12, and once vetted with your advisory board using Worksheet 13, the next chapters will help you to continue working on the one Market Vision you believe you and your team are the most inspired to work toward and where you can create the most value-add.

Chapter Review Questions

1. Why is mind mapping helpful to the visioning process?
2. What are the sub-concepts of the mind map also known as?
3. What aspects of the sub-concepts might be used to provide more detail in a mind map?

References

Buzan, T. (1974). *Use your head*. BBC Books (and NNC TV series hosted in 1974).

Holiday, B., & Dufty, W. (1956). *Lady sings the blues, the 50th-anniversary edition*. Google Books.

Reid, S. E. (2005). *Market Vision for radically new, high-tech products*. Ph.D. Thesis, John Molson School of Business, Concordia University.

Reid, S. E. (2015). Vision and radical innovation: A typology. In A. Brem & E. Viardot (Eds.), *Adoption of innovation: Balancing internal and external stakeholders in the marketing of innovation* (pp. 133–154). Springer International Publications.

Reid, S. E., & de Brentani, U. (2010). Market vision and market visioning competence: Impact on early performance for radically new, high-tech products. *The Journal of Product Innovation Management, 27*(4), 500–518.

Schwendimann, B. (2014). Concept mapping. In R. Gunstone (Ed.), *Encyclopedia of science education*. Springer.

Technology Vision Creation

Contents

© The Author(s), under exclusive license to Springer Nature Switzerland AG 2022
S. E. Reid, C. B. Crawford, *Entrepreneurial Vision*, Classroom Companion: Business,
https://doi.org/10.1007/978-3-030-77803-3_12

Learning Objectives

This chapter focuses in on a special case of vision development, which is associated with the creation of a "Technology Vision" ("TV"). This type of vision development does not pertain to the experience of all entrepreneurs, nor does it occur within all companies. It is, however, important to have a chapter devoted to it, as it plays an important role for those entrepreneurs involved with the creation and development of applied technologies and, as such, requires some discussion and differentiation from Market Vision ("MV").

The learning objectives of the following chapter, therefore, are to:

1. Highlight the need for a Technology Vision scale as a distinct measure from the Market Vision scale.
2. Outline the key components of Technology Vision.
3. Detail the importance of Technology Vision in terms of its impact on early performance for startups, where relevant.

12.1 The Need for a Technology Vision Scale

After finishing the data collection to study and develop a measure for Market Vision, Susan (Reid, 2005) realized that some people she had interviewed were more focused on creating a broad "vision for the future" for the technology they were developing, rather than on a vision of the future market for specific products which might emanate from that technology. In other words, these specific individuals were not positioned in time or place to be focused on markets, but they were certainly focused on the benefits and outcomes of the research they were conducting with their various technologies and how they might apply across a wide swath of potential products. In other words, their focus was on a Technology Vision (◘ Fig. 12.1).

12

Indeed, during the data collection for her Ph.D. research, Susan had started creating a file tentatively called "too early for developing a market vision" which she later realized was largely made up of people's stories and experiences which were focused primarily on technology development and where these researchers were not really ready yet to talk about markets. That said, however, they still were very much focusing on a vision for moving forward, but rather than the vision being focused on the market, it was focused on the outcomes of their technology development.

At the time of Susan's doctoral research, no known empirical research had been done on this specific type of technology visioning activity, and indeed, it was much more difficult to understand. This was largely due to the fact that it was occurring mostly in the heads of individual researchers and entrepreneurs (◘ Fig. 12.2), who were not yet ready to share much about their thoughts and insights with others.

In further work, largely stimulated by these insights, Reid and Roberts (2011, p. 428) employed a new level of understanding when dealing with this specific type of vision and defined it as "Technology Vision," "a mental image held by individ-

Fig. 12.1 Conceptual image to portray "Technology Vision." (Source: Image licensed and downloaded from Adobe Stock on November 9, 2020. Credit: by Christos Georghiou/▶ stock.adobe.com. License Link: ▶ https://stock.adobe.com/ca/images/a-female-woman-scientist-working-in-a-scientific-laboratory-with-microscope-and-other-science-lab-equipment/264912103)

ual organizational members regarding technical goals related to developing a new technology."

As noted in Reid et al. (2015, pp. 593–594, permission granted December 3, 2020, from John Wiley & Sons for reprint):

> "Indeed, one of the key challenges in managing technology-enabled radical innovation processes is related to the fact that much of the very early stage thinking and work is driven by one or a couple of individuals and without strategic input or knowledge of the firm (Burgelman and Sayles, 1986; Reid and de Brentani, 2004). They may either work within firms or may be entrepreneurs in the case of start-ups. If such a technology visionary is an entrepreneur, they will often be starting to think about attracting funding to their early ideas; if they are intrapreneurs, or technology visionaries working within firms, they will likely start thinking about attracting internal resources and funding to get the ball rolling. The thought processes of such individuals early on in emergent technology situations are of interest in our research. Specifically, the key questions are related to "how" the initial goals for working with a given technology are chosen, what they are, and what their impact is."

Fig. 12.2 Conceptual image to portray a Technology Vision-based idea in the individual mind of the technology entrepreneur/intrapreneur. (Source: Image licensed and downloaded from Adobe Stock on November 9, 2020. Credit: by lvnl/► stock.adobe.com. License Link: ► https://stock.adobe.com/ca/images/creativity-and-innovation-concept-human-head-line-with-light-bulb-made-of-puzzle/99712669)

12.2 Technology Vision: The Main Components

Our research (Reid & Roberts, 2011; Reid et al., 2015) offered an approach to understanding Technology Vision, and its key components, by employing a literature review, exploratory interviews, and empirical analysis, in order to create a theoretical framework for this novel area of research. It is worth describing the upshot findings of this research as it operated to distinguish between Technology Vision and Market Vision in terms of key focus, components, and potential impact on performance.

The interviews were conducted with 30 high-tech experts from academia as well as from industry, including perspectives from senior managers, CEOs, and venture capitalists involving a variety of high-tech fields. Specifically, a combination of qualitative, in-depth interviews was used with experts and academics in order to ensure the best possible understanding of the various dimensions underlying the concept.

To build further understanding, qualitative case evidence was taken into consideration from a study by Livingston (2007) on 20 high-tech company founders related to the early days of their technology development. A conceptual framework was developed by Reid and Roberts (2011) leading to the development of a set of items which were grouped into five constructs (◘ Fig. 12.3) and tested in both Reid and Roberts (2011) and Reid et al. (2015).

These five core Technology Vision elements were elucidated further in Reid et al. (2015, p. 599, permission granted December 3, 2020, from John Wiley & Sons for reprint):

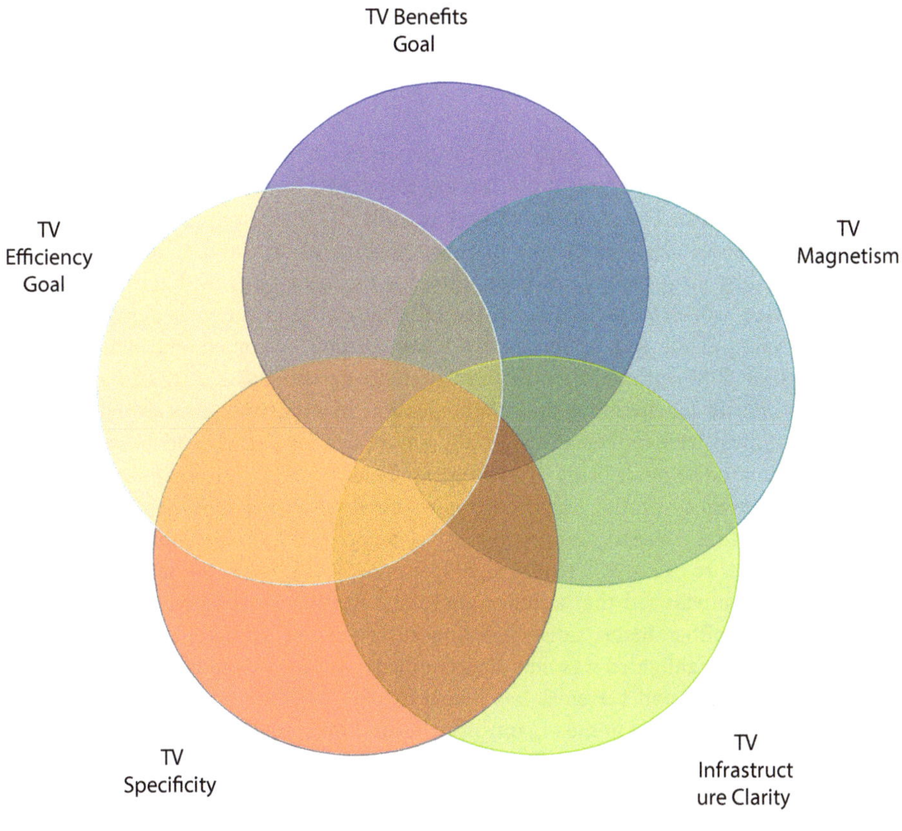

◘ **Fig. 12.3** Venn diagram to portray the components of Technology Vision. (Figure by the authors)

Fig. 12.4 The BlackBerry 950 (introduced as "Inter@ctive Pager 950," development name "Leapfrog") is an early BlackBerry model, introduced in 1998 by Research in Motion. (Source: ▶ https://upload.wikimedia.org/wikipedia/commons/0/06/RIM_BlackBerry_950.jpg. Created by Ruben de Rijcke, CC BY-SA 4.0 <▶ https://creativecommons.org/licenses/by-sa/4.0>, on April 8, 2019. Downloaded via Wikimedia Commons on November 9, 2020)

» "As a result, the notion of "goals" was further developed with interviewees and classified into two typical types: those leading to benefits and those leading to lower costs (efficiencies). For example, Mike Lazaridis of "Research in Motion" noted that while the wireless benefit to e-mail was realized as critical early on, the value was limited by the packaging and limitations of the technology of that time, and so they started working specifically on the efficiency goal in order to deliver better overall value at the end of the day to whoever their customers ended up being (Livingston, 2007); of course, while this "interactive pager" (Fig. 12.4) was developed primarily for speeding up communication in industrial sales, it eventually became a must-have tool creating initially unforeseen benefits for the mass market. This distinction of goals being of two types, efficiency goals and benefits goals, was reiterated in many of the expert interviews conducted. For example, one expert emphasized that an important component of a good technology vision was related to "the ability to eventually realize significant cost savings." At the same time, this expert also emphasized that another goal must involve focusing on "key benefits which could either better satisfy existing customers or attract new customers." Another issue highlighted was that the technology vision needs to have the potential to impact others, and therefore has a role to play in terms of offering direction ("specificity") to others in the organization beyond the initial founder, entrepreneur, or tech visionary. Finally, one expert made an interesting observation that in addition to clarity regarding the technology itself and its benefits, it was very important very early on that the requirements of the infrastructure that would be needed to get things up and running be a clear part of that vision as well (i.e., human resources, facilities, how much it would cost to develop the technology)."

Reid (2015) summarizes these five elements as follows (with permission granted on December 3, 2020, from Springer Nature for reprint):

1. *The Technology Vision benefits goal* is related to how to improve benefits for customers and employees. The benefits goals related to developing a specific technology have three main foci in terms of helping potential customers or employees: making things easier, making things more convenient, and making things more user-friendly.
2. *The Technology Vision efficiency goal* is related to solving design economics issues in the following three ways: how to most cheaply incorporate the technology into potential products, how to apply the technology more cheaply than the competition, and how to solve the economics behind the science.
3. *Technology Vision magnetism* is related to the desirability of the goal to the inventor. It requires the same underlying components as seen for Market Vision Magnetism. The vision needs to be desirable, attractive, and important enough to the vision holder(s) to motivate them to move toward the vision and break the inertia around that movement (i.e., it needs to be something the vision holders are truly passionate about).
4. *Technology Vision specificity* is related to the tangibility of the technology vision in that it needs to be clear, and specific and provides direction to others. According to Reid and Roberts (2011), the ability to build clarity into technical solutions in terms of goals and directions for people to follow is essential. Building a picture of "what might be," making the vision tangible through simple descriptions, diagrams, and the use of concepts, helps to build clarity and convince people of the technology's potential in lieu of other supporting evidence at this early stage.
5. *Technology Vision infrastructure clarity* is related to the clarity of the processes and infrastructure required during the early stages of technology conception and development. Specifically, it is related to the facilities required to enact it, the human resources required to enact it, and the cost to develop it. This may require the adoption of new and novel routines and competences from those which support the ongoing research.

These elements of Technology Vision – benefits goals, efficiency goals, magnetism, specificity, and infrastructure clarity – which were highlighted by experts in qualitative interviews, were then tested empirically both in the research of Reid and Roberts (2011) and Reid et al. (2015) to determine whether they were found to be significant factors in large-scale research.

In order to test the hypothesized underlying dimensions of Technology Vision, Reid and Roberts (2011) first conducted an exploratory factor analysis ("EFA") with a sample of 100 North American high-tech firms including those from the fields of electronics, biopharmaceuticals, energy, and sustainability. According to Reid et al. (2015, p. 599, permission granted December 3, 2020, from John Wiley & Sons for reprint):

> "In small firms, the CEO or CTO was often the person who worked directly with the technology, and in larger firms it was the CEO, CTO, or project manager. Respondents were asked to only participate if they had been involved in the early-stage development of one "high-tech" (>6% of sales spent on R & D according to the definition provided by Riche et al., 1983) and "radical innovation", as per the operational definition provided by Leifer et al. (2000): any innovation that improves performance by at least 5–10 times, reduces costs by >30%, and/or is considered new-to-the-world ("NTW")."

Second, a confirmatory factor analysis ("CFA") was run by Reid et al. (2015) on a sample of 94 firms from the UK, and the results elicited that indeed the 5 dimensions identified in the exploratory analysis were the "first-order" factors underlying the second-order factor, Technology Vision, as follows: a benefits goal (alpha = 0.95), an efficiency goal (alpha = 0.73), magnetism (alpha = 0.80), specificity (alpha = 0.89), and infrastructure clarity (alpha = 0.82) with an overall comparative fit index or CFI = 0.975 and root mean square error approximation or RMSEA = 0.45. As such, these results supported the existence of a second-order reflective model for measuring Technology Vision, and the results of these analyses are provided in ◘ Table 12.1.

In many ways, through the results of these research efforts, Technology Vision appeared to have similar characteristics to Market Vision, yet the focus was more about the technology and how these individuals working with it (i.e., the researchers, developers, and/or entrepreneurs) might eventually provide benefits or efficiencies for consumers. Specifically, the developers were training in on how to provide benefits and efficiencies for consumers by focussing on their own technology or engineering skills to provide solutions for generalized or abstracted "types" of benefits (i.e., "ease of use" or "convenience") and efficiencies (i.e., lower costs). This focus was different from how the benefits and efficiencies might actually be perceived by consumers in terms of their own prioritizations or whether there was a meaningful market for these. In other words, the magnetism of the tech solutions was often focused on the technology itself rather than the benefits for consumers.

For example, ◘ Table 12.1 shows that the types of "benefits goals" that came out as being important across the board in the confirmatory factor analysis were based on "How to make things more convenient," "How to make things easier," and "How to make things more user friendly" and not necessarily on how each of these attributes related to the development of a product might be perceived in terms of prioritization or at a higher level of consumer-focussed granularity. Similarly, the "efficiency goals" which emerged as statistically important were related to how to make things more cheaply or how to solve a problem related to economies of scale. These issues may be extremely important for manufacturers and ultimately translate to lower prices for consumers, but the question is whether this relates well to the needs and wants of a given target market. Only once vision progresses to incorporate how products and markets mesh together in a Market Vision do these relationships start to come more into focus.

Table 12.1 SEM standardized estimates and probabilities of TV based on CFA analysis

First-order TV paths tested	**Standardized estimate**
Benefits goal (alpha = .95)	.990* (λ1)
HowtoMakeThingsMoreConvenient	.950* (λ2)
HowtoMakeThingsEasier	.869* (λ3)
HowtoMakeThingsMoreUserFriendly	
Efficiency goal (alpha = .73)	
About_CheapInc	.854* (λ4)
About_HowIncMoreCheaply	.716* (λ5)
About_HowSolveEco	.547* (λ6)
Magnetism (alpha = .80)	
Goal of tech was attractive	.776* (λ7)
Goal of tech was desirable	.787* (λ8)
Goal of tech was compelling	.715* (λ9)
Specificity (alpha = .89)	
Early techvision tangible	.887* (λ10)
Early techvision clear	.889* (λ11)
Early techvision specific	.905* (λ12)
Early techvision provide direction	.619* (λ13)
Infrastructure clarity (alpha = .82)	
Clear what facilities needed	.822* (λ14)
Clear what HR needed	.968* (λ15)
Clear cost to develop	.605* (λ16)
Second-order TV paths tested	**Standardized estimate (*t*-value)**
TV to technology vision benefits goal	.364 (2.669)*
TV to technology vision efficiency goal	.561 (3.596)*
TV to technology vision magnetism	.576 (3.918)*
TV to technology infrastructure clarity	.427 (2.765)*
TV to technology vision specificity	.496 (3.343)*

Table 1 from Reid et al. (2015), permission granted December 3, 2020, from John Wiley & Sons for reprint

CFA confirmatory factor analysis, *HR* human resource, *SEM* structural equation modeling, *TV* technology vision

*$p < .05$

12.3 Why Is Technology Vision Important? Impact on Early Performance

In the research of Reid et al. (2015), a final sample of 118 firms from the UK and 82 NA firms for a total of 200 firms primarily from the biotechnology and nanotechnology sectors was utilized in order to test the structural equation model ("SEM")—or, in other words, whether there was a significant relationship and impact in terms of the measurement results for these firms for each of the five aspects of Technology Vision related to the three key aspects of early performance (as detailed in ► Chap. 2): Early Success with Customers (ESC), Technological Competitive Advantage (TCA), and Ability to Attract Capital (AAC). Basically, the findings pointed to all of the relationships are significant (Reid et al., 2015, pp. 600–602).

In sum, the results of our structural equation model specifically confirmed that the five dimensions of Technology Vision, i.e., the TV benefits goal, the TV efficiency goal, TV magnetism, TV specificity, and TV infrastructure clarity, were each separately and significantly linked to the overall Technology Vision construct. Additionally, Technology Vision had a significant impact on each of the outcome performance factors: ESC, TCA, and AAC.

- **Impact of TV on ESC**

Technology Vision had a strong positive and significant impact on Early Success with Customers *(lambda = 0.403, t = 2.906)*. Digging into the numbers more specifically, it was notable that the aspects of TV relating to goals had a particularly important impact on the ability to create a focal point for the vision specific to either delivering unique benefits or economies of scale. As such, when technology developers are focused on goals, it has an important ability to influence early success with customers because even at a very stage before considering the specifics of what a market wants, the technology visionary is attuned from the very beginning, at a broad level, on solving customer needs.

- **Impact of TV on TCA**

Not surprisingly perhaps, Technology Vision has a positive and significant impact on Technological Competitive Advantage *(lambda = 0.399, t = 2.905)*. This finding basically speaks to the fact that if the vision is focused on delivering unique benefits to consumers or developing good economies of scale in a well-defined infrastructure, then the technology visionary has a good chance of achieving these goals ahead of competition which may not have specified as clearly what their goals related to the market benefits are.

- **Impact of TV on AAC**

Lastly, Technology Vision has a significant positive impact on the Ability to Attract Capital (both social capital and financial capital) *(lambda = 0.203, t = 1.907)*. If the technology visionary is focused in such a way, that while perhaps not yet having a complete technology solution trained on a specific market, they do have specific goals related to developing the technology and are passionate about what they are doing; this translates particularly well when attracting capital from potential investors.

A final aspect of the Reid et al. (2015) study was an analysis of the potential impact of "control variables" on the main relationships of the study previously described in this chapter. In particular, the study investigated whether there were differences in the relationships between small and large firms (there were 100 firms of each size in this study and small firms were those with less than or equal to 10 employees), as well as low and high levels of resource availability. Given that this textbook is about entrepreneurial vision, it is important to gain an understanding of the factors which might be more relevant in that specific context. The results of the control variable analysis are detailed in ◘ Table 12.2.

As noted in Reid et al. (2015), as relates specifically to smaller entrepreneurial firms, and as can be seen in ◘ Table 12.2, firm size demonstrated a difference between the Technology Vision of small and large firms, in that small firms displayed a statistically greater level of focus on benefits goals and efficiency goals than large firms. On the other hand, companies with greater levels of resource availability exhibited significantly stronger levels of TV specificity and TV infrastructure clarity.

The upshot of this is that whether it is entrepreneurial startup or large, established firm, it is important for firms of all sizes and ages to keep a close eye on each of the important components of TV. In particular, for startups, it means that the aspects of specificity and infrastructure clarity do not get a pass, just because they may be more focused on delivering solutions to the end market out of the gates or because they may not have the resources to yet develop infrastructure. These aspects still need to be given serious consideration as early as possible in the development process.

The final upshot of these findings pertaining to Technology Vision and its importance is that, as noted in Reid et al. (2015, pp. 605–606, permission granted December 3, 2020, from John Wiley & Sons for reprint):

> "Investors and consumers are interested in the benefits and efficiencies provided by the technology separately from the potential impact they will have in the marketplace. Thus, securing an early TCA is inherently related to the way in which the technology is developed. Firms need earlier measures of their performance, particularly in industrial sectors where products may take several years before their launch in the marketplace may be achieved. Developing a technology vision is important in terms of attracting potential investors and early customers. Early customers also need and want to have a sense of whether the overall focus of a technology's development is going to help them along one, or all, of the following dimensions: to solve a major problem; to create a major benefit; or to do something they have done in the past, but in a much less costly way. Having clarity of vision pertains to the technology infrastructure that the firm adopts early on. This may constrain choice, but on the positive side, it provides a sense of direction in a world of seemingly infinite possibilities. This ultimately helps facilitate slower cash burn, hence improving cash flow in industries, which often require very high levels of resource commitments. Specificity of vision is helpful in providing specific direction within the broad guide-

Table 12.2 ANOVA test results for firm control variables

Firm control variables						
	Firm size			**Resource availability**		
Constructs	**Small firms Mean (n = 100)**	**Large firms Mean (n = 100)**	**ANOVA (Sig.)**	**Low RA Mean (n = 109)**	**High RA Mean (n = 91)**	**ANOVA (Sig.)**
TV first-order dimensions						
F-1 TV benefits goal	4.70	4.26	3.160 (.077)*	4.33	4.67	1.894 (.170)
F-2 TV efficiency goal	4.74	4.34	3.193 (.075)*	4.42	4.69	1.451 (.230)
F-3 TV magnetism	5.42	5.30	.527 (.469)	5.38	5.33	.066 (.797)
F-4 TV specificity	5.35	5.37	.010 (.922)	5.20	5.54	3.622 (.058)*
F-5 TV infrastructure clarity	4.54	4.66	.433 (.511)	4.40	4.84	6.332 (.013)**
TV second-order construct	4.95	4.79	1.906 (.169)	4.75	5.02	5.186 (.024)**
Early performance outcome factors						
ESC early success with customers	5.03	5.12	.223 (.637)	4.96	5.21	1.834 (.177)
TCA technical competitive advantage	5.85	5.84	.006 (.938)	5.85	5.83	.021 (.885)
AAC ability to attract capital	4.73	4.75	.015 (.902)	4.72	4.77	.070 (.791)

Table 7 from Reid et al. (2015), permission granted December 3, 2020, from John Wiley & Sons for reprint

ANOVA analysis of variance, *RA* resource availability, *TV* Technology Vision

*$p < .10$; **$p < .05$

12

lines of the technology infrastructure provided by a clear vision. Developing these two, infrastructure clarity and specificity of vision, comes from both successful past experiences, and/or an intuitive sense of where a given technology is going. Contrary to popular belief, an intuitive sense is not irrational as intuition also evolves from experience and learning (Simon, 1987). A firm's technological potential carries the promise for capitalizing on new opportunities, and the market and investors react to potential. This is precisely what technology vision and patents are able to deliver. What makes these findings interesting is the important distinction that while patents deliver a very clear technological potential, technology vision helps integrate the technological potential with a visionary's social capabilities and internal resources, which are required to be successful in the marketplace. As a result, in order to achieve true technological competitive advantage early on in the eyes of employees, potential investors, the marketplace, and other stakeholders, technology visioning is not only complementary to patenting, but in fact is required in order to be able to proceed along the product development trajectory."

Chapter Review Questions

1. Define Technology Vision
2. Compare Technology Vision with Market Vision
3. What are the key components of Technology Vision?

References

Burgelman, R, & Sayles, L. (1986). *Inside corporate innovations: Strategy, structure, and managerial skills*. NY: The Free Press.

Leifer, R., McDermott, C., Colarelli O'Connor, G., Peters, L., Rice, M., & Veryzer, R. (2000). *Radical innovation: How mature companies can outsmart upstarts*. Boston: Harvard Business School Press.

Livingston, J. (2007). *Founders at work: Stories of startups' early days*. Springer-Verlag.

Reid, S. E. (2005). *Market Vision for radically-new, high-tech products* (Ph.D. Thesis). John Molson School of Business, Concordia University.

Reid, S. E. (2015). Vision and radical innovation: A typology. In A. Brem & E. Viardot (Eds.), *Adoption of innovation: Balancing internal and external stakeholders in the marketing of innovation* (pp. 133–154). Springer International Publications.

Reid, S., & de Brentani, U. (2004). The fuzzy front-end of new product development for discontinuous innovation: A theoretical model. *Journal of Product Innovation Management, 21*(3), 170–184.

Reid, S. E., & Roberts, D. L. (2011). Technology vision: A scale development. *R&D Management, 41*(5), 442–472.

Reid, S. E., Roberts, D. L., & Moore, K. (2015). Technology vision for radical innovation and its impact on early success. *The Journal of Product Innovation Management, 32*(4), 593–609.

Riche, R. W., Hecker, D., & Burgan, J. (1983). High technology today and tomorrow: A small slice of the employment pie. *Monthly Labor Review, 106*(November), 50–58.

Simon, H. A. (1987). Making management decisions: The role of intuition and emotion. *Academy of Management Executive, 1*(1), 57–64.

Crafting the Vision Statement

Contents

© The Author(s), under exclusive license to Springer Nature Switzerland AG 2022
S. E. Reid, C. B. Crawford, *Entrepreneurial Vision*, Classroom Companion: Business, https://doi.org/10.1007/978-3-030-77803-3_13

Learning Objectives

We have covered many of the essentials involved with the construction of an entrepreneurial vision including why vision is important, what the key components are, how to create an appropriate vision framework based on your core motivators, and how to create vision context in terms of networking and market learning. We have also focused on how to effectively build up each of the core aspects specific to Market Vision and Technology Vision in a way that maximizes their potential early performance. Now it is time to take all of this upfront homework and convert it into a core message and differentiating machine through the crafting of the vision statement.

Our aims for the following chapter are to:

1. Learn why creating vision statements is important to success.
2. Learn how to create a first draft of your vision statement.
3. Assess the first draft vision statement for component strength.
4. Assess the overall structure of the vision statement.

13.1 Why Crafting a Vision Statement Is Important

A vision statement, at the end of the day, represents the final culmination of all of the efforts put forth by an entrepreneur, their team, and support network and directs it toward the marketplace (◘ Fig. 13.1).

It is important to note once again that in the case of entrepreneurs and their startups, Technology Vision and Market Vision play the largest roles from the onset because they usually begin the process with but one technology or product/market and grow from there. Suppose the startup is successful with developing and enacting their original vision. In that case, this may become the cornerstone for creating an Organizational Vision later on (please refer back to ► Fig. 2.4 in ► Chap. 2). Kirkpatrick (2016, p. 2), whose work is mainly focused on Organizational Vision, defines a vision statement as "a shared, communicated, idealistic idea of the long-term future of an organization." In the case of a Market Vision statement, the same goals of sharing and communicating the idealistic idea apply, but focused on a typically shorter-term future product/market. As noted in the findings of Baum et al. (1998, p. 51), "In small firms the two types of goals (i.e., general organizational vision goal and task-specific goal) may merge together in the CEO's vision: results-focused company goals may become the equivalent of task-specific goals (e.g., "We want to double our sales in 2 years.")." In other words, Technology Vision and/or Market Vision becomes the de facto Organizational Vision for the startup.

According to Şahin (2019, abstract), the conversion process of combining this thinking and work and putting it into a vision statement itself is mission-critical. He states that vision statements are "considered as an essential medium for conveying business values and emphasizing uniqueness and difference."

Fig. 13.1 Cartoon to portray "crafting a vision statement." (Source: Image licensed and downloaded from Adobe Stock on November 6, 2020. Credit: by cartoon resource/► stock.adobe.com. License Link: ► https://stock.adobe.com/73491152)

The research of Kirkpatrick (2016, 2017) further backs this up by providing a key conclusion from her research that it is the act of *communicating* the vision, which allows it to have an impact. As she notes (2017, p. 95) "developing a formal vision statement would have little impact unless it was communicated and put into action." The work of Kirkpatrick (2017) additionally shows that the level of formalization of vision statements varies, whereby some firms may not have a formalized statement; however, the vision is implemented through action and leadership, even if not formally stated. This is likely the case for many entrepreneurs. The entrepreneur may, then, want to actively consider how to construct a vision statement and afterward how they will communicate it and whether they will formalize it to facilitate its enactment.

According to Fiset and Robinson (2020, p. 2), "numerous studies have demonstrated the positive effects of vision statements in the prediction of employee (Fiset & Boies, 2019; Sosik & Dinger, 2007), team (Boies et al., 2015) and organizational performance outcomes (Baum et al., 1998; Kantabutra & Avery, 2010; Kirkpatrick et al., 2002)." As startups grow, then, constructing formalized visions statements may be helpful in gaining the benefits of these effects.

As such, the remainder of this chapter is focused on the creation of Market and Technology Vision statements for startup entrepreneurs. It is important to reiterate here that by necessity entrepreneurs and startups generally need to focus on one Product/Market Vision from the beginning (and where relevant, this may be preceded by the creation of a Technology Vision). Organizational Vision may become relevant later once a team has formed, an organizational structure is put in place, hiring becomes relevant, and importantly, it does so at a time where it may then be possible to focus on a broader product/service portfolio with multiple markets, and therefore a broader vision, enabling a larger envelope within which to get creative.

Starting with too much abstraction early on, however, may not be helpful to many startup entrepreneurs who need to get clear on what they are doing quickly, often with limited time and funds. This does not mean lacking in magnetism or scope, or eventually aiming longer term at a broader level of abstraction, it just means being very clear as to what the first "doable project" is out of the gates—and over time, as success will allow, blending this into a broader organizational framework and vision.

13.2 Creating a First Draft of Your Vision Statement

At this stage, we make suggestions as to how to frame your chosen vision statement and check for its current level of clarity by putting it under the microscope (◘ Fig. 13.2) to ensure it conveys an accurate and precise message around your goal.

13.2.1 Assessing Vision Statement Component Strength

Over the years, working on vision statements with students in our university incubator, as well as with entrepreneurs and organizations wishing to frame and/or rework their vision statements, we have utilized a few tools to help with this exercise. Indeed, there is no one-size-fits-all approach to building a strong vision statement. That said, if you take a look back at the vision development guidelines provided in ▶ Chaps. 11 and 12 vis-à-vis the five core vision dimensions, a vision statement should attempt to tick off as many of the following aspects of a strong vision as possible:

Vision Goal – Form is what the mental image of the vision, whether Market Vision or Technology Vision, actually looks like in the visionary's mind. In the case of Market Vision, as described in ▶ Chap. 11, this image relates to how the prod-

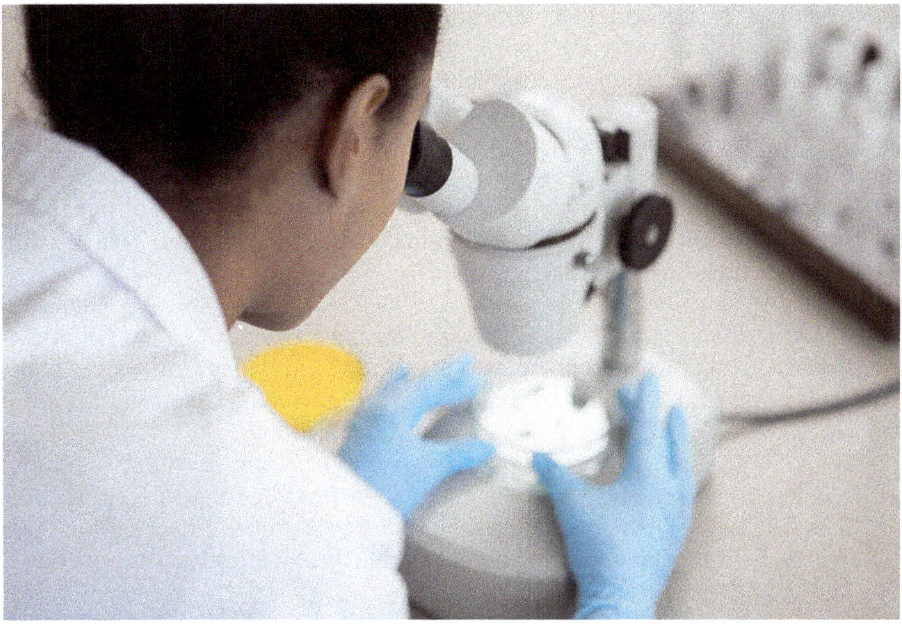

◘ **Fig. 13.2** Examining using a microscope. (Source: Image licensed and downloaded from Shutterstock on May 4, 2020. Credit: by wavebreakmedia/▸ Shutterstock.com. License Link: ▸ https://www.shutterstock.com/image-photo/scientist-examining-petri-dish-under-microscope-285650240)

◘ **Fig. 13.3** Conceptual image to portray vision scope. (Source: Image licensed and downloaded from Adobe Stock on October 20, 2020. Credit: by treenabeena/▸ stock.adobe.com. License Link: ▸ https://stock.adobe.com/images/dream-big-mixed-typography-banner-with-brush-calligraphy/266535967)

uct, possibly within a product system, might be utilized by consumers. In the case of Technology Vision, as described in ▸ Chap. 12, this image relates to benefits goals and efficiencies goals from the perspective of the technology developer.

- Does the vision statement give a specific idea of what the vision looks like in your mind?
- Does the vision statement convey a good representation of the mental model of the main goal you (and your team) are focused on in your mind(s)?

Vision Goal – Scope has to do with the size and nature of the potential target market, as well as its potential impact (◘ Fig. 13.3). For Market Vision, for example, this has to do with considering who the vision will apply to in the marketplace (both end-user groups and direct targets), as well as how much potential there is to help society, how long-term the impact will be, and the potential to create value in the marketplace and, therefore, profitability.

- Does the vision statement manage to convey the essence of the size of markets of focus?
- Does the vision statement convey information about the breadth of impact?
- Does the vision statement convey the importance of your long-term goal in terms of potential for impact?

Vision magnetism/inspiration has to do with creating a vision with a level of attraction and desirability which is proactively compelling and thereby motivating to the entrepreneurial team to break any inertia and get moving on enactment toward it (◘ Fig. 13.4).

- Does the vision statement have the ability to inspire you to move forward?
- Does the vision statement also have the ability to captivate others and get them excited about moving toward that goal as quickly and effectively as possible?

◘ **Fig. 13.4** Conceptual image to portray vision magnetism. (Source: Image licensed and downloaded from Adobe Stock on October 20, 2020. Credit: by pathdoc/► stock.adobe.com. License Link: ► https://stock.adobe.com/377429861)

Vision clarity and specificity are related to understanding the who, what, why, and by when underlying the vision. Clarity is essential in a vision as it allows the underlying ideas to be more clearly understood, shared, and bought into by others, and this, in turn, speeds up the process of vision adoption and breaks inertia in moving forward toward vision realization.

- Is your vision statement extremely clear about how you are going to distinguish your product/service/experience/company?
- If the key differentiator is a target goal, is it specific about what purpose is to be achieved (◘ Fig. 13.5)?
- If the key differentiator is an innovation goal, is it specific about the underlying technology and what it will do? Or, is it specific about the benefits that the technology delivers?
- If the key differentiator is a value-based goal, is it specific about what the target of the value is (◘ Fig. 13.6)?
- If the key differentiator is a benchmark goal, does it clearly state or imply the comparison (◘ Fig. 13.7)?

Now, thinking about each of the underlying core dimensions of your Market Vision (or Technology Vision, depending on your initiating scenario), which you started developing using Worksheet 12. It is time to put each of these underlying aspects together, to the extent which is possible, into the first draft of your Market Vision statement.

◘ **Fig. 13.5** Conceptual image to portray vision target clarity. (Source: Image licensed and downloaded from Adobe Stock on October 20, 2020. Credit: by The Cheroke/▸ stock.adobe.com. License Link: ▸ https://stock.adobe.com/217692784)

Fig. 13.6 Conceptual image to portray vision clarity for a value-based goal about inclusivity and understanding. (Source: Image licensed and downloaded from Adobe Stock on October 20, 2020. Credit: by ink drop/► stock.adobe.com. License Link: ► https://stock.adobe.com/images/people-wave-lgbtq-gay-pride-flags-at-a-solidarity-march/278984549?prev_url=detail)

Fig. 13.7 Conceptual image to portray vision clarity for a benchmark goal. (Source: Image licensed and downloaded from Adobe Stock on October 20, 2020. Credit: by annetdebar/► stock.adobe.com. License Link: ► https://stock.adobe.com/383622139)

Based on the hypothetical example we created in ► Chap. 11 (► Table 11.1) and utilizing the core components we used as an illustrative example as to how to put together a Market Vision construct in Worksheet 12, we will now continue with this example to show how to pull these ideas together as a basis for a Market Vision statement.

Our initial early Market Vision construct was centered around creating a safer, cleaner, and faster airport experience, and we wanted to specifically prioritize the following hot point: "make a cleaner and more secure way to go through the security check, in a way that people are not worried about contamination from disease." The basic product/service idea we had suggested for addressing this was a clean, soft pouch with a drawstring to be handled by a masked, gloved security employee and placed into a sterilized bin for the security check (◘ Fig. 13.8). This pouch would be sterilized between uses with a UV treatment. The idea could be developed even further and all carry-on luggage would stay in the pouch and be transported through to the overhead bin by a security employee. Another employee would bring used pouches from the overhead bins of the plane once everyone had deplaned and the pouches could be recycled, cleaned and used at the next airport.

◘ **Fig. 13.8** Conceptual portrayal of a potential soft pouch design for movement of carry-on items from arrival to destination. (Source: Image licensed and downloaded from Adobe Stock on November 10, 2020. Credit: by vipubadee/► stock.adobe.com. License Link: ► https://stock.adobe.com/386093448)

An initial Market Vision statement for this hypothetical concept might be along the following lines:

» Enhancing global traveler security through the creation of a sterile reusable soft pouch for belongings from airport arrival to destination; a simple, easily achievable solution.

Worksheet 14 offers a checklist to see how/whether the initial statement ticks all the boxes for a strong Market Vision statement for the one Market Vision you have chosen to move forward with, as follows

Market Vision Form
- Statement addresses the main hot points—safety and cleanliness.
- Statement addresses the main product form through the "pouch" concept; this word provides a visual idea of the design involved with the form; the word "soft" gives further design specifications and suggests the use of a reusable, and thus more environmentally friendly, material.

Market Vision Scope
- Statement addresses the size of market and breadth of impact by using the word "global."

Market Vision Magnetism
- The verb "enhancing" has strong imagery; the idea of innovation is conveyed through the word "creation"; the word "sterile" speaks directly to the hot point using powerful language.
- The potential for global impact across airports and the simplicity and quick turnaround time has the capability to inspire other stakeholders such as financiers or potential airport/government buyers.

Market Vision Clarity and Specificity
- The statement clearly delineates the differentiators: the innovative pouch, the sterile solution, and the idea that the service and logistics are shared across airports.
- There is an underlying connotation that the target goal implementation would be achievable in the short term through the use of the phrase "easily achievable."
- While there is no real technological innovation here, there is a service innovation, and this is conveyed through the entire statement.
- There is a values-based component to the design idea in that the word "soft" implies an eco-friendly solution which can be recycled through multiple uses.
- There is an inherent benchmark component to this goal in that it will offer a much better solution to the current status quo, particularly emphasized through the word "enhancing."

Worksheet 14: Market Vision Components Checklist

Please complete the following enhancement checklist to aid in further developing and clarifying your Market Vision statement components:

MARKET VISION FORM

List how your market vision statement specifically addresses your main differentiator hot points:

1 ______________________________
2 ______________________________

List how your market vision statement specifically addresses explaining product form:

3 ______________________________
4 ______________________________
5 ______________________________

MARKET VISION SCOPE

List how your market vision statement specifically addresses size of market:

1 ______________________________
2 ______________________________

List how your market vision statement specifically addresses breadth of market:

3 ______________________________
4 ______________________________
5 ______________________________

MARKET VISION MAGNETISM

List how your market vision statement specifically addresses incorporating powerful language:

1 ______________________________
2 ______________________________

List how your market vision statement specifically addresses incorporating powerful imagery:

3 ______________________________
4 ______________________________

List how your market vision statement specifically addresses impact:

5 ______________________________

MARKET VISION CLARITY AND SPECIFICITY

List how your market vision statement specifically addresses differentiation:

1 ______________________________
2 ______________________________
3 ______________________________

List how the goal (target,values, etc.) of the market vision statement is specifically addressed:

4 ______________________________
5 ______________________________

© Susan E. Reid and Charles B. Crawford, August 14, 2020.

13.2.2 Assessing Overall Structure of Vision Statement

Usually, once the initial Market Vision statement has been constructed, much more effort needs to go into ensuring the best potential overall structure of the statement. This is one of the more challenging components of vision construction, and the proof of this is in the pudding—the majority of vision statements are not that well-structured at all, at least initially. The problem is, while the entrepreneur and their team may have a very simple short hand that they use to communicate with one another about their primary goal(s) in terms of interfacing product with market, when it comes time to formalize these, they often suffer from what might be best described as "vision formalization-itis." Suddenly, the need to please all stakeholders weighs heavily, mission and value statements get fused in with the vision, and quite frankly, the vision statement comes out looking like an overcooked, overstuffed turkey.

To illustrate this point, we conducted a quick straw poll of a large number of North American universities to see what their online vision statements look like and how they were structured. Let's just say that most were too generic, way too long, and nondistinctive. Additionally, in general, there was just too much jargon and motherhood to remember or clearly understand most of them. To illustrate the point, we will present our takeaway as a mashup hypothetical vision statement:

> "We aim at providing interesting opportunities, knowledge, innovation and a sustainable experience that will help students be transformative leaders, meet new challenges and prepare themselves for an interesting career path in the radically changing and challenging environment of our time and moving to the future using new skills and attitudes. University X, through providing a stimulating teaching and research environment, looks to prepare students through its excellent programs and engaged faculty for a future which demands both a local and global approach to meet new challenges to help the greater good at a time when our dynamic and changing world is in need of these capabilities."

13

As you can see, such a vision statement is extremely long, is convoluted, and uses "buzz words" to tick off boxes, to the point that any reader would not be able to grasp the main objective of the school's vision. Now, these universities are good schools with good programs and good professors, but—think about the unique experience they could deliver for their students if their long-term vision was more clearly conveyed and, as a result, able to be executed.

With these aims in mind, here is our suggested approach for assessing your current vision statement structure:

1. Write your current vision statement for the Market Vision you have selected as your entrepreneurial team's "winner" on an otherwise blank paper.
2. Remove all motherhood statements. Everyone wants to be innovative, have good values, be good corporate citizens, be a good leader, and so on, so get rid of all that stuff. While these may represent highlights to include in your corporate values statement, they have no place in your vision statement. The vision

needs to do two things: (1) provide an inspiring long-term goal and (2) clearly distinguish you and your products or ideas from anyone else playing in the same game.
3. Remove all jargon statements. Your grandmother should be able to read the statement and understand what it means.
4. Shorten it down to, at most, a couple of sentences. Take a break and don't look at it again until the next day.
5. Now shorten it again to just one sentence. Remove any extra words like—"We aim to…" or "Our goal is to…". Just start with a verb or verb phrase, an action word that jumps in and uses high imagery. You will notice in the vision statement examples from ► Chap. 5 that many of them start with words like "Achieving," "To be," "There's," etc.
6. Now shorten the statement to no more than seven words (for the same reason as phone numbers are seven-number long; because it is, on average, the highest chunk of information most people can remember together based on Miller's Law, 1956)! Every word counts and should have high meaning while attempting to preserve the core aspects of your vision.

The key point here is about creating a better level of understanding of the value proposition you want to deliver and a vision that will enable you to do this in the best way possible, both to ensure success for your entrepreneurial team and value-add for your eventual customer base.

? Chapter Review Questions

1. Why is it important to put your Market Vision into a statement form?
2. Why is it possible for clarity of vision and abstraction to coexist, and at what time in the entrepreneurial process is it particularly important to focus on clarity?
3. Why is it important for a vision statement to be brief?

References

Baum, J. R., Locke, E. A., & Kirkpatrick, S. A. (1998). A longitudinal study of the relation of vision and vision communication to venture growth in entrepreneurial firms. *Journal of Applied Psychology, 83*(1), 43–54.

Boies, K., Fiset, J., & Gill, H. (2015). Communication and trust are key: Unlocking the relationship between leadership and team performance and creativity. *The Leadership Quarterly, 26*(6), 1080–1094.

Fiset, J., & Boies, K. (2019). Positively vivid visions: Making followers feel capable and happy. *Human Relations, 72*(10), 1651–1670.

Fiset, J., & Robinson, M. A. (2020). Developing foresight through the evaluation and construction of vision statements: An experiential exercise. *Organizational Management Journal,* Vol. ahead-of-print No. ahead-of-print. https://doi.org/10.1108/OMJ-03-2019-0822 (article published under the Creative Commons Attribution CC BY 4.0 license).

Kantabutra, S., & Avery, G. (2010). The power of vision: Statements that resonate. *Journal of Business Strategy, 31*(1), 37–45.

Kirkpatrick, S. A. (2016). *Build a better vision statement*. Lexington Books.

Kirkpatrick, S. A. (2017). Toward a grounded theory: A qualitative study of vision statement development. *Journal of Management Policy and Practice, 18*(1), 87–101.

Kirkpatrick, S. A., Wofford, J. C., & Baum, J. R. (2002). Measuring motive imagery contained in the vision statement. *The Leadership Quarterly, 13*(2), 139–150.

Miller, G. A. (1956). The magical number seven, plus or minus two: Some limits on our capacity for processing information. *Psychological Review, 63*(2), 81–97.

Şahin, F. (2019). An analysis of mission, vision statements. *2nd International Symposium of Bandirma and its Surroundings* UBS'19 September 17–19, 2019. Bandırma, Turkey.

Sosik, J. J., & Dinger, S. L. (2007). Relationships between leadership style and vision content: The moderating role of need for social approval, self-monitoring, and need for social power. *The Leadership Quarterly, 18*(2), 134–153.

14

Determining the Market Niche Beachhead for Testing Your Vision

Contents

© The Author(s), under exclusive license to Springer Nature Switzerland AG 2022

S. E. Reid, C. B. Crawford, *Entrepreneurial Vision*, Classroom Companion: Business, https://doi.org/10.1007/978-3-030-77803-3_14

Learning Objectives

With your initial vision statement crafted and ready to test drive, the first natural question is where to? The well-crafted vision statement will have pointed you in the direction of a port, but the question is, which actual dock/beach do we pull into? In other words, while you have narrowed things down in terms of a good port of harbor given your circumstances, now you want to narrow down your coordinates specifically.

The learning objectives of this chapter are, therefore:

1. To understand the basics behind building your first market
2. To understand what a market niche is and why it is important
3. To learn how to discover market niche options for an early product/market based on your vision
4. To learn how to create a survey to investigate the market niche options
5. To determine/identify one market niche beachhead for testing your vision

14.1 Building Your First Market

> Then the bowsprit got mixed with the rudder sometimes: a thing, as the Bellman remarked, that frequently happens in tropical climes when a vessel, is, so to speak, 'snarked'.

"The Hunting of the Snark," Lewis G. Carroll (1876) (Fig. 14.1).

We are huge Lewis Carroll fans. We love the imagery, the characters, the mixed-up world, and fun sense of it all. We've sometimes thought that some of the subjects of his works, like Alice in Wonderland, provide good metaphors for startups, particularly in the early stages of a new industry—when everyone is fumbling in the dark trying to define and create language around new products and markets that don't necessarily exist yet. In Carroll's poem, "The Hunting of the Snark" (1876), there are eight characters of various professions who set out on a journey to find a "Snark." Not only do they set out to cross an ocean with a blank map, but we never learn the nature of the "Snark" either—although it sounds to be a fictional character. In other words, the characters have no map and a very fuzzy goal.

Launching a first product can feel a little like that. Even once you have some idea of what product or service you want to develop, the market potential in the very early days, regarding geographic and psychographic targets, may feel vague at best.

So, where to start? Well, one thing is for sure. If you wait for the market to find you, you could be waiting a very long time; possibly forever. Also, looking for a "perfect market" may not be realistic, especially if the market needs to be "created" on some level. Avoid hunting the elusive Snark. It's a mythical character of epic proportion full of overblown promise. At this stage, instead, we suggest focusing on an achievable first goal. This does not mean that you let go of your longer-term vision. It's just that you need to start somewhere you can get an early win and proof of concept. So, we suggest starting by looking at potential niche markets

14 **Fig. 14.1** "Hunting of the Snark" bookplate. (Source: ▶ https://commons.wikimedia.org/wiki/File:The_Hunting_of_the_Snark_(1876).djvu. Credit: Illustrator, Henry Holiday, publications 1876. Downloaded via Wikimedia Commons on October 22, 2020. Public Domain)

whose principal purpose or inspiration resonates with your own or which offer easy locational proximity from the get-go. In the next chapter, we focus on how to go about doing just that.

14.2 The Market Niche: A Definition and Its Importance

Derived from the Latin word "nīdus," the term "niche" relates to the notion of a very small place, nook, or cranny. A higher-order level of understanding of niche puts the idea of a small environment together with a specific organism that occupies it and sometimes refers to the special relationship between the two as being highly synergistic, based on unique characteristics, attributes, or roles of each that enable their symbiosis.

The Merriam-Webster dictionary (2020, online) notes the following possible definitions for the term "niche" (related to the social and natural sciences):

» "**a:** a place, employment, status, or activity for which a person or thing is best fitted, **b:** a habitat supplying the factors necessary for the existence of an organism or species, **c:** the ecological role of an organism in a community especially in regard to food consumption, **d:** a specialized market."

One of the earliest known science-based applications of the term "niche" has been through its employment in the field of population ecology. The underlying premise of niche theory, as it is implied in the sciences, is that, as noted in the first definition provided by Merriam-Webster above, there is a close "fit" afforded in the niche environment between a given population (made up of organizations or other organisms) and various aspects/characteristics available or actively searched for in the environment itself (i.e., be they products, services, locations/habitats, supplies, attributes offering some form of benefit, or even customers themselves).

Now let us assume that limits on growth for any of the populations in a specific environment will be a result of the combination of resource availability and the level of competition for those resources between various populations. Hannan and Freeman (1977), in their well-known article *The Population Ecology of Organizations*, provide a detailed explanation of this phenomenon. Hannan and Freeman (1977, p. 934) specifically define populations as "aggregates of organizations" within the environment. A key question then, taking this view of population ecology, is what happens when two fairly similar populations (i.e., those which would be competing for resources) in the environment are sustained by the same offerings in the environment (i.e., customers)? Ecology theory would say that the population with the characteristic(s) less fit to environmental contingencies (i.e., customer demand) will not thrive unless it adapts or moves.

In fact, a specific environment has a perfect organizational partner, or as Hawley (1968) explains and as quoted by Hannan and Freeman (1977, p. 939, used with permission of the University of Chicago Press from [The population ecology of organizations, Hannan and Freeman, *The American Journal of Sociology* 82(5)]; permission conveyed through Copyright Clearance Center, Inc.): "the diversity of organizational forms is isomorphic to the diversity of environments. In each distinguishable environmental configuration one finds, in equilibrium, only that organizational form optimally adapted to the demands of the environment" (i.e., in our case, we would say that a unique market niche is one where there is a specific customer for a specific product offering). As noted by Hannan and Freeman, this level of understanding does not, however, take into account dynamism in the environment—i.e., that environments themselves can change in terms of resource offerings and levels of customer demand and organizations can change as well in terms of adaptation or movement. That said, over a short-term time horizon, one might imagine that there is indeed, in a small market niche, one best offering for one type of customer.

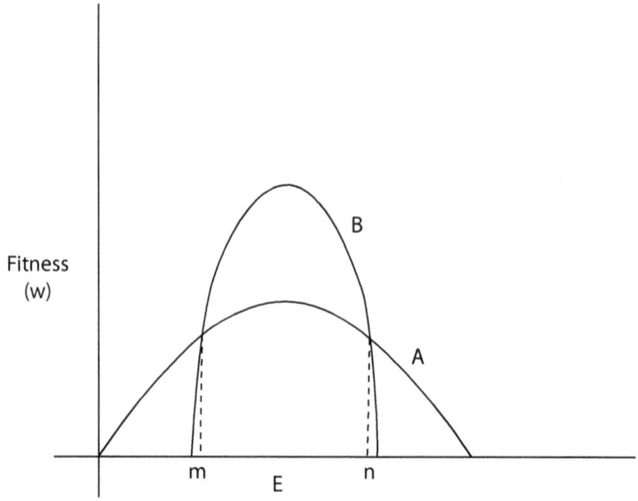

Fig. 14.2 Fitness functions (niches) for specialists and generalists. (Source: Hannan and Freeman (1977, Figure 1, p. 947, used with permission of the University of Chicago Press from [The population ecology of organizations, Hannan and Freeman, *The American Journal of Sociology* 82(5)]; permission conveyed through Copyright Clearance Center, Inc.)

As explained in Hannan and Freeman (1977, pp. 946–948, used with permission of the University of Chicago Press from [The population ecology of organizations, Hannan and Freeman, *The American Journal of Sociology* 82(5)]; permission conveyed through Copyright Clearance Center, Inc.) and illustrated in Fig. 14.2:

> "The concept of "niche," initially borrowed by biologists from early social science, plays a central role in ecological theory…The model which follows uses Hutchinson's (1957) formulation. From this point of view the (realized) niche of a population is defined as that area in constraint space (the space whose dimensions are levels of resources, etc.) in which the population outcompetes all other local populations. The niche, then, consists of all those combinations of resource levels at which the population can survive and reproduce itself.
>
> Each population occupies a distinct niche. For present purposes it suffices to consider cases where pairs of populations differ with respect to a single environmental dimension, E, and are alike with respect to all others. Then relative competitive positions can be simply summarized as in figure 1. As we have drawn this figure, one population, A, occupies a very broad niche, whereas the other, B, has concentrated its fitness, denoted W, on a very narrow band of environmental variation. This distinction, which is usually referred to as generalism versus specialism, is crucial to biological ecology and to a population ecology of organizations.
>
> In essence, the distinction between specialism and generalism refers to whether a population of organizations flourishes because it maximizes its exploitation of the environment and accepts the risk of having that environment change or because it accepts a lower level of exploitation in return for greater security."

14

Based on Hannan and Freeman (1977) and other researchers from the sciences who have contributed to this line of thinking, for entrepreneurs and startups, who, generally speaking, are able only to concentrate on one main product or service offering in the early days of their existence, it is important, particularly prior to launch when working with markets in the concept development phase, to focus exclusively on one unique niche market. In other words, entrepreneurial startups should consider themselves to be "specialists" in terms of seeking the lower levels of market and competition risk associated with a tighter level of customer specialization. This enables startups to know very clearly who their small niche market cohort is from the beginning while acknowledging that the overall potential for "mass market" exploitation levels will be lower with niche markets, but more secure. Bigger players with larger product portfolios can accept more risk, and therefore court more different types of customers in other more diverse markets which are not as much of a perfect fit for initial offerings. The strategy of the startup to stick closely to a specific market early on is truly the only one that makes sense. Sowing seeds too far afield is a very risky strategy for startups and indeed is probably one of the main reasons for their failure.

What is a "niche market", specifically, then? Effectively, a niche market is a fairly homogeneous subset of a larger market with its own particular needs and/or preferences within the larger, more heterogeneous market. "Fit" with such a market for a startup is therefore largely predicated on having special or unique relationship potential or specific characteristics or attributes such as being in a particular location or offering products or services which are highly tailored to the needs or preferences of such a market. This concept of the niche market, in relation to the market, derives from the concept of market segmentation à la Smith (1956), who explained that the heterogeneous market is basically a collection of small homogeneous markets—i.e., niche markets. Many marketing academics have touted the importance of niche markets in terms of their ability to deliver returns including Claycamp and Massy (1968), Kara and Kaynak (1997), Noy (2010), Porter (1980), and Robinson (1969).

So, for example, a market for the clothing trade is the market for athletic gear. A specialized niche market within that market would be the market for athletic gear for triathletes (◘ Fig. 14.3).

14.3 Advantages of Starting with One Market Niche

The main advantages of building a business starting with one niche market are as follows:

1. That it will naturally help you to focus and clarify your vision for that specific subsector of the market and, in so doing, will help you to get buy-in from that market because you are specifically focusing on solving their needs—likely in a way that more generic providers are not able to do. As with the previous example, a general sports retailer will not be as equipped to service the needs of a triathlete as a specialist.

Fig. 14.3 Triathletes. (Image licensed and downloaded from Shutterstock on January 14, 2018. Credit: by Pavel1964/▶ Shutterstock.com. License Link: ▶ https://www.shutterstock.com/image-photo/triathletes-groupsplash-water-while-running-sea-387220000)

14

2. Based on better access and smaller scale, you will probably also learn more quickly about the key distinctive differentiators for that target niche market, thereby enabling gaining quicker proof of concept. Then you can think about how to scale, using what you learned, to other market niches and larger markets that could potentially be serviced within the delivery of your overall longer-term vision.
3. No business, especially a startup business, can be all things to all people. As many researchers have pointed out, the essence of good business strategy is to understand this need for what is known as the "trade-off" (Porter, 1996; Maney, 2009). Porter (1996) suggests that trade-offs should be made between whether to provide a differentiated strategy or a low-cost strategy to consumers. As suggested by Maney (2009, p. 11), there is always a "fidelity-convenience trade-off" in terms of delivering products and services to consumers. Not only do consumers actively make trade-off choices, but so do producers, based on the offerings that will fit the tendencies of chosen market niche targets.

◘ **Fig. 14.4** Conceptual image to portray a market niche. (Image licensed and downloaded from Shutterstock on January 14, 2018. Credit: by ranjith Ravindran/► Shutterstock.com. License Link: ► https://www.shutterstock.com/image-illustration/focus-group-magnifying-glass-abstract-background-143505916)

Targeting a narrower range of people or companies in a niche market (◘ Fig. 14.4) doesn't mean that the task of doing the research and connecting with them is any easier, but it does give you the opportunity to get more granular in both your understanding of specific consumers and delivery of solutions, which does make the natural attraction of the market easier. If you look back at the constructive psychology approaches to interpretation and solution construction in ► Chap. 11, this resonates with the notion of granularity behind "distinction-making" and learning from experts and lead users within the niche to ensure that your product or service is crafted in the best way just for them. So, you still need to do your upfront homework with the specific market niche of interest to ensure that you've "got it right" for them in every way possible.

14.4 Discovering Market Niche Options

14.4.1 Business-to-Consumer (B2C) Bases for Segmentation

Many startups and nascent entrepreneurs find themselves in the situation where the market does not yet exist or is not yet well understood or is in the early stages of development. In these cases, an early market niche willing to try out your product or service might be quite small, at least in the beginning. Alternatively, it might be possible to use a patsy market (as described in ▶ Chap. 10—one you use in the early concept testing and developmental phases to learn more about how the attributes function and how to improve them before deciding on which market actually makes the most sense given a more developed product offering). In either case, the first step is to identify some potentially willing market niches, which might, in theory, have a lot to gain by using your product or service.

The reason why a certain market niche might be interested in a specific product or service would be that the specific product offers the differentiator(s) or "determinant attributes" of interest to them—or, in other words, it offers the unique benefits for those specific consumers that set it apart from competing products or services and is the most desirable offering.

Once you have narrowed your range of potential market niches down to a few potential targets, the next step is to collect some primary research through a survey in order to see which one of these willing niches offers the best place to start.

So, let's say, for example, hypothetically, our vision is to create a tiny AI-based drone which will fly around an indoor space and attract bugs, dust, and animal hair/fur to it quickly and then dispose of it (a sort of next-generation computer-driven vacuum cleaning system, if you will). The drone might then do a follow-on act where it would spray all surfaces with a product that attracts dirt, and then the spray would fly back to the drone for disposal. The key is to obtain relevant demographic and psychographic data from various potential niche segments, combined with their potential interest in such a product, to see which market niche offers the most potential demand out of the gates. So, for example, given that the price point for such a product would likely be relatively high vis-à-vis current computer-driven vacuum cleaning systems, we might potentially want to target high-net-worth individuals with homes larger than 10,000 square feet. We might also target suburban families with many children and pets. We could also potentially target farmers housing animals within large indoor spaces (barns) that are difficult to clean. Additionally, to do it in an easy way and to further niche it, we would start by focusing locationally as well—for example, only in Montreal and its surrounding suburban and rural areas.

What you can see that we have done here is to take one key differentiator of the product—the ability to clean very large spaces quickly and effectively without the need for labor (which is actually three attributes combined into one major differentiator)—and used those to help us think about the most likely users of such a product who would truly have their needs addressed by the combined differentiator attributes. In other words, in so much as possible, you want to think out different needs-based scenarios centered on (1) the ability for the key differentiator to respond to strong needs and (2) the ability to meet the needs of potential heavy users as much as possible.

So, in our example, heavy users might be those with large homes, large families with pets, and those with farm animals. You want to do this to give yourselves the best possible chance at getting a "hit." In addition to heavy need and high use, you can think about different demographics, psychographics, or geographical locations which might "vibe" with your differentiator for a specific reason. Given the lead user and expert interviews you have previously performed when forming market

◘ **Fig. 14.5** Lefty's Store at Pier 39. (Source: Image downloaded from Trip Advisor, January 14, 2018. Permission granted for reprint from Trip Advisor January 14, 2018, with provision of link: <"▶ https://www.tripadvisor.com/LocationPhotoDirectLink-g60713-d102779-i48498835-Pier_39-San_Francisco_California.html#48498835"><img alt=""src="▶ https://media-cdn.tripadvisor.com/media/photo-s/02/e4/08/93/pier-39.jpg"/></a>
)

vision options, you have likely already started to think about what some of these niches might be. You may have additionally utilized the pyramiding technique described in ▶ Chap. 9 as a tool for constructing as many potential niches as possible. If not, you should look back at the differentiators mentioned by your lead users and experts during interviews in order to best focus your efforts when deciding on potential niches. Additionally, you can actively start culling niche market ideas based on your own interests, experiences, ability to customize for specific clients, availability/proximity to niches, or ability to co-create with one person or a network of people operating in a niche. So, as an example, if you are creating art supplies and are left-handed (◘ Fig. 14.5), you may intuitively be interested in the left-handed niche for such products.

14.4.2 Business-to-Business (B2B) Bases for Segmentation

Typically, marketing educators like to focus on the B2C world when giving examples of how to go about segmenting a market because it is largely visible to students. That said, given that a good 90% (at least) of world business actually occurs in the B2B or business-to-business space, it is incredibly important to also consider how to segment a business market. If you've done your homework with the deep dive into your industry of interest (Worksheet 6), you may already have some of the information you will require to do this. If not, we provide some suggestions for getting started below.

There are many ways to segment the B2B market. One of the broadest ways to think about it is that the B2B market can be broken down at the "macro" level (industrial level) or at the "micro" (company) level which takes into consideration the major decision participants in a team (Wind & Cardozo, 1974).

For example, an entrepreneur starting up a supply business for university classrooms would need to first consider common macro-characteristics for segmentation. As denoted in ◘ Fig. 14.6, Hutt and Speh (2017, p. 128, Table 5.1, used with permission of Cengage Learning [Hutt, M.D., and Speh, T.W., 2017, *Business marketing management: B2B*, 12th Edition, Cengage South-Western Press]; permission conveyed through Copyright Clearance Center, Inc.) suggest that these aspects include "characteristics of buying organizations" such as organizational size or location, "product/service application," and "purchasing situation."

14

Selected macrolevel bases of segmentation

Variables	Illustrative breakdowns
Characteristics of buying organizations	
Size (the scale of operations of the organization)	Small, medium, large; based on sales or number of employees
Geographical location	USA, Asia pacific, Europe, Middle East, and Africa
Usage rate	Nunuser, light user, moderate user, heavy user
Structure of procurement	Centralized, decentralized
Product/service application	
NAICS category	Varies by product or service
End market served	Varies by product or service
Value in use	High, low
Characteristics of purchasing situation	
Type of buying situation	New task, modified rebuy, straight rebuy
Stage in purchase decision process	Early stages, late stages

◘ **Fig. 14.6** Selected macro-level bases of segmentation (originally published in Chapter 5, Table 5.1, p. 128, used with permission of Cengage Learning from [Hutt, M.D., and Speh, T.W., 2017, *Business marketing management: B2B*, 12th Edition, Cengage South-Western Press]; permission conveyed through Copyright Clearance Center, Inc.)

Hutt and Speh (2017) demonstrate that the last category of macro-segmentation, "product/service application," is often possible to investigate based on the North American Industry Classification System (NAICS) categorization. The NAICS (◘ Fig. 14.7) is a detailed numbering system developed by the USA, Canada, and Mexico, originally through NAFTA, as a way to classify North American businesses into economic sectors according to their main production processes. Essentially, a specific industrial sector is denoted by a two-digit code and industrial segments are represented by six-digit codes.

So, for example, class 541310 is the segment representing architectural services (within the overall industrial sector 54, which represents all professional, scientific, and technical services). Thus, if you are developing an online application that might be of interest to architects, where possible you may be able to go on the government website applicable to that segment to generate a list of architects who are registered under that segment in order to generate a list of potential cold call targets for your application.

◘ **Fig. 14.7** NAICS logo. (Source: ► https://commons.wikimedia.org/wiki/File:US-NAICS-Logo.svg. U.S. Government. Downloaded on November 14, 2020, via Wikimedia Commons. Public Domain)

Once the macro-segmentation has been performed for a B2B market, then, as per Hutt and Speh (2017) and Wind and Cardozo (1974), the entrepreneur should also consider the micro-characteristics of segmentation, or, in other words, who would be the right decision-makers to approach in specific universities—professors, staff, and/or administrators.

Whether you are interested in B2C or B2B market niches, or perhaps potentially both, you now may want to use Worksheet 15 to help you start building your list of potential market niches. As ideas continue to emerge over time, keep track of them along with listing key matches or mismatches between the potential niche needs and the differentiators of the offering (i.e., why you thought that the market niche might be a good one to consider).

The objective of this worksheet, Worksheet 15, is to create a list of potential niche market segments to potentially target with the vision for a product/service. The goal is, essentially, to outline the segments being considered, why and how they differ from one another, and to create a call sheet for the survey introduced in the next section. It is also a good idea to see whether you feel an affiliation with a specific segment (or not) or have natural network connections in the spaces defined by the identified segments.

Worksheet 15:
Market Niche Options

Identify at least 3 market niches that you believe will have a positive response to your product/service concept and vision. The next step, which will involve conducting a survey, is to work towards a decision on how to prioritize and make a decision on which of the 3 niche segments to go after first.

In order to best prepare for conducting the survey, this worksheet prompts you to back up your reasoning for picking these 3 segments, using your best estimates of their needs and demographics (which will be verified with your survey later). The first section provides a grid for products in the Business-to-Consumer (B2C) space and the second section provides a grid for products/services in the Business-to-Business (B2B) space. Trying to elucidate the characteristics of each niche more clearly will help you to decide the best differentiating attributes to include in the survey in order to help you make a clear decision between the 3 niche choices.

Briefly list the 3 market niches you are considering here and the main reason(s) you believe they will be interested:

Market Niche #1 ____________________

____

Market Niche #2 ____________________

____

Market Niche #3 ____________________

____

Why and how does each market niche differ?

____

____

Do you have a specific affiliation with any of the market niches?

____

____

Do you have network connections within any of the market niches? If so, list with their contact info.

____

© Susan E. Reid and Charles B. Crawford, August 14, 2020.

B2C	Level of Need/Desire (1-5)	Level of Use (1-5)	Age (1-5)	Income (1-5)	Education (1-5)	Geography (1-5)
Niche 1						
Niche 2						
Niche 3						

B2B Macro	Level of Need/Desire (1-5)	Level of Use (1-5)	Geography (1-5)	Typical Firm Size (1-5)	Typical Revenues (1-5)	List Main Product/Serv Applications
Industry Niche 1						
Industry Niche 2						
Industry Niche 3						
B2B Micro	Level of Need/Desire (1-5)	Level of Use (1-5)	Geography (1-5)	Firm Size (1-5)	Revenue (1-5)	List Key Decision Makers
Company 1						
Company 2						
Company 3						

Sample Legend for each chart:
Level of Need/Desire, Level of Use, Firm Size and Revenue: 1-5 where 5 is highest
Age: 1 = 21-30; 2 = 31-41; 3 = 41-50; 4 = 51-60; 5 = 61+ (give ranges that make sense given product/service)
Income: 1-5 (5 = highest – give ranges that make sense given product/service)
Education: 1-5 (5 = highest – give ranges that make sense given product/service)
Geography: Scale in a way that makes sense – i.e., 1 = city core; 3= suburbs; 5= rural

14

© Susan E. Reid and Charles B. Crawford, August 14, 2020.

14.5 Potential Market Niche Segment Survey

In the next Worksheet, 16, a small survey of a minimum of potential companies or customers from each potential niche segment will be used to determine one best and accessible niche segment to target with a full concept test and a "doable" test market project moving forward. In order to do this, it is suggested that at least three segments, to a maximum of five segments, be considered and a minimum of ten customers per segment be surveyed, to provide a range of at least 30–50 companies or end customer responses. With the B2B market, the low end of this range (10 × 3) may be the maximum you will be able to get; with the B2C market you may easily be able to survey far more customers per segment. So, if you can obtain more respondents, go for it if possible, up to approximately 100 total per segment. Certainly, keep a list of all niche segments that pop into your mind (you can use the previous Worksheet 15 to do this). They will come into play later on if the originally determined segments do not play out in terms of testing or if you have success and want to quickly scale to other niche segments.

Worksheet 16: Market Niche Segments Survey

In this worksheet, you will be putting together the questions which will comprise a small survey of market niche segments to determine which offers the best fit with your offering. It is suggested that a minimum of at least 3 to a maximum of 5 segments be considered and a minimum of 10 customers per segment be surveyed, to provide a range of 30-50 companies or end customer responses. With the B2B market the low end of this range (10 × 3) may be the maximum you will be able to get; with the B2C market you may easily be able to survey far more customers per segment, so if you can obtain more respondents, go for it, up to 100 total per segment. The idea is to compare the responses from potential companies or customers from each potential niche segment in order to determine one best and accessible niche segment to target with a full concept test and a 'doable' test market project moving forward. Certainly, keep a list of all niche segments that pop into your mind (you can use the previous Worksheet 15 to do this). Even once you perform the survey and decide on a fit with one target niche, they may come in to play later, if the originally determined segments do not play out in terms of testing or if you have success and want to quickly scale to other niche segments.

Here is a sample of questions as a basis to develop a survey from this worksheet. Feel free to adjust as necessary.

How well do you score on the following Scale from 1 to 5:

Definitely Not Very Unlikely	RATING Neutral	Definitely Yes Very Likely

1-----------2-----------3-----------4-----------5

PART I. PRODUCT/SERVICE SPECIFIC INDICATORS

1) How likely (1 = very unlikely; 5 = very likely) are you to use x (fill in your idea)? ________
2) How much do you need such a product/service (1 = definitely not; 5 = definitely)? ________
3) If you were likely to use a product/service like x (your idea), please rate the importance of having the following features (1 = definitely not; 5 = definitely yes):
   Feature #1 ________
   Feature #2 ________
   Feature #3 ________
   Feature #4 ________
   Feature #5 ________
   Please list the top feature you would absolutely need to have from this list: ________
4) If you were likely to use a product/service like x (your idea), please rate the importance of having the following user experience factors (1 = definitely not; 5 = definitely yes):
   User Experience Factor #1 ________
   User Experience Factor #2 ________
   User Experience Factor #3 ________
   User Experience Factor #4 ________
   User Experience Factor #5 ________
   Please list the top user experience factor you would absolutely need to have from this list: ________

© Susan E. Reid and Charles B. Crawford, August 14, 2020.

14

PART II. DEMOGRAPHIC INDICATORS

Please indicate where you are at on the following Scale from 1 to 5 for each of the demographic factors:

Lowest **Mid-Range** **Highest**

1-----------2-----------3-----------4-----------5

1) Age group (1 = 18-30; 2 = 31-40; 3 = 41-50; 4 = 51-60; 5 = 61+) ________
2) Income level (1 = no income; 3 = 50,000 household; 5 = 100,000 + household) ________
3) Education Level (1 = elementary; 2 = high school; 3 = college; 4 = undergrad; 5 = grad work) ________
4) Geography (1 = city core; 3 = suburbs; 5 = rural) ________

PART III. POTENTIAL USAGE INDICATORS

1) On average, how many hours per week do you currently spend doing x? (circle all that apply)
   a) < 1 hour per day, but daily
   b) > 1 hour per day
   c) >3 hours per day
   d) <1 x per week
   e) 1-<3 x per week
   f) 3-6 x per week
   g) <1 x per month
   h) not applicable (i.e., not a user = 0)
2) What other products/services do you use on a regular basis that help you fulfil a similar need?

____

____

____

PART IV. OTHER QUESTIONS

Please add any other questions based on your specific segments and product/service concept.

© Susan E. Reid and Charles B. Crawford, August 14, 2020.

Here is a sample list of questions which form the basis for Worksheet 16:

- Product-/service-specific questions:
  - "On a scale of 1–5, how likely (5 = very likely) are you to use × (your idea)?" This question helps you separate likely users from those who are unlikely to use.
  - "On a scale of 1–5 (5 = very likely), how much do you need such a product/service?" This question helps you to understand the level of desirability and need for the product or service.
  - "On a scale of 1–5 (5 = very likely), if you were to use a product/service like × (your idea), please rate the importance of the following *features* or *user experience factors*" (then list those attributes you want to test) (you may want to limit to 1 or 2 key attributes at this stage).
- Demographic questions:
  - Age group
  - Income level
  - Education level
  - Geographic region
- Behavioral questions related to potential usage:
  - On average, how many hours per day/week/month do you currently spend doing xxx?
  - What other products/services do you use on a regular basis that help you fulfill a similar need?
  - *Tailor other questions based on your specific segments and product/service.*

We suggest using "scaled" data, all on the same numbered scale (from 1 to 5 or 1 to 7 for even more granularity) in order to provide useful statistical analyses. For some questions, the scale will represent answers from "least likely to most likely" with the midpoint being neutral. For other questions, for example, age, each number can take on a range usually scaled toward the most meaningful or highest level. So, for example, we might want age to be scaled so that five would be the highest age category. Things like geography, which is an example of "nominal data," are a little more difficult to scale in this way unless there is some meaning to it, like progressive distance away from an urban center. See the following example provided in ◘ Table 14.1 of a scaled excel spreadsheet for our AI drone cleaning solution idea, which was provided in ► Sect. 14.4.1 of this chapter.

14

14.6 Selecting a Market Niche

The next step, once you've collected the data, is to analyze and process it into meaningful user segments. One method (although there are many), which we like to use and have used successfully with our entrepreneurship incubator students, is a statistical method known as "k-means clustering" which is available as a tool on "SPSS" (SPSS Inc., 1999, Chicago, IL), as well as to other statistics packages.

Table 14.1 AI drone cleaning solution idea example: Excel spreadsheet of responses from potential market niche segment survey on a 1–5 point scale (hypothetical)

Participant	Age	Income	Education	Location	Desire attribute
1	4	2	4	3	1
2	3	4	5	1	5
3	2	1	4	2	2
4	2	5	4	1	4
5	4	4	3	1	5
6	5	2	3	3	1
7	2	5	4	3	3
8	3	5	4	1	5
9	1	3	5	3	2
10	4	2	3	1	3
11	3	5	5	1	5
12	2	4	4	1	4
13	3	5	4	1	5
14	4	4	4	2	4
15	5	4	3	2	3
16	1	3	3	2	2
17	2	4	4	1	3
18	5	2	3	3	2
19	3	5	4	1	5
20	5	1	1	3	1

Source: The authors
Age: 1 10–20, 2 21–30, 3 31–40, 4 41–50, 5 51–60
Income: 1–5 (5 = highest)
Education: 1–5 (5 = highest)
Geographic location: 1–3 (1 = city core; 2 = suburbs; 3 = rural)
Desire for key attribute: 1–5 (5 = highest)

Clustering enables the analysis of the user data across any number of attributes (usage, demographics, etc.) and creates clusters (i.e., user segments) based on the degree to which customers cluster together in terms of similar responses based on the survey.

We usually start by collecting data from the clusters we think pre-exist. So, in our AI drone example, we presuppose that there might be three clusters: high-net-

Table 14.2 Final cluster centers using k-means clustering

Final cluster centers			
Attributes	**Cluster 1**	**Cluster 2**	**Cluster 3**
Age	5	3	2
Income	2	5	3
Education	3	4	4
Geographic location	3	1	2
Desire for key attribute	2	5	2

Source: The authors

worth individuals with large homes, suburban families with many children and pets, and dairy farmers housing animals within large indoor spaces that are difficult to clean. There may be more clusters, however. We can test out the best fit (or number of clusters, i.e., segments) by running the data with multiple numbers of clusters (e.g., we might tell SPSS to try 3, 4, or 5 clusters using an "ANOVA," or "analysis of variance" table) and see which provides the best solution to decide on the best number of clusters and fit given the data.

Table 14.2 shows the final cluster results using k-means clustering based on telling SPSS to try three clusters for hypothetical data we provided for the AI drone concept.

Once you have performed a k-means cluster analysis to generate the segments (i.e., represented by Clusters 1, 2, and 3) and have tested to see the best number of clusters which represent the data (in this case three clusters, based on our pre-assumption, did, in fact, work best), the most telling thing will be to take a close look at those segments which are the most interested in the idea (i.e., "desire for key attribute"). So, you can create a column of data from the survey responses which just speaks to how interested each person is in your idea (see the last column in Tables 14.1 and 14.2 called "desire for key attribute"). Et voilà, with the analysis, you will probably have one or two contenders for your natural first target segments. In our case, with the AI drone example, what we see in the "final cluster centers" in Table 14.2 is that Cluster 2 has the highest rating for "desire for key attribute" (5 rating on average) across the members of the second cluster (i.e., the potential niche segment). This means that the key attributes of the product—the ability to clean vast spaces quickly and without labor—are the most highly desired by Cluster 2. We can also see (by comparing back to the measurement scales in Table 14.1) that the respondents from Cluster 2 have an average age of 31–40, the highest level of income, and very high education and, using concentric circles around Montreal, are located in the city core (so likely to be a mix of large home/apartment owners or corporate space owners).

The output from the SPSS model, as shown in the cluster membership table provided in Table 14.3, also tells us specifically how many people are in each

Table 14.3 Cluster membership table

Cluster membership		
Case number	Cluster	Distance
1	1	1.667
2	2	1.106
3	3	2.280
4	2	1.291
5	2	1.633
6	1	1.054
7	3	2.098
8	2	0.577
9	3	1.483
10	1	2.028
11	2	1.054
12	2	1.333
13	2	0.577
14	2	1.599
15	1	2.261
16	3	1.265
17	3	1.612
18	1	0.667
19	2	0.577
20	1	2.404

Source: The authors

cluster and who they are (see from Table 14.3). For example, out of the 20 cases below, 6 are in Cluster 1, 9 in Cluster 2, and 5 in Cluster 3. So, we can investigate more deeply to find out specifically who these people are and why they have these needs/interests. For example, are Cluster 2 people residing in the city core interested based on home ownership, or are they commercial space owners? As such, we would probably consider these people to be the most important potential contacts for in-depth interviews and concept testing in the next stages to collect more information, as well as those who show the right combination of demographics to be part of the niche. Clusters 1 and 3 have far less desire for the product concept (as shown in Table 14.2 above under "desire for key attribute"), and so, at least at this stage, we will stick closely to the typology of the segment we will discover through more depth research with the nine cases from Cluster 2.

There might be other ways to use the data effectively, as well. For example, you could also run an analysis to investigate which cluster of customers would have the highest usage potential. Another way to look at the data might be to investigate combinations of attributes to see if there are different segments which might respond to different "arrays" or combinations of attributes and this would include key user characteristics you have pre-defined yourself.

You can delve even further into the data. For example, you could run a discriminant analysis, using a "k-means clustering tool" available through SPSS and other stats tools (as graphically depicted in ◘ Fig. 14.8) to see among the clusters which cases are outliers or right in the center of the cluster. Outliers may help you to understand micro-demographics or micro-psychographics within your niche market segment to avoid because they are not likely to get traction for you in the marketplace. Alternatively, those cases which appear closer to "centroids," or the center of the clusters, are likely good case examples of people who are in the sweet spot of your target niche and therefore also offer good potential first contacts within the niche. Such people offer the opportunity to understand the "prototype" of that first great potential consumer. The key user characteristics of people close to the centroids may be translated into what is known as a "user persona," and we give three examples of how to create them in the next chapter.

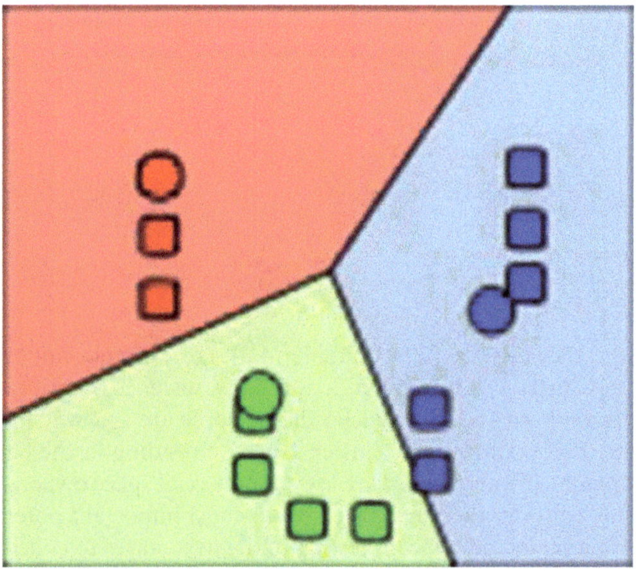

◘ **Fig. 14.8** Graphical illustration of a k-means clustering technique. (Source: ► https://en-Wikipedia.org/wiki/K-means_clustering)

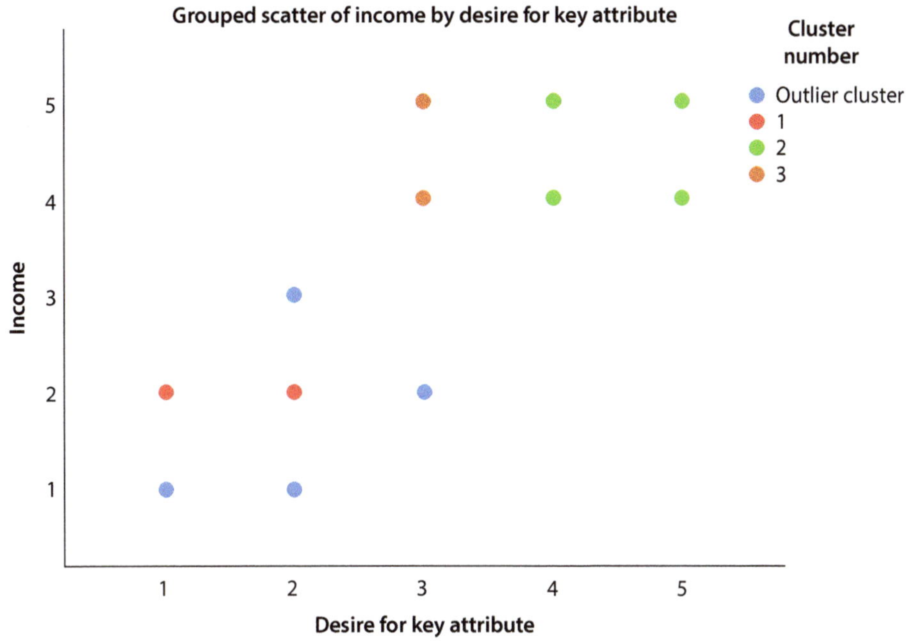

Fig. 14.9 Illustration of a two-step cluster analysis using the data provided in the example. (Source: The Authors)

One other cluster analysis-related tool might provide some interesting insights about your cluster of interest. You can perform a two-step cluster analysis, as denoted in Fig. 14.9 and Table 14.4, which essentially allows you to zero in on just two variables at a time to see what their interaction looks like. So, for example, if you wanted to specifically just look at the relationship between "income" and "desire for key attribute," you could run a two-step cluster analysis with the same data and then graph the results using a scatter plot (since with just two variables the data can exist on an x-y axis).

Please note the number of participant cases is indicated for each two-variable X-Y location from the scatterplot in Table 14.4.

Given this data, we see that Cluster 2 has the highest correlation between high income and high desire for the key attribute based on the XY locations 44, 54, 45, and 55 (Fig. 14.9 and Table 14.4). If we decide that we want to investigate the impact of income and its relationship to desire for the key attribute, in more detail for example, then we might want to specifically narrow in on the 4/9 participants who had the highest rating on income and desire for the key attribute. This is just one example; each variable combination could be analyzed in this way.

Now that we have identified some clear "sweet-spot" participants in our target cluster who we are going to begin focusing on, prior to opening up concept testing with a larger number of potential customers in the niche, we recommend going

Table 14.4 Two-step cluster analysis results

X.Y. location	Cluster number	Number of participant cases
11	Outlier	1
21	1	2
12	Outlier	1
22	1	1
32	Outlier	2
23	Outlier	1
43	3	2
53	3	1
44	2	2
54	2	1
45	2	2
55	2	4
Total # Outliers =	5	
Total # Cluster 1 =	3	
Total # Cluster 2 =	9	
Total # Cluster 3 =	3	

Source: The authors

back to these specific participants to flesh out more details for their responses to each of the attributes. We will use this information to create a "user persona" for the niche in the next chapter on concept testing, ► Chap. 15.

14

Chapter Review Questions

1. Why is picking one first market niche a particularly good strategy for an entrepreneurial startup?
2. Give a specific example of a niche market within a market.
3. What techniques or considerations can be used to construct a first list of potential B2C market niche targets? What about for B2B market niche targets?

References

Carroll, L. G. (1876). *The hunting of the Snark*. Macmillan. Public Domain.

Claycamp, H. J., & Massy, W. F. (1968). A theory of market segmentation. *Journal of Marketing Research, 5*(4), 388–394.

Hannan, M. T., & Freeman, J. (1977). The population ecology of organizations. *American Journal of Sociology, 82*(5), 929–964.
Hawley, A. (1968). Human ecology. In D. Sills (Ed.), *International Encyclopedia of the Social Sciences*. New York, NY: MacMillan, pp. 328–337.
Hutchinson, G. E. (1957). Concluding remarks. *Cold Spring Harbor Symposium on Quantitative Biology, 22*, 415–427.
Hutt, M. D., & Speh, T. W. (2017). *Business marketing management: B2B* (12th ed.). Cengage South-Western Press.
Kara, A., & Kaynak, E. (1997). Markets of a single customer: Exploiting conceptual developments in market segmentation. *European Journal of Marketing, 31*(11/12), 873–895.
Maney, K. (2009). *Trade-off: Why some things catch on and others don't*. Broadway Books, Random House, Inc.
Merriam-Webster. (2020, online). Accessed on 20 Oct 2020 at https://www.merriam-webster.com/dictionary/niche
Noy, E. (2010). Niche strategy: Merging economic and marketing theories with population ecology arguments. *Journal of Strategic Marketing, 18*(1), 77–86.
Porter, M. E. (1980). *Competitive strategy: Techniques for analyzing industries and competitors*. The Free Press & Macmillan.
Porter, M. E. (1996). What is strategy? *Harvard Business Review, 74*(6), 61–78.
Robinson, J. (1969). *The economics of imperfect competition*. Macmillan & St Martin's Press.
Smith, W. R. (1956). Product differentiation and market segmentation as alternative marketing strategies. *Journal of Marketing, 21*(1), 3–8.
SPSS Inc. (1999). *SPSS base 20.0 for windows user's guide*. SPSS Inc. (All data analyses were performed using SPSS version 20.0 (SPSS, Inc., Chicago IL).
Wind, Y., & Cardozo, R. (1974). Industrial market segmentation. *Industrial Marketing Management*. 3(3): 153–165.

Concept Testing

Contents

© The Author(s), under exclusive license to Springer Nature Switzerland AG 2022
S. E. Reid, C. B. Crawford, *Entrepreneurial Vision*, Classroom Companion: Business, https://doi.org/10.1007/978-3-030-77803-3_15

Learning Objectives

In this chapter, we focus on concept testing. It is important to invest adequate time in concept testing to discover the most important attributes/benefits to craft into the "minimum viable product" (MVP) for later development and testing with your first niche market of focus. As such, our learning objectives in this chapter are to:

1. Learn what a concept test is and why it is important.
2. Build an understanding of the core elements of a concept test.
3. Develop an understanding of some of the key challenges with concept testing.
4. Build an understanding of how to conduct a concept test.
5. Develop an understanding of the differences between concept testing for a B2C market vs. for a B2B market.
6. Develop an understanding of the appropriate types of people to survey when conducting a concept test with a new product or service idea for a startup.
7. Provide a basic tool for concept testing at an early stage.
8. Based on the feedback from your concept test, refine your understanding of your market niche in terms of who they are and what their needs are.

15.1 Concept Testing: A Definition and Its Importance

"Concept testing" in simplest terms (Wind, 1973, p. 2) is "a procedure designed to assess consumer reactions to a new product concept." Concept testing is a cornerstone of modern marketing and a field with a rich research tradition lending applicable ideas to practitioners. It's an important field of research because concept testing, done early and well, as with all "upfront homework" (Cooper, 1979), can increase chances of success in the marketplace, and also greatly reduce costs and ensure that money spent on product development with markets is done wisely.

Indeed, the earliest academic research on concept testing was focused mainly on testing concepts related to one of two areas: (1) "new product development" (Iuso, 1975, p. 228) and (2) ideas for creating advertising copy focused on the "expression of a concept" (Axelrod, 1964, p. 41). The notion of how a concept is expressed—i.e., its visual or written form—impacts how a potential consumer comprehends and interprets the idea underlying the described concept of interest and whether their comprehension of the expression of the concept maps onto the

15

intended conveyance of the idea. For example, an illustrator may draw a bird escaping from a cage to connote the notion of "freedom," but the way it is expressed may be interpreted by a viewer as "breaking away" (◘ Fig. 15.1). Although these two concepts may be related on some level, they carry a different meaning in terms of the perceived benefits between the creator and the receiver.

To begin then, the definition for the word "concept" (Dictionary.com, 2020 online) is "a general notion or idea." An earlier definition of the term "concept" from the Webster dictionary is quoted in the early research on concept testing of Axelrod (1964, p. 41) as "a mental image of a thing formed by generalization from particulars; also, an idea of what a thing in general should be."

Fig. 15.1 Conceptual image to portray "freedom." (Source: Image licensed and downloaded from Shutterstock on October 25, 2020. Credit: by fran_kie/▶ Shutterstock.com. License Link: ▶ https://www.shutterstock.com/image-photo/little-birds-escape-out-birdcage-freedom-770336959)

Tauber (1972, p. 35, used with permission from Warc Advertising Research Foundation from [What is measured by concept testing? *Journal of Advertising Research* 12(6)]; permission conveyed through Copyright Clearance Center, Inc.) provides a more specific definition related to the business context: "a concept is itself an idea for positioning new products or repositioning established ones. It is the marketing or advertising strategist's method for fixing a perception of the product in the consumer's mind." Applied to the business context of a new idea for a startup, we consider the concept to basically mean "the product or service promise" or, in other words, the consumer value proposition.

"Concept testing," then, as noted by Iuso (1975, p. 228) "has become a popular term for any number of marketing research procedures which test some sort of stimulus as a proxy for a new, revised, or remarketed product or service" and "the underlying principle of such research procedures is that it is possible to make 'go/no go' and other early strategic planning decisions from consumer inputs. This is accomplished by presenting consumers with an idea, or concept, early in the planning cycle before large amounts of development resources are committed."

Another popular definition of "concept testing" comes from Page and Rosenbaum (1992, p. 269, with permission from John Wiley and Sons, December 12, 2020, for reprint):

Fig. 15.2 Conceptual image to portray a test. (Source: Image licensed and downloaded from Shutterstock on February 6, 2018. Credit: by Number1411/► Shutterstock.com. License Link: ► https://www.shutterstock.com/image-photo/answer-sheet-pencil-education-concept-466657337)

> "a variety of marketing research-based approaches employed to assess the marketability of a product or service idea prior to its actual development. Its purpose is to provide early feedback from the market about the perceived attractiveness of a proposed new product before its development has ever begun."

In short, the main purposes of concept testing (Fig. 15.2), according to Crawford and De Benedetto (2021, p. 182/183), are "(1) to eliminate poor concepts," (2) "to estimate sales or trial rate," and (3) "to help further develop the original idea."

15

15.2 Core Elements of the Concept Test

Usually, during the stages following Technology Vision development, Product/Market Vision development, and determination of a first potential market niche of interest, the concept is starting to form in the minds of the entrepreneur and entrepreneurial team into a relationship between product features (i.e., product attributes, product form, underlying technology) and consumer benefits or a claim of proposed satisfactions. Often, there will also be one major benefit that gets highlighted in the proposition.

The concept testing exercise requires that the entrepreneurial team prepares a very early product/service description or presentation based on this early-stage proposition (as clearly as possible and with any visual representations, mind maps, white papers, early prototypes, or designs) which clearly explains the value-add the team feels they can offer this particular market. As stated by Tauber (1972, p. 35, used with permission of Warc Advertising Research Foundation from [What is measured by concept testing? *Journal of Advertising Research* 12(6)]; permission conveyed through Copyright Clearance Center, Inc.): "Two major elements in the communication of a product idea and its concept are the form of presentation – prototype of product or package, print/broadcast advertisement, or a written description – and the execution or design or what is to be conveyed, dependent on creativity, copywriting-photography skills, etc."

One core question relates to how well "developed" the concept test statement/presentation should be for potential customers in the test group. Several researchers have investigated this issue. Certainly, in the case of complex technology-based concepts which may be more difficult to explain in a concept statement, particularly in the case of industrial product concepts, reliance on prototypes and drawings is obviously important to convey the nature of the concept as much as possible. In terms of the concept statement itself, however, in the case of consumer goods, a core study conducted to compare the use of "stripped, embellished, and visual concept formulations" by Lees and Wright (2004, p. 389, with permission from John Wiley and Sons, December 12, 2020, for reprint), conducted on five consumer goods—a DVD recorder, a spray-on cleanser, a spin fryer, a baking soda toothpaste, and a disposable cell phone—suggests that:

> "respondents answers to attitude and purchase intention questions showed only minor variation with different formulations of the concept test statement... Therefore, the type of concept statement formulation may not be that important, at least for early ranking tasks performed before experiential prototypes are available. Early concept tests, therefore, may be carried out using stripped concept statements. This may reduce costs."

Concept test(s), once performed, will allow you to refine your basic concept and the value-add into a value proposition (covered in the next chapter, ▶ Chap. 16) for the specific niche you have decided to work toward, before you invest more money in further developing the product or service. The concept test may also point to components of the concept which take away from the overall value proposition and which should therefore be changed or removed.

In terms of the specific elements to consider including in a concept test, there are many prescriptive items offered up by the research. Those first denoted by Iuso (1975) are maintained on some level, as a basis for the development of most concept tests, as follows:

1. A component that tests "relevance" for those being surveyed, i.e., those "pertinent to consumer problems and wants" (Iuso, 1975, p. 230), or in other words, level of importance
2. A component that tests "comparisons" to other possible substitute products or brands
3. A component that tests "evaluation" in terms of the basic idea and its underlying attributes (Iuso, 1975, p. 230)
4. A component that tests "overall concept acceptance"

Further to this, there are additional aspects that might be tested. For example, Wind (1973, p. 3) suggests that "hard-core potential buyers are identified by requiring a choice (including a measure of 'behavioral commitment' to try or buy the concept)."

15.3 Challenges with the Concept Test

While the potential for improving the chances of success and reducing costs is an important reason for conducting concept tests, the practice is not without its challenges and critics. Axelrod (1964), for example, one of the earliest researchers on the topic, questions comparing different concepts or developing brand-new concepts based on feedback from the concept test itself—preferring instead that the use be basically limited to what he calls "monadic statement testing" where "the consumer is presented with one statement concerning the product and asked for an expression of interest in this product relative to what he now uses. He is then usually asked to explain his choice, and what likes or dislikes he may have. Clearly, this procedure simulates the realities of the marketplace" (Axelrod, 1964, p. 43). This basic idea carries through to some of the core use of concept testing today whereby one product concept idea would be tested at a time (rather than comparatively), and the focus would be on developing a more thorough understanding behind the consumer's perceived utility evaluation with the use of each specific concept.

Iuso (1975, p. 228) additionally notes challenges related to survey error (also pointed out in the empirical research of Peng & Finn, 2010) or what he calls "courtesy endorsements, which occur when a consumer does not wish to appear uncooperative or negative even though he or she actually may have little interest in the idea, or conversely, to the commonplace automatic resistance to embrace change despite the merits of an idea."

Cooper (1993) notes additional challenges with concept testing, including concepts based on sensory perception, those involved with art and entertainment, or technologies which cannot be seen or interacted with directly.

15.4 Basic Procedure for an Early-Stage Concept Test with Your First Market Niche

The basic procedure for building a concept test is as follows:

1. Prepare your concept statement (an early version of your value proposition which explains the "promise" of how your basic idea has the ability to serve the needs of your customer in a way that is differentiated from other offerings) and any related materials such as drawings or models which might provide help understanding the concept. Remember from the research discussed earlier that in the early going, a stripped-down concept statement might suffice. Have as many team members as possible involved in the exercise to gain as much agreement as possible on the wording.
2. Build your set of questions given your specific concept. See Worksheet 17 for examples, but feel free to add to these suggestions as makes sense.
3. In addition to the concept statement, include an introductory paragraph which describes your goals/why you are conducting the test, the main features of the concept, and the list of benefits for consumers which will be delivered by the product/service. You may additionally want to ask whether the participant(s) understand the concept as described. If not, you might ask them to list which elements are unclear. Ensure that as part of the concept test, you ask the participant(s) whether there are any additional features or benefits they would like to see added to the product.
4. Where possible, face-to-face interviews are a good option.
5. If not, surveys can be done virtually, online, or by email. When initially contacting participants, whether by phone or email, it's a good idea to mention that you may also be interested in conducting follow-up research later, if they are willing.

Worksheet 17 outlines a list of potential questions suggested for use in a first concept test.

Worksheet 17: Early-Stage Concept Test (1) with Market Niche

Types of Questions to Consider:

1. Warm-up Discussion
   a. Thank for coming and introductions. Ask them a little about themselves.
   b. Give them a bit of a background on how/why you got interested in the concept.
   c. Give participants an introduction paragraph including the concept statement and any accompanying descriptors or graphics. The introduction:
      i. Describes your goals with the test
      ii. Explains the main concept features
      iii. Lists customer benefits
   d. "Do you understand the general concept?" (if not, spend some time describing in a little more detail, possibly using your mind map if you think it might be helpful)
2. Background Questions:
   a. "We consider you to be a potential consumer of the product/service we are thinking of developing because…." (in the case that you have not met or previously interviewed them before).
   b. "Have you ever seen or heard something similar to these concepts before reading what we sent you? Are you aware of other companies or people who are working on anything similar?"
3. Product/Service Specific Questions:

   For questions 3 a), 3 b) and 3 d) how do you score on the following scale from 1 to 7:

   Not At All **Somewhat** **Very**
   1-----------2-----------3-----------4-----------5-----------6-----------7

   3a) How relevant/important is the product/service concept to you?_________

   3b) How interested are you in the proposed product/service concept?_________

   3c) Please elaborate:

   ____

   ____

   3d) How much do you like the proposed product/service concept?

   3e) Please give details on most/least liked features and benefits:

   ____

   ____

© Susan E. Reid and Charles B. Crawford, August 14, 2020.

15

3 f) Is there anything you would change about the basic concept? Why?

____

____

3 g) Do you think the concept is missing anything from your perspective?

____

____

3 h) Which part of the concept do you find would deliver the most value for you specifically? Why?

____

____

© Susan E. Reid and Charles B. Crawford, August 14, 2020.

Performing this early concept test will help provide your team with data to further flesh out your concept, especially the key attributes which are most important and which one of the attributes is the main priority on the whole. If you feel you have a green light from the early concept test—particularly in terms of consensus around the key discriminating feature of your product proposal—you are ready to start working on an early version of the value proposition (VP), also sometimes called the unique selling proposition (or USP). Although you might still want to add some tweaks in terms of lower priority features, the main goal is to focus on creating the USP (VP).

15.5 Running the Concept Test by Your Advisory Board

Before performing a full concept test, we suggest a quick check-in with your advisory board (personal board of directors, key lead users, and experts) to validate the market niche option you selected and the early concept and USP (VP) for your product or service. Of course, you will be working with your niche market and later with key channel members to determine a strong final value proposition and clarifying your vision based on such refinements. That said, the advisory board provides an unparalleled opportunity to ensure that there is a very good potential fit between the basic concept you have chosen to move forward with and you and your team. That fit should be fairly obvious right up front before going further. The types of questions you may want to ask of the advisory board after describing and explaining the concept are as follows:

(a) Does the market niche we have identified keep us on track with our overall long-term vision? In other words, does the niche have the potential to take us where we want to go?
(b) Does the niche offer us the ability to position differently from any other offering in that specific market and in a way that is aligned with the most desired benefits of the niche? In other words, can we be a "one-of-a-kind" in that market (◘ Fig. 15.3)?
(c) Does the niche market offer the potential for scalability to other later niche markets?

If there is a good potential match between your identified niche and your offering based on your initial cluster analysis tests and early concept test, once vetted with your advisory board, it's time to put your early ideas through a full concept test with a reasonable-sized sample from your niche market.

15.6 Full Concept Testing with a B2C Niche Market

Prior to carrying out empirical research with a B2C market, where possible it is always best to "triangulate" survey data with primary data (based on depth interviews or focus groups). These techniques are well-known and covered in the market-

Fig. 15.3 Visual image to portray "one-of-a-kind." (Source: Image licensed and downloaded from Shutterstock on January 14, 2018. Credit: by rangizzz/► Shutterstock.com. License Link: ► https://www.shutterstock.com/image-photo/individuality-standing-out-crowd-concept-close-628366715)

ing literature, and, while it is not our purpose to get into such specifics here, it is worth noting that such research can provide rich, illustrative levels of understanding of consumer reactions to concepts, which may not be possible to elicit through surveys alone. As indicated by Iuso (1975, p. 229), "this requires the conduct of rather lengthy conversations with appropriate consumers. … (it is) these conversations and not enigmatic scale-points, which provide the most reliable and complete indicators of market reactions to an idea."

So, who should the participants for primary data collection in your concept testing research effort be? The selection of key respondents has been shown to be a major contributor to variance in concept testing outcomes (Peng & Finn, 2010) and as such is a critical factor in terms of assuring the success of the outcomes of such research. Several studies based on empirical research, including the work of Ozer (2010), Reidenbach and Grimes (1984), and Schoormans et al. (1995), point to the importance of using "experts" as key contacts for such research, particularly in the early days of concept formation to positively impact test validity with concept evaluation. As such, as far as the initial depth interview and focus groups go, gaining input on a given concept from experts in the field, including "lead users" in addition to your advisory board, is definitely recommended.

Once primary research is conducted, take the early depth information from interviews and/or focus groups into account to fine-tune the concept itself. From there, we suggest surveying a minimum of 100 individuals in the B2C space if these numbers are possible given your niche market. Essentially, in so much as possible, you want to create a sample of meaningful size on which to base your decisions. Of course, there are subtleties related to sample size and method of statistical analysis, but the 100-survey rule (i.e., complete surveys collected) is usually a good rule of thumb if using basic methods of analysis and if the data distribution of your findings is considered to be within a "normal" range.

Once you and your team are ready to move onto this larger sample on which to test a fine-tuned version of the concept, it is important to go back to your market niche data, as was recommended in ▶ Chap. 14, to find as many of the "sweet-spot" consumers in the niche as possible on whom to test. Additionally, there is further research to suggest that concept testing with early adopters, or those who are likely to be first and early consumers from the niche for a new product offering, is likely to elicit the most realistic first response from the marketplace (Klink & Athaide, 2010) and one which will lend itself best to the predictability of your forecasting efforts early on.

15.7 Full Concept Testing with a B2B Niche Market

In the B2B space, we suggest surveying a minimum of 25 companies if these numbers are possible given your target market. Essentially, in so much as possible, you want to create a sample of meaningful size on which to base your decisions. This may be difficult in the B2B space, so it is a good idea to conduct surveys with a variety of individuals from within one firm, where possible (i.e., multiple data points from one firm) which represent different types of decision-making power and usage. Just as with the B2C market, psychographic data from these individuals can be used to gain a better appreciation for different responses from within the same firm. Given the numbers here, depth interviews, particularly with experts and lead users, will provide crucial information where the number of potential adopting firms may be small. Potential early adopters also take on certain importance in the B2B world and may be essential targets for launching first versions of a product or service and creating relationships that may enable alpha and beta testing sites, as a means of concept testing (Dolan & Matthews, 1993).

The main differences between Worksheet 17 (an early version of the concept test) and Worksheet 18 (a typical concept test) are that the latter introduces more detailed questions about comparing your value proposition and concept to potential competition/brands, and also begins to ask questions about potential pricing.

Worksheet 18: Concept Test (2) with Market Niche

Types of Questions to Consider:

1. **Warm-up Discussion:**
   a. Thank for coming and introductions. Ask them a little about themselves.
   b. Give them a bit of a background on how/why you got interested in the concept.
   c. Give participants an introduction paragraph including the concept statement and any accompanying descriptors or graphics. The introduction:
      i. Describes your goals with the test
      ii. Explains the main concept features
      iii. Lists customer benefits
   d. "Do you understand the general concept?" (if not, spend some time describing in a little more detail, possibly using your mind map if you think it might be helpful)
2. **Background Questions:**
   a. "We consider you to be a potential consumer of the product/service we are thinking of developing because…." (in the case that you have not met or previously interviewed them before).
   b. "Have you ever seen or heard something similar to these concepts before reading what we sent you? Are you aware of other companies or people who are working on anything similar?"
3. **Product/Service Specific Questions:**

   For questions 3 a) and 3 c) how do you score on the following scale from 1 to 5:

   Not At All Interested   Somewhat Interested   Very Interested
   1-----------2-----------3-----------4-----------5

   3 a) Are you interested in the proposed product/service concept? _________

   3 b) Please elaborate why you are so interested or not interested:

   ____

   ____

   3 c) To what extent do you like the proposed product/service concept? _____

   3 d) Please elaborate what you like the most about it:

   ____

   ____

   3 e) Please elaborate what you like the least about it:

   ____

   ____

© Susan E. Reid and Charles B. Crawford, August 14, 2020.

3 f) Is there anything you would change about the basic concept? Why?

___

___

3 g) Do you think the concept is missing anything from your perspective?

___

___

3 h) Which part of the concept do you find would deliver the most value for you specifically? Why?

___

___

4. Questions about Competitive Brands:

4 a) What other brands do you know of which satisfy the same or a similar need? Please list.

___

___

4 b) If you are already purchasing or are familiar with one or more of the brands, for the one you are most familiar with, how would you compare our concept with Brand X (circle your response on the scale from 1 to 5).

Not At All Interested Somewhat Interested Very Interested
1------------2------------3------------4------------5

4 c) Why do you like our concept more or less than Brand X?

___

___

5. Questions about potential pricing:

5 a) Assume this concept was already available on the market. How much would you expect to pay for it? (you can ask the question relative to a familiar product).

___

___

© Susan E. Reid and Charles B. Crawford, August 14, 2020.

5 b) Assume our product concept is available on the market at a price of $Y. What is the likelihood you would buy it? (circle your response on the scale from 1 to 5).

Not At All Interested **Somewhat Interested** **Very Interested**
1------------2------------3------------4------------5

5 c) Please elaborate why you answered the way you did in 5 b).

____

____

6. **Questions about the Value Proposition:**
Please take a moment to tell us what you think about our Value Proposition. What suggestions would you make to improve it?

(Fill in the blanks prior to sending out the concept test):

<u>(Product Name)</u> THE ONE

<u>(Type of Product)</u> THAT

<u>(Point of Difference)</u>

© Susan E. Reid and Charles B. Crawford, August 14, 2020.

While the format of Worksheet 18 has been adapted, the questions as denoted in ◘ Fig. 15.4 come from Cooper (2001, p. 205, Figure 7.5, used with permission of Hachette Books from [Cooper, R.G., 2001, *Winning at new products: Accelerating the process from idea to launch,* Basic Books]; permission conveyed through Copyright Clearance Center, Inc.).

1a. First, are you interested in the proposed product? You can answer on this fivepoint scale (show them the scale):

☐ not interested at all ☐ not too interested ☐ somewhat
☐ quite interested ☐ very interested

1b. Why so interested (or not interested)? ____________________

2a. To what extent do you like the product?

☐ not interested at all ☐ not too interested ☐ somewhat
☐ quite interested ☐ very interested

2b. Identify the things you like the most about it: ____________________

2c. What things do you like least about it? ____________________

3a. You are already purchasing (or familiar with) Brand X. How would you compare the new product with Brand X?

☐ not interested at all ☐ not too interested ☐ somewhat
☐ quite interested ☐ very interested

3b. Why did you like it more (or less than Brand X?) ____________________

4. Assume this new product was already available. How much would you expect to pay for it (you can ask this price question relative to a product they are familiar with or now buy)? ____________________

5a. Let's assume the new product is on the market at a price of \$Y. What is the likelihood that you would buy it?

☐ not interested at all ☐ not too interested ☐ somewhat
☐ quite interested ☐ very interested

5b. Why ... what made you answer the way you did (in 5a)? ____________________

5c. (If negative): What would you like to see changed in the product? Any suggestions? ____________________

◘ **Fig. 15.4** The typical concept test questionnaire (originally published in Chapter 7, Figure 7.5, p. 205, used with permission of Hachette Books from [Cooper, R.G., 2001, *Winning at new products: Accelerating the process from idea to launch*, Basic Books]; permission conveyed through Copyright Clearance Center, Inc.)

15.8 Refining Your Understanding of the Market Niche Using the Concept Test

Following the analysis of the results of the concept test, and in line with the earlier mentioned main recommendations of the uses of concept testing by Crawford and Di Benedetto (2021), the key questions to ask include:

1. Should we keep or eliminate the concept from further consideration?
2. If we decide to eliminate the concept, should we do a major overhaul/pivot using some of the other concepts we had considered in ► Chap. 11 (Worksheets 11 and 12) or might we be able to still work with the concept using some of the suggestions elicited by the concept test for tightening it up?
3. If we decide to move forward with the idea, what valuable, constructive feedback did we receive from experts and potential consumers to enhance and/or develop the idea further?
4. Based on a first estimate using the stated level of interest, the likelihood of buying, and importance/relevance of the idea for the market niche, what level would you estimate the trial rate and/or early sales to be? The "top-two-box" approach (Crawford & Di Benedetto, 2021) may be utilized here whereby the number of individuals scoring "very interested" and "quite interested" or "strongly agree" and "quite strongly agree," depending on the verbiage used, is used to evaluate, based on the sample from the target niche population, what percentage are likely to buy the offering. It is important to use statistical tests that can give an estimate of variability and error rate with these predictions, and keep in mind that if only early adopters were surveyed/tested, it might be a good idea to factor in that within any population, there are likely to be approximately 13.5% "early adopters" (Rogers & Shoemaker, 1971, p. 172).

Cooper (2001, pp. 209–210, used with permission of Hachette Books from [Cooper, R.G., 2001, *Winning at new products: Accelerating the process from idea to launch*, Basic Books]; permission conveyed through Copyright Clearance Center, Inc.) elaborates further on the value of the concept test and utilizing the "top box method," as follows:

> "With all its weaknesses, the concept test is still the best way of gauging likely product acceptance before you have actually developed a product. For familiar products in familiar categories (which are the bulk of product development efforts), it has proven quite predictive. The box score (the percentage of people who replied "definitely would buy") is your best early indicator of how your product will fare, short of a test market or full launch.
>
> Unfortunately, there are no simple formulas for translating this top box score into a predicted market share. Some market research firms have developed elaborate models for estimating initial trial rates for certain types of consumer market share. But such formulas and norms tend to be very specific to certain industries and even product categories within industries.

> For frequently repurchased consumer goods, for example, a top box score of 40 percent or higher is considered a strong score. In hundreds of studies comparing concept test results with test market results, such "strong" concepts result in initial trial rate in excess of 30 percent, and there is a high likelihood of positive test market results. By contrast, "average" concepts – those receiving a top box score of 30 to 39 percent – achieve an initial trial rate of somewhat less than 30 percent and result in positive test market results about one-third of the time. Any consumer brand scoring less than 30 percent "definitely would purchase" on the concept test gets a poor initial rate of well less than 20 percent and about one chance in ten that test market results will be positive."

Further questions/ideas that might be additionally considered at this point could include:

- What are the most important/salient benefits and attributes which are a part of the concept and are highlighted by the qualitative feedback of respondents?
- Are there subgroups within the niche based on their responses to the concept test, or are they relatively cohesive in terms of interest? If so, which subgroup is most interested?
- Create a "user persona" based on the subsegment or segment showing the most interest (i.e., Who are the typical individuals in your niche market? What responses are specific to them?).

15.9 User Personas

Once we have a solid idea of which market niche we want to start developing our early ideas and concepts with, based on initial feedback from the concept test, a useful tool is that of the "user persona." While the idea has existed for quite some time, the term "user persona" was coined by software developer Alan Cooper and became more widely disseminated through his book *The Inmates Are Running the Asylum* (1998). The term typically denotes a fictional character meant to be representative of the core users within a given market segment.

"Personas," according to Pruitt and Adlin (2006, p. 11), are "fictitious, specific, concrete representations of target users" able to personify data. Through the use of such personas, designers, marketers, and entrepreneurs may be in a better position to create and deliver the specific product and service solutions consumers are looking for.

Many benefits have been considered in the literature associated with the development of personas. Prime among the benefits is developing a more detailed understanding of the potential consumers themselves, including their needs and preoccupations. As detailed by Pruitt and Adlin (2006, p. 14), these benefits include the ability to "make assumptions and knowledge about users explicit, allow you to focus on and design for a small set of specific users, and engender interest and empathy toward users."

User personas have been particularly useful in the field of design. Cooper and Reimann (2002) in *About Face: 2.0* took the understanding of what is traditionally known as the product-market interface to a new level and focused on a more evolved level of understanding, calling it "interaction design," which offers a more compelling and dynamic level of the idea of an interface, where the user is an active participant rather than just a receiver of the design of the product/technology. In a user benefit study conducted utilizing a Delphi panel of experts, it was found (Miaskiewicz & Kozar, 2011, pp. 426–427) that "the most significant benefit of personas is their ability to focus product design teams on the actual goals of the target customers. Instead of talking about general consumers, personas bring the target consumers to life and help to integrate their needs and goals as a central driver of the design process."

As such, one of the main benefits of creating user personas is that developing a persona offers a much clearer and deeper understanding of "sweet-spot" consumers within the niche. Specifically, we are interested in understanding their perspective and the task(s) they are trying to complete with the product/service, in what way, and which attributes they are focused on and why. In order to do this, Go and Carroll (2004) suggest that perhaps it is better to describe a person in relation to product use or an activity/experience. As with vision, setting the context is key to promoting a much higher level of understanding. To do this, Go and Carroll suggest the use of "What if?" scenarios (just as with the strategic planning approaches described in ▶ Chap. 10) whereby the persona is taken through various "what if?" usage scenarios. Developing the user persona, especially through a use context, helps to really get a feel for these core niche market customers and also makes this information easier to share with other stakeholders such as financiers or employees.

While the concept test survey to help define the niche of interest will give you quite a bit of demographic and needs-based information related to the offering, to create a strong persona profile as recommended above, it is a good idea to narrow in on the sweet-spot participants of the survey. This will allow you to collect more data to drill down and really understand what makes these people tick. You can ask them to give you a very brief synopsis of their life story (i.e., where they were born, family situation growing up, education, experience, where they live now, family situation now, etc.).

Margaret Hagan (2014) provides a great example of the types of questions one might ask of a "persona" coming up with specific questions that would really delve into the crux of meaningful answers. For example, beyond just asking what a user's interests, values, and goals are, she asks "What enlivens her?" or instead of just asking about a user's needs, she asks "What's missing?"

As in our AI drone cleaning example in the previous chapters, we had nine participants who fell within the "high interest in the determinant attribute" cluster and four who were situated particularly in the sweet spot with regard to the specific "income" indicator variable. A sample user persona (◘ Fig. 15.5) has been created

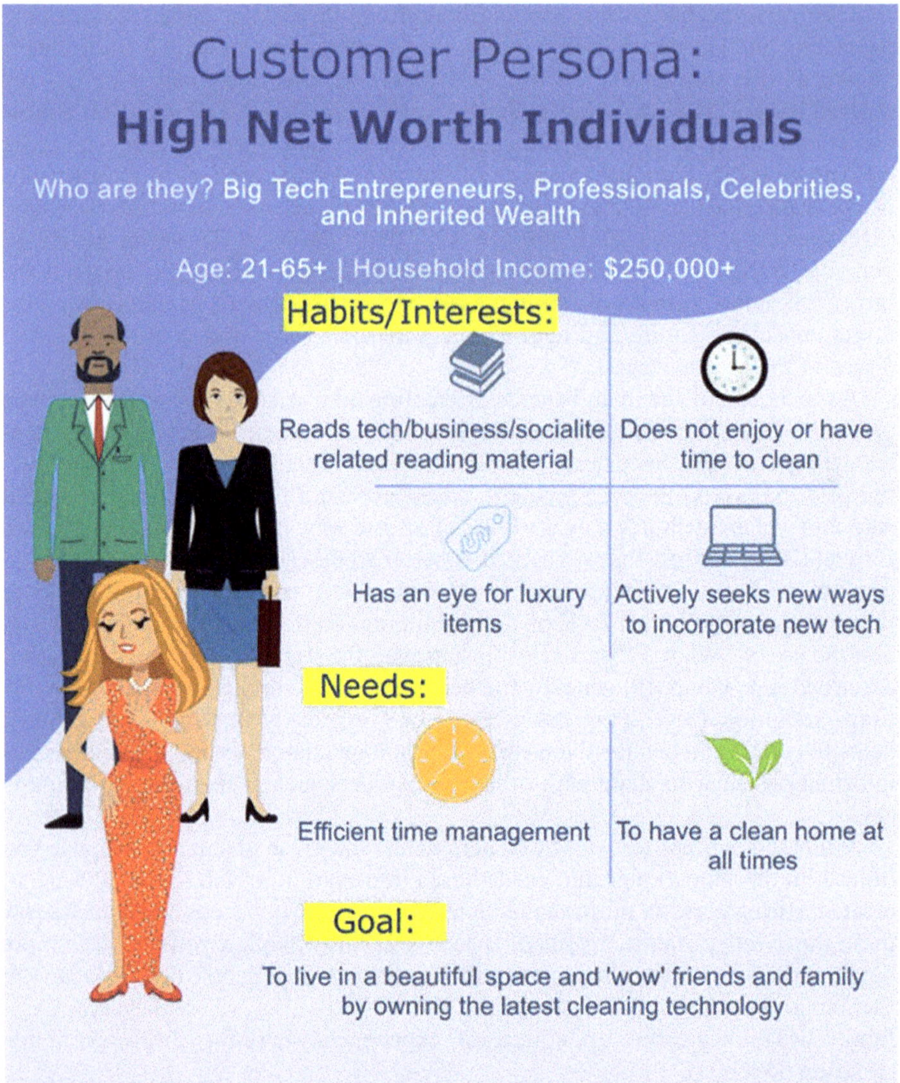

15

◼ **Fig. 15.5** User persona for Cluster #2: the urban high-income individual. (Source: Created by Research Assistant, Gillian Regnier)

to represent the sweet spot of this customer, the "high-income individual." The four individuals in the sweet spot would provide a good set of first interviews to create a persona profile. More could be done with the other five afterward to see what kinds of variation might exist within the target niche market and therefore whether it might be a good idea to create more than one profile.

Fig. 15.6 User persona for Cluster #1: the suburban family. (Source: created by Research Assistant, Gillian Regnier)

Additionally, we might create user personas for other clusters which may not represent our initial target of focus, but over time as the product life cycle progresses with the associated typical simplification and reduced cost, with some tweaks they might potentially represent a longer-run target. As such, our dairy farmers and suburban families represent potential longer-run target markets, as denoted in the user personas created in Figs. 15.6 and 15.7.

15

Fig. 15.7 User persona for Cluster #3: the dairy farmers. (Source: created by Research Assistant, Gillian Regnier)

Chapter Review Questions

1. List three reasons why concept testing is important.
2. What are some of the key challenges with concept testing?
3. In which specific case(s) is it a good idea to provide more embellishment to your concept in concept testing?
4. What are the main differences between concept testing for B2C vs. B2B markets?
5. Create a user persona to represent the aggregate personification of your initial market niche sweet-spot people.

References

Axelrod, J. N. (1964). Reducing advertising failures by concept testing. *Journal of Marketing, 28*(4), 41–44.

Cooper, R. G. (1979). The dimensions of industrial new product success and failure. *Journal of Marketing, 43*(3), 93–103.

Cooper, R. G. (1993). *Winning at new products: Accelerating the process from idea to launch* (2nd ed.). Perseus Books Group.

Cooper, A. (1998). *The inmates are running the asylum: Why high-tech products drive us crazy and how to restore sanity*. Morgan Kaufmann.

Cooper, R.G. (2001). Winning at new products: Accelerating the launch from idea to launch. Basic Books (Hachette Books Group, Inc.), 3rd edition.

Cooper, A., & Reimann, R. M. (2002). *About face 2.0*. Morgan Kaufmann (Elsevier).

Crawford, C. M., & Di Benedetto, C. A. (2021). *New products management* (12th ed.). McGraw Hill.

Dictionary.com. (2020). *Definition for the word "concept"*. Accessed on 24th Oct 2020, from https://www.dictionary.com/browse/concept

Dolan, R. J., & Matthews, J. M. (1993). Maximizing the utility of customer product testing: Beta test design and management. *The Journal of Product Innovation Management, 10*(4), 318–330.

Go, K., & Carroll, J. M. (2004). Scenario-based task analysis. In D. Diaper & N. Stanton (Eds.), *The handbook of task analysis for human-computer interaction* (pp. 117–134). Taylor & Francis.

Hagan, M. (2014). *Persona template: For user-centered design process, Open Law Lab blog by Margaret Hagan*. Accessed on 15 Nov 2020 from https://www.openlawlab.com/2014/09/19/persona-template-user-centered-design-process/

Iuso, B. (1975). Concept testing: An appropriate approach. *Journal of Marketing Research, 12*(2), 228–231.

Klink, R. R., & Athaide, G. A. (2010). Consumer innovativeness and the use of new versus extended brand names for new products. *The Journal of Product Innovation Management, 27*(1), 23–32.

Lees, G., & Wright, M. (2004). The effect of concept formulation on concept test scores. *The Journal of Product Innovation Management, 21*(6), 389–400.

Miaskiewicz, T., & Kozar, K. (2011). Personas and user-centered design: How can personas benefit product design processes? *Design Studies, 32*(5), 417–430.

Ozer, M. (2010). The moderating roles of prior experience and behavioral importance in the predictive validity of new product concept testing. *The Journal of Product Innovation Management, 28*(1), 109–122.

Page, A. L., & Rosenbaum, H. F. (1992). Developing an effective concept-testing program for consumer durables. *The Journal of Product Innovation Management, 9*(4), 267–277.

Peng, L., & Finn, A. (2010). How cloudy a crystal ball: A psychometric assessment of concept testing. *The Journal of Product Innovation Management, 27*(2), 238–252.

Pruitt, J., & Adlin, T. (2006). *The persona lifecycle: Keeping people in mind throughout product design*. Morgan Kaufmann (Elsevier).

Reidenbach, P. E., & Grimes, S. (1984). How concept knowledge affects concept evaluation. *The Journal of Product Innovation Management, 1*(4), 255–266.

Rogers, E., & Shoemaker, F. F. (1971). *Communication of innovations* (2nd ed.). The Free Press.

Schoormans, J. P. L., Ortt, R. J., & de Bont, C. J. P. M. (1995). Enhancing concept test validity by using expert consumers. *The Journal of Product Innovation Management, 12*(2), 153–162.

Tauber, E. M. (1972). What is measured by concept testing? *Journal of Advertising Research, 12*(6), 35–37.

Wind, Y. (1973). A new procedure for concept evaluation. *Journal of Marketing, 37*(4), 2–11.

Refining the Vision's Value-Add and Value Proposition

Contents

© The Author(s), under exclusive license to Springer Nature Switzerland AG 2022
S. E. Reid, C. B. Crawford, *Entrepreneurial Vision*, Classroom Companion: Business,
https://doi.org/10.1007/978-3-030-77803-3_16

Learning Objectives

This chapter provides steps to refine your vision by focusing on how to incorporate the value-add for your market niche into your vision. The value-add is crystallized through the construction of a clear value proposition statement. The value proposition is sometimes used on its own as a reflection of the product/market vision statement, or sometimes it is meaningfully incorporated into the vision statement or alternatively is provided as an adjunct to the vision statement to flesh out more meaning.

In this chapter, the focus is on:

1. Building an understanding of what value-add and value proposition mean
2. Providing formulae, with company examples, for building effective value proposition statements
3. Showing how to develop a vision-based blueprint built around delivery of the value proposition.

16.1 Definitions for Value-Add and the Value Proposition

And now, we have arrived at the value proposition. Yes, the value proposition is indeed one of, if not THE, most central tenets of marketing and strategy. It is the primary function and, at the same time, underlying aim of all businesses (or at least it should be)! It is core, not only in terms of enabling both entrepreneurial startups and larger organizations to gain success in the marketplace, but even more centrally, to being able to fulfill the promises of creation and delivery that they make to their customers (◘ Fig. 16.1).

Now, you may ask, if the value proposition is so central to marketing and strategy and the aim of all businesses, why are we only getting around to discussing it here in ▸ Chap. 16? The reason is this: that any truly spectacular value proposition can only be built with a very specific concept ready to put into motion for a very specific niche market. Without a clear understanding of these two key components—product concept and market niche—it is not really possible to construct a meaningful value proposition earlier on. By clearly elucidating the value-add for a specific market niche, which has been decided upon through the work done in all of the chapters leading up to this one, we are now ready to concretely state how the pedal hits the metal, or in other words, how the specific integration and interaction between product and market will connect and create the burst of desired value (◘ Fig. 16.2).

Essentially then, the value proposition is a statement of what the value-add is that you promise and then deliver to your customer. As marketing scholar Theodore Levitt said (1980, p. 84), "to the potential buyer, a product is a complex cluster of value satisfactions." The value-add highlights where the product/service/experience meets the consumer head-on. It is where, in a moment, all can be lost or won in terms of gaining consumer acceptance, desire, and if you're lucky, loyalty, over the longer run. Actually let's rephrase that: it may be that there is indeed some luck

■ **Fig. 16.1** Conceptual image to portray "customer promise." (Source: Image licensed and downloaded from Shutterstock on November 16, 2020. Credit: by Jemastock/► Shutterstock.com. License Link: ► https://www.shutterstock.com/image-vector/business-teamwork-ideas-1029567463)

involved, but we believe that if you work hard to create the right value-add at the right time and place for the right consumer to meet their desires, you will gain their commitment.

A value proposition is really only the statement itself—and while important for your team, organization, channel, and customers to understand your value-add, so they can communicate it, effectuate it, and share it with others, the true kernel of importance is in fact this underlying "value-add." But what does that really mean? The value-add literally means the additional value which is perceived on the part of your customer about the layered set of benefits and costs you are offering to that customer, taken together as a whole, and then compared to any potential competition, in terms of potential product offerings or those they are already using.

In the marketing and economics literatures, we talk about "utilities," which are the desired benefits that a consumer aims to gain through using a product. Indeed, the entire marketing channel, from suppliers, through to manufacturers and then through wholesalers and retailers, is involved in delivering value, or in other words, "utility" to consumers. Specifically, there are three types of utilities: place, time, and possession. This means that consumers want products where they want them,

Fig. 16.2 Conceptual image to portray "burst of desired value." (Source: Image licensed and downloaded from Shutterstock on November 16, 2020. Credit: by magic_pix/► Shutterstock.com. License Link: ► https://www.shutterstock.com/image-illustration/stylish-colorful-illustration-background-nice-design-1047518212)

when they want them, and how they want them. As a simple example, a 24/7 premium wash-and-fold laundry service offers consumers a convenient high-end laundry service, provided they are willing to pay for these combined value-added utilities (Fig. 16.3).

It is the role of the channel members to facilitate these desired utilities—or, in essence, to make the total value-add happen for the customer. Wroe Alderson was one of the first marketing scholars to speak specifically about these utilities and how they were tied to the channel (Alderson, 1954).

16

To give another simple illustrative example, a given consumer may typically eat eggs only once a week at brunch on Sundays and usually purchases them each Saturday at the market, the day before consuming them. Since this consumer hosts their whole family on Sundays and they are "foodies," the consumer would really like to have not only "cooking eggs" but also a small basket of colorful heirloom eggs for display in the center of the table to go with their brunch (and then eaten later in the week). To provide the value-add desired by this consumer means that the retailer at the marketplace (which may be the same producer who brings the eggs from their farm to the market each week) needs to recognize this desire, if pos-

■ **Fig. 16.3** Conceptual image to portray "a service delivering combined value-added utilities." (Source: Image licensed and downloaded from Shutterstock on November 16, 2020. Credit: by NotionPic/▶ Shutterstock.com. License Link: ▶ https://www.shutterstock.com/image-vector/black-white-sign-laundry-dry-cleaning-513969271)

sible—likely by having good probing conversations with the consumer that would enable finding this out—and then delivering the set of eggs as desired to the consumer, i.e., "regular" eggs for cooking in addition to colorful heirloom eggs in a smaller quantity (possession utility), at the marketplace (place utility) on Saturdays (time utility). The producer most capable of meeting these value-added requests will be the most successful with this particular type of customer (■ Fig. 16.4).

Success with figuring out the value-add therefore largely depends on the entrepreneur recognizing the need (which, as we described in a previous chapter, might not be a stated desire, but a latent one) and then being able to deliver that which is desired in line with their own interests, skills, and so forth. The value-add then would be that combination of benefits, weighed out by the cost, which in this case might come at a higher price than in the supermarket because of the higher cost of

Fig. 16.4 Conceptual image to portray "a service delivering desired possession utility—different types of eggs at the market." (Source: Image licensed and downloaded from Shutterstock on November 16, 2020. Credit: by Yohanes Herman Nggebu/▶ Shutterstock.com. License Link: ▶ https://www.shutterstock.com/image-photo/pile-chicken-eggs-badung-market-ready-1842914158)

special chickens, as well as (potentially) additional special packaging. So, it is a success, not only if the consumer desires the benefits but is also willing to take on the additional costs and profit margin affiliated with the delivery of the benefits. If yes, then the value-add equation is complete and it's onto the next customer with a similar desire for that specific proposal of value-add, or in other words, the value proposition.

16.2 Building Effective Value Proposition Statements

16

The value proposition, therefore, is a clearly stated relationship between key *product/service features/attributes* and *consumer benefits or utilities*. In other words, it represents a claim of proposed satisfactions which, if delivered properly, should elicit an outstanding experience (Fig. 16.5).

Sometimes, there will be one major benefit that gets highlighted in the value proposition, and so, a "tight" definition of the value proposition would be: a statement which conveys the single distinguishing product benefit or utility for your product/service over others in a given consumer's mind.

An easy method that many marketers use to construct a positioning statement based around a single main benefit, which is a written way to express the value proposition, is to fill in a blank template as follows:

Fig. 16.5 Image to portray the experience of a satisfied customer. (Source: Image licensed and downloaded from Shutterstock on November 16, 2020. Credit: by D.R. 3D/▶ Shutterstock.com. License Link: ▶ https://www.shutterstock.com/image-illustration/survey-form-tick-placed-outstanding-checkbox-83943241)

> "(Product Name) THE ONE
> (Type of Product) THAT
> (Point of Difference)"

Continuing with our heirloom egg example, a value proposition statement around a single benefit (based on possession utility) might be written as (Fig. 16.6):

> ""Heirloom Farm-Fresh Eggs," the ONE farm-fresh heirloom egg producer at the farmers' market THAT creates a small display (i.e., a basket, a beautiful cloth, etc.) for a ready-to-use table centerpiece."

There are many situations, however, where a single benefit may be more easily copied by the competition. This is particularly true in today's world of "hypercompetition" (D'Aveni, 1994) in almost every product category we can think of. Because of this, it is sometimes a better strategy, in order to create defensible long-term competitive advantage, to layer key benefits together in a way that is more difficult for competitors to copy. How to do this? One way is to layer *core product benefit(s)* together with *core benefits in terms of distribution strategy*—in other words, not just focusing on the possession form of utility (i.e., in terms of the product/service and how it is presented or combined with other products) but also focusing on time and place utility. This is one way to do it. So, the positioning statement might change to be:

Fig. 16.6 Conceptual image to portray a colorful display of eggs. (Source: Image licensed and downloaded from Adobe Stock on November 16, 2020. Credit: by aleksakarina/► stock.adobe.com. License Link: ► https://stock.adobe.com/192823706)

> "(Product Name) THE ONE
> (Type of Product) THAT
> (Point of Differentiation—product/service related)
> And is available (Other Point of Differentiation—delivery/channel related)"

16

In this case, then, if we were to probe even further with our heirloom egg-loving consumer, we might find out that in fact, they would actually prefer to have their order of eggs delivered directly to their home, as this would eliminate the need to go to the market as well as the risk of breaking the eggs on the way home. Consumers with these preferences may very well be willing to pay for this value-add service. So, in other words, their preferences would include "regular" eggs for cooking in addition to colorful heirloom eggs in a smaller quantity in a display (possession utility), home-delivered (place utility) on Sunday mornings just before it is time to start cooking brunch (time utility). In this case, our new value proposition would read:

> "Heirloom Farm-Fresh Eggs," the ONE farm-fresh heirloom egg producer at the farmers' market THAT creates a small display (i.e., a basket, a beautiful cloth, etc.) for a ready-to-use table centerpiece AND delivers your egg order in addition to your display directly to your home on Sunday mornings.

Another way to create multiple differentiation points is for companies to intentionally and strategically differentiate themselves using one of the "generic" strategies, first described by Porter (1980): "differentiation" or "cost leadership." On the one hand, the differentiation strategy is focused on creating differentiation through technology/products, unique design, unique branding, or unique customer service, to name a few key methods. On the other hand, the cost-focused player will attempt to utilize lower operating costs so as to be more efficient in delivering value. This strategy tends to be the game of large players with built-in economies of scale and/or scope which render their efficiencies higher than most others.

So, as mentioned above, a key question is whether you can layer more than one differentiator within these generic strategies in a way that is unique. For example, can you have both the best design and the best technology? Can you have the best operations and the lowest costs? MacMillan and McGrath (1997) suggest that the answer is a strong yes. They state (1997, p. 3) that "in fact, a company has the opportunity to differentiate itself at every point where it comes in contact with its customers…if companies open up their creative thinking to their customers' entire experience with a product or service – what we call the *consumption chain* – they can uncover opportunities to position their offerings in ways that they, and their competitors, would never have thought possible."

16.3 Blueprinting

One tool which enables consideration of many of the potential differentiators for a given "consumption chain," as described by MacMillan and McGrath (1997), is through the use of what is known as a "blueprint" (Shostack, 1984). Using a blueprint will help you start thinking about potential processes to put in place to facilitate clarifying your vision even further and allowing you to think through all of the processes that will enable you to deliver the value-add you are promising in your value proposition. A blueprint can be used to understand both the processes that need to be put in place to support a pure service as well as the service aspects of a product delivery; it can also be utilized even further to guide pre- and post-consumption activities, as will be described below, in addition to better understanding the operations that are required across the channel in order to best deliver the product/service combination. In other words, the blueprint will help you to better understand all of the interactions which may occur throughout the life of a relationship with a customer.

The first known academic article on blueprinting was written by G. Lynn Shostack (1984) where it was applied to understanding operational and marketing tasks in a firm to deliver value to the consumer throughout a product/service delivery process. The blueprinting process showed that, in addition to gaining a better handle on the overall delivery process, it was possible to focus on potential "fail points" to uncover possible improvements in the service delivery behind the "line of visibility" between customers and the company, and also that it was possible to enable profitability analysis. A straightforward example of a shoeshine is provided to illustrate that if executed in 2–3 minutes it would be profitable, but more time than that would likely lead to losses. In other words, delays and errors could result in profit losses. This article also focused on the importance of "tangible" evidence for consumers, particularly where service was a large part of the value-add. Such evidence serves as a proxy for the value-add being delivered and therefore is an important component of consumer perception.

16.3.1 Benefits of Blueprinting

In addition to the key benefits of helping to better understand and deliver the value-add desired, blueprinting has several other key advantages by facilitating:

- Better *market research*. By showing the consumer an early blueprint of what the offering will be, they can comment on their level of potential utility at each point in the blueprint—by doing this, it helps potential customers better understand the key attributes of the service (benefits and costs) and to generate feedback on level of desirability are willingness to pay.
- *Enhanced operations management and forecasting* by providing the ability to analyze potential costs, revenues, and requirements for each attribute and process involved in delivering the product/service. It also helps to evaluate potential fail points (e.g., wait times, problems with contacting customer service, etc.).
- Build effective *communication and marketing strategies* for each aspect of the entire process pre-consumption/during consumption/post-consumption, etc.
- Coordination of *workflows and related tasks* both in-house and with supply chain members (roles, timing, materials, etc.).
- Diagnosis of opportunities for more *value-add.*

Another advantage of using blueprinting is that it enables the understanding of customer and employee satisfaction at every step of the blueprint. This is important to understand, as the delivery of high-touch or very experiential services and products has the potential for creating high levels of customer satisfaction but also requires high levels of employee training in order to ensure that they are satisfied as well.

Later research and development of the blueprinting technique by Bitner et al. (2008) went beyond the concept of using blueprinting to support operations and cost analyses, to using it as a tool to better understand the entire delivery process as experienced by the consumer at the "line of interaction" between the company and customer. It also progressed to detail much more specifically what needed to happen behind the "line of internal interaction" in terms of "support processes" to foster the work of "back-stage" employees, as well as "physical evidence" to support the actions of "onstage" employees and their interactions with customers.

We have used the Creately platform (available for use from Chart, Diagram & Visual Canvas Software | Creately; presented here with permission granted from ► Creately.com on December 9, 2020) for designing the basic blueprints illustrated in this chapter. Applying the concepts from Bitner et al. (2008) and Shostack

(1984), we provide the following basic blueprint to work with as a starting point for constructing your own entrepreneurial team's blueprinting process.

BLUEPRINT WORKSHEET 19

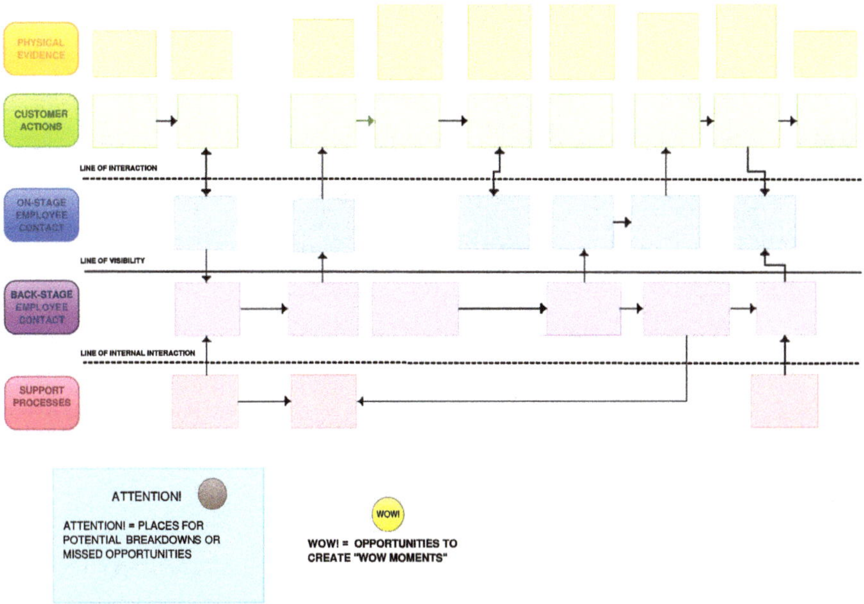

As you can see, the blueprint is a great tool for differentiating from the competition and highlighting your value propositions for your customers and employees. In order to provide some examples, we have used the basic blueprint template from ▶ Creately.com and the concepts from Bitner et al. (2008) and Shostack (1984) to create a potential value-add working document for moving forward with the two product/market visions we have been using as examples during the last several chapters: one for the airport experience (◘ Fig. 16.7) and one for the AI drone cleaning solution (◘ Fig. 16.8).

16.3.2 General How-to for Building a Blueprint

The objective of Worksheet 19 is to utilize the recommendations from all of your research and interviews conducted connected with building your value proposition, in order to build an initial blueprint for the market offering. The blueprint should clearly convey the steps required to achieve delivery of your products/service value proposition—i.e., the steps that will be experienced in the front office by the consumers in the niche market you choose to serve, as well as the steps that will be experienced by the employees in both the front and back offices (in other words, those processes that the team needs to carry out to deliver the product/service, but which are not necessarily seen or experienced by the consumers).

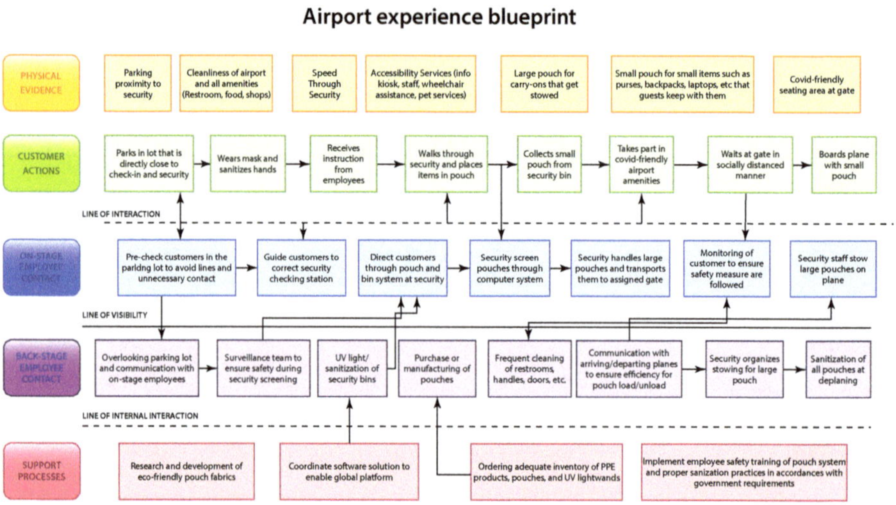

◘ Fig. 16.7 Airport experience blueprint. (Source: Blueprint created by Gillian Regnier, Research Assistant, based on the hypothetical example created by author Susan Reid)

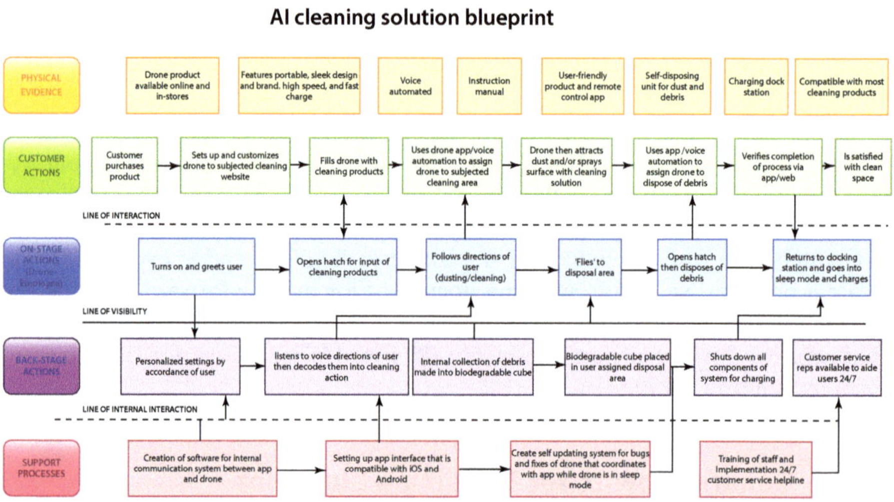

◘ Fig. 16.8 AI cleaning solution blueprint. (Source: Blueprint created by Gillian Regnier, Research Assistant, based on the hypothetical example created by author Susan Reid)

16

The activities highlighted in your blueprint might be further broken down into pre-consumption activities, consumption activities, and post-consumption activities, as suggested in Lemon and Verhoef (2016, p. 76).

In detailing *pre-consumption activities*, for example, this might include the following considerations:

- The entrepreneurial team/startup activities required to get the product/service up and running, as have been suggested and described previously in this book, including the following:
  - Individual reflection and team formation (back-stage)
  - Industry deep dive (mostly back-stage and possibly involving some support processes such as database acquisition, software for research; some on-stage contact, for example, market research with experts, lead users, potential customers)
  - Ideation (both back-stage and on-stage involvements with network, including potential co-creation activities)
  - Concept testing (both back-stage preparation and on-stage interviews and surveys with potential niche markets)
  - Vision formation (back-stage)
  - Product development (back-stage with support activities as well as parallel market testing on-stage)
- All of the pre-launch promotional activities to drive potential customer awareness and action, including PR, radio, TV, print ads, billboards, product placement, influencer campaigns, endorsements, as well as online contact through email, ads, search tools, website, blogs, vlogs, etc. Back-stage support activities will involve creating the backdrop and necessary contacts to enable each of the promotional tools and then on-stage contact for eliciting customer actions.
- All of the developmental and operational activities to produce the product and make it available through various channels to the consumer.

Considering the *consumption activities* themselves, products with a service aspect or pure services will include all of the operational activities involved during the customer experience (i.e., support activities, back-stage employee actions, front-stage employee actions and customer actions). Further, as pointed out by MacMillan and McGrath (1997), as part of the "consumption chain" you need to figure out how your customers order and pay for the product/service and then how it is delivered/enacted. On top of the direct experience of the consumer with the core product/service aspect itself, there are additional aspects of the experience and experiential environment which need to be considered including packaging and labels, instructions or phone prompts/scripts, forms to be filled out or correspondence with the consumer, and quotes/invoices/statements—and each one of these types of activities provides opportunities for differentiation and/or providing utility (especially if it differentiates from other competitors where it might be a pain point) for the consumer. It is important to also bear in mind other products or services which are complementary and/or the usage environment itself (color, music, sound, smells, etc.)—whether in the consumer's home or in a retail environment or where the product/service experience unfolds, as these offer further potential points of differentiation. For example, a runner will experience their running gear under a variety of weather conditions with different types of scenery and with or without other people accompanying them (or perhaps with their music).

Even *post-consumption activities* need to be considered, particularly during this era of cradle-to-cradle ("C-2-C") initiatives and new approaches to recycling, reusing, or renewing used materials. This component of activity is sometimes farmed out to third parties (support processes) or may be handled by retailers or wholesalers rather than the producers themselves. Further post-consumption activities include the facilitation of returns and exchanges, warranties, and product repairs and servicing. Long-term loyalty may also be enhanced by post-consumption activities such as blogs, vlogs, follow-up phone calls or emails, and corporate newsletters. Providing such contact and managing loyalty programs and facilitating customer feedback through CRM management and databases are important components of managing such activities from the back-office and support services perspective.

Here, we provide a sample blueprint (◘ Fig. 16.9) incorporating pre-, during, and post-consumption activities prepared by one of the student teams from our entrepreneurship incubator a few years ago who had agreed to sharing the blueprint with others. The basic idea for the service they developed was to offer healthy delivered meals to students during reading week and exams. The team did a great

16

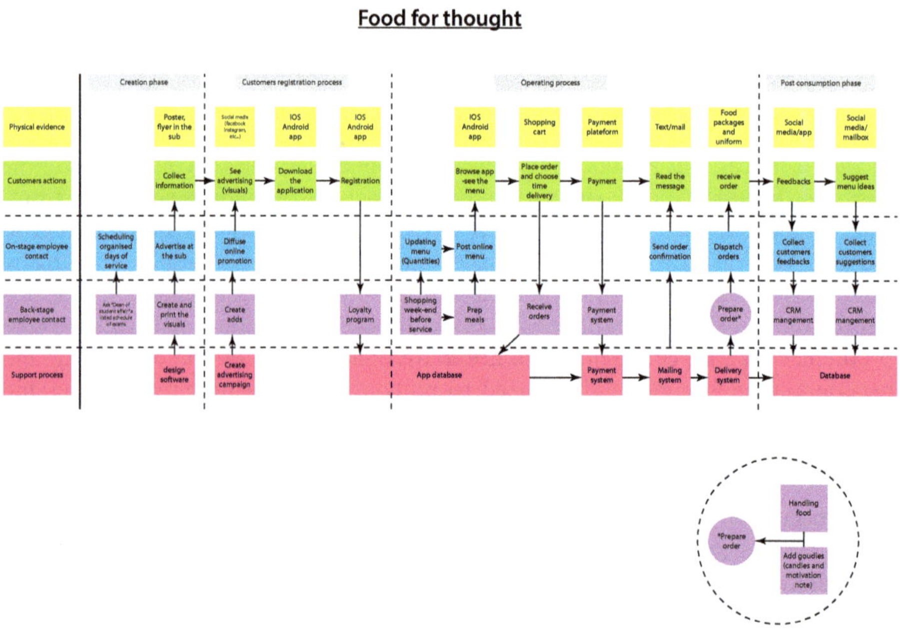

◘ **Fig. 16.9** Blueprint for a food service "Food for Thought" for students at the university. (Source: With permission from 2017 Bishop's University Student Team Pierre Gervais, Alice Robbins and Camille Truong)

job of it and provided a view of pre-, during, and post-consumption activities they included in their blueprint. What the blueprint then helps to do is a) take a look at an early-stage process flow of how the operations look from the customer perspective and (b) see how to potentially better coordinate activities. For example, this particular example shows that there is a potential opportunity to bridge together the loyalty program that people would sign up for at registration (pre-consumption) with the post-consumption CRM (customer relationship management) program. As such, the blueprint should be considered to be a dynamic document which can grow as your vision and business grows along with your customers and employees.

Now, it is time to try your entrepreneurial team's hand at building a blueprint. In order to do so, please consult Worksheet 19 previously provided in Section 16.3.1 (template from ▶ Creately.com with permission granted for template use from ▶ Creately.com on December 9, 2020).

The blueprint should specifically highlight any built-in value-add components of the offering. As in the above section and example, it is suggested that you work through all three phases, pre-consumption, during consumption, and post-consumption, in order to have a complete plan. At the bottom of Worksheet 19 you might additionally include a paragraph each to describe the potential customers in the market niche, the competition (direct and indirect), the value-add for potential customers in the niche, and the specific positioning strategy highlighting the value proposition.

1. Keep in mind that you are mapping the process from THE CUSTOMER'S POINT OF VIEW. To do this, begin by asking several questions—remember that you can add some of the questions to the concept test in the previous chapter in order to find out what they would find most desirable or easiest in terms of their participation in the consumption process. Based on all of the collected information, put together a list of the most salient issues given market information available (from your cluster analysis and concept test) and suggested strategies for enabling the desired inputs. Use these to fill in the customer interactions with the front office.
2. Map out required employee actions as well as support processes needed to make the product/service happen. Start with onstage actions and then move backstage.
3. Consider the physical evidence which will help to bring value-add and credibility to the process. This should include elements like visible features, design, brand, instruction manuals, app functionality and appearance, websites, retail displays, and so on.
4. Re-visit your vision. Are each of the above activities and processes aligned with the vision and value-add you are hoping to create? If so, you are on the right track; if there is a disconnect, how can you best address it?
5. In line with the vision, value proposition, and your blueprint, construct a series of long-term, mid-term, and short-term objectives. Ensure that the blueprint enables achieving these objectives by transparently highlighting where in the blueprint each of your main objectives begins and ends. In other words, you can do an overlay path to show how each objective gets specifically facilitated. Based on these suggestions, develop, if relevant, the following overlays along

with timelines for achievement and an action plan detailing each team member's responsibilities:
- Delivery of the value proposition's key differentiators
- Sales objectives (short, mid, long term)
- Communications, PR, and advertising objectives (short, mid, long term)
- Pricing objectives (short, mid, long term)
- Distribution channel objectives (short, mid, long term)

Chapter Review Questions

1. What is the difference between value-add and a value proposition?
2. Create a basic value proposition statement using the examples and formulae given.
3. Explain the five benefits of blueprinting and show how you see them applied to the blueprint you create.

References

Alderson, W. (1954). Factors governing the development of marketing channels: Prepared under the sponsorship of the American Marketing Association. In R. M. Clewett (Ed.), *Marketing channels for manufactured products*. Richard D. Irwin.

Bitner, M. J., Ostrom, A. L., & Morgan, F. N. (2008). Service blueprinting: A practical technique for service innovation. *California Management Review, 50*(3), 66–94.

D'Aveni, R. A. (1994). *Hypercompetition: Mastering the dynamics of strategic maneuvering*. The Free Press.

Lemon, K. N., & Verhoef, P. C. (2016). Understanding customer experience throughout the customer journey. *Journal of Marketing, 80*(6), 69–96.

Levitt, T. (1980). Marketing success through differentiation – of anything. *Harvard Business Review* (Jan-Feb), 83–91.

MacMillan, I. C., & McGrath, R. G. (1997). Discovering new points of differentiation. *Harvard Business Review*. *75*(4), 133–140.

Porter, M. E. (1980). *Competitive strategy*. The Free Press.

Shostack, G. L. (1984). Designing services that deliver. *Harvard Business Review, 62*(1), 133–139.

16

Testing Willingness-to-Adopt

Contents

© The Author(s), under exclusive license to Springer Nature Switzerland AG 2022
S. E. Reid, C. B. Crawford, *Entrepreneurial Vision*, Classroom Companion: Business,
https://doi.org/10.1007/978-3-030-77803-3_17

Learning Objectives

In this chapter, we provide a tool for measuring "willingness-to-adopt: ("W-T-A") and investigate its use across various levels of new product innovativeness and types of adopters. This tool—a questionnaire—was developed by Reid et al. (2018, 2019) in research on technology-based devices for seniors (mobile devices and stove sensors). As a result, in this chapter, we seek to:

1. Explain the concept of willingness-to-adopt and how to measure it.
2. Explain why it is important to attempt to get a reading on willingness-to-adopt prior to investing in scale-up, launch, and market testing with the final product.
3. Provide a model and measurement scales (in a questionnaire) for assessing willingness-to-adopt, and the product attributes that potentially affect it.
4. Explore the customer adoption curve to understand how willingness-to-adopt will vary across the curve and factors to consider with different types of adopters.

17.1 Willingness-to-Adopt: Definition and its Importance

Willingness-to-adopt, as a concept (◘ Fig. 17.1), has generally been associated with the level of acceptance, on the part of a consumer, to adopt a product or service at a point of time in the future.

"Willingness-to-adopt" is a somewhat fuzzy construction of the notion as it is not specific as to when adoption will occur, and it also does not map one to one onto actual purchase behavior by the consumer but merely points to the fact that there may be a certain level of interest and potential for that adoption to occur. As such, other metrics have been used to more precisely investigate when adoption intention meets purchase, moving beyond willingness-to-adopt or willingness-to-pay to the actual measurement of the payment itself. Nevertheless, understanding willingness-to-adopt is a useful metric as it allows us to understand market potential early on with a new product or service idea and, also, enables anticipation of product orders through to help with meeting demand. It is also useful to build an understanding of those factors which will likely have positive or negative impacts on these initial intentions and how to best emphasize the positive while downplaying the negative. Indeed, the conversion of potential adopters to actual adopters has been the focus of a good deal of research in the marketing literature.

New products launched into the marketplace can be considered "radical" or more "incremental." In the marketing literature, starting with Ansoff (1957), radical innovation has been defined as a product that is new both to a given company and to the marketplace. As noted in Reid (2005, p. 10): "Operationally, Colarelli O'Connor and Veryzer (2001) suggest that a radical innovation project must be viewed by the firm as having the potential to offer unprecedented performance features or embody elements that offer major potential such as: 5-to-10-fold improvement in performance or at least a 30% reduction in cost" (◘ Figs. 17.2 and 17.3).

■ **Fig. 17.1** Conceptual image to portray "willingness-to-adopt." (Source: Image licensed and downloaded from Shutterstock on November 20, 2020. Credit: by Oksana Pecherskih/► Shutterstock.com. License Link: ► https://www.shutterstock.com/image-vector/buy-button-vector-icon-hand-presses-1816505087)

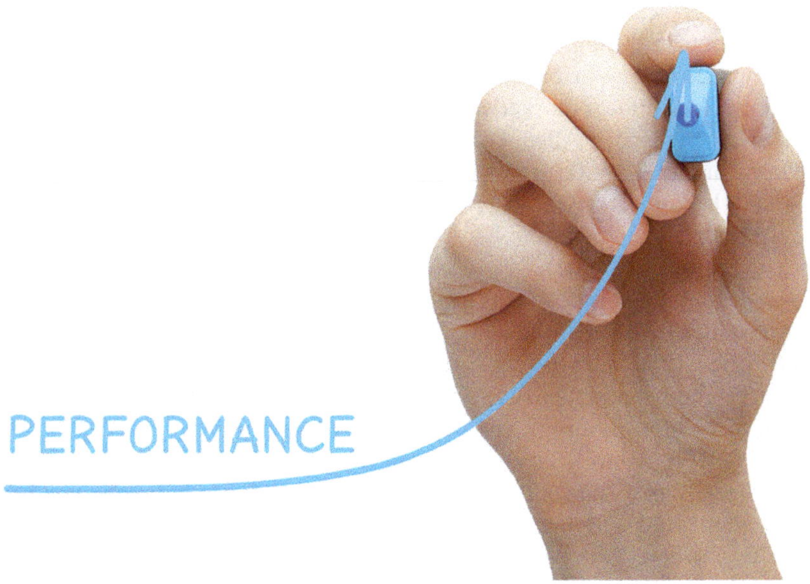

■ **Fig. 17.2** Conceptual image to portray "major increase in performance." (Source: Image licensed and downloaded on November 22, 2020, from Shutterstock. Credit: by Ivelin Radkov/► Shutterstock.com. License Link: ► https://www.shutterstock.com/image-photo/hand-drawing-increased-performance-graph-blue-611198708)

Fig. 17.3 Conceptual image to portray "major reduction in cost." (Source: Image licensed and downloaded on November 22, 2020, from Shutterstock. Credit: by pedrosek/▶ Shutterstock.com. License Link: ▶ https://www.shutterstock.com/image-illustration/word-cost-cutting-paper-scissors-240263866)

Our research (Reid, 2005; Reid & de Brentani, 2004) further points to the important involvement of individuals with radical innovation who play a major role in technology and market opportunity recognition by bringing it into a corporate context either through intrapreneurial action within a firm or through their entrepreneurial actions with their own startups. Incremental innovations (i.e., product evolution through improvements, adaptations, repositioning or adoption of existing technology or products), on the other hand, typically involve existing technologies and known market contexts.

Research by Booz, Allen and Hamilton (1982) and through the Product Development and Management Association (Griffin, 1997; Markham & Lee, 2013) shows that the launch of "radical products" sits fairly consistently at about 10% of all new products launched, whether by startups or larger firms. This means that the vast majority (approximately 90% of new product introductions) sit in the realm of more incrementally new products, which according to a well-known categorization of new products by Booz, Allen and Hamilton (1982, p. 9) exist among the following categories: 10% "new-to-the-world" (i.e., radical) products, 20% "new product lines," 28% "improvements to existing products," 26% "additions to existing product lines," 7% "repositioning," and 11% "cost reductions."

17

Relating level of innovativeness to willingness-to-adopt, research points to the fact that "really new products" may see a greater decrease between stated intentions to adopt and actual purchase behavior in comparison to more incremental products, where stated intentions may map more closely onto actual buying behavior. A distinction should be made here between "really new products," i.e., those requiring market <u>or</u> technology discontinuities, and "radical products," i.e., those with both types of discontinuities (Garcia & Calantone, 2002). As noted by Alexander et al. (2008, p. 318) in their study comparing the different types of new products (i.e., what they call "really new products" or "RNP" and "incrementally new products" or "INP") and their impact on conversion between stated and purchase behavior:

> "We would expect significant product-newness-driven differences in follow-through rates when purchase intentions are formed well in advance of expected purchase opportunities."

Specifically, Alexander et al. (2008) found that really new products were strongly correlated with lower consumer adoption intention across adopters. However, for experts and those with high consumer innovativeness, there is less need for deflation of adoption intention metrics. In other words, early adopters and experts will perform more closely to their stated intentions and therefore, in the case of RNP, will provide more accurate diagnostics. As such, for radically new and really new products, then, as is suggested in ▶ Chap. 15 on concept testing, it is important to work with early adopters, those with high consumer innovativeness and experts in consideration of data collected on "W-T-A."

17.2 A Model and Measures for Assessing Willingness-to-Adopt and Product and Consumer Attributes Which Potentially Affect It

To gain insights on how the potential consumers in your target market niche of interest may respond to your idea once it has been fleshed out after the first concept test and vision refinement, as suggested in ▶ Chaps. 15 and 16, a next step is to test consumer willingness-to-adopt with a more refined version of the concept. By doing so, we move beyond the initial feedback from consumers in the first concept tests to prune and refine the concept itself, and now focus on whether or not consumers express interest in "adopting," or buying, the product or service which will eventually be developed based on the concept.

So, a first question we asked of ourselves in previous research studies (Reid et al., 2018, 2019) was "how best to measure willingness-to-adopt a brand-new product or service. In order to garner opinion on this, we asked a group of research experts in the field what they felt would be the best measure for willingness-to-adopt. From the answers received, the most popular response cited the *Journal of Marketing Research* paper by Alexander et al. (2008) which, in a study of telecom products/services and electronics, suggested a direct measure of "intent to buy" asking consumers whether they intended to purchase (or adopt) the product in the next 6 months (1 = yes, 0 = no). Related to this they then measured the perception of product newness adapted from Hoeffler's (2003) work, which they found to be strongly correlated with willingness-to-adopt, or "Consumer Adoption Intention" ("CAI"). Alexander et al. (2008, p. 310) also specify that they "used mean newness across respondents to measure properties of products, not people – a measure of aggregate psychological response by people 'in the market' rather than a measure of individual perception." We adopted the Alexander et al. (2008)

four-item scale for use in our research (Reid et al., 2018, 2019) as detailed in ◘ Fig. 17.5.

"Consumer innovativeness" ("CI") was also postulated by Alexander et al. (2008) as having an antecedent relationship to "intent to buy," based on the previous research of Midgley and Dowling (1978), Hirschman (1980), Manning et al. (1995), and Hoeffler (2003). In other words, CI has the potential to positively impact intent to buy (i.e., willingness-to-adopt as captured through CAI) through its close relationship to the perception of product newness. Their measurement of the CI construct was captured in their research utilizing a single questionnaire item, as follows:

> I am always the first in my circle of friends to adopt a new product or service.

For simplicity sake and consistency in relation to CAI, in our research (Reid et al., 2018, 2019), we utilized the single measurement item for CI suggested by Alexander et al. (2008), as above. Building on further insights from our expert poll, we began to consider other suggested metrics as well and how they might relate to Consumer Adoption Intention in an overall model. One set of metrics, which caught our attention, during the feedback from our expert poll, was captured in the "Technology Acceptance Model" ("TAM") originally introduced by Davis (1986). The original TAM model was conceived of in Davis' 1986 thesis, where user motivations were categorized using two main factors, "Perceived Ease of Use" ("PEOU") and "Perceived Usefulness" ("PU"). These were shown to convert into an "Attitude Toward Using" ("A") resulting in further "Behavioral Intentions" ("BI") as they related to computer users (BI was introduced in a first modified version of TAM by Davis et al., 1989). Further evolutions of the model through TAM2 (Venkatesh & Davis, 2000) and beyond removed "Attitude Toward Using" as a mediator between PEOU/PU and BI and, instead, focused on the direct links from PEOU and PU to BI. Our initial research focused on the potential adoption of mobile devices by seniors, and as ease of use and usefulness are typical key benefits sought from consumer goods, in the specific case of mobile devices for seniors where usability problems might be an issue related to the shape of the device or complexity of the interface, we decided this seemed like an excellent set of factors and measures (PEOU, PU, and BI) to incorporate into our overall model along with CAI and CI.

Following a pre-test using a focus group comprised of eight seniors (65+), we tested the wording and level of understanding of the items to be used in the questionnaire. As mentioned, based on the previous Tam model developments and the work of Alexander et al. (2008), we proposed that "Perceived Ease of Use" ("PEOU") and "Perceived Usefulness" ("PU") would be potential precursors to "Consumer Adoption Intention" ("CAI") and "Behavioral Intention" ("BI"). The single measure of "Consumer Innovativeness" ("CI") was additionally included as a precursor to CAI.

In our work (Reid et al., 2018, 2019), we used a total of 22 questions in our survey including the basic model and several potential moderators. For our purposes here, we just provide the factors involved in the basic model to keep things simple. The basic model, therefore, involved 5 factors with 14 questionnaire items

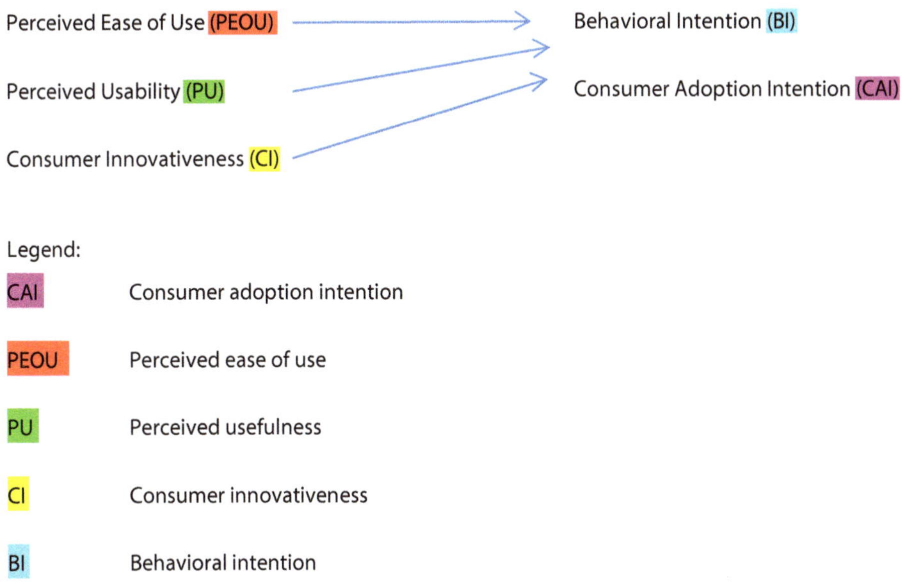

Fig. 17.4 Base model of factors impacting BI and CAI. (Source: adapted from Fig. 1, Reid et al. (2018), permission granted December 2, 2020, from *Journal of Health Science* for reprint)

(Fig. 17.4). In addition to testing whether each of these factors was valid and distinct, we also ran an exploratory analysis to test whether the relationships were significant with our data.

In this particular research (Reid et al., 2018, 2019), we were interested in looking at potential sensors for use with ovens which would help to either prevent problems before they happened or, if they did happen, to let the user or others know there was a problem. The specific device concepts were focused on safety through the reduction of risk of fire, burns, and/or intoxication for the rising global seniors' population. To test the model, a questionnaire (Fig. 17.5) was given to 57 seniors who were the study participants in order to elicit their responses to the following product/service: a sensor device that could be easily mounted on the oven itself and could automatically shut off the oven and provide a notification if any problems were detected.

We then asked the seniors to rate the concept *on a scale from 1 (never/strongly disagree) to 7 (always/strongly agree) with 4 being neutral, how would you rate yourself on the following*:

In short, the findings of this exploratory research pointed to a few key takeaways. First, the questions (i.e., the "items" adapted, as mentioned, from Alexander et al. (2008), Davis (1986), and Davis et al. (1989)) we used to measure the factors (CAI, PEOU, PU, and BI) came out as valid and reliable with our sample (see Table 17.1). We were not able to test the reliability of the single-item CI item due to measurement restrictions on single-item metrics. During the factor analysis, we did need to remove one CAI item stating: "Using this new product/service would allow me to do things that I can't easily do now." Apparently, this item, paired

		never/strongly disagree			neutral			always/strongly agree	N/A
1	I feel quite certain of the benefits I could expect to get if I bought (adopted) this product. (CAI)	☐ 1	☐ 2	☐ 3	☐ 4	☐ 5	☐ 6	☐ 7	☐
2	I'm quite sure of what the relevant trade-offs are among the costs and benefits of buying and using this product. (CAI)	☐ 1	☐ 2	☐ 3	☐ 4	☐ 5	☐ 6	☐ 7	☐
3	I'll have to change my behavior significantly to attain the potential benefits of this new product. (CAI)	☐ 1	☐ 2	☐ 3	☐ 4	☐ 5	☐ 6	☐ 7	☐
4	Using this new product would allow me to do things that I can't easily do now. (CAI)	☐ 1	☐ 2	☐ 3	☐ 4	☐ 5	☐ 6	☐ 7	☐
5	Use of such a product is clear and understandable. (PEOU)	☐ 1	☐ 2	☐ 3	☐ 4	☐ 5	☐ 6	☐ 7	☐
6	Using such a product would not require a lot of my mental effort. (PEOU)	☐ 1	☐ 2	☐ 3	☐ 4	☐ 5	☐ 6	☐ 7	☐
7	I would find the product to be easy to use. (PEOU)	☐ 1	☐ 2	☐ 3	☐ 4	☐ 5	☐ 6	☐ 7	☐
8	I would find it easy to get the product to do what I want it to do. (PEOU)	☐ 1	☐ 2	☐ 3	☐ 4	☐ 5	☐ 6	☐ 7	☐
9	Using such a product would improve my cooking performance. (PU)	☐ 1	☐ 2	☐ 3	☐ 4	☐ 5	☐ 6	☐ 7	☐
10	Using such a product would enhance my cooking effectiveness. (PU)	☐ 1	☐ 2	☐ 3	☐ 4	☐ 5	☐ 6	☐ 7	☐
11	Using such a product would increase my cooking productivity. (PU)	☐ 1	☐ 2	☐ 3	☐ 4	☐ 5	☐ 6	☐ 7	☐
12	If I had access to such a product, my intention would be to use it. (BI)	☐ 1	☐ 2	☐ 3	☐ 4	☐ 5	☐ 6	☐ 7	☐
13	If I had access to such a product, I predict that I would use it. (BI)	☐ 1	☐ 2	☐ 3	☐ 4	☐ 5	☐ 6	☐ 7	☐
14	I would use such a product. (BI)	☐ 1	☐ 2	☐ 3	☐ 4	☐ 5	☐ 6	☐ 7	☐

Fig. 17.5 Questionnaire with measurement items to capture the model denoted in Fig. 17.4. (Source: adapted from Reid et al. (2018), permission granted December 2, 2020, from *Journal of Health Science* for reprint)

Table 17.1 Final research instrument (factor analysis)

	#	Items				
Factor 1—BI	BI 4120	If I had access to such a product, my intention would be to use it				
	BI 4121	If I had access to such a product, I predict that I would use it				
	B1 4122	I would use such a product				
		Total variance	Cronbach's α	Mean	Range	Variance
		32.703%	$\alpha = 0.974$	5.099	5.019–5.185	0.007
Factor 2—PU	PU 4110	Using such a product would enhance my cooking effectiveness				
	PU 4109	Using such a product would improve my cooking performance				
	PU 4111	Using such a product would increase my cooking productivity				
		Total variance	Cronbach's α	Mean	Range	Variance
		17.295%	$\alpha = 0.835$	3.256	3.036–3.500	0.054
Factor 3—PEOU	PEOU 4108	I would find it easy to get the product to do what I want it to do				
	PEOU 4107	I would find the product to be easy to use				
	PEOU 4105	Use of such a product is clear and understandable				
	PEOU 4106	Using such a product would not require a lot of my mental effort				
		Total variance	Cronbach's α	Mean	Range	Variance
		10.328%	$\alpha = 0.830$	4.717	4.400–5.067	0.077
Factor 4—CAI	CAI 4102	I am quite sure of what the relevant trade-offs are among the costs and benefits of buying and using this product				
	CAI 4101	I feel quite certain of the benefits I could expect to get if I bought (adopted) this product				
	CAI 4103	I'll have to change my behavior significantly to attain the potential benefits of this new product				
		Total variance	Cronbach's α	Mean	Range	Variance
		8.838%	$\alpha = 0.750$	4.139	3.450–4.583	0.366

(continued)

Table 17.1 (continued)

	#	Items				
Factor 5—CI	CI 4112	I am always the first in my circle of friends to adopt a new product or service				
		Total variance	Cronbach's α	Mean	Range	Variance
		7.242%	–	–	–	–

Source: adapted from Table 3, Reid et al. (2018, p. 338), permission granted December 2, 2020, from *Journal of Health Science* for reprint

with the rest of the data set, created confusion and was therefore removed from the analysis.

In this early exploratory work, statistically significant relationships were found between PEOU and BI and between PU and CAI. The other interesting finding of this exploratory research was that 15% of the variation in senior's buying intention of the stove sensor was explained by "Perception of Ease of Use." Further research would need to be undertaken to confirm the findings of this early work; however, it indeed points to the model having a statistically significant fit.

17.3 Diffusion and Adoption: Planning for Vision Refinement through the Life Cycle

Generally speaking, when we talk about innovativeness of a consumer and relate this to their involvement with products and/or services, the relationship is often viewed through the lens of their adoption behavior. Rogers and Shoemaker (1971, p. 27) specify the nature of this relationship as being:

> "the degree to which an individual is relatively earlier in adopting an innovation than other members of his system."

This focus on the timing of adoption of innovations by a certain customer segment has led to the famous customer "adoption curve" developed by Rogers and Shoemaker (1971, p. 182), which breaks consumers down into five distinct adoption categories, based on standard deviations from the average time to adopt:

> ""Innovators" (2.5%) "Early Adopters" (13.5%) "Early Majority" (34%) "Late Majority" (34%) "Laggards" (16%)"

Diffusion is seen as a process whereby the members of the social system influence one another in direct and indirect ways leading eventually to adoption (i.e., through demonstration that creates awareness, through providing information that shows the viability of a new technology or product, through competitive pressure, etc.) (Rogers, 1983).

This process generally follows what is sometimes referred to as an "S-curve." One of the first researchers to provide empirical data to illustrate the S-curve was Sahal (1981) and by doing so demonstrated across several technology types that over time, there is a gradual improvement in understanding by the market and developers and therefore linked with progressive exploitation as the potential of a given technology becomes better recognized.

Diffusion and its related sister, adoption from the market side (represented by the product life cycle or "PLC", at the product level), tend to follow S-curve trajectories. In the early days of a new product being introduced, progress can feel at a snail's pace, because word of mouth is required, distribution channels are not well established, there is a lack of consumer data, and development and production are still undergoing a lot of fine-tuning. Innovators (◘ Fig. 17.6), however, get involved as quickly as possible because they want to be ahead of the curve, particularly if they have specific interests in the development of a new technology. If they are lead users, they are likely to also understand some of the potential solutions and major problems more than the average consumer. One approach with innovators, to better understand major problems and thereby help to create new solutions, as mentioned in ► Chap. 9, is to work hand in hand with them as co-creaters.

Early adopters and the early majority are those involved in encouraging their network to try out a new product or service and thereby effectively help to move the adoption curve along its path (for a generic product or service type, this is essentially the product life cycle) from the bottom to the top. Early adopters and the early majority actively look at what innovators are doing to emulate them and use their earlier involvement to build social capital; they are networkers and gain value

◘ **Fig. 17.6** Image to portray "innovators." (Source: ► http://commons.wikimedia.org/wiki/File:CromwellHeli.jpg. Downloaded December 14, 2020 via Wikimedia Commons)

by being in the know and trying new things (once there is some proof from innovators that these will be successful). This group of adopters needs to be attracted to multiple differentiators to ensure they connect with your product as they tend to be flightier than the innovators, lead users, and co-creators—liking to out-shop and trying different competitors' products.

Last, we have the late majority and laggards. These two groups are behind the curve but taken together they represent 50% of the market, and therefore, the wise startup will not ignore them but will consider how, at the appropriate time, to bring them into the fold. As noted in the work of Rogers (1983), these consumers tend to be risk-averse and are looking for lower price (◘ Fig. 17.7), education, and simplification to overcome adoption barriers. Therefore, startups need to provide new and different value propositions for different potential adopters at various points of the adoption curve.

Arriving toward the end of the product life cycle and adoption curve has the potential to stimulate brand-new concepts for renewal and innovation and thereby start a brand new product life cycle and adoption curve. For example, the hotel industry has a long, distinguished history, and one of the latest iterations of the product/service life cycle has been the concept of bed-spaced units for traveling salespeople (or those on a budget or who don't care about amenities—and aren't claustrophobic!) (◘ Fig. 17.8).

Rogers and Shoemaker (1971) show that each category of adopter of new products moves through five stages (regardless of the origin of the diffusion pro-

17

◘ **Fig. 17.7** Image to portray the cost-conscious consumer. (Source: Image licensed and downloaded from Shutterstock on November 21, 2020. Credit: by New Africa/► Shutterstock.com. License Link: ► https://www.shutterstock.com/image-photo/woman-putting-coin-into-piggy-bank-1354580051)

Fig. 17.8 Image of a bed-spaced unit hotel. (Source: Image licensed and downloaded from Adobe Stock, downloaded December 14, 2020. Credit: by torsakarin/► stock.adobe.com. License Link: ► https://stock.adobe.com/images/the-two-story-bedroom-area-is-combined-inside-a-modern-capsule-hotel-in-japan/370650670)

cess): "awareness," "interest," "evaluation," "trial," and finally, "adoption." Based on this perspective at the "market side" or "demand side," a market can therefore be thought of as a social system through which technologies and new products/services diffuse over time. The speed at which adoption occurs is largely impacted by the various attributes of innovation as characterized by Rogers (1983): "relative advantage," "complexity" (and perceived risk), "compatibility," "trialability," and "observability."

One of the core challenges for startups is not only how to build a brand from scratch but how to do so relatively quickly. We can apply the framework from Rogers (1983) in order to utilize the five key attributes of innovation to our advantage in order to speed up our anticipation of and preparation for the diffusion and adoption process to the marketplace in a successful way.

The majority of entrepreneurs have limited resources at the beginning of their journey. So, it is mission-critical to figure out ways to speed up the building of awareness with your potential market and conversion to adoption in order to keep ahead of your competitors, build brand equity with your sweet-spot customers, and ultimately, keep your growing business thriving. It also means that as adoption for the generic product curve moves through the population of potential adopters, if you are ahead of the competition, you can potentially gain market share from each new adopter category ahead of them by being aware of who they are, what their needs are, and how to provide them with the best value-add.

So, let's go through the five characteristics of innovation with some suggestions for capitalizing on each one. We provide a specific example from our experience developing new products together over 20 years ago—ice cider and several spirits brands—and our experience figuring out how to get the most out of our various launches while on an extremely tight budget.

1. *Relative Advantage*: What is it? Essentially, relative advantage is where you clearly convey to your market what the distinct benefits of your product are, given a specific price point.
   - *Gaining feedback from your market as early in the process as possible and as often as possible is critical for understanding customer perceptions related to your offering and how they may change over time.* We systematically worked to collect insights from our very early client base regarding all aspects of our products—not just on the taste (which, of course, was important) but also on things like the appearance of the label, bottle, cork, or stopper, as well as on promotional materials. By doing this very early on, we learned who those first "natural" sweet-spot customers were (besides our friends and family!) in terms of their demographics, psychographics, and so on and to see whether they matched the market that we had initially thought would be attracted to the offering. Additionally, once feedback is received from such customers, it is a good idea to try out refinements based on their feedback if it makes sense and if it resonates with multiple people. In our case, we kept refining the offering so we could respond to what our customers were saying. For example, within the first few months after launch, we quickly changed our packaging. When we first launched, we had outsourced a beautiful blue-satin ribbon wrapped, white crepe box as our packaging. The problem was, beyond the obvious additional expense, that it was a little bit tricky for employees to wrap and for customers to unwrap. We decided we needed a less costly simpler packaging solution. After some searching, we decided to change the packaging to a tube, which was beautiful, much easier for everyone to handle, and much less costly. It also was a great distinguisher at the shelf level and became recognized as part of the brand.
   - *Listen carefully to feedback from other stakeholders too.* In addition to gaining feedback from the market, members of your channel are also likely to give you useful feedback. Sometimes, what distinguishes your product from others in the consumer's mind has to do with various aspects in the channel (retail settings, agents, wholesalers, suppliers, and so on). We learned so much from our channel partners, for example our bottle suppliers, which had a multitude of value-adds and impacts on our business. As just one example, some of our key initial influencers were bartenders working at restaurants and/or bars who came up with creative cocktail suggestions for our ice cider.
2. *Compatibility*: How, when, and where do customers use your product/services? Creative opportunities exist from recognizing how your products interact with other products or features of the consumer's environment.
   - *Determine one key general need that your target market has and meet it directly*. It became apparent very early on in our concept testing that a key

reason for buying our product would be "gift giving." So, we needed to look at ways to find out where consumers were going when they wanted to buy gifts that might be particularly relevant to holidays. A relatively easy solution was to exhibit during major holidays at relevant markets, such as major Christmas markets. Being present at such trade shows was one of the main ways we created awareness in the marketplace for our new product in the early going.

- *Think about opportunities for bundling.* In so much as possible, if you are able to solve compatibility issues for your customer, this will help to build success. As mentioned previously, we had employed metal tubes to package our bottles. Not only did the tubes create a value-add in terms of facilitating gift packaging for our customers, but they also enabled bundling other things in the tube. As one example, we sometimes inserted annual calendars featuring local artists, thereby helping to reinforce the local roots of the brand.

3. *Complexity*: Simplicity is key to success, not just in terms of the direct impact it has on consumer understanding around products and branding, and therefore awareness, but also in terms of likability and satisfaction (except perhaps for some innovators where complexity is required as a perceived benefit!). Generally speaking, however, it is a good idea where possible to simplify the brand, its message, and product distribution.
   - *Begin marketing activities on a very small-scale level, and as directly as possible, so the early adopters and innovators know who you are, know your story, and have the opportunity to get to know you better.* Direct connections with customers save time and money and enable getting first-hand feedback. When we first launched our ice cider, we knew that our sweet-spot consumer would be one who loved trying and supporting local products, as well as being a novelty seeker. As such, we aimed our attention at local farmers' markets, events aimed at promoting local products, tourism offices, and restaurants featuring local produce and products.
   - *Using simple brand imagery in a straightforward way to clearly convey what your product is all about*, especially by focusing clearly on its distinctive advantages. In other words, use the KISS principle with your design and brand. When we first designed our brand label and logo, we used a very simple image of an apple meshed with a snowflake to show what the product, ice cider, was all about. During the first couple of years we were in business, we had a very small (i.e., almost nonexistent!) budget for marketing, and so, our label and bottle needed to do much of the talking for us. We also realized that the color we used for our label and bottle would really need to jump off the shelves compared to other products. We took a look at other products at shelf level and realized that very few, at that time a couple of decades ago, were using blue and white as a color scheme, with most instead focusing on a mixture of white, cream, gold, brown, and black with a smattering of some reds and yellows. So, we went to the other end of the spectrum with our color scheme focussing on blue and white. With these simple ideas, our first brand was born.

- *Context is key.* To build easy and early awareness of this new product category, we, quite simply, associated our name and burgeoning brand with our physical location on the southern slopes of Pinnacle Mountain in Quebec, near the Vermont border. It was an effortless way to blend our genuine terroir roots together with an authentic name which had a significant meaning—the pinnacle, or top. If it is not possible to use location, think about other contextual cues, such as your story, your why, etc. and use these together with your vision to create awareness.

4. *Communicability*: Information regarding your brand and product should always be made as easy and accessible as possible so that consumers can find you and your products and share this information with others.
   - *So, you need to make your products easy to find!* In other words, you need to make it as easy as possible for interested potential customers to find you! It is amazing that some startups don't afford themselves some of the most obvious (and often free!) tools to draw attention to themselves out of the gates such as having a map online and at the tourism office (if applicable) as to how and where to reach you; having a large, easy-to-read sign outside your physical business; a well-designed, clear website and related internet placement; listings in physical and online telephone directories (and yes, you would be surprised at how many people still look up companies and products that way!) As an example, when we started our business, we utilized local tourism offices and recruited their help with distributing flyers and publicizing who we were, that we had a boutique, and how to get to it. In other words, this type of help is great for generating word of mouth and some of it is free.
   - *Hold a social event*, either physically or virtually. For every new product we launched, we held a launch party to roll out the red carpet for everyone we knew—friends and family, neighbors, industry people, media, bar owners, bartenders, etc.—so that they could have a great time while learning about our new product and us. Sure, it cost a little bit of money (in the early days representing pretty much all of our advertising budget) but paid off in terms of ability to convey the brand message and build product knowledge. Not to mention, at this point, you and your team deserve it!
5. *Divisibility*: This last attribute of innovation essentially provides an easy and often more affordable way for your potential customers to try your product out on a limited basis.
   - *Sampling, sampling, sampling*. One of the easiest ways to provide divisibility is to offer as many opportunities to try the product in a smaller format as possible, known as sampling. In our case, we produced what were called "minis"—50 ml bottles—at the time, a fairly novel concept. This enabled one-shot sampling and, also, along the lines of our aim of targeting the gift-giving segment, provided great stocking stuffers.
   - *Think about as many ways as possible to offer your product and/or service as an experience.* To do this, we attended as many events as possible, encouraging customers to visit our boutique and tasting room to experience the product in the setting where it was produced.

These initial steps with your launch will hopefully increase your chances of gaining related adoption with your initial target niche market. Each of these steps can go a long way in terms of helping to move potential customers to becoming adopters with the goal of building through the adoption stages from awareness to loyalty.

Chapter Review Questions

1. How do really-new-products compare to more incremental products in terms of follow-through rates on purchase intentions? Why do you think this is the case?
2. Give an example of a product where "Potential Ease of Use" (PEOU) might lead to "Behavioral Intention" (BI) such as the intention to purchase that product.
3. What are the 5 adoption categories developed by Rogers and Schomaker (1971)? Think of a product or service that has gone through a typical adoption curve over time and explain what the company did to make it attractive to consumers at each stage of adoption (for simplification, early adopters and early majority can be combined and late majority and laggards can be combined).
4. List and describe the 5 characteristics of innovation developed by Rogers (1983). Using a simple product or service example, come up with tools to enhance each characteristic to facilitate adoption of that product or service.

References

Alexander, D. L., Lynch, J. G., & Wang, Q. (2008). As time goes by: Do cold feet follow warm intentions for really-new versus incrementally-new products? *Journal of Marketing Research, 45*(3), 307–319.

Ansoff, I. (1957). Strategies for diversification. *Harvard Business Review, 35*(5), 113–124.

Booz, Allen & Hamilton, Inc. (1982). *New product management for the 1980's*. Booz, Allen & Hamilton.

Colarelli O'Connor, G., & Veryzer, R. (2001). The nature of market visioning for technology-based radical innovation. *The Journal of Product Innovation Management, 18*(4), 231–246.

Davis, F. D. (1986). *A technology acceptance model for empirically testing new end-user information system: Theory and results* (Doctoral dissertation). MIT Sloan School of Management, Cambridge, MA.

Davis, F. D., Bagozzi, R. P., & Warshaw, P. R. (1989). User acceptance of computer technology: A comparison of two theoretical models. *Management Science, 35*(8), 982–1003.

Garcia, R., & Calantone, R. (2002). A critical look at technological innovation typology and innovativeness terminology: A literature review. *The Journal of Product Innovation Management, 19*(2), 110–132.

Griffin, A. (1997). PDMA research on new product development practices: Updating trends and benchmarking best practices. *The Journal of Product Innovation Management, 14*(6), 429–458.

Hirschman. (1980). Consumer innovativeness, novelty seeking and consumer creativity. *Journal of Consumer Research, 7*(3), 283–295.

Hoeffler, S. (2003). Measuring preferences for really new products. *Journal of Marketing Research, 40*(4), 406–420.

Manning, K. C., Bearden, W. O., & Madden, T. J. (1995). Consumer innovativeness and the adoption process. *Journal of Consumer Psychology, 4*(4), 329–345.

Markham, S. K., & Lee, H. (2013). Product development and management association's 2012 comparative performance assessment study. *The Journal of Product Innovation Management, 30*(3), 408–429.

Midgley, D. F., & Dowling, G. R. (1978). Innovativeness: The concept and its measurement. *Journal of Consumer Research, 4*(4), 229–242.
Reid, S. E. (2005). *Market Vision for radically-new, high-tech products* (Ph.D. Thesis). John Molson School of Business, Concordia University.
Reid, S. E., & de Brentani, U. (2004). The fuzzy front-end of new product development for discontinuous innovation: A theoretical model. *The Journal of Product Innovation Management, 21*(3), 170–184.
Reid, S. E., Abdulrazak, B., & Alas, M. (2018). Modelling willingness-to-adopt an intelligent oven: Capturing the seniors perspective. *Journal of Health Science, 6*(5), 1–10.
Reid, S. E., Abdulrazak, B., & Alas, M. (2019). Capturing the adoption intention and interest in InOvUS an intelligent oven: Segmenting senior users to evaluate the technology. In *HCII conference presentation and proceedings*, July 2019, Orlando, FL.
Rogers, E. M. (1983). *Diffusion of innovations* (3rd ed.). The Free Press.
Rogers, E. M., & Shoemaker, F. F. (1971). *Communication of innovations: A cross-cultural approach* (2nd ed.). The Free Press.
Sahal, D. (1981). *Patterns of technological innovation*. Addison-Wesley.
Venkatesh, V., & Davis, F. D. (2000). A theoretical extension of the technology acceptance model: Four longitudinal field studies. *Management Science, 46*(2), 186–204.

Designing Your Financial Vision

Contents

© The Author(s), under exclusive license to Springer Nature Switzerland AG 2022
S. E. Reid, C. B. Crawford, *Entrepreneurial Vision*, Classroom Companion: Business,
https://doi.org/10.1007/978-3-030-77803-3_18

Learning Objectives

In this chapter, we focus on building an understanding of:

1. What Financial Vision is
2. How Financial Vision relates to Entrepreneurial Vision
3. Why Financial Vision is important
4. Types of Financial Vision
5. The components of Financial Vision

18.1 What Financial Vision Is

A Financial Vision (FV) is a clear, specific, and measurable view of the financial portrait of the business over a pre-defined time horizon. FV should detail major financial milestones such as sales, profits, enterprise value, and key ratios at one or more specific points in the future as well as growth objectives and key drivers of growth, including organic product/market development, acquisitions, and strategic alliances. FV should also address the shareholder and ownership structure of the business—will it be owned individually, by family members, and key employees, or will it be sold, merged, or become a public company?

18.2 How Financial Vision Relates to Your Entrepreneurial Vision

A FV provides an unambiguous statement of where the entrepreneur sees the business from a financial point of view over a number of years and ultimately at a specific time in the future. The Financial Vision exists in parallel and in partnership with Entrepreneurial Vision, like two halves of a whole brain (Fig. 18.1). You can think of Entrepreneurial Vision as the inspiring, creative, ambitious right side of the brain and Financial Vision as the logical, calculated, analytical left side of the brain. They need to coexist and fit together to be effective.

Successful entrepreneurs and businesses should strive to pair powerful Entrepreneurial Visions with clear Financial Visions. An Entrepreneurial Vision with no accompanying Financial Vision is like an explorer with grand ambitions but with no compass or map to measure progress. On the other hand, setting an FV and ambition with no clear strategic imperative is like trying to climb a mountain without reason, cause, or mission to do so.

18.3 Why Financial Vision Is Important

Entrepreneurial Vision defines the arena and describes what the future of a new venture and related products and services will look like, while Financial Vision is the scorekeeper. FV is essential in keeping the entrepreneur on track and ensuring that the business is moving toward concrete and measurable goals. A qualitative

Fig. 18.1 Conceptual image to portray two halves of the brain. (Source: Image licensed and downloaded on December 13, 2020, from Shutterstock. Credit: by kotoffei/▶ Shutterstock.com. License Link: ▶ https://www.shutterstock.com/image-vector/creative-brain-idea-vector-concept-sciences-208792069)

vision can be open to interpretation; however, quantitative financial goals are typically more well defined.

18.4 Types of Financial Vision

FV is, at its core, driven by the overall entrepreneurial or strategic vision of the organization, but more fundamentally by the personal or individual goals of its shareholders, stakeholders, or members. FV can be divided into four different types of organizations, each with different financial priorities that will drive their vision, as shown in Table 18.1.

18.4.1 Not-for-Profit and Member-Owned Organizations

Not-for-profit (NFP) and member-owned organizations (MOOs) are not driven primarily by the imperatives of profit generation or the financial creation of shareholder value, as is the case with for-profit enterprises. The primary goal of both

Table 18.1 Financial Vision factors by organization type

Organization type	Not-for-profit organizations	Member-owned organizations	Lifestyle or family businesses	Growth-oriented businesses
Governance	Volunteer board	Members-only board	Private and closely controlled	Founders and investors; public
Primary objective	Serve a cause	Serve its members	Market niche sustainability	Market leadership and growth
Revenue source	Donations, limited fees	Fees, services	Recurring sales in existing markets	Expanding sales in new markets
Financial imperative	Sustainability while serving its cause	Maximize member benefit	Financial stability, risk reduction	Growth aided by leverage, investment
Profit objective	Small surplus for sustainability (non-profit)	Serve members, breakeven, redistribution (non-profit)	Sustainable, recurring profits (for-profit)	Market leadership and growing profitability (for profit)
Balance sheet objective	Reserves, endowments	Limited debt or liabilities	Long-term equity growth, debt reduction	Shareholder value increase; leverage as required
Risk tolerance	Low	Low	Low to moderate	Moderate to high
Financial exit/time horizon	None/long term; except in the case of project-driven causes	None/long term	Succession to family members/ long term	Share repurchase, sale of business, IPO/medium term
Relationship to entrepreneurial vision	Provide financial stability to support the cause	Provide financial stability and reserves to support members	Ensure control of the business and financial stability and reserves	Drive growth and value creation to enable exit or IPO
Typical examples of organizations	Charitable and community organizations, NGOs, religious organizations	Trade associations, unions, clubs, cooperatives	Private, closely held companies ranging from small to large	Scalable businesses with proprietary brand, technology, operations, others

Source: The authors

NFPs and MOOs, is generally, to serve a non-financial objective and mission, yet a Financial Vision remains essential for the long-term viability of these organizations. In some cases, NFPs and MOOs have a limited time horizon based on achieving specific goals or objectives (e.g., fundraising capital campaign), while in most cases these organizations are created without a defined time horizon.

NFPs in the traditional sense of the word, such as charities, nongovernment organizations, think tanks, and religious organizations among many others, exist to serve a "greater cause," be it social, political, religious, educational, economic, or others. For example, Amnesty International is a global organization that relies on donations to support its cause of defending human rights causes. Many NFPs work on a much more local level, such as The Old Brewery Mission in Montreal, Canada, which is a homeless shelter. Though the scale and scope of their work may differ, an NFP's Financial Vision is all about sustaining its core mission and values.

Similarly, MOOs are also not-for-profit from a legal point of view; however, these organizations such as unions, lobby groups, industry associations, clubs, political parties, and cooperatives exist to serve the best interests of their members. For example, Citadelle is a maple syrup cooperative organization in Quebec owned by thousands of members who are stakeholders and producers of maple syrup. Citadelle purchases maple syrup from its members at a standardized price, then grades, processes, and sells the syrup around the world. The primary goal of Citadelle is not profit-oriented, but rather to support the long-term viability of its members. Any surplus profits that are not needed for ongoing operations and investments are redistributed to members.

The Financial Vision for both MOOs and NFPs is generally one based on the sustainability of revenues to adequately and comfortably cover operating costs. In the case of MOOs, the majority of revenue comes from member dues or fees and usually represents a sustainable source of funding, assuming the mandate and performance of the organization remains relevant to its members. Generally speaking, MOOs do not maintain large, ongoing financial reserves, and in some cases, such as with cooperatives, these organizations are mandated to distribute any profits beyond a given reserve to its members. In the case of NFPs, where fees and service revenues are often inadequate to cover operating costs, these organizations rely on the funding of donations from a variety of sources including individuals, corporations, foundations, and government. As these sources of funds are not always guaranteed or recurring, financial sustainability can be a major issue for NFPs. As a result, the Financial Vision of many NFPs often goes beyond ongoing annual financial sustainability with a small operating surplus to include the building of a substantial endowment whereby the passive income from investments is adequate to be able to sustain ongoing operations on an indefinite basis.

18.4.2 Lifestyle or Family Businesses

For-profit businesses differ fundamentally from NFPs and MOOs in that financial results are a crucial measure of success. There are, however, fundamental differences between the FV for the two categories of for-profit businesses: lifestyle, or family-owned business (LFBs) and growth-oriented business (GBs). The vast majority of for-profit businesses can be considered to be lifestyle businesses, while relatively few can be high growth. Among GBs, the number of successes is relatively low, and the number of true "game-changers" is extremely rare.

LFBs are generally closely held by one individual or a limited number of other individuals or partners, all of which are generally active in the business to some degree. Often, the partners in LFBs are, in fact, family members. Generally, these businesses are closely held, and the financial objectives and vision are closely aligned with the personal objectives of the owner(s). Many owners of LFBs value their independence and seek recurring revenue and profits to maintain a personal quality of life by allowing them to do the work they love, take time off as desired, and meet their other personal lifestyle objectives. Often the Financial Vision in LFBs is not overly ambitious in terms of growth or scale but rather prioritizes security and risk minimization. In fact, many LFBs are one-person operations (e.g., consultant, tradesperson, or artist), often home-based and with minimal overhead and risk, but with little or no chance of an "exit" from the business as the person and the business (and business equity) are inextricable. Some LFBs look to pass the business along to a family member or associate, but many simply close when the entrepreneur retires.

Other LFBs look to build a steady stream of income in a protected market niche with a view to succession to family members, partners, or other key managers. In cases where the business is envisioned as an asset to be passed along to future generations, risk reduction is also often an overriding goal. LFBs may grow to become large enterprises; however, this growth is not usually built rapidly, but thoughtfully over several generations. A significant number of LFBs may also become public companies but remain family-controlled. The approach to managing a public family-owned business is that of a "steward" with a long-term view on building sustainable value and acting in the long-term interest of the company. This includes protecting it against "anything in the short-term that might harm the business" rather than as a "trader" in other public companies who are focused on enhancing short-term returns (1). As stated by Miller and Lebreton-Miller (2005, pp. 18–20):

> » "Of course, family owners are interested in having the business succeed. But typically, they are broader definitions of success and patient in their desire for return. "Returns" to them are counted in the form of substantive social or technological accomplishments and the long-term health of the enterprise… thus financial policy is conservative, with low debt, high liquidity ratios and therefore higher success rates."

18

18.4.3 Growth-Oriented Businesses

The strategic and Financial Vision of entrepreneurs in GBs is fundamentally different from those in LFBs. In GBs, entrepreneurs are focused on an innovative product or service vision that they believe can be scaled up and achieve leadership in a market accompanied by rapid growth. Since an overriding goal in GBs is growth, this implies a higher level of risk than LFBs and is generally accompanied with the need for strategic alliances to leverage growth or external "growth capital" in the form of equity. As a result, the entrepreneur very often becomes partnered with private or institutional investors seeking to obtain a suitable return on investment given the level of risk involved. Therefore, the Financial Vision for the entrepreneur inevitably becomes focused on building shareholder value over time and eventually to finding an exit for investors over a medium-term time horizon (3–7 years would be typical).

For GBs, the success of the business is viewed through an expansionist lens. Financial Vision is often measured in speed to market, the ability to gain a substantial market share in a growing or emerging market segment, and overall revenue growth. While profitability remains important, GBs are willing to take greater risks than LFBs and reinvest cash into product research and development, new products, and market development. Ultimately, GBs seek a point of "value crystallization" at some defined moment in the future whereby investors will monetize their return on investment.

18.5 The Components of Financial Vision

Just as with any type of vision, the core elements of Financial Vision remain the same: goal, magnetism, and clarity. Whereas the Entrepreneurial Vision defines the qualitative raison *d'être,* or the "why," and the nature of a venture, the Financial Vision provides a grounded counterbalance by quantifying this vision. By adding measurable and specific financial objectives to the Entrepreneurial Vision, a much stronger global vision of the business emerges that is powerful and particularly important when communicating with employees, investors, and other stakeholders. A vision to be "the leader in X" is better understood when it is also quantified with a specific Financial Vision such as "reaching $25M in revenue by 2025 with a net profit of 20%."

So how, does one build a long-term Financial Vision that is realistic, believable, and achievable? The six building blocks, as illustrated in ▫ Fig. 18.2, are in fact, similar for any type of profit or non-profit business. Time Horizon, Market Scope, and Benchmarking are the analytical building blocks from which the measurable goals of Scale, Performance, and Value are developed and summarized into a measurable and unambiguous Financial Vision statement.

18.5.1 Analytical Building Blocks of Financial Vision

The first step in developing a clear FV is to analyze the building blocks of the market you will be addressing. These building blocks include the period of time over which results will be measured (time horizon), the size and nature of the market(s) that a business will be competing in (market scope), and the performance of comparable companies (benchmarking).

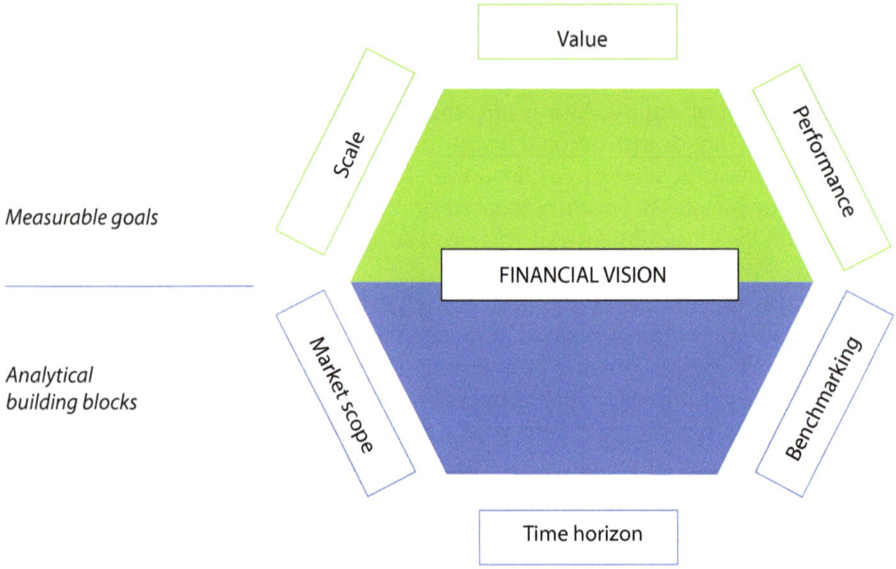

Fig. 18.2 The six building blocks of Financial Vision. (Source: The authors)

18.5.1.1 Time Horizon

The first step in developing a Financial Vision is to set a time horizon that is appropriate for the nature of the business and the objectives of the entrepreneurs and shareholders. It is important to pick a specific time horizon in order for the goals to have clarity and magnetism. A typical "strategic" or long-term view for a business would be 5 years; however, some well-established companies build much longer-term views of their financial future. At the extreme end, some Japanese firms have been known to develop 50-year (or longer!) plans and financial targets. On the other hand, a technology startup may have to develop a Financial Vision based on a series of benchmarks on a much shorter time horizon. For example, a nascent high-tech company may set goals for product launch (revenue generation) in 12 months, followed by attaining positive cash flow within 36 months and attaining a specific revenue and profit target at year 5. A company's Financial Vision needs to have a specific time horizon range that it can build upon.

18.5.1.2 Market Scope

Once a time horizon range has been established, the next step is to determine the potential market scope of the business or enterprise over that time horizon. It is essential to define the markets in which the company will be selling its products or services at a specific point in the future. For example, a startup microbrewery located in rural Vermont may begin by selling its products on a local basis, but if the time horizon it is using for its visioning process is 5 years or even 10 years, what will the business look like then? The important question to ask is what the company will be selling and in what markets at those future points in time. Is it just beer, or will it include other products such as coolers or spirits? If the Entrepreneurial Vision is to be the leading craft brewer in the state, will they be selling throughout Vermont or will they also be selling in other markets? By carefully defining the market scope, an entrepreneur can quantify the total addressable market size.

18.5.1.3 Benchmarking

In order to build a realistic FV of the future, it is also essential to benchmark the addressable market as well as competitive or comparable companies in the same or similar industries addressing the same market.

Benchmarking market size starts with reviewing any secondary market information available from published articles on an industry, market and financial analyst reports, and government statistics on the industry or census data on population. The market size may need to be pared down to the region or subregion a business will be operating in, which becomes the addressable market. The first question to ask is what market/product (or service) space will I be competing in and how big is that space? For instance, if you are planning on becoming a ski and winter sports product retailer in Canada, you need to estimate the total market size and what you expect the market size to be in the future, based upon your time horizon. For example, the total market size for winter sports equipment in Canada is estimated to be growing to C $650 M by 2025 (based on $575 m CND 2021 growing by 3.14% CAGR 2021–2025 (Statista Public Website, 2021)).

As such, if your goal is to open a chain of retail stores in the province of Quebec only, then your addressable market size would need to be estimated as a percentage of the population or the number of skiers relative to the entire Canadian market. So, given the estimated revenue growth to approximately C $650 M by 2025, if the Quebec market represents 25% of the total Canadian market, then your addressable market could be estimated at approximately C $162.5 M by 2025.

Once you have established the addressable market size, you can then try to benchmark competitors in that space. Financial filings, press releases, and annual reports from public companies in the industry should be reviewed. Additional reference sources should also be found. In the case of sporting goods stores in Canada, Statistics Canada 2018 shows that in 2018, the average store generated CAD $783 K in revenue. Further research should then be done to analyze the financial performance of companies in the industry. Various financial information services and websites publish this data. In this case, Statistics Canada also published data from 2018 (◘ Table 18.2) detailing the main financial ratios, including gross margin and net profit, for all "Ski and Winter Sports Retailers" and further detailed by quartile based on a sales level.

18.5.2 Financial Vision Goals

Financial Vision expresses concrete goals of how the business will look in the future that complement the aspirational goals set forth in the Entrepreneurial Vision.

Table 18.2 Financial performance data for ski equipment and supplies specialty stores

Revenues and expenses	Whole industry	Bottom quartile (25%)	Lower middle (25%)	Upper middle (25%)	Top quartile (25%)
Total revenue	100.00	100.00	100.00	100.00	100.00
Sales of goods and services	98.8	98.70	99.60	99.20	97.80
All other revenues	1.2	1.30	0.40	0.80	2.20
Cost of sales	57.8	64.70	59.90	56.30	52.70
Operating expenses	34.9	39.20	36.70	37.00	28.70
Total expenses	92.6	103.90	96.60	93.30	81.40
Net profit/loss	7.4	−3.90	3.40	6.70	18.60

Source: Statistics Canada – Small business profiles, 2018. Public Domain. Accessed on December 13, 2020 from ► https://www.ic.gc.ca/app/sme-pme/bnchmrkngtl/rprt-flw.pub?execution=e1s3

These goals can be viewed through one or more of three lenses or measures developed by asking three fundamental questions about a specific point in the future:

1. Scale—How big (in terms of pure size or market position) will the business be?
2. Performance—What will the financial performance and health of the business be?
3. Value—How much will the business be worth?

The importance of each of these FV goals depends on the nature of the business. For non-profit organizations, scale may be important, and performance is usually measured in terms of metrics that ensure the viability of the business, such as liquidity, reserves, and sustainability. For LFB, scale and value may be of some importance; however, performance is generally the key metric, measured in terms of cash flow, liquidity, and a healthy balance sheet with a low level of financial risk. On the other hand, GBs are often driving by growth and scale and ultimately enterprise value and specifically value to investors.

18.5.2.1 Scale

Scale is the size of the business that is envisioned, represented in market position (e.g., leader), market share, and revenue. In the case of the Quebec-based ski equipment retail chain, the financial goal can be expressed in several ways, but ideally with as much precision and clarity as possible to strengthen the vision. For example, the goal may be to open 10 ski equipment retail stores across the province with an average revenue of $1 M per store (above the industry average) for a total of $10 M in revenue representing a 5% market share of sales in the addressable market.

18.5.2.2 Performance

The second component of Financial Vision relates to financial performance. Based on industry benchmarks, the goal is often expressed in terms of operating results gross margin, net profit, cash flow, or return on investment. The financial performance goals may also be expressed in terms of balance sheet measures such as total debt load, cash position, financial reserves, or debt/equity ratio.

18.5.2.3 Value

The final Financial Vision lens is value, specifically the enterprise or share value. Ultimately, for investors looking to exit in a specific period of time, this will be the most important measure. Value, however, is not a standalone measure, but rather a function of a number of factors including revenue, growth, and market position, as well as other intangibles such as brand, technology, new product pipeline, and management team among many others. As a result, the value of the business needs to be benchmarked against other similar players in the same market space to be able to develop a reasonable estimate. Value can be expressed in terms of total company value or share value, but as with all measure of financial goals, it should be specific and unambiguous.

18.6 Building a Financial Vision Statement

The Financial Vision statement is not meant to stand alone; rather it is meant to accompany and complement the Entrepreneurial Vision statement. A clear Financial Vision enhances the three main components that make up a strong vision: goals, magnetism, and clarity. By completing a strategic vision statement with a Financial Vision, all of these objectives are enhanced. ◘ Table 18.3 illustrates the simple point that a Financial Vision statement needs to be clear, specific, measurable, easy to understand, and with no room for misinterpretation.

A Financial Vision statement is a statement of the desired destination at a determined point in time. It can include one or all elements of scale, performance, and value; however, in any case, it needs to be simple and easy to understand and to communicate. Companies often create slogans such as "The Drive for 5 in '25" to ensure that everyone in the team is working toward a known destination. These measurable and clear targets are ultimately powerful tools for rallying employees, partners, and investors together. The successful communication of Entrepreneurial and Financial Vision ultimately has a powerful influence over the achievement of these visions as we shall discover in the following chapter.

Table 18.3 Sample Financial Vision statements

Financial Vision statements	Strong	Weak
Scale	To achieve $3 M in revenue in 3 years	To maximize sales potential
	To grow revenue at a compound annual rate of 7% for each of the next 5 years	To grow faster than the competitors
	To have 10% market share of the widget market in North America	To be a market leader in widgets
Performance	To deliver a gross margin of 50% and net profit of 14% in 2025	To be highly profitable
	To have $2 M in cash reserves in 2025	To maintain a low debt/equity ratio
	To have a return on assets of 15% over the next 3 years	To provide a strong return on investment for our investors
Value	To attain an enterprise value of $25 M in 2025	Sell the business in 2025
	To go public at a market capitalization of $250 M in 2025	Complete an IPO in 2025

Source: The authors

Chapter Review Questions

1. Explain the differences between Entrepreneurial Vision and Financial Vision and how they relate to each other.
2. What are the differences in Financial Vision between non-profit and for-profit organizations?
3. What are the main differences between lifestyle/family-owned businesses and growth-oriented businesses? How do these differences impact Financial Vision?
4. What are the three analytical building blocks of Financial Vision?
5. What are the three measurable goals that can make up a Financial Vision statement?

References

Miller, D., & Lebreton-Miller, I. (2005). *Managing for the long run: Lessons in competitive advantage from great family businesses* (1st ed.). Harvard Business Review Press.

Statista Public Website. (2021). *Winter sports equipment highlights*. https://www.statista.com/outlook/cmo/toys-hobby/winter-sports-equipment/canada?currency=CAD. Accessed on 23 Feb 2021.

Communicating Your Vision

Contents

© The Author(s), under exclusive license to Springer Nature Switzerland AG 2022

S. E. Reid, C. B. Crawford, *Entrepreneurial Vision*, Classroom Companion: Business,
https://doi.org/10.1007/978-3-030-77803-3_19

Learning Objectives

As entrepreneurs move toward the launch of their products and services, often for the first time, all of the activities involved with the entrepreneurial visioning process culminate in the necessity to successfully convey their vision to others, including key stakeholders such as business partners, employees, customers, potential customers, and suppliers. As such, the key learning objectives for this chapter are to:

1. Build an understanding of the importance of visionary/transformational leadership and show that vision is a key element of such leadership.
2. Show that entrepreneurial championing and idea driving are active processes that help to not only gain commitment and involvement of other stakeholders but also impact performance.
3. Demonstrate the importance of how a vision is communicated, and provide some examples of effective vision communication strategies.
4. Provide some ideas for how to prepare for a pitch.

19.1 Why Communicating Your Vision Is Important

The importance of good vision communication has long been recognized as a key to success in business and other walks of life. Research on the key elements of success regarding how vision communication impacts performance (◘ Fig. 19.1), however, has only begun fairly recently.

◘ **Fig. 19.1** Conceptual image to portray "effective vision communication." (Source: Image licensed and downloaded from Shutterstock on November 3, 2020. Credit: by Ashalatha/▶ Shutterstock.com. License Link: ▶ https://www.shutterstock.com/image-vector/concept-brain-storming-knowledge-sharing-between-414455317)

■ **Fig. 19.2** Conceptual image to portray "transformational leadership." (Source: Image licensed and downloaded from Shutterstock on November 3, 2020. Credit: by Baimieng/▸ Shutterstock.com. License Link: ▸ https://www.shutterstock.com/image-photo/rainbow-umbrella-fly-out-mass-black-255293044)

"Visionary leaders" (Tellis, 2006), "transformational leaders" (Bass, 1985), "charismatic leaders" (House, 1977), and "champions" (Schon, 1963; Chakrabarti, 1974) have been extensively researched in the business literature and, particularly, in terms of their ability to affect change through vision.

Judge and Piccolo (2004), for example, used a meta-analysis to identify four factors related to transformational leadership, and one of the key factors is vision (■ Fig. 19.2). Indeed, Bass (1990) suggests that moving "from transactional to transformational vision" involves the ability of a leader to share their vision effectively. McLaurin and Al Amri (2008, p. 16) define "charismatic leaders" as those who "have a high self-confidence, a clear vision, engage in unconventional behavior, and act as a change agent." Clearly, vision and its communication operate as key linchpins to providing leadership.

The bulk of the early work from these various research perspectives focused mainly on the characteristics of such leaders and to a large extent, as we can see from these definitions, on their vision communication style.

19.2 Visionary Leadership for Small Firms and Startups

While organizational research has, to a large extent, focused on the relationship between transformational leadership and performance for large corporations (e.g., Baetz & Bart, 1996; Purcell et al., 2009), recent work has shed additional light on the impor-

Fig. 19.3 Conceptual image to portray "leadership." (Source: Image licensed and downloaded from Shutterstock on November 3, 2020. Credit: by Kenishirotie/▸ Shutterstock.com. License Link: ▸ https://www.shutterstock.com/image-photo/leadership-concept-using-blue-paper-ship-221682364)

tance of vision communication for small firms (e.g., van der Walt et al., 2004) as well as at different levels of the firm—individual, organizational, and team (Wang et al., 2011). For example, the work of Jing, Avery, and Bergsteiner (2014, p. 599) focused on small business in Australian retail pharmacies where they found a positive relationship between vision communication and performance: "Organizations whose managers communicate the vision to staff and whose employees share this vision outperform their peers across all business indicators and retain their employees longer."

As noted in Reid et al. (2015, p. 596), and illustrated in Fig. 19.3, "By developing a view of the future, and inspiring and motivating their followers, visionary leaders raise performance expectations and improve innovation within the organizational context (Bird, 1992; Filion, 1991; Gumusluoglu & Ilsev, 2009; Jung et al., 2003; Kirkpatrick & Locke, 1996; Larwood et al., 1995)." Additional research suggests that it is the vision, specifically, that is of importance to new ventures and entrepreneurial firms (Baron & Hannan, 2002; Breugst et al., 2012; Filion, 1991).

19.3 Vision Champions and Idea Driving

19

Championing is a cornerstone of both intrapreneurship (Rubenstein, 1994) and entrepreneurship (Schumpeter, 1934 [1911]). Idea champions need to know how to achieve and then accelerate the commitment and involvement of other stakeholders for a proposed idea. This is critical because, as Frost and Egri (2002) importantly point out, innovation at its core is a political and social process of change. Championing indeed has an element of "politicking" related to it (Argyris, 1990) and is a necessary component of visioning activity (Reid, 2005). Additionally, empirical research demonstrates that the more radical a new idea, the more political gamesmanship is likely to be an influencing factor (Fidler & Johnson, 1984; Frost & Egri, 2002; Pelz, 1983; Pelz & Munson, 1982). As such, well-focused politicking or, to put it in another way, "championing" has been shown to be an important component of driving new and contentious ideas forward (Howell & Higgins, 1990; Howell & Shea, 2001).

Visioning, and the learning that accompanies it, therefore, may be facilitated by politicking, particularly at an informal level, and especially when driven by a strong champion of innovation. As such, it is possible to see the importance of championing in the form of focused idea driving as part of the early competence involved with forming a vision.

A "champion" (◘ Fig. 19.4) is generally defined as "an individual who informally emerges in an organization and makes a decisive contribution to the innovation by actively and enthusiastically promoting its progress through the critical organizational stages" (Achilladelis et al., 1971, p. 14). The term champion has also been defined by Chakrabarti (1974, p. 58), building on earlier work of the Materials Advisory Committee, National Academy of Engineering, Washington, D.C.

◘ **Fig. 19.4** Conceptual image to portray "championing." (Source: Image licensed and downloaded from Shutterstock on November 3, 2020. Credit: by aslysun/► Shutterstock.com. License Link: ► https://www.shutterstock.com/image-photo/silhouette-super-business-woman-look-somewhere-1009393072)

(1966), as "an individual who is intensely interested and involved with the overall objectives and goals of the project and who plays a dominant role in … overcoming technical and organizational obstacles and pulling the effort through its final achievement by the sheer force of his will and energy."

Howell and Higgins (1990, p. 317), who credit Schon (1963) with identifying the role of champion, specify that "a champion is required to identify the ideas as his or her own, to promote the idea actively and vigorously through informal networks, and to risk his or her position and prestige to ensure the innovation's success." Schon (1963, p. 85) specifically notes that in some cases, established organizations will "give support to certain product champions as entrepreneurs, allowing them to push their product through from beginning to end, and establishing a new division for the resulting business"—in other words, intrapreneurs may be tasked with establishing new technology and product/market visions for the organization.

According to one of the first well-known empirical studies on champions (Howell & Higgins, 1990, p. 317), "champions reported using transformational leader behaviors to a significantly greater extent than did non-champions." Champions have also been found to be importantly related to visioning activity (Reid, 2005; Reid & de Brentani, 2010), so there is much empirical data pointing to a clear relationship between transformational vision and championing behavior.

In the specific case of entrepreneurship, championing is a good way to conceive of transformational leadership, as it additionally focuses on the nature of informal relationships, and how entrepreneurs are able to drive their own ideas forward with individuals separately from the influence of corporate culture.

Indeed, "champions" or "idea drivers," to use the terminology of Colarelli O'Connor and Veryzer (2001), provide important individual-level capabilities that are a part of Market Visioning Competence. We can think of championing in terms of the skill itself (and measure it using "strength") as well as the value behind what is being championed ("quality" of the vision).

In order to measure the level or "strength" of championing (◘ Fig. 19.5), Howell et al. (1998) developed a scale to measure the degree to which individuals lobby for support and promote innovations. They validated this study with 47 champions of radical innovations in the organizational context. They found that "stronger champions differ from weaker champions in their use of more frequent influence tactics and in their ability to monitor the impact of their actions on others" (Howell et al., 1998, p. B5). Kanter (1988), in her well-cited work in *When a Thousand Flowers Bloom*, also describes the importance of the use of "active influence attempts" on the part of leaders, and Howell et al. (1998) found a statistically significant relationship between champion strength and the use of influence tactics including ingratiation, inspirational appeals, consultation, coalition, and rational persuasion.

Howell and Shea (2001) and Howell, Shea, and Higgins (2005, p. 641) utilized a three-factor scale to measure the quality of "champion behavior" itself: "expressing enthusiasm and confidence about the innovation," "persisting under adversity," and "getting the right people involved and gaining their support" (◘ Fig. 19.5).

Fig. 19.5 Image to portray championing strength and behavior. (Source: Image licensed and downloaded from Shutterstock on November 3, 2020. Credit: by GDmitry/▶ Shutterstock.com. License Link: ▶ https://www.shutterstock.com/image-photo/joint-work-teamwork-two-men-travelers-251839777)

19.4 Impact of Championing on Performance

Vision communication research, starting mainly with the empirical work of Howell and colleagues ("championing") and Colarelli and colleagues ("idea driving"), investigates the level to which champions have been able to influence success through their actions. The study conducted by Howell et al. (2005), for example, found support for a positive relationship between their measure of "champion behavior" and "project performance." The work of de Hoogh et al. (2004) looked at the potential links between charismatic leadership, environmental dynamism, and performance and similarly found significant positive relationships. Many studies have shown an association between charismatic leadership and performance success. Howell and Frost (1989) developed this further by showing that 'charismatic leadership' could be broken down into two distinct components, 'vision' and 'charismatic personality'. Kirkpatrick and Locke (1996) performed follow-up research which found, as noted in Baum et al. (1998, p. 43), that indeed "vision was," as they said, "far more potent than charismatic personality in terms of its direct and indirect effects on follower performance and attitudes."

As such, given its importance and the research, it is clear that, in so much as possible with entrepreneurial ventures, both the way vision itself and the way in which a vision is championed and communicated should not be left to chance.

The activities and tasks involved with the role of championing should be thought out: who is involved; what are the key components of the vision itself and how will it be conveyed, who will be networked with, contacted, and consulted; what type of appeals will be used and how often; as well as how to best maintain energy in order to keep persistence and enthusiasm at the highest levels possible.

19.5 Effective Vision Communication

19.5.1 Why Effective Vision Communication Is Important

As noted in the previous sections of this chapter, there are clear links between effective vision championing and performance. In line with influence tactics as noted by Howell et al. (1998), Kanter (1988), and Yukl and Falbe (1990), it is evident that inspirational appeals and other influence tactics are a key element of successful championing through persuading others in a positive way. In other words, the way in which a vision is communicated is a critical aspect of performance.

There are several reasons underlying this importance of effective vision communication. First, it is well known that the better an idea is communicated, the more easily a shared understanding can be constructed that has high fidelity in relation to the vision originally conceived by the entrepreneur or intrapreneur. In other words, it is important to ensure proper conveyance and limited "broken telephone" (◘ Fig. 19.6) in terms of the underlying vision itself.

Second, effective vision communication is critical in terms of helping to inspire or persuade others (Reardon, 1991). In the case of intrapreneurial efforts, it can be linked to gaining organizational commitment (Dvir et al., 2004). The exact same underlying vision might be conveyed by two different people with a completely different level of impact—the measure of success is linked to the communicator's ability to inspire or persuade others to believe in and adopt the vision.

Third, the faster people understand your vision, the faster they can help you bring it to light and then market. This idea is linked to the importance of vision clarity and tangibility as core aspects of vision which have been previously described in this book. A well-understood vision, achieved by ensuring simplicity of the vision itself (◘ Fig. 19.7), is one that is often the most easily communicated to others.

19.5.2 Effective Vision Communication Strategies

The earliest known research to look at what "happens in between" vision and performance in terms of vision communication was that of Baum et al. (1998). Indeed, these researchers found that vision communication acted as an important mediator between vision (attributes and content) and performance, as measured by various factors contributing to venture growth.

Fig. 19.6 Image to portray lack of transmission fidelity. (Source: Image licensed and downloaded from Adobe Stock on November 3, 2020. Credit: by ekostsov/▶ AdobeStock.com. License Link: ▶ https://stock.adobe.com/images/two-tin-cans-attached-with-string/49116547)

Fig. 19.7 Conceptual image to portray "vision simplicity." (Source: Image licensed and downloaded from Adobe Stock on November 3, 2020. Credit: by Tierney/▶ AdobeStock.com. License Link: ▶ https://stock.adobe.com/306034619)

The most recent research on vision has brought our understanding of vision communication to a new level with regard to focusing on "how" visions are communicated and what constitutes an effective vision communication strategy when considering the potential impact on success. For example, Carton and Lucas (2018, p. 2106) focus on what they call "image-based rhetoric" (i.e., language) in terms of how vision should best be conveyed (i.e., using language charged with image, as opposed to merely relying on what they call "abstract language that cannot easily be visualized"). In our research, starting with Reid (2005), we term this aspect the "vision form" itself. Our findings showed a clear link between vision form and various measures of early pre-project performance, as described in ► Chap. 2.

Carton and Lucas provide a description to make this distinction of vision language rich with "imagery" (or "form" or "content") (2018, p. 2106):

> "Some of the most successful organizational endeavors have been credited to leaders who galvanized collective action by articulating a compelling purpose. For example, Bill Gates envisioned a "computer on every desk and in every home," John F. Kennedy challenged NASA to land "a man on the moon," and Henry Ford imagined a "motor car for the great multitude" that people could enjoy for "hours of pleasure in God's great open spaces."… The above examples of Gates, Kennedy, and Ford are telling not only because each leader articulated a compelling purpose, but because they did so by employing image-based rhetoric, which we define as language that depicts objects (e.g., "cars"), actions (e.g., "driving"), and events (e.g., "landing on the moon") that can be observed with one's senses."

Interestingly, it was found by Carton et al. (2014) that despite its intuitive appeal and the recent research showing its importance, such image-based rhetoric is used in less than 10% of communicated visions. They also note that leaders tend to use up to 15 times as much conceptual rhetoric in comparison to image-based language in the communication of vision. As such, it appears that taking a vision statement and ensuring that the verbiage converts abstract language to image-based language, as much as possible, is critical to vision communication success.

19.5.3 Vision Statement Refinement

In ► Chaps. 11, 12, and 13, you worked on developing initial vision statements and then ► Chaps. 14, 15, 16, 17, and 18 provided further fodder for refinement. Now you are in a position to take the statement(s) you have already developed and hone them further in order to communicate your vision in the most emphatic manner possible to your initial target market.

A couple of key aspects deserve repeating here. First, we have already focused extensively on the need for vision clarity (as outlined in ► Chap. 2) and, referring to the work of Carton and Lucas (2018) in this chapter, the importance of utilizing clear imagery. In fact, our research (e.g., Reid & de Brentani, 2010) found a specific link between vision clarity and various measures of performance. There is also quite a bit of consensus around the need for vision statements to be brief (Kirkpatrick, 2017). The idea of brevity for a vision in statement form is particularly important, as it is one area many vision constructors seem to struggle with. Indeed, the "vision statement" should encapsulate the intended vision itself as a brief assertion or testimony.

As noted by Fiset and Robinson (2020), the basic idea of communicating the vision through the vision statement is to engender support and mobilization around it. Indeed, Fiset and Robinson (2020, p. 2) list several studies (Baum et al., 1998; Boies et al., 2015; Fiset & Boies, 2019; Sosik & Dinger, 2007; Kantabutra & Avery, 2010; Kirkpatrick et al., 2002) which show the positive impact of well-communicated vision on employees, teams, and organizational performance outcomes. This is supported by Kirkpatrick (2017, p. 87), where she explains that "a vision statement is a prominent concept in performance improvement, talent management, and change management models." In other words, not only does vision communication act as a mediator between the vision itself and performance, but it additionally has important implications for HR and management in terms of recruiting those with whom a vision resonates, keeping people "on brand" and "on task," and enabling superior efforts toward the achievement of the vision.

19.5.4 A List of Ten Ways to Effectively Communicate Your Vision

1. If possible, have the team that was involved in creating the vision also involved with creation of the vision statement. If, however, as an entrepreneur, the vision was primarily your own, you might want to have an idea of the "envelope" you want the vision to circumscribe before team ideation around vision.
2. As per the work of Carton and Lucas, build imagery into the vision statement as much as possible (see additional vision crafting suggestions as outlined in ► Chap. 16).
3. Concept test the vision itself with potential customers and other stakeholders.
4. Have stakeholders, including lead users and experts, involved in the refinement phases of vision development.
5. Once the product/service is launched, in addition to market tests, test the effectiveness and awareness of the vision with your market and other stakeholders.
6. Have different people from the team practice delivering the vision statement with a focus on how to best communicate it.
7. Ensure that the vision is at the core of all communications strategies and messaging.
8. Develop a vision communication plan which includes communication frequency and targets.
9. Create a continuous feedback loop to check strategy, objectives, etc. with the vision and move toward building a corporate vision.
10. Continue refinement of the Entrepreneurial Vision including construction of a broader overarching Organizational Vision and how it bridges with the Financial Vision.

19.6 "The Pitch"

Each year in Susan's entrepreneurship lab course, she has done a session on how to do a pitch (or, as this session has been referred to: "Pitches that Slay Dragons"—◘ Fig. 19.8). The focus is on how to appropriately convey your product/market vision in 5 minutes—essentially, the enactment of an elevator pitch.

First, the session gives some basic advice on how to best prepare for the pitch. The session then moves on to the key elements involved with effectively conveying a vision and its importance, as follows.

19.6.1 Preparing for "The Pitch"

Pre-Pitch Prep #1: Practice makes perfect! We've all heard this axiom as a necessity in preparing for any presentation, but nowhere is it more true than in the case of the pitch. This is because you will usually have no more than 5 minutes in a luxurious setting such as our university class incubator, and much more likely, 15 seconds to a minute under more realistic pitch situations such as on the phone, in a meeting, during a chance encounter at a party, or, yes, in the elevator. As such, knowing precisely what you are going to say and how you are going to say it becomes even more mission-

◘ **Fig. 19.8** Image to portray "Pitches that Slay Dragons." (Source: Image licensed and downloaded on December 13, 2020 from Shutterstock. Credit: by Lightspring/▶ Shutterstock.com. License Link: ▶ https://www.shutterstock.com/image-illustration/children-imagination-concept-cast-shadows-on-174755942)

critical than usual and will give you the confidence that your audience will listen to what you have to say if it is well-polished and exciting.

Pre-Pitch Prep #2: Know going into the pitch that the most likely scenario is that you will receive some form of feedback, both positive and negative—so the best thing you can do to prepare for this is to acknowledge it and plan a strategy to deal with it. Some salespeople talk about using a call to action at the end of their pitch so that the audience gets put into decision mode right away; this is also a useful tool for deflecting potential rebuttals as it moves the conversation forward rather than backward. A sense of humor can go a long way, as well, in terms of turning what could be a potentially heated or negative conversation into a positive one where the audience is still actively and positively listening to what you have to say. Also, if someone criticizes your idea or objects, sometimes the best thing to do is acknowledge it, so they feel "heard" but continue on your pitch path. One trick Susan remembers hearing from many successful PhD defenders, prior to her own doctoral dissertation defense, was rather than saying "yes, but..." to say "yes, and..." so the person feels that they have been included in the discussion. It avoids them feeling like you have dismissed what they have had to say, while instead making them feel like you have included it in your consideration set for further reflection.

Pre-Pitch Prep #3: Focus on the needs of your audience instead of yourself. Another pre-dissertation defense piece of advice Susan remembers receiving was to focus on the audience as much as possible. Just as you should focus on your target customer when trying to find out about their needs with a product, the same should be done with your target pitch audience (which may be made up of potential customers, channel members or investors) so that you give them what they are looking for in your presentation. This means doing your homework so that you know who they are beforehand and can therefore specifically address each person's needs and perhaps even refer to them directly by name in your presentation, depending on the situation. It also entails thinking about their needs at that moment—are they comfortable, are you making them feel good, can they hear you properly and easily? These types of things may not seem as important as getting your message out there, but if someone is struggling to try to balance their raincoat and a heavy briefcase with several other people crowded into that elevator, their attentions may be divided, at best. So, wherever possible, it's best to try to help defray any discomforts so their full attention can be on you and what you are trying to tell them.

19.6.2 The Key Elements of "The Pitch"

- **#1 The Passion:**
  - Always begin and end with a tie into why you are passionate about what you are doing; in other words, the presentation should loop back around to give your audience closure with why this is important for you and the world—i.e., by coming full circle, it gives you the chance to begin and end with emotion.

- **#2 The Opportunity:**
  - Present 1 or 2 convincing key big opportunity stats that will wow the audience; you won't have time to give all of your background research, nor will your audience have the bandwidth to be able to process it all in a short time anyway; the key is to give them the most gobsmacking stats you have to back up why you absolutely need to pursue the gap offered by this opportunity.

- **#3 The Value Proposition:**
  - Show how your product/service threads right through a market opportunity to provide a clear value proposition for your target market and clear growth and profitability for investors.

- **#4 The Proof:**
  - What proof do you have that it is worth moving forward with your concept (from lead user tests, concept tests, market tests, expert interviews, industry stats, etc.)?
  - Where possible, provide your "proof of concept":
    - Real-life successful case studies
    - Testimonials
    - Link to a credible third-party source, name, or association for halo effect

- **#5 Expertise:**
  - If you've got specialized expertise, make sure to tout it—it gives you credibility! If not but you need it to be credible, show or explain how you're going to get it—access to experts, databanks, purchase or licensing of IP, etc.

- **#6 How It Works:**
  - Provide a clear and simple product or service demo or your product/service blueprint so the audience easily understands your offer; this is especially important if the concept is complex.

- **#7 The Experience/Your Story:**
  - Have your audience experience or imagine why someone would need the new product.
  - How you make the audience feel is important (emotion and connection through effective storytelling, visuals, metaphors, relatable analogies, familiar associations).

The following provides a good example of a short, 1-minute presentation which manages to convey many of the above-noted key elements of a good pitch. The presentation was made by a student team from the MSc in Management program at the Ivey Business School at Western University, Canada, for a course on Entrepreneurship, fall 2020 (courtesy of Haley Crawford, Melanie Dang, Chenchen

Ma, Ritika Malhotra, Vicky Qi), who gave us permission to share their ideas and presentation text, for illustrative purposes here:

» Online shopping has a trillion-dollar problem. 30–40% of clothing bought online is returned, and this has increased since the pandemic. Virtual Muse is a female-run company dedicated to helping up-and-coming women's fashion brands simulate in-person shopping experiences through the use of augmented and virtual reality, also known as AR and VR. The end goal? Increase online interaction to boost sales and reduce returns. AR shopping platforms have seen an increase of 150% in session time and 15% higher order values. Digital try-on and AR product display can increase purchases and lower return risk by helping users assess product appearance. 80% of shoppers who bought a limited-edition pair of Nike Air Jordan shoes did so after digital try-on. Unlike competitors, we offer brands pre-designed software interfaces to integrate their own products into and produce a realistic, immersive 3D experience where shoppers feel like they're truly in a store. By allowing brands to independently improve their online presence, Virtual Muse is emerging brands' bridge to next-gen shopping.

Chapter Review Questions

1. Why is vision communication important (list 3 reasons)?
2. What are some of the key behaviors of visionary leaders, champions and idea drivers? Why do you think these behaviours increase champions' likelihood of higher performance outcomes? What is the key link between championing behaviour and performance?
3. What is the difference between "image-based rhetoric" and "abstract language"? Provide an example of an "image-based" vision.
4. When creating a "pitch," how would you decide which elements to emphasize most (i.e., your "why," the value proposition, and/or the opportunity)?
5. (a) Write a short one paragraph pitch which attempts to incorporate as many of the key elements required as possible for a "Dragon's Den"-style pitch (i.e., potential investors). (b) How would you tweak the first pitch if you were delivering it to potential customers instead?

References

Achilladelis, B., Jervis, P., & Robertson, A. (1971). *A study of success and failure in industrial innovation*. University of Sussex Press.

Argyris, C. (1990). *Overcoming organizational defences: Facilitating organizational learning*. Allyn and Bacon.

Baetz, M. C., & Bart, C. K. (1996). Developing mission statements which work. *Long Range Planning, 29*(4), 526–533.

Baron, J. N., & Hannan, M. T. (2002). The economic sociology of organizational entrepreneurship: Lessons from the Stanford project on emerging companies. In V. Nee & R. Swedberg (Eds.), *The economic sociology of capitalism* (pp. 168–203). Princeton University Press.

Bass, B. M. (1985). *Leadership and performance beyond expectations*. The Free Press.

Bass, B. M. (1990). From transactional to transformational leadership: Learning to share the vision. *Organizational Dynamics, 18*(3), 19–31.

Baum, J. R., Locke, E. A., & Kirkpatrick, S. A. (1998). A longitudinal study of the relation of vision and vision communication to venture growth in entrepreneurial firms. *Journal of Applied Psychology, 83*(1), 43–54.

Bird, B. (1992). The operation of intentions in time: The emergence of the new venture. *Entrepreneurship Theory and Practice, 17*(1), 11–20.

Boies, K., Fiset, J., & Gill, H. (2015). Communication and trust are key: Unlocking the relationship between leadership and team performance and creativity. *The Leadership Quarterly, 26*(6), 1080–1094.

Breugst, N., Domurath, A., Patzelt, H., & Klaukien, A. (2012). Perceptions of entrepreneurial passion and employees' commitment to entrepreneurial ventures. *Entrepreneurship Theory and Practice, 36*(1), 171–192.

Carton, A. M., & Lucas, B. J. (2018). How can leaders overcome the blurry vision bias? Identifying an antidote to the paradox of vision communication. *Academy of Management Journal, 61*(6), 2106–2129.

Carton, A. M., Murphy, C., & Clark, J. R. (2014). A (blurry) vision of the future: How leader rhetoric about ultimate goals influences performance. *Academy of Management Journal, 57*(6), 1544–1570.

Chakrabarti, A. K. (1974). The role of champion in product innovation. *California Management Review, 17*(2), 58–62.

Colarelli O'Connor, G., & Veryzer, R. (2001). The nature of market visioning for technology-based radical innovation. *The Journal of Product Innovation Management, 18*(4), 231–246.

de Hoogh, A., den Hartog, D., Koopman, P., Thierry, H., van den Berg, P., van der Weide, J., & Wilderom, C. (2004). Charismatic leadership, environmental dynamism, and performance. *European Journal of Work and Organizational Psychology, 13*(4), 447–471.

Dvir, T., Kass, N., & Shamir, B. (2004). The emotional bond: Vision and organizational commitment among high-tech employees. *Journal of Organizational Change Management, 17*(2), 126–143.

Fidler, L. A., & Johnson, J. D. (1984). Communication and innovation implementation. *Academy of Management Review, 9*(4), 704–711.

Filion, L. J. (1991). Visions and relations: Elements for an entrepreneurial metamodel. *International Small Business Journal, 9*(2), 112–131.

Fiset, J., & Boies, K. (2019). Positively vivid visions: Making followers feel capable and happy. *Human Relations, 72*, 1651–1670. https://doi.org/10.1177/0018726718810105

Fiset, J., & Robinson, M. A. (2020). Developing foresight through the evaluation and construction of vision statements: An experiential exercise. *Organizational Management Journal*, 17 pp. https://www.emerald.com/insight/htm

Frost, P. J., & Egri, C. P. (2002). The political process of innovation. In S. Clegg (Ed.), *SAGE library in business and management: Central currents in organization studies I & II* (Vol. 8, pp. V103–V103). SAGE Publications Ltd. https://doi.org/10.4135/9781446260982.n75

Gumusluoglu, L., & Ilsev, A. (2009). Transformational leadership and organizational innovation: The roles of internal and external support for innovation. *The Journal of Product Innovation Management, 26*(3), 264–277.

House, R. J. (1977). A 1976 theory of charismatic leadership. In J. G. Hunt & L. L. Larson (Eds.), *Leadership: The cutting edge* (pp. 189–207). Southern Illinois University Press.

Howell, J. M., & Frost, P. J. (1989). A laboratory study of charismatic leadership. *Organizational Behavior and Human Decision Processes, 43*(2), 243–269.

Howell, J. M., & Higgins, C. A. (1990). Champions of technological innovation. *Administrative Science Quarterly, 35*(2), 317–341.

Howell, J. M., & Shea, C. M. (2001). Individual differences, environmental scanning, innovation framing, and champion behavior: Key predictors of project performance. *The Journal of Product Innovation Management, 18*(1), 15–27.

Howell, J. M., Shea, C. M., & Higgins, C. A. (1998). Champions of product innovations: Defining, developing and validating a measure of champion strength. *Academy of Management Proceedings, 1998*(1), B1–B6.

Howell, J. M., Shea, C. M., & Higgins, C. A. (2005). Champions of product innovations: Defining, developing and validating a measure of champion behavior. *Journal of Business Venturing, 20*(5), 641–661.

Jing, F., Avery, G., & Bergsteiner, H. (2014). Enhancing performance in small professional firms through vision communication and sharing. *Asia Pacific Journal of Management, 31*(2), 599–620.

Judge, T. A., & Piccolo, R. F. (2004). Transformational and transactional leadership: A meta-analytic test of their relative validity. *Journal of Applied Psychology, 89*(5), 755–768.

Jung, D. I., Chow, C., & Wu, A. (2003). The role of transformational leadership in enhancing organizational innovation: Hypotheses and some preliminary findings. *The Leadership Quarterly, 14*(4–5), 525–544.

Kantabutra, S., & Avery, G. (2010). The power of vision: Statements that resonate. *Journal of Business Strategy, 31*(1), 37–45.

Kanter, R. M. (1988). When a thousand flowers bloom: Structural, collective, and social conditions for innovation in organizations. In B. M. Staw & L. L. Cummings (Eds.), *Research in organizational behavior* (pp. 169–211). JAI Press.

Kirkpatrick, S. A. (2017). Toward a grounded theory: A qualitative study of vision statement development. *Journal of Management Policy and Practice, 18*(1), 87–101.

Kirkpatrick, S. A., & Locke, E. A. (1996). Direct and indirect effects of three core charismatic leadership components on performance and attitudes. *Journal of Applied Psychology, 81*(1), 36–51.

Kirkpatrick, S. A., Wofford, J. C., & Baum, J. R. (2002). Measuring motive imagery contained in the vision statement. *The Leadership Quarterly, 13*(2), 139–150.

Larwood, L., Falbe, C. M., Kriger, M. P., & Miesing, P. (1995). Structure and meaning of organizational vision. *Academy of Management Journal, 38*(3), 740–769.

Materials Advisory Board, National Academy of Engineering. (1966, July). *Report on the ad-hoc committee on principles of research-engineering interactions*. Washington, D.C.

McLaurin, J. R., & Al Amri, M. B. (2008). Developing an understanding of charismatic and transformational leadership. *Allied Academies International Conference, Reno, NV: Proceedings of the Academy of Organizational Culture, Communications & Conflict (AOCCC), 13*(2), 15–19.

Pelz, D. C. (1983). Quantitative case histories of urban innovations: Are there innovating stages? *IEEE Transactions on Engineering Management, EM-30*(2), 60–67.

Pelz, D. C., & Munson, F. C. (1982). Originality level and the innovating process in organizations. *Human Systems Management, 3*(3), 173–187.

Purcell, J., Kinnie, N., Swart, J., Raytin, B., & Hutchison, S. (2009). *People management and performance*. Routledge.

Reardon, K. (1991). *Persuasion in practice*. Sage.

Reid, S. E. (2005). *Market vision for radically-new, high-tech products.* Ph.D. Thesis, John Molson School of Business, Concordia University.

Reid, S. E., & de Brentani, U. (2010). Market vision and market visioning competence: Impact on early performance for radically-new, high-tech products. *The Journal of Product Innovation Management, 27*(4), 500–518.

Reid, S. E., Roberts, D., & Moore, K. (2015). Technology vision for radical innovation and its impact on early success. *The Journal of Product Innovation Management, 32*(4), 593–609.

Rubenstein, A. H. (1994). Ideation and entrepreneurship, Chapter 2. In W. E. Souder & J. D. Sherman (Eds.), *Managing new technology development* (pp. 15–44). McGraw-Hill.

Schon, D. K. (1963). Champions for radical new inventions. *Harvard Business Review, 41*(2), 77–86.

Schumpeter, J. A. (1934). *The theory of economic development*. Harvard University Press (Original work published 1911, German).

Sosik, J. J., & Dinger, S. L. (2007). Relationships between leadership style and vision content: The moderating role of need for social approval, self-monitoring, and need for social power. *The Leadership Quarterly, 18*(2), 134–153.

Tellis, G. J. (2006). Disruptive technology or visionary leadership? *The Journal of Product Innovation Management, 23*(1), 34–38.

Van der Walt, J. L., Kroon, J., & Fourie, B. J. (2004). The importance of a vision and mission for small, medium-sized and large businesses. *South African Journal of Economic and Management Sciences, 7*(2), 206–220.

Wang, G., Oh, I.-S., Courtright, S. H., & Colbert, A. E. (2011). Transformational leadership and performance across criteria and levels: A meta-analytic review of 25 years of research. *Group and Organization Management, 36*(2), 223–270.

Yukl, G., & Falbe, C. M. (1990). Influence tactics and objectives in upward, downward, and lateral influence attempts. *Journal of Applied Psychology, 75*(2), 132–140.

Conclusion: Bringing Your Vision to Life

Contents

© The Author(s), under exclusive license to Springer Nature Switzerland AG 2022
S. E. Reid, C. B. Crawford, *Entrepreneurial Vision*, Classroom Companion: Business,
https://doi.org/10.1007/978-3-030-77803-3_20

20

20.1 Transitioning from Entrepreneurial Product/Market Vision to Organizational Vision

Shortly after the startup's initial launch period, the entrepreneur and their team should begin to sense whether they have the makings of a viable enterprise in front of them. At this point (or probably even earlier), the entrepreneur and their team will already likely be thinking about what product #2 might look like. As such, whether a second product is timely or not, it is important for the entrepreneur and team to start considering how to migrate the focus of their vision from the product/market level to an overarching longer-term organizational level (◘ Fig. 20.1).

Product/Market Visions, by their very nature, have shorter-term time horizons than Organizational Visions do. In particular, those with medium- to high-market contexts (i.e., the market exists already) may have a focal point in the range of 1–5 years (◘ Fig. 20.2), possibly even shorter depending on the contextual situation.

On the other hand, longer-term, more broadly focused Organizational Vision looks out beyond the purview of one product or service, to a future that may include a vast product portfolio with multiple markets and a variety of stakehold-

◘ **Fig. 20.1** Conceptual image to portray transitioning to longer-term organizational vision. (Source: Image licensed and downloaded from Adobe Stock on November 26, 2020. Credit: by dragonstock/AdobeStock.com)

◘ **Fig. 20.2** Conceptual image to portray "shorter-term market vision." (Source: Image licensed and downloaded from Adobe Stock on November 26, 2020. Credit: by ATKWORK888/AdobeStock.com)

ers. Think, for example, of Apple. It wasn't long after the launch of the first Apple Computer before they were onto creating and launching products for the Apple II series and beyond.

Market Vision needs to be as clear as possible because of the necessity of focusing on a shorter-term future aimed at bringing a Product/Market Vision to fruition. For broader longer-term and overarching Organizational Vision, which may drive an organization forward for a very long time, a higher level of abstraction may be required for the vision, as noted by Baum et al. (1998), in order to enable a portfolio of products and services to be developed within it (i.e., in order to enable growth through a big envelope or umbrella of potential meaning).

Given this, a key question for the entrepreneur is how to move between one frame of thinking to the next, from Market Vision to Organizational Vision. Part of the answer lies in the ties to the entrepreneur's Financial Vision, as described in ► Chap. 18. For family firms, the Organizational Vision may always remain fairly closely aligned with the original Product/Service Market Vision through time. For example, a family bakery which started by focusing on serving only croissants may add a few additional baked goods to their menu over time, but the Organizational Vision still remains fairly consistent with the original Market Vision—to provide local fresh baked bread first thing in the morning every day of the week. For a growth-oriented firm, the need to leverage up and create a distinction between Market Vision and Organizational Vision is more obvious.

20.2 Refining and/or Pivoting Your Product/Market Vision

In addition to answering the existential question of what it means to be an organization, most startups, once their first product has launched, need to decide at the product/market level, whether to pivot, or in other words, reroute their current direction and vision focus. In essence, the decision lies with whether the entrepreneur (1) continues to refine the Product/Market Vision on the same trajectory, (2) decides to incrementally change the vision (i.e., through improvement to the current product, an addition to the same product line, repositioning the current product in a new market, or cost reduction), or (3) decides to add a completely new product line or develop something radically new (through a focus on brand-new products and new markets).

Performing test markets in the early days after launch gives the target market (or markets) the opportunity to try out your product or service on some sort of a limited basis (in time, geographical scope, as a sample, etc.) and gives the entrepreneurial team feedback related to the actual product, prior to scaling up further and investing more money into it.

At this stage, startups have likely received a flood of input and response to their Mach 1 service or product. So, depending on the feedback, your team may be doubling down and entrenching around your current core product, developing new parts of the product line and/or taking it out to new market(s) or pivoting to completely different opportunities. These are natural parts of the post-launch process. Krippendorff (2019, p. 126), in his book *Driving Innovation from Within*, describes the story of William Wrigley who started out in the American Midwest in the late 1800s selling baking soda and soap. As an early promotion he included a giveaway stick of gum along with each purchase from his detergent line. As it turned out, the gum was such a hit that he moved to focus primarily on selling the gum and, thus, an entrepreneurial legend—Wrigley's—was born.

If we had to pull together an underlying theme for the value-defining activities of entrepreneurs, it would be movement—ongoing, rapid movement both toward and away from specific market opportunities and magnetic visions. Being able to act on opportunity requires a high degree of flexibility and quick reactions and adjustments, and this puts a lot of demands on the entrepreneur's family, business partners, and other relationships.

20.3 Taking Vision to the Next Level

In Igor Ansoff's 1957 paper, *Strategies for Diversification*, he outlines four main strategies that companies can use to grow: "Market Penetration," "Market Development," "Product Development," and "Diversification." Market Penetration focuses on developing existing markets. Market Development looks at extending market reach through new target market segments, new channels of distribution, and so on. Product Development means anything from developing incremental variants of current products to developing radically new ones. Diversification offers a new perspective for companies looking to grow through a combination of both new markets and new products.

So, where to start? Some companies take a largely opportunistic approach to market and product development following the launch of a first product. However, even this early on, it is important that startups develop a strategic game plan. This is exactly why it is important to develop a long-term Organizational Vision beyond the first Product/Market Vision. The Organizational Vision can, in fact, serve as a basis for setting long-term, medium-term, and short-term objectives to stay on track with the overall vision. Much of the short-term plan will likely be built around the first product and its market, so long as it has been reasonably successful post-launch or if the entrepreneurial team can at least pinpoint what needs to be modified to make it successful. As such, the short-term is often largely about developing plans for market penetration in order to maximize that which has already been built and to wring the most out of the product life cycle by ensuring as much adoption in that market as possible. Sometimes, it makes sense to also consider market development at this stage, particularly if it would be strategic to get a head start with a new market ahead of the competition. The nature of short-term product development is often also focused on developing out a product line from the first product, or making small additions or improvements demanded by the market. Nevertheless, in line with the more medium- and long-term objectives related to the vision, research, preparation, and resource gathering (people and money) to build new products aimed at the current and new markets need to also be put into the consideration set.

At this stage, we provide one final worksheet, Worksheet 20, which may be used at various intervals to measure performance over time (i.e., post-launch, 1-year mark, 3-year mark, and so on).

20

Worksheet 20: Vision and Performance Survey

This worksheet is divided into 3 parts. The first part examines where you are at currently in terms of your 'Market Visioning Competence' (MVC). The second part looks at how strong your current Market Vision (MV) is. The last looks at how well you feel you are doing in terms of your performance (the items here are specifically related to pre-launch early performance success). As described in Chapter 2, each of the question items has been tested in previous research and has been found to be a statistically significantly reliable and valid indicator for the overall factor being examined.

There are no right or wrong answers here; rather, it is suggested that you go back and check in with how you are doing on each indicator a couple of times per year and track your progress.Additionally, you should try to identify one or two key areas where you/your team feel you have challenges/need external help, list potential ideas for improvement or resources you require and then put together a plan with your team for obtaining these.

IMPORTANT: If you are in the very early stages of entrepreneurship and do not have a specific idea or vision yet, start by filling in the networks and championing sections for now – you can fill in more as they become relevant.

How well do you score on the following scale from 1 to 7:

Definitely Not Strongly <u>DIS</u>AGREE	RATING Neutral	Definitely Yes Strongly AGREE

1------------2------------3------------4------------5------------6------------7

PART I. MARKET VISIONING COMPETENCE INDICATORS

NETWORKS

The person who first championed this idea (I, the entrepreneur…)

1) … has/have a <u>broad network</u> of relationships. ____
2) … has/have a network made up of people with a <u>variety</u> of different backgrounds. (e.g., different industries, different disciplines, different functions, etc.)
3) …is/am at the <u>center</u> of the network growing up around the new area of interest (if relevant). ____

IDEA DRIVING/CHAMPIONING

1. The person who first championed this idea (I, the entrepreneur…)
   a) … am getting/got key decision makers/experts from the field involved. ____
   b) … am sharing/shared information and campaigned for support very quickly with relevant stakeholders. ____
   c) … am securing/secured the required support. ____

MARKET LEARNING TOOLS

1. We are trying/tried to keep our market opportunity options open for as long as possible. ____
2. We are trying/tried to develop several potential market scenarios before choosing a market(s) to pursue. ____
3. Our understanding of potential markets was updated in light of new information from forecasts. ____
4. We used several forecasting and market estimation techniques <u>in combination</u> before market selection. ____

© Susan E. Reid and Charles B. Crawford, August 14, 2020.

Definitely Not Strongly DISAGREE	RATING Neutral	Definitely Yes Strongly AGREE
1-----------2-----------3-----------	4-----------	5-----------6-----------7

PROACTIVE MARKET ORIENTATION

1. We are trying to discover additional needs of our customers of which they are unaware. ____
2. We are incorporating solutions to unarticulated customer needs in our new products and services. ____
3. We brainstorm on how customers might use our products and services. ____

PART II. MARKET VISION INDICATORS

MARKET VISION FORM

1. When I/we first started thinking about what specific markets would benefit from the idea, we spent most of our time thinking and talking about …
   - a) … how the product would fit into an overall system of use for potential customers. ____
   - b) … ease of use for potential customers. ____
   - c) … the product's relationship to the customer use environment. ____
   - d) … the potential for standardizing the design. ____

MARKET VISION SCOPE

2. When I/we first started thinking about what specific markets would benefit from the idea, we spent most of our time thinking and talking about …
   - e)… what the most profitable target market would be. ____
   - f)… what the most important target market would be. ____
   - g).. what the largest target market would be. ____

MARKET VISION PASSION (MAGNETISM AND INSPIRATION)

3. Even in the very early stages of idea development, prior to product development, the market vision was …
   - a)… important. ____
   - b)… attractive. ____
   - c)… desirable. ____

MARKET VISION CLARITY

4. In the very early stages of this idea's development, it was clear…
   - a)…what target customers' needs would be. ____
   - b)… how the product would be used. ____
   - c)… who the target market (user) would be. ____

MARKET VISION SPECIFICITY

5. Even in the very early stages of idea development, prior to product development, the market vision was…
   - d)… clear. ____
   - e)… tangible (e.g., easy to visualize). ____
   - f) … very specific. ____
   - g)… able to provide direction to others. ____

© Susan E. Reid and Charles B. Crawford, August 14, 2020.

PART III. Next, we will examine the concept of EARLY PERFORMANCE INDICATORS, **or the degree to which the development of a product/market vision provides early competitive advantage for a company along various measures.**

1. Please indicate the degree of success, which you fell your company has achieved along each of the following indicators as a result of involvement with the technology (1 = 0%; 7 = 100%).

EARLY SUCCESS WITH CUSTOMERS

a) … Early customers accepted the products (even prior to sales). ____

b) … Early customers were satisfied (even prior to sales). ____

c) … Customers' needs were (will be) satisfied better by these products than existing ones. ____

ABILITY TO ATTRACT CAPITAL

d) … Cash flow. ____

e) … Ability to attract capital. ____

f) … Average growth in company employment stemming from involvement. ____

TECHNICAL COMPETITIVE ADVANTAGE

g) … Innovation's technical quality. ____

h) … Innovation's value to the organization. ____

i) … Unique benefits: perceived as superior to competitors. ____

© Susan E. Reid and Charles B. Crawford, August 14, 2020.

20.4 Parting Thoughts

Throughout this book and its accompanying worksheets, you have gone through steps conceived to help you pinpoint issues you would like the resolve, ideate products or services that could be solutions for a specific market, and test your more refined ideas with family and friends, experts, and lead users. You have developed the toolkit necessary to establish a strong vision statement and combine it with a logical financial vision, as well as a clear, longer-term organizational view, while at the same time understanding the entrepreneurial stages at which different forms of vision are at their most vital.

With your vision defined, you are now prepared to ensure that your business objectives, team motivation, and new product and service ideas are all guided by the same, uniting North Star. You have done the work, tested the concept, and boiled it down to the essence of what you would like your company to stand for, and now it's time to let your North Star light the path to long-term success.

References

Ansoff, I. (1957). Strategies for diversification. *Harvard Business Review, 35*(5), 113–124.

Baum, J. R., Locke, E. A., & Kirkpatrick, S. A. (1998). A longitudinal study of the relation of vision and vision communication to venture growth in entrepreneurial firms. *Journal of Applied Psychology, 83*(1), 43–54.

Krippendorff, K. (2019). *Driving innovation from within*. Columbia University Press.

Supplementary Information

© The Editor(s) (if applicable) and The Author(s), under exclusive license to Springer Nature Switzerland AG 2022
S. E. Reid, C. B. Crawford, *Entrepreneurial Vision*,
Classroom Companion: Business,
https://doi.org/10.1007/978-3-030-77803-3

Index

E

F

G

H

I

J

K

L

M

N

O

P

R

S

T

W

Ingram Content Group UK Ltd.
Milton Keynes UK
UKHW021419150623
423489UK00001B/107

9 783030 778026